Cape Town

Simon Richmond
Jon Murray

LONELY PLANET PUBLICATIONS
Melbourne • Oakland • London • Paris

MAP 1 – HIGHLIGHTS OF THE CAPE

MATJIESFONTEIN
Experience the vastness of the Karoo at this preserved 19th-century railway siding and grand hotel

CEDERBERG WILDERNESS AREA
True wilderness hiking in a rugged landscape with fascinating flora and ancient rock art

NORTHERN CAPE

WESTERN CAPE

Karoo

Komsberge

Roggeveldberge

Swartruggens

Witsenberg

Cederberg

Cederberg Wilderness Area

Sneeuberg (2028m)

Sutherland

Matjiesfontein

Touws River

Hottentotskloof

Prince Alfred Hamlet

Gydo Pass

Tulbagh

Porterville

Piketberg

Moorreesburg

Aurora

Hopefield

Langebaan

West Coast National Park

Saldanha

Vredenburg

Paternoster

Stompneusbaai

St Helena Bay

Bergrivier

Velddrif

Berg River

Olifants River

Citrusdal

Middelberg Pass

R303

N7

Piekenierskloof Pass

Paleisheuwel

Sandberg

Graafwater

R364

Clanwilliam

Pakhuis Pass

Tweefontein

Cederberg

Lamberts Bay

Doring Bay

Strandfontein

Papendorp

Vredendal

Vanrhynsdorp

Klawer

St Helena Bay

Saldanha Bay

SWELLENDAM
One of South Africa's most historic towns, in a splendid location at the foot of the Langeberge range

HERMANUS
View mighty southern right whales in Walker Bay between June and November

CAPE OF GOOD HOPE NATURE RESERVE
Wildlife, hiking and deserted beaches await visitors to the tip of the peninsula

WINELANDS
Explore centuries-old towns and vineyards set amid beautiful scenery

ROBBEN ISLAND
Once a notorious prison, where Mandela spent 18 years; now a UN World Heritage Site

TABLE MOUNTAIN
A dramatic urban backdrop with a breathtaking view from the top

CLIFTON & CAMPS BAY
Cape Town's trendiest beaches, pounded by freezing surf, are the place to come for sundowners

ELEVATION

1200m
900m
600m
300m
0

5km
25
15
30mi
0
0

Cape Town
3rd edition – January 2002
First published – February 1996

Published by
Lonely Planet Publications Pty Ltd ABN 36 005 607 983
90 Maribyrnong St, Footscray, Victoria 3011, Australia

Lonely Planet offices
Australia Locked Bag 1, Footscray, Victoria 3011
USA 150 Linden St, Oakland, CA 94607
UK 10a Spring Place, London NW5 3BH
France 1 rue du Dahomey, 75011 Paris

Photographs
Many of the images in this guide are available for licensing from
Lonely Planet Images.
email: lpi@lonelyplanet.com.au
Web site: www.lonelyplanetimages.com

Front cover photograph
City Bowl and part of Table Mountain, as seen from Signal Hill
(Daniel Birks)

Map section title-page photograph
Aerial view of Cape Town with Table Mountain behind
(Manfred Gottschalk)

ISBN 0 86442 759 X

text & maps © Lonely Planet Publications Pty Ltd 2002
photos © photographers as indicated 2002

Printed by Craft Print International Ltd
Printed in Singapore

Contents – Text

CAPE TOWN ARCHITECTURE 101

PLACES TO STAY 109

PLACES TO EAT 118

ENTERTAINMENT 129

GAY & LESBIAN CAPE TOWN 137

SHOPPING 144

EXCURSIONS 148

CAPE WINERIES 180

LANGUAGE 189

GLOSSARY 193

INDEX 195

METRIC CONVERSION inside back cover

Contents – Maps

MAP 1 – Highlights of the Cape

THINGS TO SEE & DO

EXCURSIONS

CAPE WINERIES

CAPE TOWN MAP SECTION (colour)   see back pages

MAP LEGEND   back page

The Authors

Simon Richmond

In his 30-odd years of travel Simon Richmond has covered fair chunks of the world's continents. He jumped at the chance to explore one of Africa's most visually stunning and happening cities. Such were Cape Town's attractions it took some effort for him to actually leave and get on with his research further afield, but the rest of Western Cape province did not disappoint. An award-winning author of guidebooks on Japan, South-East Asia, India, South America and Australia, Simon has worked on various projects for Lonely Planet including *Istanbul to Kathmandu*, *Central Asia* and the Out to Eat series. He calls Sydney home, whenever it's time to clean out the backpack.

Jon Murray

Jon Murray spent time alternately travelling and working with various publishing houses in Melbourne, Australia, before joining Lonely Planet as an editor. He coauthored Lonely Planet's *South Africa, Lesotho & Swaziland* and has written and updated books on destinations including West Africa, Papua New Guinea, Bangladesh and Hungary. He lives in country Victoria, on a bush block he shares with quite a few marsupials and a diminishing number of rabbits.

FROM SIMON

This book couldn't have been completed without the steadying hands of Virginia Maxwell and Vince Patton back at base. Thanks also to Kerryn Burgess for doing a careful and considerate job on the editing.

Virginia Haddon at South African Tourism in Sydney was a great help and gave me a glimpse of the friendliness that would be waiting for me in South Africa. Thanks also to Diana Lyon for some contacts, particularly Anne Wallis Brown and her colleagues. In Cape Town, the dynamic Sheryl Ozinksy and her staff (in particular the marvellous Vicky) pulled out all stops to check details and make arrangements. André Vorster gave me an insight into the gay side of the city, Barbara and Barry unveiled its adventurous streak. Donald Paul, Gina Schauffer and Gary de Klerk of *SA Citylife* and Patricia Davison at the South African Museum were all generous with their time and knowledge. Much thanks to Lee and Toni, Tony and Barbara, and Barry for nights off.

Finally, thanks to two women who more than anything summed up the hopeful, reconciling spirit of the new South Africa, Vicky Ntozini and Tammin Barker. They showed there's little to separate the Xhosa word *ubuntu* from the Afrikaans word *kuier*: Both mean hospitality, pure and simple.

This Book

The first edition of *Cape Town*, written by Jon Murray, was published in 1996. Jon wrote the second edition too. Simon Richmond updated the text for this edition.

FROM THE PUBLISHER

This edition of *Cape Town* was coordinated by Kerryn Burgess (editor) and Huw Fowles (cartographer and designer). Both of them admire the way author Simon Richmond handled their 'pesky queries' from Internet cafes in Tobolsk and other Siberian outposts.

Back at head office in Melbourne, Jenny Mullaly proofread the entire manuscript, Vince Patton checked artwork and changed nappies, and Kim Hutchins checked artwork and drove through snow. Language guru Emma Koch sorted the *koeksesters* from the *drankwinkels*, while Mick Weldon drew illustrations of our favourite Cape Town characters, and Jenny Jones designed the cover. Support crew comprised Matt King, illustrations coordinator; Annie Horner in LPI; Hunor Csutoros, who got out his rain gauge to create the climate chart; the legendary Anna Judd; tech man David Burnett, who can bring files back from the far side; and Quark expert Mark Germanchis, who knows all the layout quirks.

THANKS
Many thanks to the travellers who used the last edition and wrote to us with helpful hints, advice and interesting anecdotes. Your names appear on the following page.

Thanks

Thanks to the folk at Cape Town Tourism for their good-humoured help throughout the production process, and to readers of the last edition who wrote to us with anecdotes and helpful hints:

Ben Allison, Caroline Bay, Jesse Berenos, Andrew Bergwald, Sebastiaan Biehl, Steinar Bjornstad, Peter Boodell, Bob & Anne Bown, M Brown, Debbie Bruk, Helen Bull, Christina Campbell, Ian Campbell, David Child, Nicholas Clive, Gary Colite, Blake Congdon, J Cooper, J Copeland, Ivor Crews, Monique Cuthbert, Rob Davidowitz, Liz Davis, Trudy Delong, Dax Denneboom, Regina Dinneen, Keith Dixon, Eileen Eggerton, Caroll Everest, Catherine Van Den Eynde, the Evans family, Tomasz Fidytek, Andrew Florides, MW Friedlander, Aleksandra Golebiowska, Bryn Gooding, Michael Hanford-Arnold, Manuela Hanni, Steve Harris, Philip J Hartog, Mark Higgitt, Richard Hill, Lorinda Houghton, Hari Iyer, Bridgett James, Pascal Jfri, Claus Kellenberger, Bob Lipske, Iain Mackay, Helena & Rod MacPhail, Adrian S Man, RMS Maude, Lauren McDonald, Osacr Nagtegaal, Claire Newey, Lindsey Nickolls, Dirk Jan Parlevliet, Giorgio Perversi, Bernd Pfefferkorn, Dan Potter, Kate Prout, Simon Rose, Alex Ross, Ali Rowlett, Ian Rummery, John Schmit, Davide Selva, Jean Smith, Joost & Conny Snoep, Saskia Soeterbroek, Dan Sparks, Nicole Staal, Marc Tebrugge, David & Evonne Templeton, Ria Timmerman, Marjolein Van Rest, Slavica & Jilles Van Werkhoven, Antonia Vettermann, Hedwig Vollers, Andy Ward, Peter Ward, Jean A Wilsen, S Zienoger.

Foreword

ABOUT LONELY PLANET GUIDEBOOKS

The story begins with a classic travel adventure: Tony and Maureen Wheeler's 1972 journey across Europe and Asia to Australia. Useful information about the overland trail did not exist at that time, so Tony and Maureen published the first Lonely Planet guidebook to meet a growing need.

From a kitchen table, then from a tiny office in Melbourne (Australia), Lonely Planet has become the largest independent travel publisher in the world, an international company with offices in Melbourne, Oakland (USA), London (UK) and Paris (France).

Today Lonely Planet guidebooks cover the globe. There is an ever-growing list of books and there's information in a variety of forms and media. Some things haven't changed. The main aim is still to help make it possible for adventurous travellers to get out there – to explore and better understand the world.

At Lonely Planet we believe travellers can make a positive contribution to the countries they visit – if they respect their host communities and spend their money wisely. Since 1986 a percentage of the income from each book has been donated to aid projects and human rights campaigns.

Updates Lonely Planet thoroughly updates each guidebook as often as possible. This usually means there are around two years between editions, although for more unusual or more stable destinations the gap can be longer. Check the imprint page (following the colour map at the beginning of the book) for publication dates.

Between editions up-to-date information is available in two free newsletters – the paper *Planet Talk* and email *Comet* (to subscribe, contact any Lonely Planet office) – and on our Web site at www.lonelyplanet.com. The *Upgrades* section of the Web site covers a number of important and volatile destinations and is regularly updated by Lonely Planet authors. *Scoop* covers news and current affairs relevant to travellers. And, lastly, the *Thorn Tree* bulletin board and *Postcards* section of the site carry unverified, but fascinating, reports from travellers.

Correspondence The process of creating new editions begins with the letters, postcards and emails received from travellers. This correspondence often includes suggestions, criticisms and comments about the current editions. Interesting excerpts are immediately passed on via newsletters and the Web site, and everything goes to our authors to be verified when they're researching on the road. We're keen to get more feedback from organisations or individuals who represent communities visited by travellers.

Lonely Planet gathers information for everyone who's curious about the planet – and especially for those who explore it first-hand. Through guidebooks, phrasebooks, activity guides, maps, literature, newsletters, image library, TV series and Web site we act as an information exchange for a worldwide community of travellers.

Research Authors aim to gather sufficient practical information to enable travellers to make informed choices and to make the mechanics of a journey run smoothly. They also research historical and cultural background to help enrich the travel experience and allow travellers to understand and respond appropriately to cultural and environmental issues.

Authors don't stay in every hotel because that would mean spending a couple of months in each medium-sized city and, no, they don't eat at every restaurant because that would mean stretching belts beyond capacity. They do visit hotels and restaurants to check standards and prices, but feedback based on readers' direct experiences can be very helpful.

Many of our authors work undercover, others aren't so secretive. None of them accept freebies in exchange for positive write-ups. And none of our guidebooks contain any advertising.

Production Authors submit their manuscripts and maps to offices in Australia, USA, UK or France. Editors and cartographers, all experienced travellers themselves, then begin the process of assembling the pieces. When the book finally hits the shops, some things are already out of date, we start getting feedback from readers and the process begins again ...

WARNING & REQUEST

Things change – prices go up, schedules change, good places go bad and bad places go bankrupt – nothing stays the same. So, if you find things better or worse, recently opened or long since closed, please tell us and help make the next edition even more accurate and useful. We genuinely value all the feedback we receive. A well-travelled team reads and acknowledges every letter, postcard and email and ensures that every morsel of information finds its way to the appropriate authors, editors and cartographers for verification.

Everyone who writes to us will find their name listed in the next edition of the appropriate guidebook. They will also receive the latest issue of *Planet Talk*, our quarterly printed newsletter, or *Comet*, our monthly email newsletter. Subscriptions to both newsletters are free. The very best contributions will be rewarded with a free guidebook.

We may edit, reproduce and incorporate your comments in all Lonely Planet products, such as guidebooks, Web sites and digital products, so let us know if you don't want your comments reproduced or your name acknowledged.

Send all correspondence to the Lonely Planet office closest to you:

Australia: Locked Bag 1, Footscray, Victoria 3011
USA: 150 Linden St, Oakland, CA 94607
UK: 10a Spring Place, London NW5 3BH

Or email us at: talk2us@lonelyplanet.com.au

For news, views and updates see our Web site: www.lonelyplanet.com

HOW TO USE A LONELY PLANET GUIDEBOOK

The best way to use a Lonely Planet guidebook is any way you choose. At Lonely Planet we believe the most memorable travel experiences are often those that are unexpected, and the finest discoveries are those you make yourself. Guidebooks are not intended to be used as if they provide a detailed set of infallible instructions!

Contents All Lonely Planet guidebooks follow roughly the same format. The Facts about the Destination chapters or sections give background information ranging from history to weather. Facts for the Visitor gives practical information on issues like visas and health. Getting There & Away gives a brief starting point for researching travel to and from the destination. Getting Around gives an overview of the transport options when you arrive.

The peculiar demands of each destination determine how subsequent chapters are broken up, but some things remain constant. We always start with background, then proceed to sights, places to stay, places to eat, entertainment, getting there and away, and getting around information – in that order.

Heading Hierarchy Lonely Planet headings are used in a strict hierarchical structure that can be visualised as a set of Russian dolls. Each heading (and its following text) is encompassed by any preceding heading that is higher on the hierarchical ladder.

Entry Points We do not assume guidebooks will be read from beginning to end, but that people will dip into them. The traditional entry points are the list of contents and the index. In addition, however, some books have a complete list of maps and an index map illustrating map coverage.

There may also be a colour map that shows highlights. These highlights are dealt with in greater detail in the Facts for the Visitor chapter, along with planning questions and suggested itineraries. Each chapter covering a geographical region usually begins with a locator map and another list of highlights. Once you find something of interest in a list of highlights, turn to the index.

Maps Maps play a crucial role in Lonely Planet guidebooks and include a huge amount of information. A legend is printed on the back page. We seek to have complete consistency between maps and text, and to have every important place in the text captured on a map. Map key numbers usually start in the top left corner.

Although inclusion in a guidebook usually implies a recommendation we cannot list every good place. Exclusion does not necessarily imply criticism. In fact there are a number of reasons why we might exclude a place – sometimes it is simply inappropriate to encourage an influx of travellers.

Introduction

Whichever way you look at it, Cape Town occupies one of the world's most stunning locations. A large part of that impact comes down to the 1073m-high mountain slap-bang in the centre of the city. Table Mountain and its attendant peaks – Devil's Peak and Lion's Head – are the city's most enduring image. As beautiful as the surrounding beaches and vineyards are, it's this rugged wilderness, covered in a unique flora, that is the focus of everyone's attention.

More than matching Cape Town's visual drama has been its tumultuous recorded history of over 350 years. Walk through the lovely Company's Gardens and you are literally walking through the history of a place Capetonians still call 'the Mother City': past the vegetable garden planted by the city's founder, Jan Van Riebeeck; the graceful Cape Dutch architecture of the 18th-century Tuynhuis; the awful reality of the old Slave Lodge; the staunch majesty of St George's Cathedral, focus of Archbishop Desmond Tutu's struggle against the madness of apartheid; and the houses of parliament, where Nelson Mandela was proclaimed the country's first democratically elected president. It's soul-stirring stuff.

Like many of the world's ports, Cape Town is also a longtime master of the art of showing visitors a good time. Its mix of trendy hostelries matches up favourably to those in any other cosmopolitan city. There's a lively cultural scene, particularly when it comes to music, which seems to pervade every corner of the city. The locals are generally open-minded and the mood is relaxed.

Sadly, the scars of the republic's terrible history still run deep. Like all South African cities, Cape Town is two-faced – European but not European, African but not African; a volatile mixture of the Third and First Worlds. Apartheid allowed whites to reserve some of the world's most spectacular real estate, and the stark contrast between poverty-stricken Crossroads and ritzy Clifton remains – black and white.

And yet you simply must visit the ever-growing Cape Flats townships, home to an estimated 1.5 million people, to truly understand this city and to glimpse its future. Not everything you see will appal you. On the contrary, it can be argued that a stronger sense of optimism and pride are found in the shacks of Khayelitsha than in the mansions of Tamboerskloof. The experience of the city's large coloured community, presented movingly in the District Six Museum, is equally fascinating, and essential for putting Cape Town fully into context.

The capital of Western Cape province and the parliamentary capital of the republic, Cape Town works as a city in a way that so few on the African continent do. Historic buildings have been saved, and there are restaurants, cafes and bars, parks and gardens, markets and shops – all the things that make living in a city worthwhile. And then there are a few things that most cities don't have: mountains, magnificent surf beaches and outstanding vineyards. Give yourself at least a week to explore all Cape Town offers. You may well find – like many before you – that a week is far too short.

11

Facts about Cape Town

HISTORY

Signs of the first humans have been found in several places in South Africa. At Langebaan Lagoon (north of Cape Town), the discovery of 117,000-year-old fossilised footprints prompted one researcher to speculate that 'Eve' (the very first human; the common ancestor of us all) lived here.

Little is known about the early humans in South Africa but there are signs that they conducted funerals, an indication of at least basic culture. Academics don't know whether the earliest recorded inhabitants of South Africa – the San peoples – are direct descendants or if they returned to the area after aeons of travel.

San & Khoikhoi Peoples

The San (also known as Bushmen) were nomadic hunters and gatherers, and the Khoikhoi (formerly known as Hottentot) were seminomadic hunters and pastoralists. However, both groups were closely related, so the distinction was by no means clear, and the term Khoisan is now widely used to describe these peoples. Culturally and physically, they developed differently from the Negroid peoples of Africa.

It is believed the Khoikhoi developed from San groups in present-day Botswana. Perhaps they came into contact with pastoralist Bantu-speaking tribes, as in addition to hunting and gathering food, they became pastoralists, with cattle and sheep. They migrated south, reaching the Cape of Good Hope about 2000 years ago. For centuries, perhaps even millennia, the San and the Khoikhoi intermarried and coexisted. It was not uncommon for impoverished Khoikhoi to revert to a hunter-gatherer existence, or for the San to acquire domestic animals.

The migration of the Bantu-speaking peoples into Southern Africa (by about AD 500 they had settled what is now KwaZulu-Natal) resulted in many Khoisan peoples being dislodged or absorbed in other parts of South Africa, but the Bantu-speaking peoples did not reach the Cape Town area. Their westward expansion halted around the Great Fish River (in Eastern Cape Province, about 700km east of Cape Town) because they were agricultural people and further west there was not enough rainfall to support their crops.

The Portuguese Visit & Move On

The Portuguese came to the Cape Town area on their search for a sea route to India and for that most precious of medieval commodities: spice. Bartholomeu Dias rounded the Cape in 1487, naming it Cabo da Boa Esperanca (Cape of Good Hope), but his eyes were fixed on the trade riches of the east coast of Africa and the Indies.

In 1503 Antonio de Saldanha became the first European to climb Table Mountain. But the Portuguese had no interest in a permanent settlement. The Cape offered them little more than fresh water, since their attempts to trade with the Khoisan often ended in violence, and the coast and its fierce weather posed a terrible threat to their tiny caravels.

The Dutch Come to Stay

By the end of the 16th century English and Dutch traders were beginning to challenge the Portuguese, and the Cape became a regular stopover for their scurvy-ridden crews. In 1647 a Dutch vessel was wrecked in Table Bay; its crew built a fort and stayed for a year before they were rescued.

This crystallised the value of a permanent settlement in the minds of the directors of the Dutch East India Company (Vereenigde Oost-Indische Compagnie; VOC). They had no intention of colonising the country, but simply wanted to establish a secure base where ships could shelter and stock up on fresh supplies of meat, fruit and vegetables.

Jan Van Riebeeck was the man they chose to lead a small expedition from the flagship *Drommedaris*. His specific charge was to build a fort, barter with the Khoisan for meat, and plant a garden. He reached

Table Bay on 6 April 1652, built a mud-walled fort not far from the site of the stone castle that survives today, and planted the gardens now known as the Company's Gardens (or the Botanic Gardens).

In 1660, in a gesture that took on an awful symbolism, Van Riebeeck planted a bitter-almond hedge to separate the Khoisan and the Europeans. It ran around the western foot of Table Mountain down to Table Bay, and a section of it can still be seen in the Kirstenbosch Botanical Gardens. The hedge may have protected the 120 Europeans, but the settlement, having excluded the Khoisan, suffered a chronic labour shortage. In another move that would have consequences for centuries ahead, Van Riebeeck then proceeded to import slaves from Madagascar, India, Ceylon, Malaya and Indonesia.

The Settlement Grows

The European men of the community were largely employees of the VOC, and were overwhelmingly Dutch. They comprised a tiny official elite and a larger number of little-educated soldiers and sailors, many of whom had been pressed into service. In 1685 they were joined by about 200 Huguenots, French Calvinists who had fled from persecution by King Louis XIV.

There was a shortage of women in the colony, so the female slaves and the Khoisan survivors were exploited both for labour and for sex. In time, the slaves intermixed with the Khoisan. The offspring of these unions formed the basis of sections of today's coloured population.

Under the VOC's almost complete control Cape Town thrived, providing a comfortable European lifestyle for a growing number of artisans and entrepreneurs servicing ships and crews. Cape Town became known as 'the Tavern of the Seas', a riotous port used by every navigator, privateer and merchant travelling between Europe and the East (including Australia).

The Boers Begin to Trek

The white population did not reach 1000 until 1745, by which time small numbers of free (meaning non-VOC) burghers were

drifting away from the close grip of the company into other areas of Africa. These were the first of the Trekboers (literally 'Trekking Farmers'), later known just as Boers, who developed a unique culture and eventually their own language, Afrikaans, based on the argot of their slaves.

They were fiercely independent and lived lives based on rearing cattle. In many ways their lives were not all that different from those of the Khoisan with whom they came into conflict as they drifted into the interior. The timing of their voluntary withdrawal from the outside world is significant. The Boers, many of whom were illiterate and most of whom had no source of information other than the Bible, missed out on the great social, political and philosophical developments of Europe in the 18th century.

The Boers' inevitable confrontations with the Khoisan were disastrous. The indigenous people were driven from their traditional lands, ravaged by introduced diseases and almost destroyed by superior weapons. The survivors were left with no option but to work for Europeans in a form of bondage little different from slavery.

The British Take Over

The fourth Anglo-Dutch War was fought between 1780 and 1783. French regiments were sent to Cape Town to help the Dutch defend the city. The British eventually prevailed at the Battle of Muizenberg in 1795 and took control of the Cape from the VOC, which by then was bankrupt.

Under the Treaty of Amiens (1803) the British ceded the Cape back to the Dutch, but this proved just a lull in the Napoleonic Wars. In 1806 at Bloubergstrand, 25km north of Cape Town, the British again defeated the Dutch. The colony was ceded to the British on 13 August 1814.

The British abolished the slave trade in 1808 and the remaining Khoisan were finally given the explicit protection of the law (including the right to own land) in 1828. These moves contributed to Afrikaners' dissatisfaction and their mass migration, which came to be known as the Great Trek, inland from the Cape Colony.

MOMENTS IN CAPE TOWN'S & SOUTH AFRICA'S HISTORY

100,000 BC	**c.100,000 BC**	San people settle Southern Africa
	c.AD 500	Bantu-speaking peoples arrive in KwaZulu-Natal area
	1487	Bartholomeu Dias sails around the Cape of Good Hope
AD 1600	**1652**	The Dutch establish a settlement in Table Bay (Cape Town)
	1688	French Huguenots arrive at the Cape
1700	**c.1690**	Boers move into the hinterland around present-day Cape Town
	1779	Boers fight Xhosa at Great Fish River
1800	**1795**	British capture Cape Town
	1806	British defeat Dutch in battle at Bloubergstrand
	1808	Slave trade abolished
	1814	Cape Colony ceded to British
	1830s	Voortrekkers undertake the Great Trek
	1834	Slaves emancipated
	1838	Boers defeat the Zulu at Battle of Blood River
1850	**1852**	Boer Republic of Transvaal created
	1854	Lower house of parliament created in Cape Town
	1864	Cape Town–Wynberg railway line completed; links to Kimberley (1885) and Johannesburg (1892) follow
	1869	Diamonds found near Kimberley
	1871	Gold discovered in eastern Transvaal
	1877	British annex the Boer Republic of Transvaal
	1881	Boers defeat British, and Transvaal becomes the South African Republic
	1886	Gold discovered on the Witwatersrand (the area around Johannesburg)
	1899	Anglo-Boer War starts
1900	**1901**	Ndabeni, Cape Town's first black township, established
	1902	Anglo-Boer War finishes
	1905	Government commission recommends separate development for blacks, with inferior education
	1910	Union of South Africa created, federating the British colonies and the old Boer republics; blacks denied the vote
	1912	South African Native National Congress established (forerunner to the ANC)
	1913	Natives Land Act restricts black ownership of land to 7.5% of the country
1920	**1919**	Industrial & Commercial Union formed by coloured and African workers in Cape Town; it counts over 200,000 members by late 1920s

SARAH JOLLY

MARTIN HARRIS

SARAH JOLLY

SARAH JOLLY

KATE NOLAN

1928	Communist Party begins agitating for full democracy
1948	National Party wins government and retains control until 1994; apartheid laws, such as the ban on interracial marriages and sex, begin to be passed
1955	ANC adopts Freedom Charter
1959	Pan-African Congress (PAC) formed
1960	Sharpeville massacre; ANC and PAC banned
1961	South Africa leaves the Commonwealth and becomes a republic
1963	Nelson Mandela, Walter Sisulu and others jailed for life
1967	Christiaan Barnard carries out world's first heart transplant at Cape Town's Groote Schuur Hospital
1975	South Africa invades Angola; Zulu cultural movement Inkatha revived by Mangosuthu Buthelezi
1976	Soweto uprisings begin
1977	Steve Biko murdered
1985	State of emergency declared in South Africa; official murder and torture become rife, black resistance strengthens
1986	Nobel peace prize winner Desmond Tutu elected Anglican archbishop of Cape Town
1990	ANC ban lifted, Nelson Mandela freed
1991	Talks on a new constitution begin, political violence escalates
1992	Whites-only referendum agrees to reforms
1993	New constitution enacted, signalling end of apartheid and birth of new South Africa
1994	Democratic elections held; Nelson Mandela succeeds FW De Klerk as South African president
1996	Truth & Reconciliation Commission hearings begin; final constitution signed into law; Robben Island decommissioned
1997	Mandela retires as ANC president, succeeded by Thabo Mbeki
1999	ANC wins landslide victory in second democratic elections; Robben Island declared a UN World Heritage Site
2000	Oil spill in Table Bay leads to world's largest rescue effort for stricken African penguins
2001	Mbeki rejects calls for a state of emergency despite an estimated 4.7 million South Africans thought to be infected with HIV/AIDS

SARAH JOLLY

Travelling by wagon, the Trekboers moved inland to make a living beyond the reach of the Dutch East India Company's settlement on the Cape.

Despite outlawing slavery, the British introduced new laws that laid the basis for an exploitive labour system little different from slavery. Thousands of dispossessed blacks sought work in the colony, but it was made a crime to be in the colony without a pass – and without work. It was also a crime to leave a job.

Cape Economy Booms

The British introduced free trade, which greatly benefited Cape Town's economy. Cape wines, in particular, were a huge hit, accounting for some 10% of British wine consumption by 1822. During the first half of the 19th century, before the Suez Canal opened, British officers serving in India would holiday at the Cape.

Capetonians successfully managed to stop the British government's attempt to turn the colony into another Australia when their governor, Sir Harry Smith, forbade 282 British prisoners from leaving the ship *Neptune* when it docked in Cape Town in 1849. The *Neptune* continued to Tasmania and the locals, who had challenged the might of the empire, became bolder in their demands for self-government.

In 1854, a representative parliament was formed in Cape Town, but much to the dismay of Dutch and English farmers to the north and east, the British government and Cape liberals insisted on a multiracial constituency (albeit with financial requirements that excluded the vast majority of blacks and coloureds).

In 1860 construction of the Alfred Basin in the docks commenced, finally giving Cape Town a stormproof port. The opening of the Suez Canal in 1869 dramatically decreased the amount of shipping that sailed via the cape, but the discovery of diamonds and gold in the centre of South Africa in the 1870s and '80s helped Cape Town maintain its position as the country's premier port. Immigrants flooded into the city and the population trebled from 33,000 in 1875 to over 100,000 at the turn of the century.

Boer War & After

After the Great Trek the Boers established several independent republics, the largest being the Orange Free State (today's Free State province) and the Transvaal (today's Northern Province, Gauteng and Mpumalanga).

When the world's richest gold reef was found in the Transvaal (a village called Johannesburg sprang up beside it), the British were miffed that the Boers should control such wealth and precipitated war in 1899. The Boers were vastly outnumbered but their tenacity and knowledge of the country resulted in a long and bitter conflict. The British finally defeated them in 1902.

Cape Town was not directly involved in any of the fighting but it did play a key role in landing and supplying the half a million imperial and colonial troops who fought on the British side. The Mount Nelson Hotel was used as headquarters by Lords Roberts and Kitchener.

Bubonic plague in 1901 gave the government an excuse to introduce racial segregation. Africans were moved to two locations, one near the docks and the other at Ndabeni on the western flank of Table Mountain. This was the start of what later would develop into the townships of the Cape Flats.

After the war, the British made some efforts towards reconciliation, and instituted moves towards the union of the separate South African provinces. In the Cape, blacks and coloureds retained a limited franchise (although only whites could become members of the national parliament, and eligible blacks and coloureds constituted only around 7% of the electorate), but did not have the vote in other provinces.

The issue of which city should become the capital was solved by the unwieldy compromise of making Cape Town the seat of the legislature, Pretoria the administrative capital, and Bloemfontein the judicial capital. The Union of South Africa came into being in 1910.

Racism Rules

Afrikaners were economically and socially disadvantaged compared with the English-speaking minority, who controlled most of the capital and industry in the new country. This, plus lingering bitterness over the war and Afrikaners' distaste at having to compete with blacks and coloureds for low-paying jobs, led to strident Afrikaner nationalism and the formation of the National Party.

In 1948 the National Party came to power on a platform of apartheid (literally, 'the state of being apart'). In a series of bitter court and constitutional battles, the right of coloureds to vote in the Cape was removed and the insane apparatus of apartheid was erected.

Mixed marriages were prohibited, interracial sex was made illegal and every person was classified by race. The Group Areas Act defined where people of each 'race' could live and the Separate Amenities Act created separate public facilities: separate beaches, separate buses, separate toilets, separate schools and separate park benches. Blacks were compelled to carry passes at all times and were prohibited from living in or even visiting towns without specific permission.

The Dutch Reformed Church justified apartheid on religious grounds, claiming the separateness of the races was divinely ordained. The volk (literally, 'the people', but it means Afrikaners) had a holy mission to preserve the purity of the white race in its promised land.

A system of Homelands was set up, whereby just 13% of South Africa was allocated to blacks, who made up about 75% of the population. The idea was that each black group had a traditional area where it belonged – and must now stay. The government defined 10 such groups, based largely on dubious 19th-century scholarship.

Apart from the inequity of the land allocation, not to mention the injustice of making decisions about people who couldn't vote, this plan was crazy, as it ignored the huge numbers of blacks who had never lived in 'their' Homeland. Millions of people who had lived for generations in other areas were forcibly removed and dumped in bleak, unproductive areas with no infrastructure. Starvation was a real possibility.

The Homelands were regarded as self-governing states and it was planned that they would become independent countries. Four of the 10 Homelands were nominally independent by the time apartheid was demolished (they were not recognised as independent countries by the UN), and their dictators held power with the help of the South African military.

Of course, the white population depended on cheap black labour to keep the economy booming, so many black 'guest workers' were admitted to South Africa. But unless a black had a job and a pass, he or she was liable to be jailed and sent back to the Homeland.

This caused massive disruption to black communities and families. Not surprisingly, people without jobs gravitated to towns and cities to be near their husbands, wives and parents.

No new black housing was built. As a result, illegal squatter camps mushroomed on the sandy plains to the east of Cape Town. In response, government bulldozers flattened the shanties, and their occupants were dragged away and dumped in the Homelands. Within weeks, inevitably, the shanties would rise again.

The western half of what was then known as Cape Province (now covering most of Northern Cape, Eastern Cape and Western Cape provinces) was declared a 'coloured preference area', which meant no black person could be employed unless it could be proved there was no coloured person suitable for the job.

In 1960 the African National Congress (ANC) and the Pan-African Congress (PAC) organised marches against the hated pass laws, which required blacks and coloureds to carry passbooks authorising them to be in a particular area. At Langa and Nyanga on the Cape Flats, police killed five protesters. In response to the crisis, a warrant for the arrest of Nelson Mandela and other ANC leaders was issued. In mid-1963 Mandela was captured and sentenced to life imprisonment. Like many black leaders before him, Mandela was imprisoned on Robben Island, in the middle of Table Bay.

The government tried for decades to eradicate squatter towns, such as Crossroads, which were focal points for black resistance to the apartheid regime. In its last attempt between May and June 1986, an estimated 70,000 people were driven from their homes and hundreds were killed. Even this brutal attack was unsuccessful in eradicating the towns, and the government accepted the inevitable and began to upgrade conditions. Vast townships have sprung up across the Cape Flats, and are now home to possibly 1.5 million or more people – no-one really knows how many.

District Six

Under apartheid Cape Town's coloured communities had no more of an easy time of it than the blacks. District Six, immediately east of the city centre, was the suburb that, more than any other, gave Cape Town its cosmopolitan atmosphere and life. It was primarily a poor, overcrowded coloured ghetto but people of every race lived there. The streets were alive with people, from children to traders, buskers to petty criminals. Jazz was its life blood, and the district was home to many musicians, including the internationally known pianist Dollar Brand (now called Abdullah Ibrahim). Being so close to the centre, it infected the whole city with its vitality.

This state of affairs naturally did not appeal to the National Party government, so, in 1966, District Six was classified as a white area. Its 50,000 people, some of whose families had been there for five generations, were gradually evicted, and were dumped in bleak and soulless townships like Athlone, Mitchell's Plain and Atlantis. Friends, neighbours, even relations were separated. Bulldozers moved in and the multiracial heart was ripped out of the city, while in the townships, depressed and dispirited youths increasingly joined gangs and turned to crime.

Today District Six largely remains an open wasteland, a depressing monument to the cruelty and stupidity of the government. A ray of hope, though, came on 27 November 2000 when President Thabo Mbeki signed a document handing back the confiscated land to the former residents of District Six. Although it would be impossible for all the 8000 or so forcibly removed families to return (new constructions such as the Cape Technikon college now occupy part of the area), some do plan to reclaim their property and live again in a rejuvenated District Six.

The Bo-Kaap

The history of the Bo-Kaap, the largely Cape Muslim area on the north-eastern edge of Signal Hill, provides an interesting contrast to that of District Six. Home to Cape Town's first mosque (the Auwal Mosque on Dorp St dates back to 1798), the district was once known as the Malay Quarter because

Nelson Mandela

No person has been as important in South Africa's recent history as Nelson Rolihlahla Mandela. It is a testament of his force of personality, transparent decency and integrity that Mandela, a man once vilified by the ruling whites, helped unite all South Africans at the most crucial of times.

The son of the third wife of a Xhosa chief, Mandela was born on 18 July 1918 in the small village of Mveso on the Mbashe River. When he was very young the family moved to Qunu, south of Umtata, where he grew up in a mud hut. He attended school in the Transkei before going to Johannesburg where, after a few false starts, he became a lawyer and set up a practice with Oliver Tambo.

In 1944 he helped form the Youth League of the African National Congress (ANC) with Walter Sisulu and Oliver Tambo. Its aim was to end the racist policies of the white South African government. He met Nomzamo Winifred Madikizela ('Winnie') and married her in 1958, after receiving a divorce from his first wife, Evelyn.

In 1956 he was one of 156 ANC and Communist Party members charged with treason; all were found not guilty at the subsequent trial. But in 1964, having established the ANC's military wing and gone underground, Mandela was captured and sentenced to life imprisonment in the infamous Robben Island prison. He remained there until 1982 when he was moved to Pollsmoor Prison on the mainland.

By the time the ANC was declared a legal organisation, Mandela had again been transferred, this time to a house in the grounds of the Victor Vester Prison near Paarl. It was through the gates of this jail that Mandela walked, at last a free man, in 1990. In 1991 he was elected president of the ANC and continued the long negotiations (which had started secretly while he was in prison) to end minority rule. He shared the 1993 Nobel peace prize with FW De Klerk and, in the first free elections the following year, was elected president of South Africa.

The prison years had inevitably taken their toll on the Mandelas' marriage and in 1992, the couple separated, Nelson saying 'I part from my wife with no recriminations'. They were divorced in 1996.

Mandela's gift for reconciliation was best demonstrated by his famous 'Free at last!' speech made on 2 May 1994, when he said, 'This is the time to heal the old wounds and build a new South Africa'.

In 1997, Mandela (or Madiba, his traditional Xhosa name, which is frequently used as a mark of respect) retired as ANC president and on his 80th birthday in July 1998 he married Graca Machel, the widow of a former president of Mozambique. Despite suffering ailments caused by decades of harsh prison life, Mandela maintains a schedule of international engagements, and comments on domestic political and social developments as an elder statesman.

For more information on this charismatic man read his autobiography, *Long Walk to Freedom*, the first draft of which was written while he was still on Robben Island, and Anthony Sampson's exhaustive *Mandela, the Authorized Biography*. Also check out **w** www.pbs.org/wgbh/pages/front line/shows/mandela, the informative Web site of a PBS documentary series on Mandela.

---

it was where many of the imported slaves from the start of the Cape Colony lived with their masters.

In 1952 the entire Bo-Kaap region was declared a coloured area under the terms of the Group Areas Act. There were forced removals, but the residents of the community, which was more homogenous than that of District Six, banded together to successfully fight for and keep ownership of their homes, many of which were declared National Monuments in the 1960s (so at least they were saved from the bulldozers). Today, though, the area's Muslim character is noticeably diminishing as economic realities take hold. Defunct mosques on Long St indicate how far Bo-Kaap once extended into the city, and on its north-western flank, the trendy Waterkant district increasingly encroaches as yuppies snap up the characterful houses.

Path to Democracy

In the 1980s, amid deepening economic gloom caused by international sanctions and the increasing militancy of black opposition groups (which began with the Soweto student uprising in 1976), it became obvious that continuing with apartheid would lead to disaster.

In 1982, Nelson Mandela and other ANC leaders were moved from Robben Island to Pollsmoor Prison in Cape Town. (In 1986 senior politicians began secretly talking with them.) In 1983, the United Democratic Front (UDF) was formed when 15,000 anti-apartheid activists gathered at Mitchell's Plain in the Cape Flats. At the same time the state's military crackdowns in the townships became even more brutal.

In early 1990, President De Klerk began to repeal discriminatory laws, and the ANC, the PAC and the Communist Party were legalised. On 11 February Nelson Mandela was released. His first public speech since he had been incarcerated 27 years earlier was delivered from the balcony of City Hall to a massive crowd filling the Grand Parade.

From this time onwards virtually all the old apartheid regulations were repealed, and in late 1991, the Convention for a Democratic South Africa (Codesa) began negotiations on the formation of a multiracial transitional government and a new constitution extending political rights to all groups.

Months of negotiations and brinkmanship finally produced a compromise and an election date, although at considerable human cost. Political violence exploded across the country during this time. It's now known that elements within the police and the army contributed to this violence. There have also been claims that high-ranking government officials and politicians ordered, or at least condoned, massacres.

Across the country at midnight on 26 April 1994, *Die Stem* (the old national anthem) was sung and the old flag was lowered. Then the new rainbow flag was raised and the new anthem, *Nkosi Sikelele Afrika (God Bless Africa)*, was sung – in the past people had been jailed for singing this beautiful hymn. The election was amazingly peaceful and there was an air of goodwill throughout South Africa.

The ANC won 62.7% of the vote, less than the 66.7% that would have enabled it to rewrite the constitution. In Western Cape, though, the majority coloured population voted in the National Party as the provincial government, seemingly happier to live with the devil they knew than with the ANC.

Truth & Reconciliation Commission

Crimes of the apartheid era were exposed by the Truth & Reconciliation Commission (1994–99). This admirable institution carried out Archbishop Desmond Tutu's dictum: 'Without forgiveness there is no future, but without confession there can be no forgiveness'. Many stories of horrific brutality and injustice were heard by the commission, offering some catharsis to indivduals and communities shattered by their past.

SARAH JOLLY

Former archbishop of Cape Town Desmond Tutu

The commission operated by allowing victims to tell their stories and perpetrators to confess their guilt, with amnesty offered to those who made a clean breast of it. Those who chose not to appear before the commission face criminal prosecution if their guilt can be proven, and that's the problem. Although some soldiers, police and 'ordinary' citizens have confessed their crimes, it seems unlikely that the human-rights criminals who gave the orders and dictated the policies will appear (former president PW Botha was one famous no-show), and gathering evidence against them has proven difficult.

The catalogue of crimes committed by the apartheid government and its servants is truly horrific, ranging from beatings, torture, murders and massacres to twisted science, including attempts to design poisons that would kill only nonwhite people. Widespread abuses aside, the simple fact remains that apartheid led to tens of millions of people being denied basic human rights because of their skin colour.

1999 Election

In December 1997, Mandela stepped down as ANC president and was succeeded by his deputy, Thabo Mbeki. Jacob Zuma was appointed the new deputy president.

In 1999, after five years of learning about democracy, the country held the second free elections in its history. There had been speculation that the ANC vote might drop, but in fact it increased to put the party within one seat of the two-thirds majority that would allow it to alter the constitution.

The NP, restyled as the New National Party (NNP), lost two-thirds of its seats, and the revitalised Democratic Party (DP) became the official opposition. This party has shifted to the right since the apartheid years when the DP's Helen Suzman represented a solitary voice of opposition to the NP. The new United Democratic Movement (UDM) attempted to exploit disillusionment with the ANC, but fared poorly. The mainly Zulu Inkatha Freedom Party (IFP) lost some support but its leader, Chief Buthelezi, still wields power in the government as home affairs minister.

Since the general election the NNP and the DP have joined together in opposition as the Democratic Alliance. In 2000, the alliance won control of Western Cape and of the city in provincial and metropolitan elections.

Cape Town Today

During the 1990s drugs became such a problem in the Cape area that communities, and in particular the coloured community, began to take matters into their own hands. People against Gangsterism and Drugs (Pagad) was formed in 1995, but the movement quickly turned sour in 1996 with the horrific (and televised) death of gangster Rashaad Staggie. A lynch mob burned then repeatedly shot the dying gangster, and Pagad was labelled as a group of violent vigilantes by both white and black politicians.

Pagad members are mainly coloured Muslims living in the bleak townships of Mitchell's Plain. The group sees itself as defending the coloured community from the crooked cops and drug lords who allow gangs to control the coloured townships.

But this is South Africa and nothing is as simple as it might seem. The gangs in the coloured townships grew out of a desperate need for the coloured community to organise itself against criminals from the neighbouring black townships. Gang members saw themselves as upright citizens defending their community. Many blacks bitterly resented the coloureds because they received 'favoured' treatment from the apartheid government, and also because blacks perceived the coloureds as not being active in the fight against apartheid.

To further complicate the issue, Pagad is in danger of being hijacked by an Islamic fundamentalist group. The battles between Pagad and the gangsters continue; a series of bombings of Cape Town police stations in 1999 and a bomb at the Waterfront have been blamed on the group. The trial of five Pagad members for the murder of Staggie only began, after much legal wrangling, in May 2001.

Suspicion and mistrust between the black and coloured communities remains one of

SARAH JOLLY

Thabo Mbeki succeeded Nelson Mandela as South Africa's president in 1999.

the more heartbreaking legacies of the apartheid era. In an effort to work towards what former archbishop Desmond Tutu called the Rainbow Nation, the local media launched a 'One City, Many Cultures' program in 1999. It has proved popular. The process of integration and mutual acceptance and understanding is being further helped along by the restructuring of Cape Town's local government to create six councils each covering a broad range of communities, rich and poor, black, white and coloured.

GEOGRAPHY

Cape Town is at the northern end of a peninsula that juts into the Atlantic Ocean on the south-west tip of Southern Africa. The peninsula has a steep, high spine of mountains, beginning at Devil's Peak in Cape Town and running all the way down to Cape Point. Table Mountain, the most prominent feature of these mountains, is more than 1000m high, starting close to sea level. The escarpment running down the Atlantic (west) coast south of Table Mountain forms a striking series of buttresses known as the Twelve Apostles (although there are more than 12 of these formations).

The suburbs and towns on the Atlantic coast, and those on False Bay, west of Muizenberg, cling to a very narrow coastal strip. East of these mountains the land slopes more gently down to the Cape Flats, a sandy plain. Looking east across the Cape Flats you can see more mountain ranges rising up around Stellenbosch and, to the south-east, the Hottentots Holland area. They are sometimes snowcapped in winter. Behind these ranges are others which rise to the Great Southern African Plateau and the semidesert of the Karoo.

There is no major river in the city area, although there is a system of lakes northeast of Muizenberg, near the Cape Flats.

GEOLOGY

Some 600 million years ago, all of what today is Cape Town lay beneath the sea. Volcanic activity pushed the land briefly out of the ocean but it wouldn't be until roughly 400 million years later that another series of cataclysmic earth movements would force the land back up again for good. The continent of Africa began to form around 125 million years ago, and the bit of the plateau around Cape Town gradually eroded to leave behind Table Mountain.

All this geological activity has left the Cape Peninsula with three main types of rock. The lower reaches of the mountains are made up of Malmesbury shale, a soft, finely textured rock that is easily weathered. Under the shale, and sticking out in places such as Simon's Town and along the Atlantic coast, is Cape granite. The mountains themselves are Table Mountain sandstone, which is a combination of sandstone and quartzite that starts off grey and weathers to red-brown.

The sandy deposits that make up the Cape Flats are a comparatively recent addition.

CLIMATE

Weather is not really a critical factor in deciding when to visit Cape Town. Great extremes of temperature are unknown, although it can be relatively cold and wet for a few months in winter.

One of the Cape's most characteristic phenomena is the famous Cape doctor, a south-easterly wind that buffets the Cape and lays Table Mountain's famous 'tablecloth' (a layer of cloud that covers the City Bowl). It can be a welcome breeze in summer, but it can also be a wild gale, particularly in spring. When it really blows you know you're clinging to a peninsula at the southern end of Africa, and there's nothing between you and the Antarctic.

In winter, between June and August, temperatures range from 7°C to 18°C, with

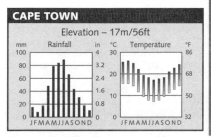

pleasant, sunny days scattered between the gloomy ones. The prevailing winds are north-westerly. If the wind is blowing from the chilly inland mountains it can be cold; otherwise the temperature is tolerable. The rain tends to come in heavy showers, with long, fine breaks. However, it is not unknown for a rainy spell to set in and Table Mountain to be invisible for a week.

Between September and November the weather is unpredictable, with anything from bright warm days to howling south-easterly storms and winds of up to 120km/h. (The wildflowers are at their best during August and September.)

December to March can be very hot, although the average maximum temperature

Do-It-Yourself Forecasting

As if Table Mountain is not spectacular enough in itself, for much of the summer it is capped by a seemingly motionless cloud that drapes itself neatly across the summit. The cloud is known as the tablecloth. An Afrikaner legend explains this phenomenon by telling of an old burgher, who was fond of his pipe, attempting to outsmoke the devil in a competition.

Meteorologists have come up with a more prosaic explanation. The south-easterly wind (the Cape doctor) picks up moisture as it crosses the Agulhas current and False Bay. When it hits Table Mountain it rises, and as it reaches cooler air around 900m above sea level it condenses into thick white clouds. As the clouds pour over the plateau and down into the City Bowl they once more dissolve in the warmer air at around 900m.

Table Mountain happens to be at the perfect height and place, and the tablecloth is a dynamic and hypnotic sight.

Many people use the mountain as a weather forecaster, and it's apparently quite accurate. Some things to watch for:

• If there is heavy cloud on Lion's Head, rain is coming.

• If the tablecloth shrouds the mountain, the Cape doctor is coming.

• If there is no cloud around the upper cableway station (visible from all over town), there is no wind on Clifton Beach.

is only 26°C and the Cape doctor generally keeps things bearable (it is usually relatively calm in the mornings). From March to April, and to a lesser extent in May, the weather remains good and the wind is at its most gentle.

The Cape is the meeting point for two great ocean currents that have a major impact on the climate of Southern Africa, and the Cape itself. The cold Benguela current (about 8°C) runs up the west side of the Cape from Antarctica. The warm Agulhas current (about 20°C) swings around Madagascar and the east coast from the equatorial waters of the Indian Ocean and, if you're lucky, into False Bay. If you're unlucky, the spring and summer south-easterly blows cold water into the bay.

ECOLOGY & ENVIRONMENT

So special is the environment of the Cape Peninsula that the whole area has been nominated for UN World Heritage status. Yet four centuries on from European settlement it is also an environment that has been radically and often detrimentally changed, with the indigenous flora and fauna now surviving mainly in reserves and on agriculturally unviable land.

Dense evergreen forests that were once home to large mammals have long since vanished. Forests of nonindigenous trees such as oak, pine and eucalypt have been planted in their place. In the Cape's kind climate these aliens have thrived, but have also wreaked havoc on the environment.

The wind-sculpted pines that coat the lower slopes of Table Mountain are draining the Cape of its precious water supplies; the whole peninsula regularly suffers water shortages. Their presence also contributed to the devastating forest fires that swept across the mountain in January 2000.

The Cape's unique *fynbos* (see Flora following) is also under attack from alien flora, which include black wattle *(Acacia mearnsii)* and Port Jackson wattle *(Acacia saligna)*. Sydney golden wattle *(Acacia longifolia)*, introduced to the Cape early last century, has also become a pest. Probably the worst offender is *Hakea sericea* (known

locally as silky hakea), imported as a hedge plant in the 1830s and now declared a noxious weed in South Africa.

Australian plants were often imported for special purposes (the bark of the black wattle, for example, was used in leather-making, and Port Jackson wattle served to bind soil), but the results have been devastating to local flora. These introduced species require more water than native plants do, but thrive without natural enemies; water sources dry up and fynbos is choked out of certain areas as a result.

In 1997 an alien-clearance program was started within and around what has now become the Cape Peninsula National Park. It is the largest such program of its type and has shown positive results so far.

In the huge townships and squatter camps on the Cape Flats, Third-World economic imperatives mean poor environmental standards. The most obvious sign of this is the smoke that sometimes drifts around the mountain and over the city, building up into quite heavy pollution after a few windless days. Luckily for those on the city side of the mountain, successive windless days are uncommon. The airport is close to the townships and planes sometimes have to make instrument landings because of the smoke.

Most of the smoke is from fires used for cooking and heating (people trudging back to the townships carrying loads of wood is a common sight on the roads east of the city) but some is from burning tyres. A few scraps of metal can be gleaned from a tyre and then sold.

Pollution is also a threat to the marine environment, as demonstrated by an oil spill in Table Bay in June 2000 (see the boxed text 'Saving the African Penguin' in the Things to See & Do chapter).

FLORA

Cape Town and Western Cape are home to the fascinating Cape floral kingdom, the richest and smallest of the world's six floral kingdoms. (The other five are the Holarctic, Paleotropical, Neotropical, Australian and Holantarctic floral kingdoms.)

KATIE BUTTERWORTH

Daisies are among the flowers commonly encountered in and around Cape Town.

All told there are nearly 8500 plant species in the Cape floral kingdom, more than three times as many per square kilometre as in South America. In part this is a result of ecological isolation, as South Africa's mountain ranges harbour miniuniverses of biodiversity. At least as impressive as the number of species is their colour; the profusion of hues could drive a would-be post-impressionist back to the banks of the Seine.

The Cape floral kingdom extends from Cape Point east to Port Elizabeth (or Grahamstown, depending on how the flora is defined) and north to the Olifants River. Table Mountain and the peninsula alone contain some 2285 plant species, more than all of Britain.

The most common type of vegetation is fynbos (literally 'fine bush', from the Dutch). Fynbos somehow thrives in the area's nitrogen-poor soil – it's supposed that the plants' fine, leathery leaves improve their odds of survival by discouraging predators. Fynbos is composed of three main elements: proteas (South Africa's national emblem), heaths and reeds.

The family with the largest number of species is actually Asteraceae (daisies) – there are nearly 1000 species, of which nearly two-thirds are endemic.

Orchids are also found throughout the region, mainly in marshlands and grasslands. Red disa and blue disa are especially worth watching for.

Many species of the family Iridaceae not only thrive in the fynbos, they have also taken root in gardens around the world (eg, freesia, iris and watsonia).

Apart from fynbos, on Signal Hill and the lower slopes of Devil's Peak you'll find *renosterbos* (literally 'rhinoceros bush'), a vegetation type that is composed predominantly of a grey ericoid shrub, and peppered with grasses and rich in geophytes (plants that grow from underground bulbs). In the cool, well-watered ravines on the eastern slopes of Table Mountain you'll also find small pockets of Afro-montane forest and thicket.

FAUNA

Cape Town and Western Cape support few large animal species, but there is much fauna to look out for, especially in the Cape Peninsula National Park.

Lions, elephants, black rhinos and hippos used to live on the peninsula. Except for the hippos, which have been reintroduced to Rondevlei Nature Reserve, all these large mammals have long gone, and the closest you'll get to an elephant these days in Cape Town is by spotting its nearest living relative, the ubiquitous dassie, also known as the rock hyrax, on Table Mountain.

Table Mountain is home to 111 invertebrates and one vertebrate (the Table Mountain ghost frog) not found anywhere else on Earth. The birdlife is particularly impressive.

Among the feral population of introduced fallow deer that roam the lower slopes of Table Mountain around the Rhodes Memorial, you may spot an animal long regarded as extinct: the quagga. This partially striped zebra was formerly thought to be a distinct species, but DNA obtained from a stuffed quagga in Cape

Birdlife on the Cape

Cape Town is a fine place for an aspiring bird-watcher. The unique vegetation *fynbos* (fine bush), the rugged escarpment of Table Mountain, the wetlands and the rich coastal waters all support an exciting variety of birdlife. Cape Town also makes a good base for trips further afield: There are some excellent natural areas on the very edge of the city, and numerous national parks and nature reserves are only a day trip away.

Apart from carrying a field guide and a pair of binoculars, try the following tips to get the most out of bird-watching:

- Start early, particularly in hot weather. Most birds are more active during the cooler hours of the day.
- Approach birds slowly and avoid sudden movements or loud talk.
- Dress in drab clothing so as not to stand out.
- Birds are not usually too concerned about people in vehicles, and stunning views can often be obtained from the road side.
- Water birds and waders respond to tidal movements and are usually best seen on a falling tide as they search for food.
- Always ask permission before birding on private property.
- Do not disturb birds unnecessarily and never handle eggs or young birds in a nest. Adults will readily desert a nest that has been visited, leaving their young to perish.

City Centre (Map 13)

Even while walking around town you may notice some wild birds – this is Africa, after all. Parks and gardens are a good place to start, and among the portly pigeons being fed at lunch time you may see the more graceful red-eyed dove and the smaller laughing dove. Male Cape sparrows are recognisable by their striking black-and-white head pattern.

Table Mountain (Map 12)

Sharing the view with you and the dassies at the top of Table Mountain will be a few hopeful rock pigeons, recognisable by their red eye patch and white-spotted wings, and the noisy and garrulous red-winged starlings. Walking one of the trails on the mountain you will encounter a variety of habitats and birds. Larger species include birds of prey, such as black eagles and rock kestrels. Swifts and martins dart through the air, while the iridescent green malachite sunbird and its pied relative, the dusky sunbird, feed on emergent flowers.

Town's South African Museum showed it to be a subspecies of the widespread Burchell's zebra. A breeding program which started in 1987 has proved successful in 'resurrecting' the quagga.

Mammals in the Cape of Good Hope section of the national park include eight antelope species, Cape mountain zebras and a troupe of Chacma baboons. Many signs warn you not to feed the baboons (and you shouldn't – they're potentially dangerous).

Both the southern right whale and the humpback whale breed in False Bay and along the southern coast (for more information see Hermanus in the Excursions chapter). Dolphins can also be spotted in False Bay, while Cape fur seals entertain visitors to the Waterfront and can be seen in a more natural environment at Duiker Island, which can be reached from Hout Bay.

GOVERNMENT & POLITICS
National Government

South Africa's constitution is one of the most enlightened in the world – not surprising when you consider the people's long

Birdlife on the Cape

Kirstenbosch Botanical Gardens (Map 11, #13)

Be especially on the lookout for two of the region's specialities: the Cape sugarbird and the orange-breasted sunbird. Each has a down-curved beak with which it probes for nectar; the male sugarbird is recognisable by his long showy tail and the male sunbird by his green iridescent plumage and orange-yellow breast.

Boulders Beach (Map 11)

A must for any bird enthusiast is the colony of African penguins at Boulders Beach. There's also a colony on Robben Island.

Cape of Good Hope Nature Reserve (Map 11)

Some 240 species of birds, including cormorants, have been recorded here; you'll see their nests on the cliffs at Cape Point and Cape Maclear. Shore birds feeding at the water's edge can include oyster-catchers, plovers and sandpipers; you should be able to see sugarbirds and sunbirds feeding along the road sides. You may be lucky enough to spot a majestic albatross, particularly when onshore winds drive them close to land. Look out for marauding skuas: large, dark relatives of the gulls that harass sea birds and force them to drop their catch.

West Coast National Park (Map 1)

Just south of the Berg River Estuary (which is also an excellent bird-spotting location), this national park is famous for sea birds and waders. It shelters the lovely Langebaan Lagoon and features a good cross-section of habitats in which some 250 bird species have been recorded. There are several colonies of the beautiful European bee-eater around the park.

Strandfontein Sewage Works (Map 11)

These ponds between Muizenberg and Strandfontein are no longer used for treating sewage, but they attract an impressive number of birds. Look for ducks, herons, egrets and pelicans; smaller birds frequent the waterside vegetation.

Rondevlei Nature Reserve (Map 11)

Situated at Zeekoevlei, 24km south-east of Cape Town, the fluctuating water levels of this small nature reserve attract egrets, herons, ducks and waders. The striking African fish-eagle is sometimes seen patrolling the ponds, as are flocks of greater flamingos. Facilities include a waterside trail, two viewing towers and hides.

David Andrew

struggle for freedom. Apart from forbidding discrimination on practically any grounds, among other things it guarantees freedom of speech and religion, and access to adequate housing, adequate health care and basic adult education.

There are two houses of parliament: the National Assembly with 400 members and the National Council of Provinces (NCOP) with 100 members. Members of the National Assembly are elected directly using the proportional representation method (there are no constituencies), but members of the NCOP are appointed by the provincial legislatures. Each province, regardless of its size, appoints 10 councillors, then there are 10 more from the South African Local Government Association, representing the six metropolitan districts: Johannesburg, Pretoria, East Rand, Cape Town, Nelson Mandela Metropole (an area that includes Port Elizabeth) and Durban.

The head of state is the president, currently Thabo Mbeki, leader of the ANC. The president is elected by the National Assembly (and thus is always the leader of the majority party) rather than directly by the people. A South African president has more in common with a Westminster-style prime minister than with a US president, although as head of state he or she does have some executive powers denied most other prime ministers.

National elections will next be held sometime between May and July of 2004.

In addition to the Western-style system of democracy there is a system of traditional leadership. All legislation pertaining to indigenous law, tradition or custom must be referred to the Council of Traditional Leaders. Although the council cannot veto or amend legislation it can delay its passage. There are no recognised traditional authorities in Western Cape.

Cape Town was, and remains, one of the three capitals of South Africa. Pretoria is the administrative capital, Bloemfontein is the judicial capital and Cape Town is the seat of the nation's parliament (it's also home to the legislature of Western Cape province). The talk of moving parliament to Pretoria to save money remains just that – talk.

Provincial Government

Each province has its own legislature and a premier. Provincial governments have strictly limited powers and are bound by the national constitution. There are the six metropolitan governments, too, covering South Africa's largest conurbations, which include Cape Town.

Cape Town is the capital of Western Cape province, one of only two provinces in the country not to have an ANC government. In the 1999 elections the ANC won 42% of the vote but was kept out of power by a coalition of the New National Party and the Democratic Party.

It seems astounding that one of the most liberal areas of South Africa should elect the party that created and enforced apartheid. However, those who identify themselves as coloured make up the largest voting group in Western Cape province. Coloureds are largely Afrikaans-speaking and under apartheid they received slightly better treatment than blacks. It's believed many coloureds voted for parties other than the ANC out of fear of a black government. Many blacks resented the coloureds' favoured status and perceived them as uncommitted to the struggle against apartheid. An ANC government might, the coloureds feared, seek revenge.

ECONOMY

South Africa's economy is a mixture of First World and Third World, with marked disparities in incomes, living standards, education standards and work opportunities. On one hand there is a modern, industrialised urban economy; on the other there is a subsistence agricultural economy little changed since the 19th century. In the middle are the mainly black and coloured urban workers.

While there is tremendous poverty in South Africa, on an African scale the country's economy is not only reasonably successful, it dwarfs all others on the continent. The success is based, to a large degree, on tremendous natural wealth, First-World industrialisation, and an abundance of low-paid black labour.

Until the discovery of diamonds at Kimberley (1869) and the gold reef on the Witwatersrand (1886), the economy was exclusively agricultural. Since then, mineral wealth has been the key to development. Mining remains central to the economy, and South Africa is the world's leading supplier of gold, chromium, manganese, vanadium and platinum. Mining accounts for some 40% of exports and 6.5% of gross domestic product (GDP). The manufacturing industry grew rapidly during and after WWII, mostly to meet local demand. Oddly, it was the aggressively antisocialist apartheid governments that instituted massive state ownership of industry, and it is the quasi-socialist ANC government that is privatising industry.

Previous national governments successfully sought the redirection of wealth into Afrikaner hands through economic intervention. The private sector is highly centralised and is dominated by De Beers and the Anglo American Corporation, which are enormous and interrelated. Their combined stockmarket capitalisation is more than four times greater than that of their closest competition.

Western Cape accounts for 14.2% of the country's total GDP, and many of South Africa's petroleum, insurance and retail corporations are based in Cape Town. Viticulture, clothing, textiles, agriculture and fishing are all important sectors of the local economy. Like the rest of the country, Western Cape has well-developed infrastructure with an excellent transport system.

Nationally, both inflation (running at 7.8% in February 2001) and massive unemployment remain problems. Moreover, even if the economy recovers to its boom-time peak, almost the only people to benefit immediately will be whites. Blacks and coloureds have never shared in the fruits of their labour and it will be very difficult for the government to ensure that they do in the future. The economy is still geared to an unlimited pool of black and coloured workers (who are paid Third-World rates), and restructuring will be a long and slow process.

The challenges facing South Africa are not dissimilar to those facing the rest of the First World. Is it ever possible to justify gross economic inequality that is based on race or nationality? Can, for instance, a Californian justify their wealth to a Mexican (who by a stroke of fate was born a mile south of an arbitrary border)? Can an Australian justify their wealth to an Indonesian?

While the word debates the merits and problems of globalisation, South Africa, like many countries, must also find a way to create and redistribute wealth within its own borders – without alienating the white community, foreign investors or the many poverty-stricken people. (For tips on how you can help in some small way as a traveller, see Responsible Tourism in the Facts for the Visitor chapter.)

POPULATION & PEOPLE
Of South African's population of 43 million people, 33.2 million are African (or black), 4.5 million are white, 3.8 million are coloured (ie, of mixed race) and 1.1 million are of Indian or Asian descent, leaving 400,000 others. There are reported to be

several million illegal immigrants from various other African countries.

Aside from the Afrikaners, the majority of white South Africans (around 1.9 million) are of British extraction. There is also a large and influential Jewish population (around 90,000). There are significant minorities of Portuguese (some 30,000), many of whom are refugees from Angola and Mozambique, as well as Germans, Dutch, Italians and Greeks.

Cape Town and Western Cape's racial mix is different from that of the rest of the country. Of the province's population of 4.6 million, coloureds account for 2.5 million, blacks for around 1 million, and whites and others the balance.

Blacks
Although most blacks in Cape Town are Xhosa hailing from Eastern Cape province, they are not the only group in the city. Cape Town's economy has attracted people from all over Southern Africa including a fair few immigrants from the rest of the continent, as you'll easily discover strolling around the craft markets outside the train station and at Green Point.

Xhosa culture itself is diverse, with many clan systems and subgroups. Politics makes for another division, with most people supporting the ANC but a sizable minority supporting the more hardline PAC. There are also economic divisions, with some owning their own houses in the townships; and subgroups based on culture, such as the Rastafarian community.

Few Xhosa in the Cape Flats maintain a traditional lifestyle, but among the women, in particular, different subgroups wear different costumes, colours and arrangements of beads. The Tembu and Bomvana favour red and orange ochres in the dyeing of their clothing, while the Pondo and Mpondomise use a very light blue (chemical dyes, which are nontraditional, are now much in use).

The Xhosa's deity is known variously as umDali, Thixo and Qamata. This deity also figured in the San religion and it's probable that the invading Xhosa adopted it from them. There are numerous minor

Dealing with Racism

In this book we make use of the old apartheid terms: white, black, coloured and Indian. It is impossible to pretend that these distinctions, as distasteful as they may seem, have disappeared from South Africa. Many South Africans proudly identify themselves with one or other of these groups – so, for example, you'll meet black South Africans who happily refer to themselves as black rather than South Africans or Africans (which is the ANC's preferred collective expression for all people of African, Indian and mixed-race origin).

We have no problem with someone arguing that there are cultural differences (based on language, shared beliefs, ancestry, place of birth, tribe, political beliefs or religion) that sometimes correlate to some degree with skin colour. However, when such differences are used to justify inequality, intolerance or prejudgment, problems arise.

Visitors to South Africa will find that although the apartheid regime has been dismantled, cultural apartheid still exists. To an extent, discrimination based on wealth is replacing that based on race (so most visitors will automatically gain high status), but there are still plenty of people (mainly whites) who sincerely believe that a particular skin colour means a particular mind-set. A few believe it means inferiority.

If you aren't white, many white South Africans will register this. The constant awareness of race, even if it doesn't lead to problems, is an annoying feature of travel in South Africa, whatever your skin colour.

Racial discrimination is illegal, but it's unlikely that the overworked and underresourced police force will be interested in most complaints. Tourism authorities are likely to be more sensitive. If you encounter racism in any of the places mentioned in this book, please let us know.

African

If you are of African descent, you may well encounter some white resentment. The lies perpetuated about blacks during the apartheid era are taking some time to wear off. On the other hand, do not assume a special bond with black South Africans. The various indigenous peoples of South Africa form distinct and sometimes antagonistic cultural groups. Pan-Africanism is a force in politics here, but not the dominant force. Thus travellers of African descent from France or the USA will not necessarily receive a warmer welcome than anyone else.

White

If you are of European descent, it will be assumed by most white South Africans that you are essentially the same as them. However, if you've saved for your trip by, say, cleaning offices or working in a petrol station, you will get some startled reactions from some white South Africans. You may also find yourself having to listen to some obnoxious racist remarks.

Indian

Although Indians were discriminated against by whites during apartheid, blacks saw them as collaborating with the whites. If you are of Indian descent this could mean some low-level antagonism from both blacks and whites.

Asian

East Asians were a problem for apartheid – Japanese were granted 'honorary white' status, and people from other East Asian countries are probably indistinguishable from the Japanese to insular South Africans. Grossly inaccurate stereotyping and cultural ignorance will probably be the main annoyances you will face.

spirits, and a rich folklore persists in rural areas.

A belief in witches (male and female) is strong and witch-burning is not unknown.

Most witchcraft is thought to be evil, and the Xhosa's main fear is that they will be possessed by depraved spirits. The main source of evil is the tokoloshe (a mythical manlike creature), which lives in water but is also kept by witches. One reason why many Xhosa keep their beds raised high off the ground is to avoid being caught in their sleep by the tiny tokoloshe.

Water is not always seen as containing evil. If someone drowns and their body is not recovered, it is assumed, joyously, that they have gone to join 'the people of the sea'. It is also believed that the drowned are reincarnated with special knowledge and understanding.

The *igqirha* (spiritual healer), being able to deal with both the forces of nature and the trouble caused by witches, holds a very important place in traditional Xhosa society. The *ixhwele* (herbalist) performs some magic but is more concerned with health. *Mbongi* are the holders and performers of a group's oral history and are something like a cross between a bard and a court jester.

While there is a hierarchy of chiefs, the structure of Xhosa society is much looser than that of the Zulu.

Many people have the top of their left-hand little finger removed during childhood to prevent misfortune. Puberty rituals also figure heavily. Boys must not be seen by women during the three-month initiation period following circumcision; during this time the boys disguise themselves with white clay or in intricate costumes made of dried palm leaves. In the female puberty ritual, a girl is confined in a darkened hut while her friends tour the area singing for gifts.

Marriage customs and rituals are also important. Unmarried girls wear short skirts, which are worn longer as the wedding ceremony approaches. Married women wear long skirts and cover their breasts. They often put white clay on their faces and wear large, turban-like cloth hats. Smoking long-stemmed pipes is also popular among married women.

Beadwork and jewellery are culturally important. The *isi-danga* is a long turquoise necklace which identifies the wearer to their ancestors. The *ngxowa yebokwe* is a goat-skin bag carried over the left shoulder on important occasions.

Coloureds

Coloureds, sometimes known as Cape coloureds or Cape Malays and including Cape Muslims, are South Africans of long standing. Although many were brought to the early Cape Colony as slaves, others were political prisoners and exiles from the Dutch East Indies. People were brought from countries as far apart as India and modern Indonesia, as well as East Africa, but their lingua franca was Malay (at the time an important trading language), which is why they came to be called Cape Malays.

Although Islam could not be practised openly in the colony until 1804, the presence of influential and charismatic political and religious figures among the slaves helped a cohesive Cape Muslim community to develop. The Cape Muslim culture has survived intact over the centuries, and has even resisted some of the worst abuses of apartheid. The strongest evidence of it is in Cape Town's Bo-Kaap district; in the circle of 20 or so *karamats* (tombs of Muslim saints) that circle the city; and, to a lesser extent, in Simon's Town. (For more details see the boxed text 'Islamic Cape Town' in the Things to See & Do chapter.)

The slaves who moved out with the Dutch to the hinterland, many losing their religion and cultural roots in the process, had a much worse time of it. And yet practically all the coloured population of the Western Cape and Northern Cape provinces today are bound by the unique language that began to develop from the interaction between the slaves and the Dutch over three centuries ago. One of the oldest documents in Afrikaans is a Koran transcribed using Arabic script.

The most public secular expression of Cape-coloured culture today is the riotous Cape Minstrel Carnival (see the boxed text 'Cape Minstrel Carnival' in the Facts for the Visitor chapter). At the end of Ramadan thousands of Muslims pray on Cape Town's Sea Point promenade, where they gather to sight the new moon.

Whites

The Boers' history of geographical isolation and often deliberate cultural seclusion has created a unique people who are often called 'the white tribe of Africa'. (For details on their history, see History earlier in this chapter.) The Boers' lifestyle and culture, both real and idealised, have been the dominant factors shaping Afrikaners' view of themselves and their place in Africa.

The ethnic composition of Afrikaners is difficult to quantify but it has been estimated at 40% Dutch, 40% German, 7.5% French, 7.5% British and 5% other. Some historians have argued that the '5% other' figure includes a significant proportion of blacks and coloureds.

Afrikaans, the only Germanic language to have evolved outside Europe, is central to the Afrikaner identity but it has also served to reinforce their isolation from the outside world. The Afrikaners are a religious people and their brand of Christian fundamentalism based on 17th-century Calvinism is still a powerful influence.

Urbanised middle-class Afrikaners tend to be considerably more moderate. The further the distance between the horrors of the apartheid era and the 'new South Africa', though, the more room there is for Afrikaners to be proud of their heritage. One expression of such pride is the growing success of an annual all-Afrikaans arts festival, the Klein Karoo Nasionale Kunstefees (Little Karoo National Arts Festival), held in the Western Cape town of Outdshoorn. This annual festival attracts an audience of over 70,000 in March or April each year, and embraces a diverse range of drama and music.

Most other white South Africans are of British extraction. The British are much more urbanised than the Afrikaners and, particularly up until the 1960s, dominated the mining, manufacturing, financial and retail sectors, much to the resentment of the Afrikaners.

Cape Town, as the seat of British power for so long, is somewhat less Afrikaner in outlook than other parts of the country. Liberal Capetonians were regarded with suspicion by more conservative whites during the apartheid years, and even today the city is tantalisingly cosmopolitan in outlook.

EDUCATION

Western Cape has the highest literacy rate in the country, but on the whole South Africa continues to suffer from the education policies of the apartheid era. There's a whole generation of people who received little or no schooling at all because of the colour of their skin. Many black students took to the streets at the height of the struggle for political freedom chanting 'Liberation before education'. Nearly one in five South Africans aged 20 or older is considered illiterate.

Education now accounts for a large share of the national budget (21% of government spending in 2000–01), but still the system remains racked with difficulties. There's a desperate shortage of teachers, particularly in maths and the sciences; violence in schools is a major problem, as is attendance; and classrooms are overcrowded, with textbooks and other facilities in short supply. Sexual abuse of girls in schools is another enormous problem. Even the education minister, Kadar Asmal, admits that 30% of the nation's schools are not fit to be used.

There are some signs, though, that things are improving. In 2000, 57.9% of pupils nationally passed their final high-school exams, up from a dismal 48.9% in 1999. The pass rate of one school in a poor area of KwaZulu-Natal made an extraordinary leap from 7% to 94%. The proportion of students who did well enough to qualify for university courses rose from 12.5% to 14%. The improvements were attributed to a number of factors; for example, many pupils sat mock exams before their real ones for the first time, and more marks were allocated to course work than to final exams.

ARTS

Artists of all races were involved in the anti-apartheid campaign and some were placed under the equivalent of house arrest. In a society where you could be jailed for owning a painting deemed politically suspect, serious art was forced underground and blandness ruled in the galleries and theatres.

It is ironic then that the political freedom that accompanied the end of apartheid was not especially kind to local artists on several levels. First there was the lack of government funding now that there were considerably more serious problems to be addressed in the country. Second, with the fight against apartheid won, many artists were left initially floundering to find inspiration and expression for their work. Third came the inevitable attack on elitist European arts such as classical music, ballet and opera.

Several years down the line, the situation is beginning to look a little less bleak. Private companies are starting to fill the funding gap with much-needed sponsorship. Artists are finding their feet with contemporary subjects, or, more excitingly, returning to their roots for inspiration; witness the success of the theatre of the coloured community in Cape Town. The classical performing arts have fared the worst, but the relaunch of the city's philharmonic provides hope for the future.

Visual Arts

South Africa's oldest art is undoubtedly that of the San, who left their mark on the landscape in the form of rock paintings and subtle rock engravings. Despite having been faded by aeons of exposure these works of art are remarkable; for a fantastic example, have a look at the Linton Panel in the South African Museum.

While subject to strict conservation regulations, a number of rock-art sites are open to the public and it's worth seeing them (for details, see Cederberg Wilderness Area in the Excursions chapter). Today, San motifs are commonly employed on tourist art such as decorative mats and carved ostrich eggs.

The art of the Bantu-speaking peoples is similar to that of the San as a result of their long history of cultural interaction. Their traditional lifestyle led to their artefacts being portable and generally utilitarian (see the boxed text 'Crafts of the Region' in the Shopping chapter). Snuff containers, headrests, spoons and beadwork are not created as mere commodities: They are individual statements of self and have always entailed long hours of careful labour.

For a good overview of South African art during apartheid, see *Resistance Art in South Africa* by Sue Williamson. Her follow-up book *Art in South Africa: The Future Present* takes a look at the contemporary scene, which, as a wander around any of South Africa's major public and private galleries demonstrates, is tremendously exciting and imaginative.

In Cape Town you won't fail to notice the many examples of public art including murals, monuments and memorials. It's amazing how many of the old statues and icons of the apartheid era remain, perhaps testament to the tolerance of the black majority. Contrast these with the bright murals of the townships and the amusing *Africa* sculpture in St George's Mall, a piece of public art that blends a Côte d'Ivoire curio figure with the cartoon character Bart Simpson.

Cinema

Foreign movies about South Africa, such as *Zulu*, *Cry Freedom* and *A World Apart*, have found an international audience, but the South African film industry itself has had a harder time establishing a reputation. During the apartheid era the only film to make any kind of stir outside of South Africa was the bush comedy *The Gods Must Be Crazy*.

Part of the problem is the lack of support the film industry receives at home; you'll search in vain at South Africa's multiplexes for any locally made movies. So what are all those film makers doing every time you turn a corner in Cape Town? Well, most of them are making commercials, and most of those are for overseas clients – they like Cape Town's bright weather, its picturesque and quirky locations, and most of all its high-quality labour and low costs.

At the 2001 Oscars South Africa was represented, albeit at one remove, by an American documentary, *Long Night's Journey into Day*. This Sundance Film Festival winner follows four cases from the Truth & Reconciliation Commission hearings and is very moving.

Performing Arts

There's much breast-beating in South Africa about the state of performing arts, but, from an outside perspective at least, you only have to look at the success of arts festivals such as Outdshoorn's Klein Karoo Nasionale Kunstefees and the annual Festival of the Arts in Grahamstown, Eastern Cape, to see that the situation is far from bleak.

Theatre was important for blacks during the apartheid era, both as an art form and as a means of getting messages across to illiterate comrades. In the 1960s, Welcome Msomi had a huge hit with his Zulu version of Macbeth, *Umabatha*, which toured the world. Jo'burg's Market Theatre, where a lot of black theatre was staged, was and is the most important venue in South Africa.

Athol Fugard is the country's best-known playwright; his famous works include *Woza Albert*, *The Road to Mecca*, and collaborations with actors John Kani and Winston Ntshona such as *Sizwe Bansi is Dead*, about getting around the hated pass laws.

Capetonians David Kramer and Taliep Peterson scored an international hit with their jazz musical *Kat & the Kings*, which swept up awards in London in 1999 and received standing ovations on Broadway. Local successes include *Meet Joe Barber*, a comedy by Oscar Petersen and David Issacs, and Petersen's *Suip!*, a play about the homeless which has had outings in Australia and London. Concurrently, there's serious talk of the development of an indigenous Cape theatre.

Government subsidy for European cultural expressions no longer exists. However, collaboration between performing-arts companies and business is providing a solution; an example is the annual Summer Festival sponsored by South African Airways and held on the Spier Wine Estate near Stellenbosch. The 2001 program, performed by an ensemble cast of all races, embraced Bizet's *Carmen*, Brecht's *The Silver Lake*, Fugard's play *Hello & Goodbye,* and the Broadway musical *West Side Story*.

Literature

A number of excellent authors have helped unlock something of South Africa's soul, beginning with feminist Olive Schreiner (1855–1920), whose *Story of an African Farm*, first published in 1883 under a male pseudonym, was immediately popular and established her enduring reputation as one of South Africa's seminal novelists.

In a similar vein is *Jock of the Bushveld* by Sir James Percy Fitzpatrick, written in 1907. As well as being a story about the relationship between a man and his dog, it is a vivid portrayal of the time when the country was still dependent on ox-wagons for transport.

Nadine Gordimer's first book, *The Lying Days*, was published in 1953. In her subsequent novels she has explored South Africa, its people and their interaction with a merciless eye. The 1991 Nobel prize winner's more recent work homes in on the country's interracial dynamics and white liberal consciousness.

Gordimer is also represented in *Being There*, edited by Robin Malan, a good introductory collection of short stories from Southern African authors. *Transitions*, compiled by Craig MacKenzie, is a similar collection covering roughly half a century of South African short stories and including one by the country's most famous exponent of the form: Herman Charles Bosman.

Bosman, who wrote mainly in the 1930s and '40s, is an accessible writer and is widely popular for stories that blend humour and pathos, and capture the essence of rural South Africa. His most popular collection is *Mafeking Road*.

Alan Paton's *Cry the Beloved Country*, written in 1948 and one of the most famous South African novels, is an epic that follows a black man's suffering in white urban society. Paton returned to the theme of apartheid in *Ah but Your Land Is Beautiful*.

Circles in a Forest by Dalene Mathee, translated from Afrikaans, is a historical novel about woodcutters and elephants in the forests around Knysna, written from an Afrikaner point of view. It's a good one to read while travelling the Garden Route. Evocative of the Northern Cape and another fine translation from Afrikaans is Etienne Van Heerden's *Ancestral Voices*, which captures the tangled and tragic history of several generations of a Voortrekker family.

Cape Town is home to several prominent South African writers. The novels of JM Coetzee, twice winner of the coveted Booker Prize (in 1983 for *The Life and Times of Michael K* and in 1999 for *Disgrace*), like those of Gordimer, grapple with the white situation in the new South Africa. André Brink, another celebrated local, is seen as the foremost literary opponent of apartheid. His *Age of Iron* covers the end of apartheid and the lives of the homeless, known as Bergies in the Capetonian vernacular.

The books of Alex La Guma, a coloured writer who died in exile in 1985, are worth reading; they include *A Walk in the Night*, a collection of short stories set in the District Six area of Cape Town.

For obvious reasons black writers had a difficult time of it under apartheid. One area they could shine in, though, was the liberal press. The Johannesburg-based *Drum* magazine, for example, launched the career of Todd Matshikiza, among others. Today there is no shortage of books by black writers. Sindiwe Magona is a black female writer whose *Mother to Mother* is a fictionalised account of the correspondence between the mother of Amy Biehl, a white American woman murdered in the Cape Flats in 1993, and the mother of her killer. Another author to look out for is Zakes Mda, whose *Ways of Dying* is now a set text in schools. His recent *Heart of Redness* has been hailed as the most ambitious work of fiction by a black South African writer in a decade.

For information on nonfiction books about South Africa, see Books in the Facts for the Visitor chapter.

SOCIETY & CONDUCT

Traditional cultures do survive in South Africa, but very few people are able to live a purely traditional lifestyle, especially those living in cities like Cape Town. Teaching urban children about their heritage has become a growth industry in the new South Africa. Fortunately, indigenous languages remain strong.

There is nothing new in this – culture is never static and always responds to external events. Even during the short recorded history of the black peoples of Southern Africa, there have been several huge cultural changes (such as those caused by forced migration and white invasion). The idea that a people can have an intrinsic and unchangeable cultural identity and way of life was one of the racist myths promulgated by the apartheid regime to justify its Homelands policy. For example, if people prefer to live in square brick houses with tin roofs rather than circular mud huts with thatched roofs, it might mean fewer photo opportunities for visitors but it does mean a more comfortable life for the residents.

During the apartheid years, the Homelands kept alive some of the traditional cultures to an extent, but in a static form. The day-to-day realities of traditional and contemporary cultures were ignored, trivialised or destroyed. The most striking example of this in Cape Town was the bulldozing of District Six (see History earlier in this chapter).

Superficially, urban culture in South Africa today doesn't differ much from that found in Western countries. A small proportion of blacks and coloureds have lives not dissimilar from those of middle-class people anywhere, and the same can be said of most white South Africans.

What makes South Africa's urban culture different from that of other Western countries is that everyone is acutely aware of class and culture. Whites of Afrikaner and British descent form distinct subgroups, just as distinct from each other as the subgroupings of blacks from different language groups.

Although there are several majority and many minority groupings in the traditional black cultures, there are broad similarities. All are based on belief in a masculine deity, ancestral spirits and various supernatural forces. Marriage customs and taboos differ (though they are always important), but polygamy (which here means men can have more than one wife but women can have only one husband) is permitted. A *lobolo* (dowry) is usually paid to the groom's family. First-born males have inheritance rights.

Cattle play an important part in many cultures, as symbols of wealth and as sacrificial animals.

The British have always had a slightly equivocal position in South African society, exemplified by the not-so-friendly Afrikaans term *soutpiel*, literally 'salt dick', referring to a man with one foot in South Africa and one in Britain, his penis dangling in the ocean. Afrikaners have often felt (justifiably in many cases) that the English-speakers' commitment to Africa was lesser than their own. Apart from anything else, many of the British who arrived in the 20th century can return 'home' if things get really tough.

RELIGION

Over three-quarters of the population is Christian, but among Christians there is enormous diversity. This includes everything from the 4000 African indigenous churches to the racist sects that have split from the Dutch Reformed churches.

The indigenous churches are run by and for blacks, independent of the mainstream white churches. They broadly follow either the Ethiopian line, which broke away from the early Methodist missions, or the later Zionist line, which developed as a result of American Pentecostal missionary activity early this century.

The Dutch Reformed churches cover at least three major groups of Afrikaner churches, all of which are conservative. The largest and most influential is the Neder-

duitse Gereformeerde Kerk (the NG Kerk), once referred to as 'the National Party at prayer'. The Church of England is also represented; it gained a high profile because of the anti-apartheid battles of Archbishop Desmond Tutu.

About 580,000 people, virtually all of whom are of Indian descent, are Hindu.

There are roughly 600,000 Muslims, mainly from the coloured and Indian communities. In Cape Town there are few Indians but there is a large Muslim population that is not of recent Indian descent.

A minority of blacks follow traditional religions. Among different peoples, beliefs and practices vary, although there is usually a belief in a supreme deity (but with more emphasis on ancestor worship). Magic plays a large part in beliefs and ceremonies. The distinction between religion and what would be considered folklore in Western societies is blurred on a day-to-day level. Many blacks combine Christianity with traditional beliefs, in much the same way that Christianity adopted some 'pagan' rituals in its spread through Europe.

LANGUAGE

In the Cape Town area three languages are prominent: Afrikaans (spoken by many whites and coloureds), English (spoken by nearly everyone) and Xhosa (spoken mainly by blacks). For more information on languages, see the Language chapter near the back of this book.

Facts for the Visitor

WHEN TO GO

There's not really any best or worst time to visit Cape Town, although different seasons have their advantages.

From late December to the end of January accommodation can be hard to find and prices rise. Easter and the other school holidays are also busy times. You're more likely to encounter one of the famous south-easterly gales during spring (September to November), but this might be an attraction, with huge waves rolling up from the Antarctic and pounding the coastline. In winter (June to August) the weather can be a bit gloomy and, if the wind blows from the snowy peaks inland, chilly. However, there are plenty of clear days and the crowds have gone.

In pricing terms, peak season is from Christmas to late January. High season is the rest of summer (November to February) and sometimes October and March as well. Easter is also considered high season. Summer school holidays fall in high season; other school holidays (see School Holidays later in this chapter) are considered high season at some places, midseason at others. Low season is winter (June to August). Midseason is the rest of the year (ie, autumn and spring).

ORIENTATION

Cape Town's commercial centre, known as the City Bowl, lies to the north of Table Mountain and east of Signal Hill. The old inner-city suburbs of Tamboerskloof, Gardens and Oranjezicht are all within walking distance of it. On the other side of Signal Hill, Green Point and Sea Point are densely populated seaside suburbs.

The city sprawls quite a distance to the north-east (this is where you'll find the beach-side district of Bloubergstrand and the enormous Canal Walk shopping centre, but little else of interest to visitors). To the south, skirting the eastern flank of the mountains and running down to Muizen-

Street Names with a Past

Some streets in the city centre have been there for a long time. Castle St and Hout (meaning 'wood') St were two of the three original streets in Cape Town, although they were then called Heere St and Oliphant St. Spin St was named during an unsuccessful attempt to begin a silk-weaving industry. Bree St advertises its width, and Plein St runs from Grand Parade or Grootplein. Parliament St was the first street to be paved.

You'll notice that a number of streets in the city centre have 'buiten' in their names. Buiten means 'near', so Buitengracht St, for example, was near a canal.

Waterkant (meaning 'waterfront') St and Strand St were left high and dry after seafront land was reclaimed in the 1930s. Adderley St's original name was Heerengracht (meaning 'gentlemen's canal'), after a canal in Amsterdam, and that name was given to Adderley St's continuation in the area of reclaimed land.

To see how apartheid bureaucrats named streets in townships, by contrast, have a look at the Cape Flats pages in a street directory. After exhausting the usual lists of names of plants, animals and so on, the bureaucrats moved on to other things. You'll find pockets of streets with names such as Karate, Ludo, Scrabble and Korfball! Other names include Volvo, Chevrolet, Peugeot, Austin and – for you Australians – Holden.

berg at False Bay, is a string of salubrious suburbs including Observatory, Newlands and Constantia.

Further down the Atlantic coast, exclusive Clifton and Camps Bay are accessible by coastal road from Sea Point or through Kloof Nek, the pass between Table Mountain and Lion's Head. Camps Bay is a 10-minute drive from the city centre and can easily be reached by public transport, but as you go further south, the communities of

Llandudno, Hout Bay and Noordhoek are better explored with your own car or bike. The False Bay towns from Muizenberg to Simon's Town can all be reached by rail.

Stretching along the N2 south-east of Table Mountain, the vast black townships of the Cape Flats are also accessible by rail, but this is not how you'd want to get there (unless you have a burning desire to be mugged).

The spectacular Cape of Good Hope (which is not Africa's southernmost point; Cape Agulhas is) is 70km south of the city centre by road. The area's extraordinary indigenous flora is protected within the Cape of Good Hope Nature Reserve.

MAPS

Lonely Planet's *Cape Town City Map* includes an index of street names. Cape Town Tourism produces a free map that will serve most short-term visitors' needs.

If you're staying for more than a week or so, and have a car, consider buying Map Studio's Cape Town street directory. Map Studio (☎ 462 4360) at Struik House, 80 McKenzie Rd, Gardens, also sells Michelin maps and government topographic maps, which are excellent for hiking. It's open from 8.30am to 4.30pm Monday to Friday.

RESPONSIBLE TOURISM

In a country so riven by economic inequality you might want to make an effort to spend your rands where they'll help most. For instance, take a township tour run by township people, not a big company; stay at one of the township B&Bs; buy your souvenirs from the people who make them, not a dealer; shop for fruit at road-side stalls rather than supermarkets. All such businesses need your support.

Remember to pay the guys who look after cars in the city centre and towns; in general, they're helping to make the streets safer for everyone. And don't forget to tip waiting and hotel staff – they rely on this income to supplement their low wages.

South Africa's national parks and reserves are well managed, but, in general, its environmental laws are weak, and some activities permitted here wouldn't be allowed in some other countries. Shark-diving, sand-surfing and 'adventure' 4WD tours, for example, can have a negative effect on the environment, so try to get a feel for operators' commitment to treading lightly on the Earth before you make arrangements.

TOURIST OFFICES
Local Tourist Offices

Cape Town Tourism **(Map 13, #113)** (☎ 426 4260, fax 426 4266, **W** www.cape town.org), on the corner of Castle and Burg Sts, is a very impressive and busy facility. Here you'll find advisers who can book accommodation, tours and rental cars. Western Cape Tourism has a desk here, and you can get advice on Cape Nature Conservation parks (☎ 426 0723) and the national parks and reserves (☎ 423 8005). There's also a booking desk for the Baz Bus, an adviser for safari and overland tours, a travel clinic, an Internet cafe, a craft shop and a foreign-exchange booth. Opening hours are 8am to 5pm Monday to Friday, 8.30am to 1pm Saturday and 9am to 1pm Sunday.

There's a Cape Metropolitan Tourism desk at the airport, open 7am to 5pm daily. The visitor centre at the Waterfront **(Map 14, #45)** (☎ 418 2369, **W** www.waterfront .co.za) is good and can assist with information on the whole city and Western Cape as well as the facilities close by. It's open from 9am to 5pm Monday to Friday (until 6pm at weekends and from December to February).

Travelling outside Cape Town you'll find that practically every town has its own tourist office. Some are extremely helpful, others not. While some of them are obviously for-profit booking offices for tours and accommodation, you should be aware that even major tourist offices, such as Cape Town Tourism, will only recommend the services of members – you may well have to push to find out about *all* the possible options.

Tourist Offices Abroad

South African Tourism (formerly known as Satour) is the main government tourism organisation, but it only operates outside of the country. It produces useful brochures and maps, mostly geared to short-stay, relatively wealthy visitors. The head office is in Pretoria (☎ 012-482 6200, fax 347 8753, W www.southafrica.net) at 442 Rigel Ave South, Erasmusrand 0181.

South African Tourism offices abroad include:

Australia (☎ 02-9261 3424, fax 9261 3414, e info@satour.com.au) Level 6, 285 Clarence St, Sydney, NSW 2000
France (☎ 01 45 61 01 97, fax 01 45 61 01 96, e satour@afriquedusud-tourisme.fr) 61 rue La Boëtie, 75008, Paris
Germany (☎ 069-92 91 29 0, fax 28 09 50, W www.satour.de) Alemania Haus, An der Hauptwache 11, D-60313 Frankfurt
Japan (☎ 03-3478 7601, fax 3478 7605, e satour_t@netjoy.ne.jp) Akasaka Lions Bldg, 1-1-2 Moto Akasaka, Minato-ku, Tokyo 107
UK (☎ 020-8971 9350, fax 8944 6705, e satour@satbuk.demon.co.uk) 5 & 6 Alt Grove, Wimbledon, London SW19 4DZ
USA (☎ 212-730 2929, fax 764 1980, e satourny@aol.com) 500 Fifth Ave, 20th floor, New York, NY 10110
Zimbabwe (☎ 04-746 487, fax 746 489, e satour@internet.co.zw) Office 106, Sanlam Centre, Newlands, Harare

TRAVEL AGENCIES

Most hotels and hostels offer tour bookings, although not always a full range of options. Many have good deals on car hire and they are usually better informed about budget options than mainstream travel agencies.

For international travel, STA Travel **(Map 13, #99)** (☎ 418 6570) at 31 Riebeeck St in the city centre is part of the worldwide chain and offers some good fares, as does Flight Centre **(Map 15, #45)** (☎ 461 8658) in the Gardens Centre, Mill St, Gardens.

Rennies Travel has agencies throughout South Africa. The City Bowl branch **(Map 13, #121)** (☎ 423 7154) is at 101 St George's Mall. The Sea Point branch **(Map 16, #11)** (☎ 439 7529) is at 182 Main Rd, Sea Point. There's also a branch at the Waterfront **(Map 14, #29)** (☎ 418 3744). Rennies is the agent for Thomas Cook travellers cheques and handles international and domestic bookings. It can arrange visas for neighbouring countries for a moderate charge.

The Visa Service (☎ 421 7826), 9th floor, Strand Towers, 66 Strand St, also arranges visas for countries outside South Africa.

The Africa Travel Centre **(Map 13, #76)** (☎ 423 5555, fax 423 0065) at The Backpack, 74 New Church St, City Bowl, books all sorts of travel and activities, including day trips, hire cars and extended truck tours of Africa. Its rates are good. As the centre has been in business for some time, it has vetted many of the operators – and there are some cowboys out there.

Other hostels with reputable travel agencies are Ashanti Lodge **(Map 15, #13)** (☎ 423 8721, fax 423 8790, W www.ashanti.co.za), 11 Hof St, Gardens; and Aardvark Backpackers **(Map 16, #18)** (☎ 434 4172, fax 439 3813, e aardbp@ mweb.co.za), 319 Main Rd, Sea Point.

For a host of activities and overland trips, Adventure Village **(Map 13, #85)** (☎ 424 1580), 229B Long St, is a handy one-stop shop.

For more options, see Information in the special section 'Gay & Lesbian Cape Town'.

DOCUMENTS
Visas

Entry permits are issued free on arrival to visitors on holiday from many Commonwealth and most Western European countries, as well as Japan and the USA. You are entitled to a 90-day visa but if the date of your flight out is sooner than this, the immigration officer will use it as the date of your visa expiry.

If you aren't entitled to an entry permit, you'll need to get a visa (also free) before you arrive. These aren't issued at the borders. It's worth getting a visa before you depart for South Africa, but allow a couple of weeks for the process. South Africa has consular representation (at the least) in most countries.

If you do need a visa (rather than an entry permit), get a multiple-entry visa if you plan to go to a neighbouring country (such as Lesotho or Swaziland) then return to South Africa. This avoids the hassle of applying for another South African visa in a small town such as Maseru or Mbabane.

On arrival you may have to satisfy an immigration officer that you have sufficient funds for your stay in South Africa. Obviously, 'sufficient' is open to interpretation, so it pays to be neat, clean and polite. We've heard that UK visitors of Indian descent are sometimes given a hard time by immigration officers, and there's general paranoia about illegal immigrants from other African countries, so if you're of African descent (especially if you live in Africa), you might get a chilly reception.

If you arrive by air, you must have an onward ticket of some sort. An air ticket is best but an overland ticket seems to be OK.

Visa Extensions You can apply for a South African visa extension or a re-entry visa at the Department of Home Affairs **(Map 13, #137)** (☎ 462 4970), 56 Barrack St.

Travel Insurance

A travel-insurance policy to cover theft, loss and medical problems is a good idea. Although there are excellent private hospitals in South Africa, the public health system is underfunded and overcrowded, and is not free. Services such as ambulances are often run by private enterprise and are expensive. There is a wide variety of policies available, so check the small print.

You may prefer a policy that pays doctors or hospitals directly rather than requiring you to pay on the spot and claim later. If you have to claim later make sure you keep all documentation. Some policies ask you to call back (reverse charges) to a centre in your home country where an immediate assessment of your problem is made. Check that the policy covers ambulances or an emergency flight home.

Some policies exclude 'dangerous activities', which can include scuba-diving, motorcycling and even trekking. If such activities are on your agenda you don't want such a policy. A locally acquired motorcycle licence is not valid under some policies.

Driving Licence

As a visitor, you can use any foreign driving licence that carries your photo. You might experience difficulties if your licence is in a language that a traffic officer cannot easily read. It's best to carry other forms of ID as well.

Hostel Cards

You'll save a few rands at Hostelling International South Africa (HISA) hostels and affiliated hostels with a Hostelling International (HI) card. There are eight such hostels in the Cape Town area.

VIP is an Australian-based backpacker promotion agency with members in South Africa. Its card is useful for getting discounts at several hostels not affiliated with HISA. Contact VIP in Australia (☎ 07-3395 6777, fax 3395 6222, e backpack@backpackers.com.au).

Most hostels, whatever their affiliation (or lack of it), arrange discounts with local businesses.

Student & Youth Cards

There's no real advantage in having a student card here; student discounts apply only to South African nationals.

EMBASSIES & CONSULATES
South African Embassies & Consulates

Diplomatic representation abroad includes the following (for a full list see W www.gov.za/structure/samissions):

Australia (☎ 02-6273 2424, fax 6273 3543, e info@rsa.emb.gov.au) Rhodes Place, Yarralumla, Canberra, ACT 2600
Brazil (☎ 561-312 9500, fax 322 8491, e saemb@brnet.com.br) Avienda das Nações, Lote 6, Brasilia DF CEP70406-900
Canada (☎ 613-744 0330, fax 741 1639, e rsafrica@sympatico.ca) 15 Sussex Dr, Ottawa, Ontario K1M 1M8
France (☎ 01 53 59 23 23, fax 01 53 59 23 33, e 101754.1762@compuserve.com) 59 Quai d'Orsay, 75343 Paris, Cedex 07
Germany (☎ 030-22 0730, fax 22 07 3190, e botschaft@suidafrika.org) 4th floor, Atrium Bldg, Friedrichstrasse 60, Berlin 101117
Israel (☎ 03-525 2566, fax 525 3230, e saemtel@isdn.net.il) 16th floor, Top Tower, 50 Dizengoff St, 64332, Tel Aviv

Kenya (☎ 02-215616, fax 223687,
  e sahc@africaonline.co.ke) Lonrho House,
  Standard St, Nairobi
Malawi (☎ 265-783 722, fax 782 571) British
  High Commission Bldg, Capital Hill,
  Lilongwe
Mozambique (☎ 01-49 1614, fax 49 3029,
  e sahcmap@mail.tropical.co.mz) Avenida
  Eduardo Mondlanc 41, Caixa Postal 1120,
  Maputo
Namibia (☎ 061-205 7111, fax 22 4140) RSA
  House, Corner of Jan Jonker St & Nelson
  Mandela Ave, Windhoek 9000
Netherlands (☎ 70-392 4501, fax 346 0669,
  e info@zuidafrika.com) Wassenaarseweg 40,
  The Hague 2596 CJ
Sweden (☎ 08-24 39 50, fax 660 71 36,
  e saemb.swe@telia.com) Linnégatan 76,
  11523 Stockholm
UK (☎ 020-7451 7299, fax 7451 7283,
  e general@southafricahouse.com) South
  Africa House, Trafalgar Square, London
  WC2N 5DP
USA (☎ 202-232 4400, fax 265 1607, e safrica@
  southafrica.net) 3051 Massachusetts Ave NW,
  Washington DC 20008 (also consulates in New
  York, Chicago and Los Angeles)
Zimbabwe (☎ 04-753147, fax 757908,
  e sahcomm@harare.iafrica.com) 7 Elcombe
  St, Belgravia, Harare

Foreign Consulates in Cape Town

Most countries have their main embassy in
Pretoria or Johannesburg (Jo'burg), with an
office or consulate in Cape Town that becomes the official embassy during Cape
Town's parliamentary sessions.

The following is not an exhaustive list. If
your consulate is not listed, consult a telephone directory.

Most diplomatic offices listed here are in
the city centre; many are open only in the
morning.

Australia (Map 13, #102) (☎ 419 5425,
  fax 419 7345) 14th floor, BP Centre, Thibault
  Square
Botswana (Map 13, #111) (☎ 421 1045,
  fax 421 1046) 4th floor, Southern Life Centre,
  8 Riebeeck St
Canada (Map 13, #38) (☎ 423 5240, fax 423
  4893) 19th floor, Reserve Bank Bldg, 60 St
  George's Mall
France (Map 15, #27) (☎ 423 1575, fax 424
  8470) 2 Dean St, Gardens

Germany (Map 13, #81) (☎ 424 2410, fax 424
  9403) 825 St Martini, Queen Victoria St,
  Gardens
Ireland (Map 13, #89) (☎ 423 0431, fax 423
  0433) 54 Keerom St
Italy (Map 15, #26) (☎ 424 1256, fax 424
  0146) 2 Grey's Pass, Queen Victoria St,
  Gardens
Japan (Map 13, #105) (☎ 425 1695, fax 418
  2116) Standard Bank Centre, 2100 Main
  Tower, Heerengracht
Mozambique (Map 13, #22) (☎ 426 2944,
  fax 418 3396) Pinnacle Bldg, 8 Burg St
Netherlands (Map 13, #5) (☎ 421 5660,
  fax 418 2690) 100 Strand St
UK (Map 13, #111) (☎ 425 3670, fax 452
  1427) Southern Life Centre, 8 Riebeeck St
USA (Map 13, #106) (☎ 421 4280, fax 425
  3014) Monte Carlo Centre, Heerengracht

CUSTOMS

South Africa, Botswana, Namibia, Swaziland and Lesotho are members of the South
African Customs Union, which means that
their internal borders are effectively open
from a customs point of view. When you
enter the union, however, there are the usual
duty-free restrictions. You're only allowed
to bring in 1L of spirits, 2L of wine and 400
cigarettes. Motor vehicles must be covered
by a carnet. For more information, contact
the Department of Customs & Excise
(☎ 012-28 4308) in Pretoria.

MONEY
Currency

The unit of currency is the rand (R), which
is divided into 100 cents. There is no black
market for foreign exchange.

The only old note you might see is the R5
(which has been replaced by a coin), but old
coins are still common. The coins are one,
two, five, 10, 20 and 50 cents, and R1, R2
and R5. The notes are R10, R20, R50, R100
and R200. The R200 note looks a lot like the
R20 note, so check them carefully before
handing them over. There have been forg-
eries of the R200 note and some businesses
are reluctant to accept them.

Exchange Rates

The rand is a shaky currency, and it's likely
that you will get more rands for your unit of

currency when you arrive than when you leave. However, it's also likely that many costs will rise as the rand falls (see Costs later).

country	unit	rands
Australia	A$1	R4.46
Canada	C$1	R5.43
Euro zone	€1	R7.63
India	Rs 10	R1.78
Japan	¥100	R6.96
New Zealand	NZ$1	R3.68
UK	UK£1	R12.07
USA	US$1	R8.36

Exchanging Money

Opening a bank account in South Africa is not really possible, as no bank will accept a foreign address from an account holder.

Travellers Cheques Rennies Travel, a large chain of travel agencies, is the Thomas Cook agent. Rennies Travel also changes other brands of travellers cheques; its rates are good and it doesn't charge fees for changing travellers cheques (but does for cash). Thomas Cook has travellers cheques in rands for South Africa, useful for here but not anywhere else (given the instability of the rand, buy these just before departure). (For details of Rennies Travel offices in Cape Town, see Travel Agencies earlier in this chapter.)

There are American Express (AmEx) offices in Cape Town and other big cities; these, like foreign-exchange bureaus, don't charge commission but will give you a lower rate of exchange than you'll generally get from a bank. AmEx has offices on Thibault Square at the end of St George's Mall **(Map 13, #101)** (☎ 408 9700); outside the arcade at the Victoria & Alfred Hotel at the Waterfront **(Map 14, #53)** (☎ 419 3917); and at Cape Town Tourism **(Map 13, #113)**. The Waterfront office is open from 10am to 5pm daily.

Most banks change travellers cheques in major currencies, with various commissions. First National Bank is an AmEx agent and its branches are supposed to change AmEx travellers cheques without

Beating the ATM Scams

If you become a victim of crime in South Africa, it is most likely to occur at an ATM. There are dozens of scams that involve stealing your cash, your card or your personal identification number (PIN) – usually all three – while you're using an ATM. Thieves are just as likely to operate in Stellenbosch as they are in downtown Jo'burg and they are almost always well-dressed and well-mannered men.

The ATM scam you're most likely to encounter involves the thief tampering with the machine so your card becomes jammed. By the time you realise this you've entered your PIN. The thief will have seen this, and when you go inside to report that your card has been swallowed, he will take the card and leave you several thousand rands shorter. We make no guarantees, but if you follow the rules listed here you stand a better chance of avoiding this and other scams.

- Avoid ATMs at night and in secluded places. Rows of machines in shopping malls are usually the safest.

- Watch carefully the people using the ATM ahead of you. If they look suspicious, go to another machine.

- Use ATMs during banking hours and if possible take a friend. If your card is jammed in a machine then one person stays at the ATM and the other seeks assistance from the bank.

- When you put your card into the ATM press cancel immediately. If the card is returned then you know there is no blockage in the machine and it should be safe to proceed.

- Don't hesitate to be rude in refusing any offers of help to complete your transaction.

- If someone does offer, end your transaction immediately and find another machine.

- Carry your bank's emergency phone number and if you do lose your card report the loss immediately.

- If you think you might need help using an ATM, seek it *before* arriving in South Africa.

charging commission, but some don't seem to know this and you might have to pay a transaction fee anyway.

Keep at least some of your receipts when exchanging money because you'll need to reconvert leftover rands when you leave.

Credit Cards & ATMs Credit cards, especially MasterCard and Visa, are widely accepted. Nedbank is an official Visa agent and Standard Bank is a MasterCard agent – both have branches across the country. Many ATMs give cash advances; if your card belongs to the worldwide Cirrus network you should have no problem using it across the country. However, it pays to follow some basic procedures to ensure safety (see the boxed text 'Beating the ATM Scams').

Costs

Although South Africa is certainly not as cheap to travel in as many poorer African countries, it is very good value by European, US and Australian standards. This is largely a result of the collapse in the value of the rand, which has given those converting from a hard currency a major advantage. Don't expect imported or manufactured goods (including books) to be cheap, though.

Inflation is high, so the prices in this book can be expected to rise at a corresponding rate. However, the rand is also likely to continue to devalue, so inflation and devaluation may well cancel out each other. For example, hostel beds have stayed at around US$7 for years now, even though the price in rands has more than doubled from R20 to R50.

There is a value-added tax (VAT) of 14% added to most transactions but some of this can be claimed back upon departure (see Taxes & Refunds later).

Shoestring travellers will find that camping or staying in hostels, on-site caravans or bungalows where they can self-cater are the cheapest options. Sit-down meals in restaurants (without getting into *haute cuisine*) cost between R40 and R60 per person (less in pubs). Steak dishes, in particular, are incredibly cheap. Fresh produce is good value.

The distances in South Africa are large, so transport can be sparse and expensive;

How Much Is...?	
item	**cost**
cottage, sleeping two	from R150
hostel dorm bed	R50
hostel double room	about R140
two-star double hotel room	from R150
five-star double hotel room	from R1000
36-exposure print film	R40
36-exposure slide film	R50
36-exposure processing	R44
hamburger & chips	R25
steak	from R35
small beer	R6
one-way economy air ticket from Jo'burg to Cape Town	R923
deluxe bus from Jo'burg to Cape Town	R375
shared taxi from Jo'burg to Cape Town	R240

hiring or buying a car is certainly worth considering, for convenience and economy.

Cape Town, with its current popularity as a destination for foreign visitors, tends to be a little more expensive than the rest of the country but it still isn't prohibitive. The exception is top-end accommodation. It is not especially expensive compared to, say, London, but is way overpriced when you consider average incomes in South Africa.

Tipping & Bargaining

Tipping in bars and restaurants is usual; 10% to 15% is reasonable. Staff are often paid very low wages (or even no wages). This results in overfriendly service, which can be irritating. Tipping taxi drivers, petrol-pump attendants and so on is also common. A rand or two is sufficient.

Bargaining is not a South African habit, but you'll often find that you can lower the price of accommodation and perhaps other expenses when business is slow. It's definitely worth asking about special deals whenever you're inquiring about places to stay. When buying handicrafts from street hawkers, bargaining is expected, but it isn't usually the sophisticated game that it is in Asia. Don't press too hard.

Taxes & Refunds

South Africa has a value-added tax (VAT) of 14% but foreign visitors can reclaim some of their VAT expenses on departure. This applies only to goods that you are taking out of the country; you can't claim back the VAT you've paid on food or car rental, for example. Also, the goods have to have been bought at a shop participating in the VAT foreign tourist sales scheme.

To make a claim, you need your tax invoice. This is usually the receipt, but make sure that it includes the following:

• the words 'tax invoice'
• the seller's VAT registration number
• the seller's name and address
• a description of the goods purchased
• the cost of the goods and the amount of VAT charged, or a statement that VAT is included in the total cost of the goods
• a tax invoice number
• the date of the transaction

For purchases over R500, your name and address and the quantity of goods must also appear on the invoice. All invoices must be originals, not photocopies. The total value of the goods claimed for must exceed R250.

At the point of your departure, you will have to fill in a form or two and show the goods to a customs inspector. At airports, make sure you have the goods checked by the inspector before you check in your luggage. After you've gone through immigration, you make the claim and pick up your refund cheque – at some airports you can then cash it immediately at a bank (in any major currency). If your claim comes to more than R3000, your cheque is mailed to your home address.

To save time, there are facilities available for you to prepare the paperwork for your VAT claim at the bureau in Cape Town's V&A Waterfront complex.

You can claim at the international airports in Jo'burg, Cape Town and Durban, and at the following local airports: Bloemfontein, Gateway, Lanseria, Mmabatho, Nelspruit, Port Elizabeth and Upington. It's also possible to claim at the Beitbridge (Zimbabwe) and Komatipoort (Mozambique) border crossings and at major harbours.

POST & COMMUNICATIONS
Post

Most post offices are open from 8.30am to 4.30pm Monday to Friday and 8am to noon Saturday. Sending aerograms (handy prepaid letter forms) and standard-size postcards costs R1.90. Airmail letters cost R2.30 per 10g, internal letters R1.30.

Internal delivery can be very slow and international delivery isn't exactly lightning-fast. If you ask someone in South Africa to mail you something, even a letter, emphasise that you need it sent by airmail, otherwise it will probably be sent by seamail and could take months to reach you. If you're mailing anything of value consider using one of the private mail services; Postnet is the one most commonly found in cities and large towns.

Cape Town's main post office (Map 13, #125) is on the corner of Darling and Parliament Sts (upstairs, above the new shopping centre). It has a poste restante counter; identification is (theoretically) required.

Central Cape Town's postcode of 8001 covers Camps Bay, Clifton, Gardens, Green Point, Sea Point, Oranjezicht and Tamboerskloof. Some other postcodes you may find useful are:

Bloubergstrand	7436
Claremont	7700
Constantia	7848
Hout Bay	7800
Kalk Bay	7975
Khayelitsha	7784
Kommetjie	7975
Muizenberg	7945
Newlands	7700
Noordhoek	7985
Observatory	7925
Simon's Town	7975
Woodstock	7925

Telephone

Except in remote country areas, phones in South Africa are fully automatic, with direct dialling available to most parts of the world.

Local phone calls are timed and you get three minutes for each 70-cent unit. The most expensive domestic calls (for distances over 200km) cost R1.24 per minute. If you're calling any government department, expect to rack up several units.

Phone directories carry long lists of numbers that are due to change. The phone system seems to be being perpetually upgraded so it's possible that some of the numbers (including some area codes) in this book will have changed by the time you get to South Africa.

The following are some useful directory services:

Inquiries (local and national)	☎ 1023
Inquiries (international)	☎ 0903
Collect calls (national)	☎ 0020
Collect calls (international)	☎ 0900

Finding a Phone There are many privately run 'phone centres' where you can make calls without coins. These are more convenient than public phones but are also more expensive. Expect charges for calls from hotel rooms to be outrageous – never less than double what you would pay at a public phone and often a lot more.

When using a coin phone you might find that you have credit left after you've finished a call. If you want to make another call don't hang up or you'll lose the credit. Press the black button under the receiver hook.

Cardphones are even easier to find than coin phones, so it's certainly worth buying a phonecard if you're going to make more than just the odd call. Cards are available in denominations of R10, R20, R50, R100 and R200 and you can buy them at Cape Town Tourism, newsagents and general stores.

If you're looking for a quiet public phone in the city centre, there's one in the foyer of the Cultural History Museum at the Slave Lodge **(Map 13, #49)**, as well as a couple at Cape Town Tourism **(Map 13, #113)**. The Telekom office **(Map 14, #46)** (☎ 419 3944)

at the Waterfront, open 9am to 9pm daily, has private phone booths and Internet facilities, and is a good place to make a long-distance or international call.

Mobile Phones The mobile phone (cellphone) network covers most of the densely populated parts of South Africa and the major roads. It operates on the GSM digital system, as you'll need to know if you're thinking of bringing your phone from home. Mobile-phone ownership is very widespread and although you won't absolutely need a mobile during your travels here, it can come in very handy; when you're out on the town and need to call a taxi late at night, for example.

There are two competing networks (Vodacom and MTM) but there's likely to be another in the near future. Hiring a mobile phone is relatively inexpensive; both Vodacom and MTM have desks at Cape Town airport, but you'll get cheaper rates if you wait until you're in town. Cellurent (☎ 418 5656, ⓔ service@cellurent.co.za) charges from R5 a day for a phone plus R3.50 for optional insurance. Call rates start at R2.18 a minute. Cellurent will deliver a phone to wherever you are in the city and pick up from you before you leave.

Prepaid cards for use with your own phone are readily available, with Vodacom and MTN stores in every mall and plenty of other places too. Vodacom sells SIM cards for R90, and cards for prepaid services for R29, R55, R110 and R275.

The prefix ☎ 083, among others, indicates a mobile telephone number.

Area Codes All long-distance calls (ie, calls from one region to another) involves dialling the area code. When you are calling within an area, there is no need to dial the code. For example, if dialling a Cape Town number from within Cape Town, there's no need to dial the ☎ 021 code; if dialling the same number from KwaZulu-Natal, you would include the code.

Cape Town's area code is ☎ 021, as is Stellenbosch's, Paarl's and Fraschhoek's. If a number given in this book doesn't have an area code, you can assume that it is in the ☎ 021 area.

Sometimes you'll come across phone numbers beginning with ☎ 0800; this prefix indicates a toll-free number.

International Calls To make an international call, dial ☎ 09 then your country's access code. Some international access codes are given here:

Australia	☎ 61
Botswana	☎ 267
Canada	☎ 1
Denmark	☎ 45
France	☎ 33
Germany	☎ 49
Japan	☎ 81
Netherlands	☎ 31
New Zealand	☎ 64
Spain	☎ 34
Sweden	☎ 46
UK	☎ 44
USA	☎ 1

International phone calls are cheaper after 8pm Monday to Thursday, and from 8pm Friday to 8am Monday; during these times you'll pay economy rates. (Standard rates apply at other times.) Rates per minute for international calls include:

to	standard rate	economy rate
Australia	R3.65	R3.31
Canada	R4.58	R3.53
France	R4.09	R3.53
Germany	R4.10	R3.29
UK	R4.10	R3.29
USA	R4.58	R3.53

To avoid high charges when calling home, dial your 'Direct' number. This puts you through to an operator in your country. You can then either place a call on your 'phone home' account, if you have one, or place a reverse-charge call.

Australia Direct	☎ 0800 990061
Belgium Direct	☎ 0800 990032
Canada Direct	☎ 0800 990014
Denmark Direct	☎ 0800 990045
Ireland Direct	☎ 0800 990353
Japan Direct	☎ 0800 990081
Netherlands Direct	☎ 0800 990031
New Zealand Direct	☎ 0800 990064
UK Direct (BT)	☎ 0800 990044
UK Direct Call (UK)	☎ 0800 990544
USA Direct (AT&T)	☎ 0800 990123
USA Direct (MCI Call US)	☎ 0800 990011
USA Direct (Sprint Express)	☎ 0800 990001

eKno Communication Card
There's a wide range of local and international phonecards. Lonely Planet's eKno Communication Card is aimed specifically at travellers and provides cheap international calls, a range of messaging services and free email. For local calls, you're usually better off with a local card. To access eKno services in South Africa, call ☎ 0800 992921 or ☎ 0800 997285. Check the eKno Web site for updates. You can join via the Web at 🅦 www.ekno.lonelyplanet.com.

Fax
Most businesses and places to stay have fax facilities. All South African telephone directories include fax numbers.

Email & Internet Access
Cape Town is one of the most wired cities in Africa. All the hostels have Internet facilities and in the city there are several handy Internet cafes, including one at Cape Town Tourism **(Map 13, #113)**; it charges R10 for the first 15 minutes and R5 per five minutes thereafter.

If you're looking for a quiet and cheap place to surf head to the National Library (see Libraries & Archives following), or its annexe, the Centre for the Book **(Map 13, #90)**, at 62 Queen Victoria St. Both places charge R10 per 30 minutes.

Internet cafes line Long St and Main Rd at Sea Point **(Map 16)**. At the Waterfront, there's the Telekom office **(Map 14, #46)**, and Odyssey Internet **(Map 14, #28)** (☎ 418 7289) above Cinema Nouveau in the Victoria Wharf shopping mall. It's open from 10am to midnight daily.

DIGITAL RESOURCES

It's possible these days to plan and book your entire trip using the Internet. There's no better place to start your Web explorations than the Lonely Planet Web site (W www.lonelyplanet.com). Here you'll find succinct summaries on travelling to most places on Earth, postcards from other travellers, and the Thorn Tree bulletin board, where you can ask questions before you go or dispense advice when you get back. You can also find links to the most useful travel resources elsewhere on the Web.

The Internet has been embraced enthusiastically by South Africans. Listed here are some useful sites, but it's worth spending a few hours searching the Web for more.

ananzi South African Internet gateway.
W www.ananzi.co.za

ANC The official site of the ruling party. Includes daily press releases, plenty of facts and figures and links to other government and useful South African sites.
W www.anc.org.za

Daily Mail & Guardian Web version of the weekly *Mail & Guardian*.
W www.mg.co.za/mg

Ecoafrica.com Useful for wildlife information and for making bookings for the national parks.
W www.ecoafrica.com/saparks

GaySA Listings information with links to other useful sites. Warning: Some links are to explicit erotic images.
W www.GaySouthAfrica.org.za

iafrica.com South African Internet gateway.
W www.iafrica.com

Internext South African Internet gateway.
W minotaur.marques.co.za

South African National Parks All you need to know about the country's national parks. Go on an Internet safari with Web cams trained on national park water holes.
W www.parks-sa.co.za

South African Tourism New site of the government's international tourism promotion organisation. (For other official tourism sites, see Tourist Offices earlier in this chapter.)
W www.southafrica.net

Womensnet Government-sponsored women's Internet resource.
W www.Womensnet.org.za

BOOKS

For an overview of South African literature, see Arts in the Facts about South Africa chapter. The Shopping chapter has detailed information on bookshops in Cape Town.

Lonely Planet

Lonely Planet publishes *South Africa, Lesotho & Swaziland* and covers South Africa in great depth; *Southern Africa Road Atlas* to help you get around; *Southern Africa*, with information on the whole region; and the classic *Africa on a shoestring* for budget travellers setting out to explore the continent. For novice travellers there is also *Read This First: Africa*, and if you want to stay healthy there's *Healthy Travel Africa*.

Architecture

Phillida Brooke Simons' *Cape Dutch Houses & Other Old Favourites* is a well-illustrated guide to Western Cape vernacular architecture. Christina Muwanga's *South Africa: A Guide to Recent Architecture* is a pocket guide to 20th-century South African architecture, and includes a section on Cape Town.

Astronomy

If you're from the northern hemisphere, you might want a guide to all those unfamiliar stars. Try the *Struik Pocket Guide to the Night Skies of South Africa* by Peter Mack.

Flora & Fauna

Wild About Cape Town by Duncan Butchart is a very useful, comprehensive photo guide to the Cape Peninsula. It covers the full range of habitats and species, with descriptions of mammals, birds, reptiles, fish, and all kinds of vegetation.

Southern African Trees by Piet Van Wyk is a handy little guide full of information and photos. *Wildflowers of South Africa* by Braam Van Wyk is a pocket-size photo guide covering 260 species.

Mammals of Southern Africa by Chris & Tilde Stuart includes a great deal of information and many excellent photos. *Whale Watch* by Vic Crockcroft & Peter Joyce gives details of whale-watching spots from Namibia all the way down the Western Cape coast. *Signs of the Wild* by Clive Walker is a field guide to the spoors and signs of South African mammals.

Newman's Birds of Southern Africa by Kenneth Newman is an excellent, comprehensive field guide with full-colour paintings. Ian Sinclair's pocket-size *Southern African Birds* is an excellent guide with colour photos. It's particularly suitable for the short-term visitor because it does not cover obscure birds.

Restaurants

Tony Jackman's *Cape on a Plate* is the most comprehensive of the locally produced guides to the dining scene. Also useful are the annual *Wine Magazine's Top 100 Restaurants in South Africa* and the *Eat Out* restaurant guide. Both cover the whole country but include good sections on Cape Town.

Surfing

Guide to Surfing South Africa by Steve Pike covers some 300 surf spots, each rated, and has colour photos and maps.

Walking

Mike Lundy's books include *Easy Walks in the Cape Peninsula* and *Weekend Trails in the Western Cape* and are all recommended.

Wine

John Platter's South African Wine Guide is updated annually and is incredibly detailed, covering all available wines. It's highly recommended. For a cheaper selection of wines consult David Briggs' *The South African Plonk Buyer's Guide*.

History & Politics

The best general history is Rodney Davenport's *South Africa: A Modern History*, now in its 5th edition. It includes a section on the Truth & Reconciliation Commission (TRC). *South Africa: From the Early Iron Age to the 1970s* by Paul Maylam is a detailed and fascinating read.

A fine introduction to white South African history is *The Mind of South Africa* by Allister Sparks. It's opinionated, readable, insightful and delightfully controversial. Sparks' *Tomorrow is Another Country*, the inside story of the Convention for a Democratic South Africa (Codesa) negotiations,

is also a fascinating read. Out of print, but worth searching out, is *The Afrikaners – Their Last Great Trek* by Graham Leach. It gives a detailed analysis of the Afrikaner people and their political development.

The history of the ANC is recounted in *The African National Congress* by Jonathan Ball & Saul Dubow, a concise and up-to-date account. For a disturbing insight into the forces opposed to the ANC, read *A Long Night's Damage: Working for the Apartheid State* by Eugene de Kock & Jeremy Gordon. De Kock was highly placed in the government's Covert Operations Branch, and his story is horrific.

For a passionate but logical reckoning of the evil of apartheid, read *Reconciliation Through Truth* by Asmal, Asmal & Roberts. Antjie Krog's *Country of My Skull* is an award-winning and compelling personal account of the TRC hearings.

If you're at all interested in the political process, read *Election '94 South Africa*, edited by Andrew Reynolds, and its follow-up *Election '99 South Africa*. Anthony Sampson's *Mandela: The Authorized Biography* is a weighty and balanced companion to Mandela's own autobiography.

Culture

Indaba My Children is an interesting book of folk tales, history, legends, customs and beliefs, collected and retold by Vusamazulu Credo Mutwa. *Vanishing Cultures of South Africa* by Peter Magubane is quite a good compromise between a glossy picture book and authoritative text, covering 10 peoples.

Religion in Africa, published by the David M Kennedy Centre at Princeton University, is thick and scholarly but is one of the few books that gives an overview of this subject. More readable is *African Religion* by Laurenti Magesa.

Africa: The Art of a Continent, edited by Tom Phillips, includes an authoritative section on South African art.

Personal Accounts

There can be no more obvious or important book to read before coming to South Africa than Nelson Mandela's autobiography, *Long*

Walk to Freedom, which despite its 750-odd pages is a compelling and easy read.

If you want more of Mandela's words, look for the collections of his writings and speeches in *The Struggle Is My Life*. Though pretty dry, they offer an insight into the steadfastness of this amazing man – and also into how he changed the focus of his message depending on his audience.

Singing Away the Hunger by Mpho 'M'atsepo Nthunya is a fascinating collection of autobiographical stories by a Basotho woman who grew up in rural Lesotho but also experienced life in apartheid-era South African cities.

For a white perspective on the apartheid years, read Rian Malan's outstanding *My Traitor's Heart*, about his attempt to come to grips with his Afrikaner heritage and his country's uncertain future. Gillian Slovo, novelist and daughter of Joe Slovo and Ruth First, key figures in the struggle against apartheid, writes movingly about her family's turbulent life in *Every Secret Thing*. It's a fascinating book on the same subject covered by the screenplay her sister Shawn Slovo wrote for the movie *A World Apart*, and more far-reaching.

Nobel peace prize winner and former archbishop of Cape Town Desmond Tutu weighs in with his own thoughts on the TRC in *No Future Without Forgiveness*. He was chairman of the commission and clearly describes what was obviously a harrowing but ultimately inspirational experience.

The Lost World of the Kalahari and *The Heart of the Hunter* by Laurens Van Der Post both chronicle the author's exploration of the Kalahari and give a poetic, sympathetic and thought-provoking interpretation of the nomadic San's culture.

Travel Literature

The redoubtable Dervla Murphy comes up with another corker in *South of the Limpopo: Travels Through South Africa*, which follows her cycle journeys through the country in the years either side of and during the 1994 elections. More up-to-date, although it lacks Murphy's panache, is award-winning journalist Gavin Bell's

entertaining *Somewhere over the Rainbow: Travels in South Africa*.

Not Home Yet by Booker Prize–winning author Justin Cartwright is a slim but illuminating study of the expat South African's trips home between 1994 and 1996.

NEWSPAPERS & MAGAZINES

The *Cape Times* (morning) and the *Cape Argus* (afternoon) are tabloids masquerading as broadsheets and print practically the same news.

The tabloid *Sowetan* is the biggest-selling paper in the country. Although it caters to a largely poorly educated audience, it has a more sophisticated political and social outlook than most of the major white papers. The *Nation* and *South* are other black papers that upheld journalistic standards during the apartheid years.

The best weekly read, although it can at times take itself too seriously, is the *Mail & Guardian*, which includes excellent investigative and opinion pieces, a good arts review supplement and a week's supply of the Doonesbury cartoon strip. The *Independent on Sunday* is also worth a look.

Cape Review is a monthly arts and listings magazine dedicated to what's going on around town. The glossy monthly *SA Citylife* is one of the better arts and lifestyle magazines available, covering politics and social issues as well as giving decent listing information. Pick up a copy of the *Big Issue*, the weekly magazine that helps provide an income for the homeless – it's a good read and a worthy cause.

For information on the gay and lesbian press, see the special section 'Gay & Lesbian Cape Town'.

RADIO & TV

South African Broadcasting Corporation (SABC) was the monolithic mouthpiece of previous governments, and although times have changed you'll still find most of its fare bland. There are now some privately owned radio and TV stations but the SABC still dominates. English is the dominant language on TV, even though there are news broadcasts in several other languages.

Most SABC radio stations (AM and FM) are broadcast nationally and play dreary music and stodgy chat, although the hour-long current affairs programs are good and

you should certainly tune in to Tim Modise's decent morning talk show on SABC's FM station. Stations broadcasting in African languages other than Afrikaans play the best music.

Cape Town's talk radio station Cape Talk 567MW is a quick way to tune into local views and opinions on a variety of subjects. Many other local radio stations pump out a bland range of pop.

The BBC World Service is available on short-wave, medium-wave and, if you're near Lesotho (where the transmitter is), FM. If you're about to travel through Africa, then the Beeb's nightly *Focus on Africa* program is essential listening.

The SABC has three TV channels and there's also e-tv, a new, privately owned free-to-air station. Its news services are marginally more international than those of the other stations. Only the cheapest places to stay won't have M-Net, a pay station that shows standard fare and some good movies. CNN is much less widely available than it was. If you're lucky you'll get BBC World. Satellite digital TV is on the way.

Programming is similar to that in any US-dominated TV market: Soaps, sitcoms, chat shows and infomercials dominate. On the free-to-air stations 'blasphemy' is edited out, and sudden gaps in the dialogue make you realise how often characters in US sitcoms say 'Oh my God'.

Locally made programs include tacky game shows, some reasonable children's programs, a few music shows, and soaps such as *Isidingo* and *E Goli*. *Yizo Yizo*, set in a school and reflecting current realities, is one of the better dramas and caused a storm in 2001 when an episode included a male prison rape scene (funnily enough there had been no outcry at the previous episodes' inclusion of violence, sexual or otherwise, towards women). Dali Tambo's talk show *People of the South* is worth watching, as is the current affairs program *Agenda*.

Zebulon Dread

Hei Voetsek! is the wildly outspoken, satirical magazine of self-proclaimed 'cultural terrorist' Zebulon Dread. Zebulon, known to his family and friends as Elliot Joseph, is not only the publisher but also the writer, photographer and sole distributor; chances are high that you'll come across him hawking a pile of his magazines and books around the city's most popular watering holes.

Often dressed in a pastel-shaded sarong with a bundle of dreadlocks tumbling over his forceful face and large frame, Zebulon is not a man to be ignored. *Don't* take his photograph; he's been known to tip beers over tourists who've ignored his warnings. *Do* buy his magazine. It's mostly in Afrikaans (a language that this black man speaks as proudly as any white) but it contains enough visual gags – many of them explicit – to be worth the cover price.

PHOTOGRAPHY

Cape Town and the Winelands are very photogenic. Remember that the harsh midday sun will wash out colours. Morning and

evening are the best times to take photos. Keep your film cool and have it processed promptly.

Prolab **(Map 13, #58)** at 177 Bree St is a good place to buy film (especially pro film) that has been stored correctly, and it does quick and competent slide processing.

For regular film you'll find camera shops and fast developers all over the city; try Shap's Cameraland **(Map 13, #24)** (☎ 423 4150) at Camera House, 68 Long St. It's open from 8am to 8.30pm Monday to Friday and 8am to 1pm Saturday. There are various other outlets at the Waterfront.

For camera repairs, the Camera Repair Centre **(Map 13, #30)** (☎ 423 3757) is on the 2nd floor, Dental House, 165 Longmarket St. It is open from 8am to 5pm Monday to Friday, and 9am to 1pm Saturday; it has been recommended.

Travel Photography: A Guide to Taking Better Pictures by Richard I'Anson is a lavishly illustrated Lonely Planet guide that will help you in doing just what the title says.

TIME

South African Standard Time is two hours ahead of Greenwich Mean Time (GMT; at noon in London it's 2pm in Cape Town), seven hours ahead of USA Eastern Standard Time (at noon in New York it's 7pm in Cape Town) and eight hours behind Australian Eastern Standard Time (at noon in Sydney it's 4am in Cape Town). There is no daylight saving.

ELECTRICITY

The electricity system is 220/230 volts AC at 50 cycles per second. Appliances rated at 240 volts AC will work. Plugs have three large round pins. Adaptors aren't that easy to find; we found one at the national camping supply and clothing store Cape Union Mart for around R50 (see the Shopping chapter for details).

If your appliance doesn't have a removable lead, you can always buy a South African plug and have it wired on (assuming that the appliance takes AC and is rated at the correct voltage).

WEIGHTS & MEASURES

South Africa uses the metric system. For more information, see the metric conversion tables on the inside back cover of this book.

LAUNDRY

Laundrettes are scattered throughout the city, although most hostels and many hotels will have either a laundry on the premises or a laundry service.

To have a medium-size bag of laundry washed, dried and folded for you will cost around R20.

TOILETS

Toilets are the standard Western style (although the flush will be unfamiliar to North Americans). There aren't many public toilets, but plenty of hotels and restaurants will let you use their facilities. The main long-distance bus lines have on-board toilets.

LEFT LUGGAGE

There's a left-luggage facility next to platform 24 in the main train station **(Map 13)**; it's open from 6am to around 2pm daily.

HEALTH

South Africa is facing a terrible health crisis in the form of HIV/AIDS, so you must take precautions against this. Otherwise, apart from malaria and bilharzia in some areas (but not Cape Town), and the possibility of hikers drinking contaminated water, there are few health issues visitors need be concerned about.

If you're planning to venture into less developed areas of Africa, you might want to read *Healthy Travel Africa*, by Dr Isabelle Young, which is a Lonely Planet guide to staying healthy while on the road in Africa. *Travel with Children* by Maureen Wheeler is another Lonely Planet guide that includes helpful basic advice on travel health for young children.

Predeparture Planning

If you wear glasses take a spare pair and your prescription; there are plenty of optometrists in South Africa where you can get new ones if you run into problems.

If you use a particular medication regularly, take the prescription; better still, take part of the packaging showing the generic name rather than the brand (which may not be locally available), as it will make getting replacements easier. In South Africa you can buy drugs over the counter that would require a prescription in some other countries but it's still a wise idea to have a prescription with you to show that you legally use the medication.

For information on health insurance, see Travel Insurance earlier in this chapter.

Immunisations If you're travelling only to Cape Town it's not necessary to get any special vaccinations, but if you plan to travel further afield in South Africa seek medical advice at least six weeks before travel. Some vaccinations require more than one injection, while some should not be given together. Some vaccinations should not be given during pregnancy or to people with allergies. Discuss your requirements with your doctor, but vaccinations you might need to consider for South Africa are diphtheria, tetanus, hepatitis A, hepatitis B, typhoid and yellow fever.

Problem Areas

Malaria is mainly confined to the eastern half of South Africa (northern KwaZulu-Natal, Mpumalanga, and Northern Province), especially on the lowveld. Parts of North-West Province are also malarial. Cases are occasionally reported outside these areas.

Bilharzia is found mainly in the east but outbreaks can occur elsewhere. It's wise to always check with knowledgeable locals before drinking water or swimming in the east.

Wherever you find yourself drinking from streams, make sure there isn't a village upstream, even if there is no bilharzia. Typhoid is rare but it does occur, as does hepatitis A. There was an outbreak of cholera in the eastern provinces in 2001.

Industrial pollution is common in more settled areas.

For more information see also Natural Hazards under Dangers & Annoyances later in this chapter.

Medical Services

Medical services are of a high standard in Cape Town. In an emergency, you can go directly to the casualty department of Groote Schuur Hospital **(Map 17, #17)** (☎ 404 9111), Main Rd, Observatory. As every local will proudly tell you while driving past on the N2, this is where in 1967 the late Dr Christiaan Barnard made the world's first successful heart transplant.

In the City Bowl, City Park Hospital **(Map 13, #26)** (☎ 480 6271), at 181 Longmarket St, is the best private hospital; reception is on the 8th floor.

Contact the police (☎ 10111) to get directions to the nearest hospital. Many doctors make house calls; they're listed under Medical in the phone book, and hotels and most other places to stay can arrange a visit.

Glengariff Pharmacy **(Map 16, #2)** (☎ 434 1685), on the corner of Main Rd and Glengariff St, Sea Point, is open daily until 11pm. There's also the Lite Kem Pharmacy **(Map 13, #131)**, open daily until 11pm, in the city centre on Darling St between Plein and Parliament Sts.

For vaccinations, the British Airways Travel Clinic **(Map 13, #103)** (☎ 419 3172, fax 419 3389) is at Room 314 in the Fountain Medical Centre on Adderley St. It's open from 8am to 5pm Monday to Friday and 9am to 1pm Saturday. The SAA Netcare Travel Clinic (☎ 423 1401) is in the Cape Town Tourism office **(Map 13, #113)**.

Women's Health

Gynaecological Problems Antibiotic use, synthetic underwear, sweating and contraceptive pills can lead to fungal vaginal infections, especially in hot climates. Fungal infections are characterised by a rash, itch and discharge and can be treated with a vinegar or lemon-juice douche, or with yogurt. Nystatin, miconazole or clotrimazole pessaries or vaginal cream are the usual treatment. Maintaining good personal hygiene and wearing loose-fitting clothes and cotton underwear may help prevent these infections.

Sexually transmitted infections are a major cause of vaginal problems. Symptoms include a smelly discharge, painful intercourse and sometimes a burning sensation when urinating. Medical attention should be sought and sexual partners must also be treated.

Pregnancy If you're pregnant and considering a trip to Cape Town and Western Cape, you should have few worries. If you're going further afield and need some vaccinations, you should know some are not advisable during pregnancy (eg, yellow fever). In addition, some diseases (eg, malaria) are much more serious for the mother during pregnancy, and may increase the risk of a stillborn child.

Most miscarriages occur during the first three months of pregnancy. Miscarriage is not uncommon and can occasionally lead to severe bleeding. The last three months should be spent within reasonable distance of good medical care. A baby born as early as 24 weeks stands a chance of survival but only in a good modern hospital. Pregnant women should avoid all unnecessary medication, although vaccinations and malarial prophylactics should still be taken where needed. Extra care should be taken to prevent illness and particular attention should be paid to diet and nutrition. Alcohol and nicotine, for example, should be avoided.

Water Purification

High-quality water is available practically everywhere in Cape Town and you need not fear drinking from taps. Hikers drinking from streams might be at risk of waterborne diseases (eg, gastroenteritis or, rarely, typhoid), especially if they take water downstream of unsewered villages.

The simplest way to purify water is to boil it thoroughly for 10 minutes. However, at high altitude, water boils at a lower temperature, so germs are less likely to be killed.

Simple filtering doesn't remove all dangerous organisms, so if you can't boil water you should treat it chemically. Chlorine tablets (Puritabs, Steritabs or other brand names) will kill many but not all nasties, including giardia and amoebic cysts, which are resistant to chlorine. Iodine is very effective

Medical Kit Check List

Following is a list of items you should consider including in your medical kit – consult your pharmacist for brands available in your country.

☐ **Aspirin or paracetamol (acetaminophen in the USA)** – for pain or fever
☐ **Antihistamine** – for allergies, eg, hay fever; to ease the itch from insect bites or stings; and to prevent motion sickness
☐ **Cold and flu tablets, throat lozenges and nasal decongestant**
☐ **Multivitamins** – consider for long trips, when dietary vitamin intake may be inadequate
☐ **Antibiotics** – consider including these if you're travelling well off the beaten track; see your doctor, as they must be prescribed, and carry the prescription with you
☐ **Loperamide or diphenoxylate** – 'blockers' for diarrhoea
☐ **Prochlorperazine or metaclopramide** – for nausea and vomiting
☐ **Rehydration mixture** – to prevent dehydration, which may occur, for example, during bouts of diarrhoea; particularly important when travelling with children
☐ **Insect repellent, sunscreen, lip balm and eye drops**
☐ **Calamine lotion, sting-relief spray or aloe vera** – to ease irritation from sunburn and insect bites or stings
☐ **Antifungal cream or powder** – for fungal skin infections and thrush
☐ **Antiseptic (such as povidone-iodine)** – for cuts and grazes
☐ **Bandages, Band Aids (plasters) and other wound dressings**
☐ **Water purification tablets or iodine**
☐ **Scissors, tweezers and a thermometer** – note that mercury thermometers are prohibited by airlines
☐ **Sterile kit** – just in case you need injections in a country with medical hygiene problems; discuss with your doctor

in purifying water and is available in tablet form (such as Potable Aqua); remember to follow the directions carefully as too much iodine can be harmful.

If you can't find tablets, use tincture of iodine (2%). Four drops of tincture of iodine per litre of clear water is the recommended dosage; the treated water should be left to stand for 20 to 30 minutes before drinking. Iodine crystals (very dangerous things to have around as they are highly toxic and give off toxic gas when exposed to air) can also be used to purify water, but this is a more complicated process, as you have to first prepare a saturated iodine solution.

WOMEN TRAVELLERS
Attitudes Towards Women

Sexism is a common attitude among South African men, regardless of colour. Modern ideas such as the equality of the sexes haven't filtered through to many people, especially away from the cities. Women are usually called 'ladies' unless they play sport, in which case they are called 'girls'.

Fortunately times are changing and there are plenty of women who don't put up with this sort of rubbish, but South African society as a whole is still decades behind most developed countries. Also, ironically, there has been something of an antifeminist backlash without there having been many feminist gains in the first place. The fact that black women were at the forefront in the liberation struggle and that many of them have entered politics may change this, however.

Not surprisingly, there are big differences between the lives of women in South Africa's various cultures. In traditional black cultures, women often have a very tough time but this is changing to some extent because a surprising number of girls have the opportunity to stay at school while the boys are sent away to work. In South Africa's white communities, however, the number of girls finishing secondary school is significantly lower than the number of boys, which goes against international trends.

The practice of female genital mutilation (female circumcision) is not part of the traditional cultures of South Africa.

There's a very high level of sexual assault and other violence against women in South Africa, the majority of which occurs in townships and rural areas. The extremely high level of HIV/AIDS in the country compounds the problem.

A large part of the problem in South Africa is the leniency of the judicial system, which repeatedly lets perpetrators of sex offences off with short sentences. This, particularly in recent times, has had women's groups around the country voicing their concerns and demanding the government step in and take tougher action.

There have been incidents of female travellers being raped, but these cases are isolated, and cause outrage in local communities. For most female visitors paternalistic attitudes, rather than physical assault, are the main problem.

Safety Precautions

Single female travellers have a curiosity value that makes them conspicuous but it may also bring forth generous offers of assistance and hospitality. It is always difficult to quantify the risk of assault – and there is such a risk – but plenty of women do travel alone safely in South Africa.

Obviously the risk varies depending on where you go and what you do. Hitching alone is extremely foolhardy, for instance.

Everyday Health

Normal body temperature is around 37°C (98.6°F); a temperature more than 2°C (4°F) higher indicates a high fever. The normal adult pulse rate is 60 to 100 beats per minute (children 80 to 100, babies 100 to 140). As a general rule the pulse increases about 20 beats per minute for each 1°C (2°F) rise in fever.

Respiration (breathing) rate is another indicator of illness. Count the number of breaths per minute: from 12 to 20 is normal for adults and older children (up to 30 for younger children, 40 for babies). People with a high fever or serious respiratory illness breathe more quickly than normal. More than 40 shallow breaths a minute may be an indicator of pneumonia.

What risks there are, however, are significantly reduced if two women travel together or, even better, if a woman travels as part of a mixed-sex couple or group. But while the days of apartheid have long gone, a mixed-race couple will almost certainly attract attention and could get antagonistic reactions (old attitudes die hard).

However you travel, it's best to behave conservatively, especially inland and in the more traditional black communities. On the coast, casual dress is the norm, but elsewhere dress modestly (in full-length clothes that aren't too tight) if you do not wish to draw attention to yourself.

Common sense and caution, particularly at night, are essential.

DISABLED TRAVELLERS

People with limited mobility will not have an easy time in South Africa and although there are more disabled people per capita here than in the West, facilities are few. Most wheelchair users will find travel easier with an able-bodied companion. The sight- or hearing-impaired traveller should have fewer problems.

There is some good news: An increasing number of places to stay have ramps and wheelchair-friendly bathrooms. Many buildings (including safari lodges and huts in the national parks) are single-storey, car hire is easy, and assistance is usually available on regional flights. Details of disability-friendly accommodation are included in a guide available from South African Tourism.

Carpe Diem Tours (☎/fax 027-217 1125) specialises in tours for the physically challenged and the elderly. Cheshire Homes, an international organisation that works with the disabled, also runs the Enabled Traveller program (W enabled.24.com), which can help with travel arrangements.

Other useful places for advice on what facilities are available across the country include the following:

National Council for Persons with Physical Disabilities in South Africa
  (☎ 011-726-8040, e ncppdsa@cis.co.za)

Independent Living Centre
  (☎ 011-482-5475, e ilcafrica@icon.co.za)
Association for Persons with Disabilities
  (☎ 555-2881, e apd-wc@mweb.co.za)
Access-Able Travel Source
  (W www.accessable.com)

SENIOR TRAVELLERS

Much of South Africa's tourist infrastructure (which was, until recently, geared to wealthier domestic tourists) caters well to senior travellers. You won't, however, find seniors' discounts, special tours or other 'grey power'–related goodies.

Service in the more upmarket hotels, guesthouses and B&Bs is very good indeed, and even less expensive hotels have porters. If you're concerned about the logistics of travel, chances are you can prebook and prepay for everything from your own country.

CAPE TOWN FOR CHILDREN

Cape Town, with its beaches, parks, and fun family attractions such as the Two Oceans Aquarium and the Ratanga Junction amusement park, is a great place to bring the kids. South Africans tend to be family oriented, so most places cope easily with kids' needs. 'Family' restaurants, such as the Spur chain, offer children's portions, as do some of the more upmarket places.

Many of the sights and attractions of interest to parents will also entertain kids. The Table Mountain cableway, the attractions at the Waterfront (especially the seals, which can usually be seen at Bertie's Landing), and Cape Point, with its baboons and other animals, will delight kids. The South African Museum has plenty to offer the younger visitor, including special shows at the Planetarium.

At the beach you'll have to watch out for rough surf, but there are some quiet rock pools as well as some sheltered coves. The Things to See & Do chapter has information on many beaches in Cape Town. The Sea Point Pavilion has a great family swimming pool that is significantly warmer than the surrounding ocean.

There are few services such as nappy-changing facilities in large stores (many don't even have public toilets). Short-term daycare is becoming more common. Your hotel should be able to arrange a baby-sitter, or you can contact an outfit such as Super-sitters (☎ 439 4985).

For tips on keeping children (and parents) happy on the road, check out Lonely Planet's *Travel with Children* by Maureen Wheeler.

LIBRARIES & ARCHIVES

The National Library of South Africa **(Map 13, #95)** (☎ 424 6320), Company's Gardens, Government Ave, is the national reference library; it doesn't lend books but you can consult them from 9am to 5pm Monday to Friday. The library has an Internet cafe, a small bookshop and an exhibition space on the 2nd floor.

Several other organisations have reference libraries. The library of the British Council **(Map 15, #31)** (☎ 462 3921, **W** www.britishcouncil.org/southafrica), 21 St John's St, is open from 9am to 4.30pm Monday, Tuesday and Thursday, 9am to 1pm Wednesday and 9am to 4pm Friday. The Alliance Française's library **(Map 13, #59)** (☎ 423 5699, **e** afducap@iafrica.com), 155 Loop St, is open from 2pm to 6pm Monday to Thursday, 10am to 2pm Friday and 10am to 1pm Saturday.

The Mayibune Centre **(Map 11, #5)** (☎ 959 2954) at the University of Western Cape, Modderdam Rd, Modderdam, houses a large archive of materials concerned with the anti-apartheid struggle, including letters written by former Robben Island prisoners. Visits are by appointment only.

Western Cape Archives **(Map 15, #36)** (☎ 462 4050), 72 Roeland St, Gardens, holds some immensely important documents relating to Cape Town's history. It's open from 8am to 4pm Monday, Tuesday, Wednesday and Friday, and 8am to 7pm Thursday.

DANGERS & ANNOYANCES
Crime

Despite an increase in street crime in recent years, Cape Town remains one of the most relaxed cities in Africa, which can instil a false sense of security. People who have travelled overland from Cairo without a single mishap or theft have been known to be cleaned out in Cape Town – generally doing something stupid like leaving their gear on a beach while they go swimming.

Paranoia is not required but common sense is. There is tremendous poverty on the peninsula and the informal redistribution of wealth is reasonably common. The townships on the Cape Flats have an appalling crime rate and unless you have a trustworthy guide or are on a tour they are off-limits.

Take care when driving along the N2 near the airport; reports of rocks being thrown off the cross bridges onto passing cars, so that they'll be forced to stop (and then robbed), are fairly constant. Whatever happens, if at all possible, *never* stop on this stretch of highway.

The rest of Cape Town is reasonably safe. Care should be taken in Sea Point and quiet areas of the city centre at night, and walking to and from the Waterfront is not recommended, day or night. As always, listen to local advice. There is safety in numbers.

There's a police Tourism Assistance Unit (☎ 418 2853) at 2 Pearl House, Tulbagh Square. The main city police station (☎ 467 8000) **(Map 13, #138)** is on Buitenkant St between Albertus and Barrack Sts. There are always police at the Waterfront.

Natural Hazards

Swimming at all the Cape beaches is potentially hazardous, especially for those inexperienced in surf. Always check for warning signs about rips and rocks and don't swim outside patrolled areas unless you really know what you're doing.

The mountains in the middle of the city are no less dangerous just because they are in the city. Weather conditions can change rapidly, so warm clothing, water and a good map and compass are always necessary if you're hiking.

Another hazard of the mountains is ticks, which can latch on to you when you brush past vegetation. A strong insect repellent can help, and serious hikers should consider having their boots and trousers impregnated with benzyl benzoate and dibutylphthalate.

You should always check all over your body if you have been walking through a potentially tick-infested area as ticks can cause skin infections and other more serious diseases, including typhus. You should seek medical advice if you think you may have any of these diseases.

If you find a tick attached, press down around the tick's head with tweezers, grab the head and gently pull upwards. Avoid pulling the rear of the body as this may squeeze the tick's gut contents through the attached mouth parts into the skin, increasing the risk of infection and disease. Clean and apply pressure if the point of attachment is bleeding. Smearing chemicals on the tick will not make it let go and is not recommended.

There are also some poisonous snakes in the area, although they are rarely aggressive and will generally get out of your way if they sense you coming. But to minimise your chances of being bitten, wear boots, socks and long trousers when walking through undergrowth where snakes may be present. Don't put your hands into holes and crevices, and be careful when collecting firewood.

Snake bites do not cause instantaneous death, and antivenins are usually available. Keep the victim calm and still, wrap the bitten limb tightly, as you would for a sprained ankle, and attach a splint to immobilise it. Then seek medical help.

If the snake is definitely dead take it along with you for identification. Don't waste time or risk your life trying to catch a live snake. Tourniquets and sucking out the poison are now comprehensively discredited first-aid methods.

Although reaching medical assistance is of paramount importance, weigh up the dangers of moving the victim. Physical exertion will increase the rate at which the poison travels, so if at all possible, bring medical assistance to the victim.

EMERGENCIES

The phone numbers for emergency services are:

Ambulance	☎ 10177
Automobile Association	
(AA) emergency rescue	☎ 0800 033007
AA sales	☎ 086 111 1994
Fire brigade	☎ 535 1100
Lifeline	☎ 461 1111
Police	☎ 10111
Rape Crisis Centre	☎ 447 9762
Tourist police	☎ 418 2853

LEGAL MATTERS

South Africa's legal system is a blend of the Dutch-Roman and British systems. The British influence is most prevalent in criminal justice procedures. Cases are tried by *landdrosts* (magistrates) or judges without juries, at the instigation of police 'dockets' or private actions. Clients are represented by solicitors (*prokureurs* in Afrikaans) and advocates (*advokates* – the equivalent of barristers).

Under apartheid, South Africa was a police state. The country may have radically changed since then, but the police generally continue to suffer from a poor image and many people don't trust them. Private security firms are in high demand and many people own firearms and dogs.

It's highly unlikely that the police will bother you for petty breaches of the law, such as breaking the speed limit. This might sound like a pleasant state of affairs, but after you've encountered a few dangerous drivers or some brawling upcountry farmers on a spree, strict cops seem more attractive.

If your skin colour isn't white, you might receive less than courteous treatment if, say, you're pulled over for a traffic violation. A Western passport should fix things quickly, and make sure you have your driving licence to hand too.

Drugs

Dagga or *zol* (marijuana) was an important commodity in the Xhosa's trade with the San. Today it is illegal but widely available. There are heavy penalties for use and possession but many people still use the drug – often quite openly, as you'll discover in some of the backpacker hostels and bars you might frequent. The legal system doesn't distinguish between soft and hard drugs.

Ecstasy is just as much part of the rave and clubbing culture in South Africa as it is anywhere. South Africa is also reputed to be the world's major market for the barbiturate Mandrax, which is now banned in many countries (including South Africa) because of its effects. Drugs such as cocaine and heroin are becoming widely available and their use accounts for much property crime.

BUSINESS HOURS

Banking hours vary but are usually from 9am to 3.30pm Monday to Friday. Many branches also open from 8.30am to 11am Saturday. Post offices are usually open from 8.30am to 4.30pm Monday to Friday and 8am to noon Saturday. Both banks and post offices close for lunch in smaller towns.

Most shops are open from 8.30am to 5pm Monday to Friday and on Saturday morning. Bars usually close around 11pm except in the major cities. Outside the cities it's difficult to get a drink without a meal on Sunday during the day.

PUBLIC HOLIDAYS

The public holidays system underwent a dramatic shake-up after the 1994 elections. For example, the Day of the Vow, which celebrated the massacre of Zulus, has become the Day of Reconciliation. The officially ignored but widely observed Soweto Day, marking the student uprisings that eventually led to liberation, is now celebrated as Youth Day. Human Rights Day is held on the anniversary of the Sharpeville massacre.

Public holidays and dates in South Africa include the following:

New Year's Day 1 January
Good Friday March or April
Easter Sunday March or April
Easter Monday March or April
Human Rights Day 21 March
Family Day 17 April
Constitution or Freedom Day 27 April
Workers' Day 1 May
Youth Day 16 June
Women's Day 9 August
Heritage Day 24 September
Day of Reconciliation 16 December
Christmas Day 25 December
Boxing Day (Day of Goodwill) 26 December

SCHOOL HOLIDAYS

It's useful to know the dates of school holidays, because accommodation at reserves and resorts – especially beach resorts in summer – is at a premium during these times. Cape Town also experiences a big influx of domestic tourists in the summer school holidays.

The dates differ slightly from year to year and from province to province, but are roughly mid-April (two weeks), late June to mid-July (three weeks), late September to early October (about one week) and early December to early February (about eight weeks). Contact South African Tourism for the exact dates.

SPECIAL EVENTS

Whichever month you're in Cape Town you can be sure that there'll be some special event in the offing. The year-long party kicks off in style with the Cape Minstrel Carnival (see the boxed text) and the Jazzathon at the Waterfront (early January).

Cape Minstrel Carnival

Cape Town's longest-running annual street party is the Cape Minstrel Carnival, held on 1 and 2 January and the following two Saturdays. It was first officially documented in 1907, but dates back to the early 1800s when slaves enjoyed a day of freedom over the New-Year period. The carnival was inspired by visiting American minstrels of the time, hence the face make-up and colourful costumes that are all part of the ribald song-and-dance parades.

The highlight is the parade, which is traditionally held on 2 January and known as *tweede nuwe jaar*; it runs through the city towards Green Point Stadium. Around 13,000 revellers organised into separate troupes participate in the parade, and each troupe competes to win trophies in various categories over the course of the carnival, including for best dressed, most flamboyant, best band and best singer.

The J&B Met, held at Kenilworth Racecourse in February, is the city's top horse-racing event, the equivalent of Australia's Melbourne Cup or the UK's Grand National (with the fashion stakes to match). March sees the running of the Cape Argus cycle tour and the North Sea Jazz Festival. And so it goes with various film, performing-arts and food festivals, marathons and sporting fixtures, ending up in December with a fabulous costume party by Mother City Queer Projects (W www.mcqp.co.za). Contact Cape Town Tourism for a list of events.

DOING BUSINESS

South Africa's free-enterprise economy is still in the process of recovering from the distortions imposed on it by apartheid governments. The ANC government is privatising many of the huge state-owned monopolies and the very cosy relationship between these and favoured contractors is disappearing.

The tax system will be familiar to businesspeople from developed countries, as will commercial practice. Labour unions are well organised in some industries. South Africans complain loudly about the unions – until recently strikes were seen as weapons in a revolution – but they are probably less disruptive than in many other countries.

The Reconstruction and Development Program is the government's major tool in opening up the economy to people previously shut out. Small (and tiny) businesses owned by the 'disadvantaged sector' (blacks and coloureds) are the main beneficiaries.

At the small-business end, this is pretty much a 'me too' economy. Good ideas, such as franchised pubs, are seized upon and quickly done to death. There is room for new ideas but there are pitfalls for outsiders. Currency controls on international transactions are expected to ease as the economy improves.

The Cape Chamber of Commerce & Industry **(Map 12, #12)** (☎ 418 4300, fax 418 1800, W www.capechamber.co.za) is on the 2nd floor at 19 Louis Gradner St, Foreshore, and is open from 8.30am to 4.45pm Monday to Friday. It produces *The Cape of Good Hope Business Guide*, which is free and contains some useful contact details and background information.

Some other business contacts include:

Development Bank of Southern Africa (☎ 011 313 3911, fax 313 3086) PO Box 1234, Midrand 1685, Gauteng
Department of Trade & Industry (☎ 012-310 9791, fax 322 0298) Private Bag X84, Pretoria 0001, Gauteng
Deloitte & Touche (☎ 670 1500, fax 683 8259) PO Box 578, Cape Town 8000

WORK

Because of high unemployment and fears about illegal immigration from the rest of Africa, there are tough penalties for employers taking on foreigners without work permits. So far this doesn't seem to have stopped foreigners getting jobs in restaurants or bars in tourist areas, but this might change. Don't expect decent pay – something like R12 per hour plus tips (which can be good) is usual.

The best time to look for work is from October to November, before the high season starts and before university students begin holidays.

In Western Cape, hostels might know of fruit-picking work, especially in the Ceres, Citrusdal and Piketberg areas. The pay is negligible but you'll probably get free accommodation. It's uncommon for travellers to do this, so don't count on it.

Getting There & Away

AIR

Cape Town International Airport (☎ 937 1200) is served by direct flights from many countries, although several touch down first in Johannesburg (Jo'burg) before flying on to Cape Town.

International airlines with offices in Cape Town include:

Air Mauritius (☎ 421 6294, fax 421 7371) 11th floor, Strand Towers, 66 Strand St, City Bowl
Air Namibia (☎ 936 2755, fax 936 2760) Cape Town International Airport
British Airways (☎ 934 0292, fax 934 0959) Cape Town International Airport
KLM (☎ 0806-247747, fax 670 2501) Slade House, Boundary Terraces, 1 Mariendahl Lane, Newlands
Lufthansa (☎ 415 3888, fax 415 3636) 9th floor, Picbel Arcade, 58 Strand St, City Bowl
Malaysia Airlines (☎ 419 8010, fax 419 7017) 8th floor, Safmarine House, 22 Riebeeck St
SAA (☎ 936 1111, fax 936 2308) Cape Town International Airport
Singapore Airlines (☎ 674 0601, fax 674 0710) 3rd floor, Sanclaire, 21 Dreyer St, Claremont
Swissair (☎ 434 8101, fax 934 8106) Cape Town International Airport
Virgin Atlantic (☎ 683 2221, fax 683 3359) Claremont

Departure Tax

There's an airport departure tax of R34 for domestic flights, R57 for flights to regional (African) countries, and R179 for other international flights. The tax will usually be included in the price of your ticket.

Other Parts of South Africa

South African Airways (SAA; ☎ 936 1111, Ⓦ www.flysaa.com) is the main domestic carrier as well as the international flag carrier. Its subsidiaries, SA Airlink and SA Express, also service domestic routes. There are plenty of flights daily to most destinations.

Fares aren't cheap; if you plan to do a lot of flying check with a travel agency before you leave home for special deals. If you book and pay 21 days in advance there's a

50% discount on the regular fare; for 10 days in advance there's a 30% discount.

The baggage allowance is 40/30/20kg in 1st/business/economy class; excess baggage is charged at R17 per kilogram.

For domestic services the one-way fares quoted here are full economy. SAA flies between Cape Town and major centres, including Port Elizabeth (R570), Upington (R992), Durban (R1174), Kimberley (R992), Jo'burg (R1083) and East London (R1106).

Comair (☎ 936 9000), an airline operating in conjunction with British Airways, flies to Cape Town, Durban, Jo'burg and Port Elizabeth.

Nationwide Airlines (☎ 936 2050, Ⓦ www .nationwideair.co.za) is a domestic airline that operates in conjunction with Sabena. Nationwide's destinations include Cape Town, Durban, Jo'burg and George.

There are also several smaller airlines, such as National Airlines (☎ 934 0530), which flies between Cape Town, Springbok, Alexander Bay and tiny Kleinsee (Northern Cape), and Civair (☎ 934 4488,

W www.civair.co.za), which operates services between Cape Town, Plettenberg Bay and Port Elizabeth.

Other African Countries

SAA has inter-Africa flights, and most regional African airlines fly to and from South Africa. Some European airlines stop in various African countries en route to South Africa.

Connections with South Africa's closest neighbours are mainly via Jo'burg. The exceptions are Comair and Air Namibia, which have flights between Cape Town and Windhoek (R1200/1500 one way/return). Comair also flies to Harare (Zimbabwe) and Victoria Falls (Zimbabwe).

The UK

The majority of travel agencies in Britain are registered with the Association of British Travel Agents (ABTA). If you have bought your ticket from an ABTA-registered agency that then goes out of business, ABTA guarantees a refund or will arrange an alternative flight. Check out its Web site at **W** www .abta.com.

Buying your ticket from an unregistered bucket shop is riskier but sometimes cheaper. London is the national centre for bucket shops, although all major cities have unregistered agencies as well.

The following companies are reliable:

Africa Travel Centre (☎ 020-7387 1211, **W** www.africatravel.co.uk) 4 Medway Court, 21 Leigh St, London WC1H 9QX. Specialising in Africa, with a video library.

STA Travel (☎ 020-7361 6262, **W** www.statravel .co.uk) 86 Old Brompton Rd, London SW7 3LQ. The largest worldwide student/budget travel agency.

Trailfinders (☎ 020-7938 3939, **W** www.trail finders.com) 194 Kensington High St, London W8 7RG. A complete travel service, including foreign exchange, a bookshop, an information centre, a visa service and an immunisation centre. It also puts out a useful quarterly magazine.

Usit Campus (☎ 020-7730 8111, **W** www.usit campus.co.uk) 52 Grosvenor Gardens, London SW1W 0AG. Formerly Campus Travel, this company has outlets in large YHA offices and at university campuses around the UK.

Fares from the UK are very competitive. It's worth shopping around but you should be able to get a return flight to Jo'burg or Cape Town for anything between £350 and £450. Some airlines (eg, British Airways, KLM, SAA) will allow you to fly into Cape Town and leave from Jo'burg or vice versa. The fare if you're under 26 is around £450.

Although it is a long-haul flight, it's pretty easy to handle (nothing like flying to Asia or Australia). The flight takes about 13½ hours but it is overnight and as South Africa is only two hours ahead of Greenwich Mean Time (GMT) the body clock doesn't get too badly out of whack.

There are also interesting tickets available from the UK that include other ports in Africa, such as Cairo (Egypt), Nairobi (Kenya) and Harare (Zimbabwe). If you have plenty of time up your sleeve, you may find some good-value round-the-world tickets that include Jo'burg. Return tickets to Australia via Jo'burg and Asia are also worth looking at (£800 to £900 if you're under 26).

One-way fares from Cape Town to the UK start at as little as R2730.

Asia

Air India, Cathay Pacific, Malaysia Airlines, Singapore Airlines, Thai Airways International and other Asian airlines fly to South Africa – most to Jo'burg.

Air Mauritius flies to South Africa via Mauritius from Singapore, Hong Kong and Mumbai (Bombay).

From Cape Town to Kuala Lumpur (Malaysia) or Singapore costs about R3170; cheap one-way fares from Cape Town to Mumbai (India) start at R4615.

Australia

STA Travel and Flight Centres International are major dealers in cheap air fares. For competitive fares on the Internet check out **W** www.travel.com.au and **W** www.sta travel.com.au.

There are direct flights from Sydney on Qantas and SAA and from Perth on SAA to Cape Town and Jo'burg, however, there are no direct flights from New Zealand. You can expect to pay around A\$2200 for a standard shoulder-season economy fare, but as little as A$1600 for special deals. If you're thinking of including South Africa as a stop on a round-the-world ticket or as a stopover on a return ticket to Europe you'll be looking at around A$2300.

Air Mauritius has an interesting fare that involves a direct flight from Perth to Mauritius, a stopover in Mauritius, then a direct flight to Jo'burg, for around A$1300.

Singapore Airlines and Malaysia Airlines often have the cheapest flights from Australia to Jo'burg and Cape Town. The hassle is that you travel via Singapore or Kuala Lumpur, which adds considerably to the flying time. There are more-or-less direct connections but you may want to take advantage of the airlines' stopover deals for each city.

From Cape Town, one-way cheapies to Sydney go as low as R3780 on Malaysia Airlines. It's cheaper to fly to Perth (R3320), but you'd spend a lot more than R450 getting from Perth to Sydney (even hitching you'd spend more than that on food), so it's definitely worth spending the extra if you're heading for Australia's east coast.

The USA & Canada

North America's largest student travel organisations, Council Travel (W www.counciltravel.com), and STA Travel (W www.statravel.com) have offices in major cities throughout the USA. You may have to produce proof of your student status and in some cases be under 26 years of age to qualify for their discounted fares.

In Canada, Travel Cuts (☎ 800 667 2887, W www.travelcuts.com) has offices in all major cities, as does Flight Centre. Vancouver-based Great Expeditions (W www.greatexpeditions.com) is also useful.

North America is a relative newcomer to the bucket-shop traditions of Europe and Asia so ticket availability and the restrictions attached to them need to be weighed against what is offered on the advance-purchase excursion (APEX) or full-economy tickets.

It's often cheaper to fly first to London on an inexpensive airline, then buy a bucket-shop or on-line ticket from there to Africa. Do some homework before setting off.

From the US west coast it should be possible to get a good deal via Asia. Malaysia Airlines flies from Los Angeles to Kuala Lumpur and from there to Jo'burg and Cape Town. There are no direct flights but there are usually good stopover deals. Malaysia Airlines flies from Cape Town to Buenos Aires, so you could put together a very interesting trip.

SAA flies to and from New York, Miami and Atlanta. You should be able to purchase a one-way/return ticket from New York for US$1600/2200, and from Los Angeles for US$2000/2200.

From Cape Town, cheap one-way fares to Los Angeles start at R5000; to New York R4250; and to Toronto about R4670.

South America

SAA and Varig airlines link Jo'burg and Cape Town with Rio de Janeiro and Sao Paulo. Malaysia Airlines offers good deals on flights to Buenos Aires: A one-way ticket from Cape Town is around R2260.

BUS
Major Bus Companies

The booking offices of all three major bus lines (Greyhound, Intercape Mainliner and Translux) and their main arrival and departure points are at the Meriman Square end of Cape Town train station (Map 13). There's little to choose between their prices but check with each before making a booking; their services and routes are similar.

Tickets must be booked 24 hours in advance. You can get on without a booking if there's a spare seat but you won't know that until the bus arrives. You usually can't book a seat to a nearby town, but prices for short sectors are exorbitant anyway – you're better off looking for a local bus or a shared taxi.

Computicket (☎ 918 8910, W www.computicket.com) and many travel agencies take bookings. The bus companies' main offices are as follows:

Greyhound (☎ 418 4310) Open from 7am to 7pm daily
Intercape Mainliner (☎ 386 4400) Open from 6am to 8pm daily

Translux (☎ 449 3333) Open from 7am to 7pm daily. Phone bookings are taken 8am to 5pm Monday to Friday and 8am to noon Saturday.

Durban Both Greyhound and Translux run services to Durban via either Port Elizabeth (R395, 26 hours) or Bloemfontein (R395, 22 hours). Intercape's service takes 29 hours via Port Elizabeth and is slightly cheaper at R385.

Eastern Cape On all three services, the route to Durban via Port Elizabeth goes through Grahamstown (R205), East London (R240) and Umtata (R300 with Intercape, R320 with Greyhound and Translux).

Garden Route Translux runs along the Garden Route daily from Cape Town to Port Elizabeth (R190) via Paarl (R85), Worcester (R95), Swellendam (R95), Mossel Bay (R115), George (R130), Knysna (R145), Plettenberg Bay (R155) and Storms River (R175). Greyhound also has a bus on this route.

Intercape runs the Garden Route twice daily at slightly lower fares. (If you plan to visit several Garden Route towns, check out the hop-on, hop-off options on the Baz Bus).

Karoo Route Translux runs daily overnight services from Cape Town to East London (R240) via the Karoo, stopping at Beaufort West, Graaff-Reinet and Cradock (all R220).

Jo'burg From Cape Town to Jo'burg, Translux/Greyhound/Intercape buses run at least daily for R410/415/370, via either Bloemfontein or Kimberley (about 19 hours). Intercape also runs to Jo'burg via Upington (you may have to change buses) four times a week for the same fare.

West Coast & Namibia Intercape runs buses every Sunday, Monday, Wednesday and Friday from Cape Town to Upington (R195, 10½ hours) via Citrusdal (R120 from Cape Town), Clanwilliam (R130) and Calvinia (R170). From Upington you can connect with an Intercape bus to Windhoek (Namibia) for R250.

Baz Bus

The Baz Bus (☎ 439 2323, fax 439 2343, Ⓦ www.bazbus.com) is a good, if pricey, alternative to the major bus lines. While it's aimed at backpackers, its routes, organisation and service levels make it very useful for travellers on any budget.

The Baz Bus offers hop-on, hop-off fares between Cape Town and Jo'burg via Northern Drakensberg, Durban and the Garden Route. It also does a very useful loop from Durban up through Zululand and Swaziland and back to Jo'burg, passing close by Kruger National Park. This loop passes through arguably the most interesting part of the region and no other mainstream transport options cover it.

The major routes and one-way fares from Cape Town are Durban via the Garden Route (R930), Jo'burg via Northern Drakensberg (R1100); and Jo'burg via Swaziland (R1350).

These fares are significantly more than similar ones on the big three bus companies (although you should factor in being taken door to door at most places). You can also buy sector tickets, but these work out more expensive, so weigh up how important the flexibility of a hop-on, hop-off fare is to you. For example, if your itinerary is just Cape Town-Knysna-Durban you'd probably be better off travelling with one of the big three.

The Baz Bus drops off and picks up at many hostels along the way, and has transfer arrangements with some hostels in less accessible places, such as Coffee Bay and Port St Johns in the Transkei. Most hostels take Baz Bus bookings.

SHARED TAXI

Shared taxis cover most of South Africa with an informal network of routes. A shared taxi is not a taxi you share with your friends and acquaintances, but a form of public transport also known as a minibus taxi, long-distance taxi or black taxi. Used predominantly by blacks and some adventurous whites, mainly foreign backpackers who are keen to meet locals, they're a cheap and generally efficient way of getting around. The driving can occasionally be hair-raising but it is mostly OK, especially compared with similar transport in other African countries. As their clientele is largely black, they'll often travel via townships and will usually depart very early in the morning or in the early evening to cater to the needs of commuting workers and shoppers.

In Cape Town, most shared taxis start picking up passengers in a distant township, especially Langa and Nyanga, and perhaps make a trip into the main train station if they need more people, so your choices can be limited. The townships are not great places to be wandering around in the early hours of the morning carrying a pack, so *do not* go into them without accurate local knowledge; it's best to go with a reliable local guide.

Langa is currently relatively safe (however, these things can change) and shared taxis leave from the Langa shopping centre early in the morning. A shared taxi from the main train station to Langa costs about R3. A shared taxi to Jo'burg costs about R240 (compared with R370 on Intercape) and departs around 7pm. The trip is long, uncomfortable and potentially dangerous because of driver fatigue. Between a few people, hiring a car would be cheaper.

TRAIN

All long-distance trains leave from the main Cape Town train station **(Map 13)**, where the booking office (☎ 449 3871) is open from 7.30am to 3.55pm Monday to Friday and 7.30am to 10.30am Saturday. It can take a long time to get to the front of the queue.

There's a left-luggage facility next to platform 24 but it closes at 2pm after the last train has arrived from Jo'burg.

Trains are a good way to travel between major cities, and economy class (the old 3rd class) is very affordable. Another advantage is that fares on short sectors are not inflated (unlike those for long-distance buses).

On overnight journeys the 1st- and 2nd-class fares include a sleeping berth, but there's a charge of R20 for bedding hire. Alternatively, you can hire a private compartment (sleeping four in 1st class and six in 2nd class) or a coupe (sleeping two in 1st class and three in 2nd class). Meals are available in the dining car or can be taken in your compartment.

First, 2nd and economy class must be booked at least 24 hours in advance (you can book up to three months in advance). Most stations accept bookings, or you can call the Main Line Passenger Services call centre (☎ 086 000 8888).

Routes

The fares given here are for one-way travel from Cape Town. Return fares are double the one-way fares. For further details, see Spoornet's Web site (W www.spoornet .co.za). Also useful is ferroequinologist David Forsyth's South African Railways Page (W terrapin.ru.ac.za/~iwdf/) – he provides some information that the Spoornet site doesn't.

Jo'burg & Pretoria The daily *Trans Karoo* is competitive in price, but much slower than the bus (about 27 hours instead of 17). Still, this is an interesting journey, and stops include Kimberley and Beaufort West. 1st-/2nd-/economy-class fares are R450/R305/R190; a 1st-/2nd-class compartment costs R1830/1800 and a coupe is R915/900. There is also a new 'premier class' that provides a bit more comfort and style than 1st class.

Durban It's possible to travel between Cape Town and Durban on the weekly *Trans Oranje*. The price is competitive but the trip takes an awfully long time – 30½ hours. The service departs Cape Town on Monday at 6.50pm, and Durban on Wednesday at 5.30pm. Stops include Wellington, Beaufort West, Kimberley, Bloemfontein, Kroonstad, Bethlehem, Ladysmith and Pietermaritzburg. 1st-/2nd-/economy-class fares are R560/R380/R235. A 1st-/2nd-class compartment costs R2280/2240 and a 1st/2nd-class coupe is R1140/1120.

Oudtshoorn The weekly trip on the *Southern Cross* takes 14½ hours and follows an interesting route – stops include Huguenot (in Paarl), Robertson, Ashton (near Montagu), Swellendam and George. The train departs Cape Town on Friday at 6.15pm, and Outdshoorn on Sunday at 5.40pm. 1st-/2nd-/economy-class fares are R185/125/75. A 1st-/2nd-class compartment costs R750/740 and a coupe is R375/370.

Blue Train

Some people come to South Africa just to ride on the famous *Blue Train* (W www.bluetrain.co.za). Travel agencies, both in South Africa and abroad, take bookings; it's worth inquiring about special packages. Some deals include a one-way flight from Jo'burg to Cape Town and a night's accommodation. Direct bookings can be made in Cape Town (☎ 449 2672, fax 449 3338) or in Pretoria (☎ 012-334 8459, fax 334 8464).

The low season for fares is from 1 May to 31 August. You can choose between the deluxe cabins and the luxury suites, which are more spacious, some including a bathtub rather than a shower.

From Cape Town the Blue Train runs to Pretoria on Monday, Wednesday and Friday, taking 27 hours. The train departs Cape Town at 11am, or Pretoria at 8.50am. Single/double suites cost from R7600/10,800. These fares are for deluxe class in the high season of 2001 and are likely to rise. There's also a monthly service to Port Elizabeth along the Garden Route. Single/double suites cost from R10,300/13,700, and the journey takes 40 hours.

CAR & MOTORCYCLE

The main road routes to Cape Town are the N1 from Jo'burg, the N7 from Springbok (and Namibia) and the N2 from the Garden Route and Durban. If speed is your aim, stick to these highways. However, there are often alternative routes on smaller roads, passing through some interesting country and sleepy towns

For detailed information on car and motorcycle rental and purchase, see the Getting Around chapter.

Road Rules & Etiquette

You can use your driving licence if it carries your photo; otherwise you're supposed to have an international driving permit, obtainable from a motoring organisation in your country.

South Africans drive on the left-hand side of the road just like drivers in the UK, Japan and Australia.

On freeways, faster drivers will expect you to move into the emergency lane to let them pass. If you do, they will probably say 'thank you' by flashing their hazard lights; you may say, 'you're welcome' by flashing your high-beam lights.

Among the local variations on road rules is the procedure at a 'four-way stop' (crossroad), which can occur even on major roads. If you are familiar with a system where drivers on major roads always have priority over drivers on smaller roads you'll definitely need to stay alert. When you arrive at a four-way stop, you must stop. If there are other vehicles at the intersection, those that arrived before you get to cross before you. Before you proceed, make sure that it *is* a four-way stop – if it is, you can safely cross ahead of approaching cars. If you've mistaken an ordinary stop sign for a four-way stop, the approaching cars won't be slowing down!

In many places, particularly in rural areas, you'll see hitchhikers, who will be predominantly black and coloured people. Use your judgment on who to pick up (a group of young men in the city might not be a wise idea), but in general giving lifts is a great way to meet locals and have conversations that you'd otherwise never have.

The speed limit is 100km/h (roughly 60mph), and 120km/h on most major highways. Some dangerous sections of rural roads have a limit of less than 100km/h, while the usual limit in towns is 60km/h.

If you stick to the highway speed limit you'll feel lonely – most traffic travels either much faster or much slower.

Driving Hazards

South Africa has a horrific road accident rate. Hundreds of people die whenever there's a long weekend and the annual death toll is pushing 10,000. A further 150,000 people are injured on the roads annually – appalling figures given that the vast majority of the population don't own cars.

Road deaths are evenly divided between drivers, passengers and pedestrians, which suggests that multiple-fatality shared-taxi accidents aren't the only things you need to worry about.

Road Conditions Around Cape Town you won't have to worry about road conditions, but you don't have to get very far away from the city to find yourself on dirt roads. Most are regularly graded and reasonably smooth and it's often possible to travel at high speed. Don't!

If you're cruising along a dirt road at 100km/h and you come to a corner, you won't go around that corner, you'll sail off into the veld. If you put on the brakes to slow down you'll probably spin or roll. If you swerve sharply to avoid a pothole you'll go into an exciting four-wheel drift then find out what happens when your car meets a telephone pole. Worst of all, if another car approaches and you have to move to the edge of the road, you may lose control and collide head-on.

On dirt roads that are dry, flat, straight, traffic-free and wide enough to allow for unexpected slewing as you hit potholes and drifted sand, you could, with practice, drive at about 80km/h. Otherwise, treat dirt as though it were ice.

Pedestrians & Animals In rural areas slow down and watch out for pedestrians and animals on the roads. Standard advice is don't stop if you hit an animal in a poor area – drive to the nearest police station and report it there. This might be paranoia but then again it might not be. If the animal you hit is a cow or a horse, leaving the scene might not be an option.

Other Drivers On highways, fast cars coming up behind you will expect you to move over into the emergency lane to let them pass. However, there might be pedestrians, slow-moving vehicles or even animals already in the emergency lane. Don't move over unless it's safe!

It is possible that an overtaking car will rely on *oncoming* traffic to move into the emergency lane! This is sheer lunacy and you must remain constantly alert. When two cars travelling in opposite directions decide that they will overtake despite oncoming traffic, things get really hairy, especially if the protagonists are travelling at the usual 150km/h.

Drivers on little-used rural roads often speed and they often assume that there is no other traffic. Be careful of oncoming cars at blind corners on rural roads.

Breath-testing for alcohol exists but given the lack of police resources and the high blood-alcohol level permitted (0.08%), drunk drivers remain a danger.

Weather Dense mists can reduce visibility to a few metres on roads over mountain passes, so take care.

Crime Car theft and theft from cars are big problems. Take precautions. Carjacking, a problem in Jo'burg, is not so common. Still, it pays to stay alert and keep windows wound up at night. If you are car-jacked, make it clear that it's a rental car and you don't give a damn about losing it.

HITCHING

No country in the world is ever entirely safe from hitching, and we don't recommend it. Travellers who decide to hitch should understand that they are taking a small but potentially serious risk. People who do choose to hitch will be safer if they travel in pairs and let someone know where they plan to go.

If you want to hitch long distances, despite our warnings not to, either start in the city centre, or catch public transport to one of the outlying towns such as Paarl for Jo'burg, Somerset West for the Garden Route and Durban, and Malmsbury or Citrusdal for regions in the north. Do not hitch anywhere near the Cape Flats, where safety is a real issue.

In the city centre, make a sign and start at the foreshore near the entry to the Waterfront, where the N1 (to Jo'burg), the N7 (to

The Overland Route to Cape Town

The traditional Cairo to Cape Town route is now notoriously difficult as a result of the fraught relations between Sudan and Ethiopia. However, we have had reports from travellers who managed to cross the border between these countries at Metema. If your starting point in Africa must be Egypt, you could take a flight from Cairo – or at best from Khartoum – to Kampala (Uganda) or Nairobi (Kenya). Alternatively, fly to Ethiopia and travel south to Kenya from there.

On the Sahara route through North and West Africa, your options are limited to starting in Morocco or Mauritania, then travelling into Senegal and the rest of West Africa, as the routes through Algeria into Mali and Niger are blocked as a result of political unrest. There's war in Congo (Zaïre), so a flight will be necessary from Accra (Ghana) or Lagos (Nigeria) to Nairobi.

From Nairobi, the most popular route south seems to be the Tazara railway between Dar es Salaam in Tanzania (which is accessible by bus or plane from Nairobi) and Kapiri Mposhi in Zambia, from where it's possible to pick up another train on to Lusaka and Livingstone (both also in Zambia). It's extremely inexpensive for the distance travelled but be prepared for uncomfortable conditions and a slow pace.

Another option takes you across Tanzania to Kigoma on Lake Tanganyika, then by steamer to Mpulungu (Zambia) and overland to Chitipa (Malawi) or Lusaka (Zambia). It's also possible to enter Zambia at Nakonde or Malawi between Mbeya and Karonga. There's no public transport along the latter route so it will require hitching.

Once you're in Zambia, it's fairly straightforward continuing to Zimbabwe, Botswana or Namibia. The most direct route to Cape Town is from Namibia; there are direct buses from Windhoek to Cape Town. The border post west of Upington in the Northern Cape is at Nakop (open 24 hours). There's also one further west at Vioolsdrif (open from 7am to 7pm).

Make sure you take a copy of Lonely Planet's *Africa on a shoestring*.

Windhoek), and the N2 (to the Garden Route) all converge.

Hostel notice boards often have offers of lifts and rental-share arrangements.

BOAT

Cape Town is a major port of call for cruise ships, and the Royal Cape Yacht Club (**Map 12, #13**) (☎ 421 1354) is also popular with round-the-world sailors. Races known as 'the Wags' are held every Wednesday afternoon at the club and this would be a good time to come looking for crewing work if you have sailing experience.

Many container lines take a limited number of passengers, and while the voyage will be considerably more expensive than flying, the cost per day can be reasonable. Accommodation can be anything from the owner's suite to a bunk in a self-contained cabin.

The best source of information about routes and the shipping lines plying them is the *OAG Cruise & Ferry Guide*, published quarterly by the Reed Travel Group in the UK. Your travel agency might have a copy.

A few companies take bookings for freighters, including:

Freighter World Cruises (☎ 626-449 3106, fax 449 9573) 180 South Lake Ave, Suite 335, Pasadena, CA 91101, USA

Strand Cruise & Travel Centre (☎ 020-7836 6363, fax 7497 0078) Charing Cross Shopping Centre Concourse, London WC2N 4HZ, UK

Sydney International Travel Centre (☎ 02-9299 8000, fax 9299 1337) Level 8, 75 King St, Sydney 2000, Australia (Note that at the time of research, no freighter companies were taking passengers between South Africa and Australia.)

South Africa's Safmarine (☎ 408 6911, fax 408 6660), Ⓦ www.safmarine.co.uk) is actively seeking passengers for its container ships, which sail to many of the world's major ports. Fares are relatively high (eg, from US$2200/3000 per single/double between Cape Town and the UK, much more in high season or with a better cabin), but the company says costs are definitely negotiable. Fares *from* South Africa seem to be lower than fares *to* South Africa.

ORGANISED TOURS

Quite a few overland operators have taken up the trans-Sahara route through Morocco and West Africa, across to Central Africa, then flying over Congo (Zäire) to East Africa and on to Zimbabwe, Botswana and South Africa. These trips are very popular but are designed primarily for first-time travellers who feel uncomfortable striking out on their own or for those who prefer guaranteed social interaction to the uncertainties of the road.

If you have the slightest inclination towards independence or would feel confined travelling with the same group of 25 or so people for most of the trip (quite a few normally drop out along the way), think twice before booking something like this.

UK-Based Operators

All of the following overland operators are based in the UK (Exodus has offices in Australia, New Zealand, the USA and Canada as well as the UK):

Dragoman (☎ 01728-861133, fax 861127, W www.dragoman.co.uk) Camp Green, Kenton Rd, Debenham, Suffolk IP14 6LA

Exodus Expeditions (☎ 020-8675 5550, fax 8673 0779, W www.exodustravels.co.uk) 9 Weir Rd, London SW12 0LT

Guerba Expeditions (☎ 01373-826611, fax 858351, W www.guerba.co.uk) Wessex House, 40 Station Rd, Westbury, Wiltshire BA13 3JN

Kumuka Expeditions (☎ 020-7937 8855, W www.kumuka.co.uk) 40 Earls Court Rd, London W8 6EJ

Top Deck (☎ 020-244 8641, fax 7373 6201, W www.topdecktravel.co.uk) 131–135 Earls Court Rd, London SW5 9RH

South Africa–Based Operators

Truck Overland truck journeys from South Africa to other African countries are popular. Most are round trips. Once again, these

are mainly for people who haven't the confidence to travel on their own or who are looking for a party with changing scenery. Many hostels will book you on a truck trip but there are some cowboys out there, so deal with an agency that's been in business a while. Reliable companies include:

African Routes (☎ 031-569 3911, fax 569 3908, e aroutes@iafrica.com) PO Box 1835, Durban 4000

Drifters (☎ 011-888 1160, fax 888 1020, W www.drifters.co.za) PO Box 48434, Roosevelt Park, Johannesburg 2129

Nomad (☎ 559 4133, fax 559 4134, W www.nomadtours.co.za) 186 Vryburger Ave, Bothasig, Cape Town 7441 (Nomad's retail branch, the Nomad Adventure Centre **(Map 13, #65)**, is on Long St in the City Bowl.)

Which Way Adventures (☎ 845 7400, fax 845 7401, e whichway@iafrica.com) PO Box 2600, Somerset West 7129

Bus The main coach tour operators are Springbok Atlas (☎ 460 4700, W www.springbokatlas.com) and Connex (☎ 011-884 8110, fax 884 3007). They have a wide range of fairly expensive tours covering popular routes, as well as day tours. Their clientele tend to be older travellers.

Train Mike and Rachel Barry (☎/fax 023-230 0665, e uzahamba@telekomsa.net) organise an interesting range of one- and two-day package trips by train from Cape Town to Tulbagh, the Klein Cedarberg reserve near Ceres (not to be confused with the Cederberg Wilderness Area), and Matjiesfontein in the Karoo. Prices range from R150 for the day trip to Tulbagh to R700 for the two-night trip combining Tulbagh and the Klein Cedarberg reserve. Bookings can be made directly or at Computicket outlets in Cape Town (☎ 918 8910, W www.computicket.com).

Union Ltd Steam Rail Tours (☎ 449 4391, fax 449 4395, W www.steamsa.co.za), a division of Spoornet, runs restored steam trains. The *Union Limited* was the pre–*Blue Train* king of the line, running to Cape Town with passengers who were meeting liners to Europe. The luxurious compartments are roomier than they once were, as two people now share four-berth compartments and singles the two-berth ones. The six-day Golden Thread tour runs from Cape Town along the coast to Outdshoorn and back. It costs R4900/9800 per single/double or R19,600 for two people in a deluxe suite, including meals and a few side trips. There are also six- and 15-day 'steam safaris' from about R9000 per person.

A safari by train is also what Shongololo Express (☎/fax 011-486 2902, **W** www .shongo.co.za) package tours are about. They're not quite as luxurious as the other classic trains, but still quite acceptable. The concept entails travelling by night on a sleeper train and then disembarking to go on a day's sightseeing – a bit like a cruise, but on land. Options include trips from South Africa to Namibia, Zimbabwe, Botswana and Zambia.

Rovos Rail (☎ 012-323 6052, fax 323 0843, **W** www.rovos.co.za) rivals the *Blue Train* as the most luxurious and expensive service in Africa. Regular trips include Pretoria–Cape Town over two nights and three days (as opposed to the *Blue Train*'s one night and two days), with stops both ways at Matjiesfontein and Kimberley. Or you can travel from Pretoria to Kruger National Park; from Cape Town to George; or on a longer trip from Pretoria to Victoria Falls (Zimbabwe) and Dar es Salaam (Tanzania).

Getting Around

TO/FROM THE AIRPORT

Cape Town International Airport **(Map 11)** is 20km east of the city centre, around a 20-minute drive depending on traffic. People returning rental cars to the airport should note that there is no petrol station at the airport, so refuel before you get there.

Several companies offer a shuttle service between the airport and the city and some hostels will pick you up for free if you have a booking. Backpacker Bus (☎ 082-809 9185, ⓔ bpackbus@mweb.co.za) picks up from hostels and hotels in the city and does airport transfers for R70 per person.

Nonshared taxis are expensive; expect to pay nearly R150 one way.

BUS

Cape Town's Golden Arrow public bus network is reliable, if a little run-down. Most services stop running early in the evening. Buses are most useful for getting along the Atlantic coast from the city centre to Hout Bay (trains service the suburbs to the east of Table Mountain). When travelling short distances, most people wait at the bus stop and take either a bus or a shared taxi, whichever arrives first.

The main bus station, the Golden Acre Terminal **(Map 13, #126)**, is on Grand Parade. Here there's also a helpful bus information kiosk **(Map 13, #129)** (☎ 461 4365 or ☎ 0801 21 2111), open from 8am to 5.30pm Monday to Friday and 8am to 1.30pm Saturday.

Destinations and off-peak fares (applicable from 8am to 4pm) from the city include the Waterfront (R1.90), Sea Point (R2.30), Kloof Nek (R2.30), Camps Bay (R2.80) and Hout Bay (R5.20). Peak fares are about 30% higher. If you're using a particular bus regularly, it's worth buying 'clipcards', which offer 10 discounted trips.

TRAIN

Metro commuter trains are a handy way to get around, although services have been cut back and there are few (or no) trains after 6pm on weekdays and after noon on Saturday. The Metro Rail information office (☎ 449 4045) is in the main train station **(Map 13)** next to ticket offices 7 and 8. It's open from 6am to 6pm Monday to Friday and 6.30am to 5pm at weekends.

Metro trains have 1st- and economy-class carriages only. The difference in price and comfort is negligible, although you'll find the 1st-class compartments to be safer on the whole.

The most important line for visitors is the Simon's Town line, which runs through Observatory and then around the back of Table Mountain through upper-income white suburbs such as Rosebank, down to Muizenberg and along the False Bay coast. These trains run at least every hour from around 5am to 7.30pm Monday to Friday (to 6pm on Saturday), and from 7.30pm to 6.30pm on Sunday. (Rikkis meet all trains and go to Boulders.) On some of these trains you'll find Biggsy's, a restaurant carriage and rolling wine bar. There's a small extra charge to use it.

Metro trains run some way out of Cape Town, to Strand on the eastern side of False Bay, and into the Winelands to Stellenbosch and Paarl. They are the cheapest and easiest means of transport to these areas but we have received reports of muggings, so take care to travel at peak times.

Some economy-/1st-class fares include Observatory (R3.80/4.50), Muizenberg (R4.50/7.50), Simon's Town (R5.50/9.50), Paarl (R5.50/9.50) and Stellenbosch (R5.50/9.50).

The Spier steam train (☎ 419 5222) runs occasional trips to the Spier wine estate and Darling. Every month it runs to Simon's Town; the return trip costs R60/30 for adults/children.

CAR & MOTORCYCLE

Cape Town has an excellent road and freeway system that, outside of the morning and early-evening rush hours, carries surprisingly little traffic. Driving in Cape Town is on the whole a pleasure. The only downside is getting used to the sometimes erratic breaking of road rules by fellow drivers.

Road signs alternate between Afrikaans and English. You'll soon learn, for example, that Linkerbaan isn't the name of a town – it means 'left lane'.

Petrol stations are often open 24 hours. Petrol costs around R3.30 per litre, depending on the octane level you choose, but prices are constantly rising. Not all petrol stations accept credit cards and of those that do some will charge you a fee, typically 10%, to do so. An attendant will always fill up your tank for you, clean your windows and ask if the oil or water needs checking – you should tip them 10% for their service.

For details on road rules, speed limits and driving hazards in South Africa, see the Getting There & Away chapter.

Car Rental

Major international companies such as Avis **(Map 13, #3)** (☎ 080 002 1111), at 123 Strand St, and Budget **(Map 13, #4)** (☎ 080 001 6622), at 120 Strand St, are represented.

The larger local companies, such as Imperial **(Map 13, #8)** (☎ 0800 131 000) on the corner of Loop and Strand Sts, offer service comparable to the major companies at slightly lower rates.

Smaller, cheaper companies come and go; you'll find plenty of brochures for them at Cape Town Tourism and all the hostels. The deals may look tempting, but read the small print (R99 a day is a rate that is seldom, if ever, available).

If you hire a 'category B' car (usually a smallish Japanese car such as a Toyota Corolla with a 1.6L motor, manual transmission and air-con) for five days with at least 200 free kilometres per day, and collision and theft insurance, you'll pay in the region of R300 per day with the larger companies and from about R250 with the smaller companies. Many backpacker hostels can arrange better deals from around R200 per day or less.

If all you're looking for is a wreck in which to tootle around the city, contact Christine at Milnerton Car Hire (☎ 082 892 9959) for deals at around R75 a day.

South Africa is a big country but unless you are a travel writer on a tight schedule, you probably don't need to pay higher rates for unlimited kilometres. For meandering around, 400km a day should be more than enough, and if you plan to stop for a day here and there, 200km a day might be sufficient.

However, if you're renting with an international company and you book through the branch in your home country, you'll probably get unlimited kilometres at no extra cost. At peak times in South Africa (mainly summer), even your local branch might tell you that unlimited-kilometre deals aren't available. Your travel agency might be able to get around this.

One-way rentals are usually possible with the larger companies if you are driving between the major cities. This may not be the case with the smaller companies. There's also likely to be a drop-off charge with some companies.

When you're getting quotes make sure that they include value-added tax (VAT), as that 14% slug makes a big difference.

Choose a car powerful enough to do the job. The smallest cars are OK for one person but with any more they'll be straining on the hills, which even on major highways are steep. Steep hills can also make automatics unpleasant to drive.

One problem with nearly all car-rental deals is the excess: the amount you are liable for before the insurance takes over. Even with a small car you can be liable for up to R5000 (although there's usually the choice of lowering or cancelling the excess for a higher insurance premium). Visitors with little experience of driving on dirt roads have a high accident rate on the region's roads, so this could be an important consideration.

A few companies offer 100% damage and theft insurance at a more expensive rate. You may be charged extra if you nominate more than one driver. If a non-nominated driver has an accident, then you won't be covered by insurance.

Rental Car Check List

One reader sent us this list of things to watch out for when hiring a car; they're particularly useful if you opt for a cheaper deal where the car maintenance might not have been so stringent.

• Check the tyres to see if they have sufficient tread.

• Ask when the car was last serviced.

• Check the oil and water before you go, and get the petrol station attendants to check them regularly for you while you're on the road.

• Check the spare tyre and whether there's a jack.

• Check the wipers and windscreen-washer water.

• If the car is delivered to you with a 'full' tank of petrol, make sure it's full.

• Ask how the car alarm works.

• As you drive away, put the brakes on fully to see if the car keeps a straight line; faulty brakes could be lethal in wet weather.

• Check the insurance details and make sure you know what is and isn't covered.

Jonathan Sibtain

Read the contract carefully before you sign. Hail damage is a distinct and costly possibility, so see if it's covered. Many contracts used to stipulate that you couldn't enter townships – maybe that has changed but check. If you plan to visit another country (eg, Swaziland), make sure the rental agreement permits this, and make sure you get the standard letter from the rental company granting this permission.

Motorcycle & Scooter Rental

Le Cap Motorcycle Hire **(Map 13, #78)** (☎ 423 0823, **W** www.lecapmotorcycle hire.co.za) at 3 Carisbrook St hires motorcycles (from R200 a day) and scooters (from R125 a day), and also runs longer tours. It's open from 8.30am to 5pm Monday to Friday and 9am to 1pm Saturday.

African Buzz **(Map 13, #63)** (☎ 423 0052), 202 Long St, charges R160 a day for scooter hire.

Harley-Davidson Cape Town **(Map 13, #9)** (☎ 424 3990, **e** hdcape@mweb.co.za), 45 Buitengracht St, rents a Harley 1340cc Big Twins or an MG-B convertible sports car for R912 for 24 hours. It's open from 9am to 5pm Monday to Saturday.

Buying a Car

Cape Town is by far the most pleasant place in South Africa to spend the week or two that it will inevitably take to buy a car. Prices do tend to be a bit higher here, so it's not a bad place to sell, but as the market is smaller you might wait longer. Cars that have spent their lives around Cape Town are more likely to be rusty than those kept inland, but as one dealer told us, 'What's wrong with rust? It just means that the car is cheaper'.

Dealers The main congregation of used-car dealers is on Voortrekker Rd **(Map 12)** between the suburbs of Maitland and Bellville. Voortrekker Rd is the R102; the dealers start around Koeberg Rd and extend east for about 10km.

Some dealers might agree to a buy-back deal – try John Wayne at Wayne Motors **(Map 15, #32)** (☎ 465 2222, **e** wancars @mweb.co.za), 21 Roeland St. He'll guarantee a buy-back price but he reckons that you'd have a fair chance of selling the car privately for more than that. He doesn't deal in rock-bottom cars, though.

Dealers have to make a profit, so you'll pay less if you buy privately. The weekly classified-ads paper *Cape Ads* is the best place to look, or try its Web site (**W** www .capeads.com). Other useful Web sites include **W** www.autotrader.co.za and **W** www .autonetmail.co.za, both of which advertise thousands of cars around the country.

Making the Deal Whoever you're buying a car from, make sure its details correspond accurately with those on the ownership (registration) papers, that there is a *current* licence disk on the windscreen and that there's police clearance on the vehicle. The police clearance department can be contacted on ☎ 945 3891. Check the owner's name against their identity document, and check the engine and chassis numbers. Consider getting the car tested by the Automobile Association (AA; ☎ 462 4462). A full test can cost up to R300; less detailed tests are around R100.

Cheap cars will often be sold without a roadworthy certificate. This certificate is required when you pay tax for a licence disk, and register the change-of-ownership form. 'Roadworthies' used to be difficult to get but now some private garages are allowed to issue them, and some will overlook minor faults. A roadworthy costs R135.

Unfortunately, there seem to be very few quality used cars at low prices; a good car will cost about R25,000. You will be lucky to find a decent vehicle for much less than R13,000 (anything cheaper than R8000 is definitely a gamble).

You might be thinking of getting a 4WD for a trans-Africa trip – Series 1, 2 and 3 Land Rovers will cost anything in the region of R15,000 to R30,000 depending on their condition. A recommended contact in Cape Town is Graham Duncan Smith (☎ 797 3048), who's a Land Rover expert and has helped people buy these 4WDs in the past; he charges a consultation fee of R80, and R130 per hour for engineering work.

Paperwork To register your newly purchased car, present yourself along with the roadworthy, a current licence disk, an accurate ownership certificate, a completed change-of-ownership form (signed by the seller), a clear photocopy of your ID (passport) along with the original, and your money to the City Treasurer's Department, Motor Vehicle Registration Division (☎ 400 2385/6/7/8/9) in the Civic Centre **(Map 13, #109)**, Cash Hall, on the foreshore. It's open from 8am to 2pm Monday to Friday and distributes blank change-of-ownership forms. Call ahead to check how much cash you'll need, but it will be under R300.

Insurance for third-party damages and damage to or loss of your vehicle is a very good idea as repairs are horrendously expensive. It's easy enough to take out a year's insurance but most travellers don't want that much. Unfortunately, if you want to buy insurance by the month it is surprisingly difficult to find an insurance company to take your money if you don't have a permanent address or a local bank account. Try the AA. You might be able to negotiate paying for a year's worth of insurance then getting a pro-rata refund when you sell the car, but get an agreement in writing, not just a vague promise. One recommended insurance agent is First Bowring (☎ 425 1460).

Membership of the AA is highly recommended. It has an efficient vehicle breakdown service and a good supply of maps and information. (The important things to get are the window stickers you're given for breakdown service.) The initial joining fee is waived for members of many foreign motoring associations, so bring your membership details from home.

NONSHARED TAXI

It's worth considering taking a nonshared taxi late at night or if you're in a group, but they're expensive (about R10 per kilometre. There is a taxi rank **(Map 13, #118)** at the Adderley St end of the Grand Parade in the city, or call Marine Taxi (☎ 434 0434) or Unicab Taxis (☎ 447 4402). There are often taxis outside the Cape Sun Hotel **(Map 13, #116)** on Strand St or at the Waterfront. (For a cheaper alternative, see Rikki later.)

SHARED TAXI

Shared taxis cover most of the city with an informal network of routes. They're a cheap and efficient way of getting around. Useful routes are from Adderley St opposite the Golden Acre Centre **(Map 13, #119)** to Sea Point along Main Rd (R2.50) and up Long St to Kloof Nek (R2).

The main rank is on the upper deck of the main train station **(Map 13)**, accessible from a walkway in the Golden Acre Centre or from stairways on Strand St. It's well organised, and finding the right rank is

Shared-Taxi Etiquette

- People with lots of luggage (usually women) sit in the first row behind the driver.
- Pay the fare with coins, not notes. Pass money forward (your fare and those of the people around you) when the taxi is full. Give it to one of the front-seat passengers, not the driver. If you're sitting in the front seat you might have to collect the fares and give change.
- If you sit on the folding seat by the door it's your job to open and close the door when other people get out. You'll have to get out of the taxi each time.
- Say 'Thank you, driver!' when you want to get out, not 'Stop!'.

easy. Anywhere else, you just hail shared taxis from the side of the road. There's no way of telling which route a shared taxi will be taking except by asking the driver.

RIKKI

These tiny, open vans, called Rikkis (☎ 423 4888), provide Asian-style transport in the City Bowl and nearby areas for low prices. They operate from 7am to 7pm Monday to Friday, and 7am to 2pm Saturday. They can be booked or hailed on the street and travel as far afield as Camps Bay and Observatory. A single-person trip from the main train station to Tamboerskloof costs R10; to Camps Bay is R15. A Rikki from the City Bowl to Kirstenbosch Botanical Gardens costs R50 for the first four people and R10 for each extra person. Rikkis also operate out of Simon's Town (☎ 786 2136); they meet all trains to Simon's Town and go to Boulders.

Although cheap and fun, Rikkis may not be the quickest way to get around, as there is usually a certain amount of meandering as passengers are dropped off, and they can be notoriously slow to turn up to a booking.

BICYCLE

The Cape Peninsula is a great place to explore by bicycle, but there many are hills, and distances can be deceptively large – it's nearly 70km from the centre to Cape Point. Unfortunately, you aren't supposed to take bicycles on suburban trains.

If bringing your own bike to South Africa, fill your repair kit with every imaginable spare to be on the safe side. Airlines will transport bicycles as luggage, but check with them well in advance – some just want you to cover the chain, remove the pedals and turn the handlebars sideways; others require the bike to be completely dismantled and stored in a box. Cardboard bike boxes are available for a small charge or free from bike shops. Your bike is probably safer if it's *not* in a box, as it will probably be stowed upright or on top of the other luggage. These days cargo holds are pressurised, so it isn't necessary to let down your tyres.

For bicycle hire contact Downhill Adventures **(Map 13, #79)** (☎ 422 0388, W www.downhilladventures.co.za), Orange St, Gardens. Le Africa Express **(Map 16, #3)** (☎ 439 0901), 16A Main Rd, Three Anchor Bay, has scooter hire from R150 a day, bike hire for R50.

ORGANISED TOURS

For a quick orientation on a fine day, you can't beat the Cape Town Explorer open-top double-decker bus tour (☎ 426 4260), which runs regularly on a circular route from the Waterfront via Cape Town Tourism and Camps Bay. A full trip (you can hop on and off) costs R60 and takes two hours.

Major tour companies include Springbok Atlas Tours (☎ 417 6545) and Hylton Ross (☎ 511 1784, W www.hyltonross.co .za); their tours are professional but tend to be expensive and aimed at older travellers.

Day Trippers (☎/fax 531 3274, W www .daytrippers.co.za) gets excellent reports. Mountain bikes are taken along on most trips, so you can do some riding if you want to. Most tours cost around R195 and include Cape Point, the Winelands and, in season, whale-watching (an extra R250). Downhill Adventures **(Map 13, #79)** (☎ 422 0388, W www.downhilladventures .co.za), Orange St, Gardens, is another good company that runs a wide range of adventure trips.

Apart from the specialist tours described following, Cape Town Tourism can fill you in on myriad other options.

Township & Cultural Tours

Lots of operators offer township tours. The half-day tours are sufficient – the full-day tours tack on a trip to Robben Island that is best done separately and for which you don't need a guide. You might want to ask a prospective tour operator how much of what you spend actually goes to help people in the townships, since not all tours are run by Cape Flats residents. Bookings for most can be made directly or via Cape Town Tourism.

Grassroute Tours (☎ 706 1006, ☒ www .grassroutetours.co.za) runs a highly recommended tour that costs R195. The guide Arlene is very enthusiastic and knowledgeable, and tours drop by Vicky's B&B (see the Places to Stay chapter) for a chat with this Khayelitsha legend. The company also runs an unusual trip (R300) exploring the culture of the Cape fishermen on board one of their boats.

Sam's Cultural Tours (☎/fax 423 5417, ☎ 082 970 0564) is run by the ebullient and informed Sam Ntimba, who also works for Day Trippers on its township tours. His half-day trip (R170) includes visits to a dormitory and shebeen (unlicensed drinking establishment) in Langa and a creche project in Khayelitsha. A two-hour tour on Sunday to see a gospel choir in a Baptist church in Langa is R100.

Our Pride Tours (☎/fax 423 2971, ☒ our pride@mweb.co.za) offers the excellent Township Music Tour (R260) on Wednesday and Friday nights, as well as other cultural tours. The guides know their stuff.

Other companies to check out include Roots Africa Tours (☎ 988 7848), which offers a full day in the townships for R240 (excluding the traditional African lunch); and major operator Legend Tourism Services (☎ 697 4056, ☒ www.legendtourism.co.za), whose half-day Walk to Freedom tour (R210) includes a walk around Langa.

Green Turtle Tours & Safaris (☎ 082 558 2963, 082 882 7884, ☒ grturtle@mweb .co.za) is a good operator whose half-day walking tour is an eye-opening, relaxed alternative to the largely bus-based tours of the Cape Flats. Tours of the Hout Bay township of Imizamo Yethu (also known as Mandela Park) are available too.

Margaret Whiteing (☎ 790 2406, ☒ white ing@mweb.com.za) offers tours with lunch and choir singing (with 48 hours notice) at the community centre.

To learn something of the Cape Muslim and Cape coloured experience, contact Bo-Kaap Community Guided Tours (☎ 422 1554) for a good history-based walking tour of the Bo-Kaap district (R60), or Tana Baru Cultural Tours (☎ 424 0719) for a tour that focuses more on people, and includes tea at the guide's home (R70). (This company can also arrange B&B accommodation in the Bo-Kaap for R200 per person.)

History lecturer Andrew Bank (☎ 447 8467, ☒ abank@uwc.ac.za) leads the Slave Tour, a highly informative walking tour of the City Bowl past locations associated with Cape Town's period of slavery. The tour costs R75 per person and takes around two hours.

Air Tours

Spectacular air tours from the Waterfront are available with Civair Helicopters (☎ 419 5182, ☒ civair@mweb.co.za) and the Seaplane Company (☎ 0800 006 878, ☒ www.seaplane.co.za). There are various deals but you can expect to pay at least R320 for a flight over the peninsula with guaranteed amazing views.

Wildlife Tours

Green Turtle Tours & Safaris (see Township & Cultural Tours earlier) offers a full-day Cape Peninsula Wildlife Tour including viewing of hippos, flamingos, penguins and bonteboks, as well as custom itineraries.

Richard Grant runs Birdwatch Cape (☎/fax 762 5059, ☒ arg@iafrica.com). He is a birding expert who runs Cape Town tours pointing out the many unique species of the Cape floral kingdom. He also offers trips further afield in the Karoo, the Kalahari and along the Garden Route. Local tours start at R150 per person.

Winery Tours

Plenty of companies offer day trips to the Winelands, but unless you're tight for time it's better (and possibly cheaper) to stay overnight in, say, Stellenbosch and take a tour there.

The popular backpacker option (but not the one for those who are seriously into their wines) is to go with Ferdinand's Tours & Adventures (☎ 465 8550, ⓦ www.ferdi nandstours.co.za). The tours (R200) take in at least four wineries and include lunch.

Things can get pretty raucous: 'A merry rockin' time. Hell, we danced our way back to Cape Town', said one enthusiastic patron. (Ferdinand also arranges para-gliding and hiking trips to the marvellous Cederberg Wilderness Area.)

Mother City Tours (☎ 448 3917, ⓦ www .mctours.co.za) offers a reasonably priced package (R200) that includes a cellar tour at KWV in Paarl and tastings of wine and cheese at Fairview.

Easy Rider Wine Tours (☎ 886 4651) is well established. Its day tour is good value at R180 including lunch, and covers five wineries: Eikendal, Boschendal, Fransch-hoek Vineyards, Fairview and Ruitersvlei.

Things to See & Do

MUSEUMS & GALLERIES

One thing that Cape Town isn't short of is museums and galleries, with over 15 in the City Bowl area alone. Many, including the South African Museum and the Michaelis Collection, are banded together as the Iziko Museums of Cape Town (W www.museums .org.za/iziko).

The following museums are listed in order of, in our opinion, the most interesting to see on a short visit to Cape Town. For other recommendations see the Southern Suburbs and False Bay sections of this chapter and the special section 'Cape Town Architecture'.

District Six Museum (Map 13, #139)

If you see only one museum in Cape Town make it this one; note that almost all township tours stop here first to explain the history of the pass laws. The museum (☎ 461 8745, 25A Buitenkant St; admission by donation; open 9am-4pm Mon-Sat) is as much for the people of the now-vanished District Six as it is about them. The displays are moving and poignant: a floor covered with a large-scale map of District Six, former residents having labelled where their demolished homes and features of their neighbourhood were; reconstructions of home interiors; faded photographs and recordings. Most memorable of all are the staff, practically all displaced residents themselves, each with a heartbreaking story to tell. By appointment it's also possible to arrange walking tours of the old District Six for R20.

South African Museum & Planetarium (Map 15, #30)

The South African Museum (☎ 424 3330, 25 Queen Victoria St; adult/child R8/free, Wed free; open 10am-5pm daily), at the mountain end of the Company's Gardens, is the oldest museum in South Africa and is beginning to show its age. This said, there are plans to upgrade it, and the building contains a truly fascinating collection of objects, starting with a fossilised human footprint believed to be 117,000 years old! Next comes the Linton Panel, one of the most amazing examples of San rock art you'll see anywhere. Most of the startlingly lifelike displays of San (made in 1911 from casts of living people, some of whom died in the process) have now been removed.

Other displays to look out for include the terracotta Lydenburg Heads, the earliest known examples of African sculpture (AD 500–700); the Whale Well, hung with giant skeletons of these mammals and sometimes used as a venue for concerts; a stuffed quagga foal (the very exhibit that provided the DNA to start the rebreeding of the thought-to-be-extinct quagga); the fascinating Wonders of Nature Gallery; and the 2m-wide nest of the sociable weaver bird, a veritable avian apartment block.

Attached to the museum is a planetarium (☎ 424 3330; adult/child R10/5, evening shows adult R12). If you want to unravel the mysteries of the southern hemisphere's night sky, shows are given on Tuesday (8pm including a 3D star show, and 2pm), Thursday (2pm) and Saturday (2.30pm). There are more frequent shows during school holidays.

Noor Ebrahim's Story

'I used to live at 247 Caledon St', begins Noor Ebrahim, pointing at the street map covering the floor of the District Six Museum. Noor is one of the 60,000-plus people forcibly removed from the inner-city district during the 1960s and '70s. His story is one of the many you can discover on a visit to the District Six Museum.

Noor's grandfather came to Cape Town in 1890 from Surat in India. An energetic man who had four wives and 30 children, he built up a good business making ginger beer. Noor's father was one of the old man's sons to his first wife, a Scot called Fanny Grainger, and Noor grew up in the heart of District Six. 'It was a very cosmopolitan area. Many whites lived there – they owned the shops. There were blacks, Portuguese, Chinese and Hindus all living as one big happy family.'

'We didn't know it was going to happen', remembers Noor of the 1966 order declaring District Six a white area under the Group Areas Act. 'We saw the headlines in the paper and people were angry and sad but for a while little happened.' Then in 1970 the demolitions started and gradually the residents moved out.

Noor's family hung on until 1976, when they were given two weeks to vacate the house that his grandfather had bought some 70 years previously. By that time they'd seen families, neighbours and friends split up and sent to separate townships determined by their race. They'd prepared by buying a new home in the coloured township of Athlone – otherwise they'd have been forced to go to Mitchell's Plain, today one of the most violent suburbs on the Cape Flats.

Noor will never forget the day he left District Six. 'I got in the car with my wife and two children and drove off, but only got as far as the corner before I had to stop. I got out of the car and started to cry as I saw the bulldozers move in immediately. Many people died of broken hearts – that's what apartheid was. It was really sick.'

As a way of reclaiming his destroyed past Noor, like several other former District Six residents, wrote a book, and, since 1994, has worked as a guide at the museum. He was naturally delighted when the land was officially handed back to former residents in 2000 (see History in the Facts about Cape Town chapter).

'My life was in District Six', he says. 'My heart and home was there. I'm really looking forward to going back.'

South African National Gallery (Map 15, #39)

This exquisite gallery (☎ 465 1628; adult/child R5/free, Sun free; open 10am-5pm Tues-Sun) in the Company's Gardens always has some very interesting exhibitions as well as permanent displays. Check out the portrait of Desmond Tutu, the remarkable carved teak door in the courtyard, and a dinosaur sculpture made from wire. There's a pleasant cafe and a good shop with some interesting books.

South African Jewish Museum (Map 15, #40)

One of the newest of the city's museums is the imaginative South African Jewish

Museum (☎ 445 1546, 88 Hatfield St, ⓦ www.sajewishmuseum.co.za; adult/child R20/10; open 10am-5pm Sun-Thur, 10am-2pm Fri). Entry is through the beautifully restored Old Synagogue (1862), from where a wooden gangplank leads to state-of-the-art galleries with displays on the vibrant history of the nation's Jewish community, which today numbers around 90,000. Downstairs you'll find a partial recreation of a Lithuanian shtetl (village); many of South Africa's Jews fled this part of Eastern Europe during the pogroms and persecution of the late 19th and early 20th centuries.

Across from the main complex, don't miss the Cape Town Holocaust Centre (☎ 462

*5553; admission free; open 10am-5pm
Sun-Thur, 10am-1pm Fri).* This admirable
museum is small, but packs a lot in with a
considerable emotional punch. The history
of anti-Semitism is set in a South African
context with parallels drawn to the local
struggle for freedom. Stop to watch the video
tales of Holocaust survivors at the end.

It's possible also to visit the beautifully
decorated baroque **Great Synagogue** *(guided
tours 10am-2pm Mon-Thur, 10am-4pm
Sun).* The Gardens Shul, as it was known,
was consecrated the same year that Cape
Town elected its first Jewish mayor, Hyman
Liberman.

Bo-Kaap Museum (Map 13, #17)
The small but engaging Bo-Kaap Museum
*(☎ 424 3846, 71 Wale St; admission R3;
open 9.30am-4.30pm Mon-Sat)* gives an insight into the lifestyle of a prosperous 19th-
century Cape Muslim family and a
somewhat idealised view of Islamic practice in Cape Town. The house itself, built in
1763, is the oldest in the area.

Cultural History Museum (Map 13, #49)
The rather muddled Cultural History Museum *(☎ 461 8280, 49 Adderley St; adult/
child R7/2; open 9.30am-4.30pm daily)*
occupies the former **Slave Lodge** of the
Dutch East India Company (Vereenigde
Oost-Indische Compagnie; VOC) and contains displays on that period as well as bits
and pieces from ancient Egypt, Greece and
Rome and the Far East. Worth pottering
around, particularly for history buffs, it is
likely to be recurated in the near future as a
museum about slavery in the Cape.

One of the oldest buildings in South
Africa, dating back to 1660, the Slave Lodge
has a fascinating history in itself. Until 1811
the building was home, if you could call it
that, to as many as 1000 slaves, who lived in
damp, insanitary, crowded conditions. Up to
20% died each year. The slaves were bought
and sold just around the corner on Spin St.

From the late 18th century the lodge was
used as a brothel, a jail for petty criminals

Islamic Cape Town

Many Muslim Bo-Kaap residents are descendants of the slaves brought to Cape Town by
the Dutch East India Company (Vereenigde
Oost-Indische Compagnie; VOC) from the
Indian subcontinent and Indonesia (hence the
term Cape Malays, although few of them actually hailed from what is today called
Malaysia).

The VOC also used Cape Town as a place
of exile for Islamic leaders such as Tuan Guru
from Tidore, who arrived in 1780. During his
13 years on Robben Island he accurately
copied the Quran from memory. In 1794 he
helped establish the Auwal Mosque, the city's
first mosque.

Tuan Guru is buried in Bo-Kaap's Tana Baru
cemetery (Map 13, #1), one of the oldest in
South Africa, at the western end of Longmarket St. Within the cemetery (which has
fallen into disrepair and is subject to a local
preservation campaign) his grave is one of
the 20 or so *karamats* (tombs of Muslim
saints) encircling Cape Town and visited by
the faithful on a minipilgrimage. Other karamats are found on Robben Island (that of
Sayed Abdurahman Matura), at the gate to
the Klein Constantia wine estate, and by the
Eerste River in Macassar (that of Sheik Yussof,
the most significant Muslim leader of his time).

A sizable Muslim community also lived in
Simon's Town before the Group Areas Act
evictions of the late 1960s. Their history can
be traced in the Heritage Museum in Simon's
Town (see Simon's Town later in this chapter).

and political exiles from Indonesia, and a
mental asylum. In 1811 it became Cape
Town's first post office. Later it became a
library, and it was the Cape Supreme Court
until 1914. The walls of the original Slave
Lodge flank the interior courtyard, where
you can find the tombstones of Cape
Town's founder, Jan Van Riebeeck, and his
wife Maria De La Queillerie. The tombstones were moved here from Jakarta where
Van Riebeeck is buried.

Michaelis Collection
(Map 13, #40)

Donated by Sir Max Michaelis in 1914, this art collection (☎ 424 6367, Greenmarket Square; adult/child R3/free; open 10am-5pm) is in the Old Townhouse, which used to be the City Hall. The Dutch and Flemish paintings and etchings from the 16th and 17th centuries (including works by Rembrant, Frans Hals and Anthony Van Dyck) suit the somewhat gloomy atmosphere. Nip upstairs for views from the balcony overlooking the square, or come for lunch or a drink in the relaxed Ivy Garden Restaurant (see Restaurants under City Bowl in the Places to Eat chapter).

Rust-en-Vreugd (Map 15, #33)

This delightful 18th-century mansion (☎ 465 3628, 78 Buitenkant St; admission by donation; open 8.30am-4.30pm Mon-Sat) was once the home of the state prosecutor. It now houses part of the William Fehr collection of paintings and furniture (the major part is in the Castle of Good Hope). Paintings by John Thomas Baines show early scenes from colonial Cape Town, while the sketches of Cape Dutch architecture by Alys Fane Trotter are some of the best you'll see. There's also a pleasant garden.

Cape Medical Museum
(Map 14, #23)

On the way to the Waterfront from Green Point, the Cape Medical Museum (☎ 418 5663, Portswood Rd, Green Point; admission by donation; open 9am-4pm Tues-Fri) is worth a few minutes. Of particular interest is its display on Dr James Barrie, a woman who kept herself disguised as a man for years so she could practise as a doctor; she performed the Cape Colony's first successful Caesarean operation in 1818.

HOUSES OF PARLIAMENT
(Map 13, #96)

Visiting the houses of parliament (☎ 403 2537, Entrance on Plein St; admission free; tours by appointment Mon-Fri) is one of the most fascinating things you can do in Cape Town. If parliament is sitting, fix your tour for the afternoon so you can see the politicians in action. Opened in 1885 and enlarged several times since, this is where British prime minister Harold Macmillan made his famous 'Wind of Change' speech in 1960. The articulate tour guides will proudly fill you in on the mechanisms and political make-up of their new democracy. You must present your passport to gain entry.

CASTLE OF GOOD HOPE
(Map 13)

Built to defend Cape Town, the stone-walled Castle of Good Hope (☎ 469 1084, Entrance on Buitenkant St; adult/child R15/6.50 Mon-Sat, R8/4 Sun; open 9am-4pm daily; tours 11am, noon & 2pm Mon-Sat) has never seen action in all its 350 years, unless you count the more recent stormings by hordes of school kids and tourists.

It's worth coming for one of the tours (the noon tour on weekdays coincides with the changing of the guard, since the castle is still the headquarters for the Western Cape military command), although you can quite easily find your own way around. A key ceremony is held at 10am weekdays.

There are extensive displays of militaria and some interesting ones on the castle's archaeology and the reconstruction of the so-called Dolphin Pool. The highlight is the bulk of the **William Fehr Collection** (open 9.30am-4pm daily). It includes some fabulous bits of Cape Dutch furniture, such as a table seating 100, and more paintings by John Thomas Baines.

Also within the castle grounds are Wine Concepts (a noted wine store), a cafe, and a good restaurant, De Waterblommetjie (see Restaurants under City Bowl in the Places to Eat chapter).

LONG ST (Map 13)

Narrow and overhung with balconied buildings, Long St has undergone a renaissance, with restaurants, bars and backpacker accommodation appearing among the junk and antiques shops. It's a lively area and forms the link between the city centre and suburbs such as Tamboerskloof. It was once the red-light district, and a few prostitutes (both male and female) still hang out at its less-reputable north-east end.

Long St was once part of the nearby Bo-Kaap, also known as the Muslim quarter. The old Noor el Hamedia Mosque (1884) (Map 13, #52) is on the corner of Dorp St. The Palm Tree Mosque (Map 13, #56) at No 185 is the last 18th-century house on the street.

LONG ST BATHS (Map 13, #80)

The Long St Baths (☎ 400 3302, Cnr Long & Buitensingel Sts) are something of an anachronism, but they have been restored, they're heated and they're very popular. At the **Turkish baths** (admission R40; open to men 9am-7pm Tues, Wed & Fri, 9am-noon Sun; open to women 9am-7pm Mon, Thur & Sat) a massage costs R30, and a massage with bath costs R55. The Turkish baths are segregated, unlike the **heated swimming pool** (admission R6; open 7am-7pm Mon-Sat, 8am-7pm Sun).

SIGNAL HILL (Map 12)

Once also known as Lion's Rump, as it is attached to Lion's Head by a 'spine' of hills, Signal Hill separates Sea Point from the City Bowl. There are magnificent views from the 350m-high summit, especially at night. Head up Kloof Nek Rd from the city and take the first turn-off to the right at the top of the hill. At this intersection you also turn off for Clifton (also to the right) and the lower cableway station (left).

Signal Hill was the early settlement's lookout point, and it was from here that flags were hoisted when a ship was spotted, giving the citizens below time to prepare their goods for sale and dust off their tankards.

At noon Monday to Saturday, a cannon known as the **Noon Gun (Map 14, #19)** is fired from the lower slopes of Signal Hill. You can hear it all over town. Traditionally this allowed the burghers in the town below to check their watches. It's a stiff walk up here through Bo-Kaap – take Longmarket St and keep going until it ends. The Noon Gun Tearoom & Restaurant is a good place to catch your breath (see Restaurants under City Bowl in the Places to Eat chapter).

TABLE MOUNTAIN (Map 12)
Cable Car

The cable car (☎ 424 8181, W www.table mountain.co.za; adult one way/return R40/75, child one way/return R28/40; open 7.30am-9pm daily) is such an obvious and popular attraction that you might have difficulty convincing yourself that it's worth the trouble and expense. It is. The views on the way up and from the top of Table Mountain are phenomenal, and there are some good easy walks on the summit.

There's a small self-service restaurant and shop at the top, where you can also post letters. Ride 'n' Dine tickets cover a return trip on the cable car plus breakfast (R100), lunch (R120) or dinner (R120). For an adrenaline rush like no other, consider doing the abseil (see the boxed text 'Cape Town Adrenaline' later in this chapter).

The cable cars don't operate when it's dangerously windy, and there's obviously not much point going up if you are simply going to be wrapped in the cloud known as 'the tablecloth'. Call in advance to see if they're operating. Weather conditions permitting, they operate every 10 minutes in high season and every 20 minutes in low season. The last car down the mountain leaves at 10pm (these times can change, so check). The best visibility and conditions are likely to be first thing in the morning or in the evening.

To get here from central Cape Town by car take Kloof Nek Rd and turn off to the left (signposted). If you don't have your own transport, Rikkis will come up here for R10; a nonshared taxi will cost around R45.

It's possible to walk up (or down) the mountain from the Kirstenbosch Botanical Gardens side (see Kirstenbosch Botanical Gardens later in this chapter) or the City Bowl side.

Climbing Table Mountain

At first glance, climbing Table Mountain looks deceptively easy. Over 300 routes up and down the mountain have been identified, perhaps giving you a clue as to how easy it is to get lost. Hikers die here from time to time, so make sure you're properly equipped with warm and waterproof clothing, sufficient water and some food before setting off.

Bear in mind that the mountain is over 1000m high and conditions can become treacherous quickly. Thick mists can make the paths invisible, and you'll just have to wait until they lift. You should always tell someone where you are going and you should never walk alone; check with Cape Town Tourism if you want a guide. Climbing the mountain is such a popular pastime that there's a good chance you'll meet someone who will invite you along.

None of the routes is easy but the Platteklip Gorge walk on the City Bowl side is at least straightforward. Unless you're fit, try walking down before you attempt the walk up. It took us about 2½ hours from the upper cableway station to the lower, taking it fairly easy. A better walk is the one called Indian Windows that starts from directly behind the lower cableway station and heads straight up. The hikers you see from the cable car, perched like mountain goats on apparently sheer cliffs, are taking this route, and it's the one you'll end up on if you do the abseil from the summit.

Shirley Brossy's *Walking Guide to Table Mountain* details 34 walks, while Mike Lundy's *Best Walks in the Cape Peninsula* is also recommended.

WATERFRONT (Map 14)

The Victoria & Alfred Waterfront (always just called the Waterfront), popular with both tourists and locals, is an atmospheric, buzzing place where pockets of dockside life remain alongside good attractions, especially the aquarium.

Apart from the main visitor centre (see Tourist Offices in the Facts for the Visitor chapter) there's also an information kiosk (Map 14, #29) in the Victoria Wharf shopping centre; it's open until 9pm in summer.

Despite all the development, the Waterfront remains a working harbour and that is the source of much of its charm. Most of the redevelopment has been undertaken around the historic Alfred and Victoria Basins (constructed from 1860). Although these wharves are too small for modern container vessels and tankers, the Victoria Basin is still used by tugs, harbour vessels of various kinds, and fishing boats.

Cape Town's Best Viewpoints

Cape Town has more than its fair share of places that show off its beauty. If you're lucky, the first unforgettable sight will be on arrival, should your plane come in low past Table Mountain, or, even better, if you arrive by cruise ship into the port.

The most famous view of Table Mountain is from the beach at Bloubergstrand (Map 1), north of the city. The mountain as seen from a boat cruise on Table Bay is pretty special too, but for a view with a thrill, take one of the short helicopter or seaplane flights on offer (see Organised Tours in the Getting Around chapter).

Once you've had your fill of views *of* Table Mountain, there are the views to be had *from* Table Mountain (Map 12). Take the cable car to the top, then follow one of the trails to take in the sweeping vistas. There are also decent views of the City Bowl and the sea from the road running past the lower cableway station towards Devil's Peak.

The Noon Gun (Map 14, #19) area of Signal Hill is one of the few places offering a good prospect of the shipping activity in Cape Town's busy port.

Driving from the city to Camps Bay via Kloof Nek Rd you cross Kloof Nek (just past the cableway turn-off), with a breathtaking view of the beaches and the Twelve Apostles (Map 11). This view is best appreciated on a climb of Lion's Head, something best done to coincide with sunset.

Travelling down the coast, the best views of Hout Bay are from Chapman's Peak Drive (Map 11). Further out of town, the road between Strand and Hermanus has superb views back across False Bay.

Large modern ships use the adjacent Duncan and Ben Schoeman docks. These were constructed from the mid-1930s and the sand excavated was used to reclaim the foreshore area north-east of Strand St. The Castle of Good Hope used to be virtually on the shore front, and the old high-water line actually passes through the Golden Acre Centre **(Map 13, #119)** on Adderley St.

The Waterfront has quite a lot of nightlife. There is strict security, and although it is safe to walk around, there are plenty of merry men, so lone women should be a little cautious. See the Places to Eat and Entertainment chapters for information on the numerous restaurants and bars, although you'll find something that appeals if you just go for a wander.

Although it's tempting, don't walk between the city and the Waterfront; muggings do happen here. Shuttle buses run from Adderley St in front of the main train station **(Map 13)**, then up Strand St, with a stop near Cape Sun Hotel **(Map 13, #116)**, to the centre of the Waterfront (R1.20). They also leave from near the Sea Point Pavilion **(Map 16, #25)** in Sea Point (R2). They depart half-hourly from early until late. Rikkis also regularly ply this route.

If you're driving, there are free parking spaces around the Waterfront, and if they're full, there's plenty of paid parking at fairly inexpensive rates.

Cruises

A trip into Table Bay should not be missed. Few people nowadays have the privilege of reaching Cape Town by passenger ship, but something of the feeling can be captured by taking a harbour cruise. The view of Table Mountain hasn't changed.

Waterfront Adventures (Map 14, #37) *(☎ 418 5806)* beside Quay 5 offers a variety of cruises, from one-hour trips into Table Bay (adult/child R40/20) to the highly recommended 1½-hour sunset cruises (R90) on the handsome 58-foot schooner *Spirit of Victoria*.

Nomad Adventure Centre (Map 13, #65) *(☎ 426 5445, W www.nomadtours.co.za)* offers half-day sailing trips for R180, and

four-hour sunset cruises down to Clifton and back, which includes dinner on board, for R235.

See Robben Island, following, for details of cruises to this UN World Heritage Site.

Two Oceans Aquarium (Map 14, #55)

The Waterfront's best attraction is its excellent aquarium *(☎ 418 3823, Dock Rd, Waterfront, W www.aquarium.co.za; adult/child R40/20; open 9.30am-6pm daily)*. It features denizens of the deep from both the cold and the warm oceans that border the Cape Peninsula, including great white sharks. There are seals, penguins, turtles an astounding kelp forest open to the sky, and pools in which kids can touch sea creatures; these things alone are worth the entry fee.

Qualified divers can get into the tank – sharing it with five ragged-tooth sharks, a 150kg short-tailed stingray, other predatory fish and two delightful turtles wouldn't be everyone's idea of fun, but for experienced divers (certificate required) this is a great way to get really close to the ocean action. The cost is R325 including hire of diving gear.

Get your hand stamped on entrance and you can return again any time during the same day for free.

South African Maritime Museum (Map 14, #54)

There are lots of model ships and some full-sized ones at this museum *(☎ 419 2505, Dock Rd, Waterfront; adult/child R10/3; open 10am-4.30pm daily)*, which is a bit of a poor relation at the glitzy Waterfront. Admission includes entry to SAS *Somerset*, a wartime vessel now permanently docked beside the museum.

ROBBEN ISLAND (Map 1)

Proclaimed a UN World Heritage Site in 1999, Robben Island is unmissable. Most likely you will have to endure crowds and being hustled around on a guided tour that at 2½ hours is woefully too short – such is the price of the island's infamy. It's likely to be truly swamped in the future as the island's tourist infrastructure is developed to include accommodation and better roads. Still, you must go to see this shrine to struggle.

Used as a prison from the early days of the VOC right up until the first years of majority rule, Robben Island's most famous involuntary resident was Nelson Mandela. You will learn much of what happened to Mandela and other inmates, since one will be leading your tour. The guides are happy to answer any questions you may have, and although some understandably remain bitter, as a whole this is the best demonstration of reconciliation you could hope to see in Cape Town.

Booking a **tour** (☎ 419 1300, W www .robben-island.org.za, adult/child R100/50; hourly ferries 8am-3pm daily, sunset tours at 5pm & 6pm in summer) is essential as they are extremely popular; otherwise be prepared for a long wait. At the time of research boats were departing from Jetty 1 **(Map 14, #36)** at the Waterfront's Quay 5, but in the future there will be a new departure point **(Map 14, #48)** from beside the clock tower on Fish Quay.

The tour entails being guided through the old prison, and includes a 45-minute bus ride around the island with commentary on the various places of note, such as the prison house of Pan-African Congress (PAC) leader Robert Sobuke, the lime quarry in which Mandela and many others slaved, and the church used during the island's stint as a leper colony. There will be a little time for you to wander around on your own; you could check out the penguin colony near the landing jetty (see the boxed text 'Saving the African Penguin').

All tours have a set departure and return time, but when you book, consider asking to extend your time on the island so you can see **Cell Stories**, a remarkable exhibition in the prison's A Section and not on the regular tour. Here in each of 40 isolation cells is an artefact and story from a former political prisoner: chess pieces drawn on scraps of paper; a Christmas card from a forgotten wife; an intricately patterned belt made from fishing nets and old shoe leather; a soccer trophy. It's all unbelievably moving.

SOUTHERN SUBURBS

Heading south around the bulk of Devil's Peak will take you into the expensive residential suburbs clinging to the eastern slopes of Table Mountain.

While the studenty area of Observatory **(Map 17)** has a laid-back, hippy air, by the time you reach leafy Newlands you'll be in no doubt that this is still a rich and mainly white place to live. This said, the area around Claremont station is a fascinating study in contrasts, with black and coloured

Saving the African Penguin

The fate of the African penguin (also known as the jackass penguin) hit the headlines across the world when a cargo ship sank 8km off Robben Island in June 2000, spilling vast quantities of oil into the sea. Over 40% of the penguin population was threatened by the resulting slick, the worst ever suffered along the notoriously treacherous Cape coast.

The penguin colonies at Robben and Dassen Islands received immediate attention from several conservation bodies, the local authorities and even the army, in what turned out to be the world's biggest rescue operation of its kind, affecting over 21,000 oiled birds. Over 28,000 volunteers from as far away as New Zealand, Japan and Canada also took part.

Remarkably, given the scale of the spill and the extensive rehabilitation process for the penguin victims, practically all the birds were eventually released back into the wild. The world held its breath as Peter, Percy and Pamela – three of the penguins removed to Port Elizabeth during the cleanup and released with transmitters on their backs – swam home through shark-infested waters, their progress being monitored on their own Web site.

The cost of the operation nudged the R20 million mark and has impressed the need for South Africa to toughen up its maritime regulations and penalties for negligent shipping.

traders crowding the streets around the ritzy Cavendish Square shopping centre (see the Shopping chapter). Higher up on the slopes are views across the Cape Flats towards the mountain ranges around Stellenbosch and, on a clear day, to the succeeding ranges that eventually rise up into the great Southern African Plateau.

The Simon's Town railway line is a useful way to get to most of these suburbs, but a car will mean you don't have to do so much walking or be at the mercy of the train timetables.

Take the N2 (Map 13) from the city centre or the M3 (Map 15) from Orange St in Gardens. These freeways merge near the Groote Schuur Hospital (Map 17, #17) in Observatory, then run around Devil's Peak. The M3 sheers off to the right soon after (it can be a dangerous manoeuvre getting into the right lanes!) and then runs parallel to the east side of the mountain.

If you were to follow the M3 you'd arrive in Muizenberg, on False Bay, but to visit the attractions of the southern suburbs, you'll have to keep a sharp eye out for the exits.

The Baxter Theatre (Map 12, #22) is on the corner of Woolsack Dr and Main Rd (the M4). Main Rd continues south past Newlands, a Holiday Inn and several large shopping centres, to the suburb of Claremont, where you'll find the Cavendish Square (Map 11, #11) shopping centre.

Transplant Museum
(Map 17, #17)
Although Observatory is primarily a place to visit for something to eat or drink, if you find yourself here during the day drop by the quirky Transplant Museum (☎ 404 5232, Groote Schuur Hospital, Observatory; adult/child R5/2; open 9am-2pm Mon-Fri). Detailing the history of the world's first heart transplant in the very theatre in which it all happened in 1967, the displays have a fascinating Dr Kildare quality to them, especially given the heart-throb status of Dr Christiaan Barnard at the time.

To reach the hospital from Observatory station, walk west along Station Rd for about 10 minutes.

If you're driving from the city, take the UCT (University of Cape Town) exit off the M3; turn left at the T-intersection and travel along Woolsack Dr.

Irma Stern Museum
(Map 12, #18)
The most worthwhile museum to visit in the southern suburbs is the UCT's Irma Stern Museum (☎ 685 5686, Cecil Rd, Rosebank; adult/child R5/2.50; open 10am-5pm Tues-Sat), based in the charming home of this pioneering 20th-century artist. Irma Stern (1894–1966) lived in this house for 38 years and her studio has been left intact, as if she'd just stepped out into the verdant garden for some fresh air. Her ethnographic art and craft collection from around the world is as fascinating as her own expressionist art, which has been compared to Gauguin's.

To reach the museum from Rosebank station walk a few minutes west to Main Rd, cross over and walk up Chapel St.

University of Cape Town
(Map 12)
For the nonacademic there is no real reason to visit the University of Cape Town (UCT), but it is an impressive place to walk around. Unlike most universities it presents a fairly cohesive architectural front, with ivy-covered neoclassical facades, and a fine set of stone steps leading up to the templelike Jameson building. Check out Smuts and Fuller Halls halfway up the steps.

On the main campus, there's a bland cafeteria and a South African Students' Travel Service (SASTS) office in the new student union building.

As you're following the M3 from the city, just after the open paddocks on Devil's Peak, you'll pass the old Mostert's Mill (Map 12, #19), a real Dutch windmill dating from 1796, on the left. Just past the old windmill, also on the left, is the exit for the university. To get there, turn right at the T-intersection after you've taken the exit.

Alternatively, if you approach UCT from Woolsack Dr, you'll pass The Woolsack (Map 12, #21), a cottage designed in 1900 by Sir Herbert Baker for Cecil Rhodes, who

Cecil Rhodes: Empire Builder

Cecil John Rhodes (1853–1902), the sickly son of an English vicar, was sent to South Africa in 1870 to improve his health. After working on his brother's farm in Natal, Rhodes left for the new diamond fields near Kimberley in 1871. By 1887 he had founded the De Beers company and could afford to buy Barney Barnato's Kimberley Mine for UK£5 million. By 1891 De Beers owned 90% of the world's diamonds and Rhodes also had a stake in the fabulous reef of gold discovered on the Witwatersrand (near Johannesburg).

Rhodes was not satisfied with merely acquiring personal wealth and power. He personified the idea of 'empire' and dreamed of painting the map red, of building a railway from the Cape to Cairo (running through British territory all the way). He even had far-fetched ideas of bringing the USA back under British rule. The times were right for such dreams, and Rhodes was a favourite of Queen Victoria and of the voters in the Cape (both Boer and British). In 1890 he was elected prime minister of the Cape Colony.

To paint Africa red, Rhodes pushed north to establish mines and develop trade. Although he despised missionaries for being too soft on the 'natives', he used them as stalking horses in his wrangling and chicanery to open up new areas. He was successful in establishing British control in Bechuanaland (later Botswana) and the area that was to become Rhodesia (later Zimbabwe), but the gold mines there proved to be less productive than those on the Witwatersrand.

The Transvaal Republic in general and Boer leader Paul Kruger in particular had been causing Rhodes difficulty for some time. Both Kruger and Rhodes were fiercely independent idealists with very different ideals, and there was no love lost between them. It greatly irked Rhodes that Kruger's pastoralist republic should be sitting on the richest reef of gold in the world, and the republic was also directly in the path of British expansion.

The miners on the Witwatersrand were mainly non-Boers, and were denied any say in the politics of the republic. This caused increasing resentment, and in late 1895 one Dr Leander Starr Jameson led an expedition into the Witwatersrand with the intention of sparking an uprising among the foreigners.

The Jameson raid was a fiasco. All the participants were killed or captured, and Jameson was jailed. The British government was extremely embarrassed when it became apparent that Rhodes had prior knowledge of the raid and probably encouraged it. He was forced to resign as prime minister and the British government took control of Rhodesia and Bechuanaland, his personal fiefdoms.

Rhodes' health deteriorated after these disasters. His empire-building days were over, but one more stock episode from the Victorian omnibus awaited: An honourable chap becomes entangled in the schemes of a glamorous and ruthless woman, in this case the Princess Randziwill. She was later jailed for her swindles.

After his death in Cape Town in 1906, Rhodes' reputation was largely rehabilitated by his will. He devoted most of his fortune to the Rhodes scholarship, which sends recipients to Oxford University.

once owned the entire area (see the boxed text 'Cecil Rhodes: Empire Builder'). The cottage was the winter residence of Rudyard Kipling from 1900 to 1907 and it's said he wrote the poem *If* here.

Visitors can usually get parking permits at the university – call at the information office on the entry road, near the bottom of the steps.

Rhodes Memorial (Map 12, #20)

In 1895 Cecil Rhodes purchased the eastern slopes of Table Mountain as part of a plan to preserve a relatively untouched section. He bequeathed the property to the nation on his death in 1906.

An impressive granite memorial to Rhodes was constructed, commanding a view of the Cape Flats and the mountain ranges beyond – and by implication, right into the heart of Africa. Despite the classical proportions of the memorial and the eight large bronze lions, Rhodes looks somewhat bored and testy.

There's a pleasant tearoom, the Rhodes Memorial Restaurant, in an old stone cottage nearby (see Southern Suburbs in the Places to Eat chapter).

The exit for the memorial is at the Princess Anne Interchange on the M3.

Newlands

Most visitors will come to Newlands to visit either its pretty cricket ground or the neighbouring rugby stadium (see Spectator Sports in the Entertainment chapter).

If there's no game on you may still want to come here to take a very quick look around the tiny **Rugby Museum (Map 11, #9)** (☎ 695 3038, Boundary Rd, Newlands; admission free; open 9am-5pm Mon-Fri), which contains a predictable collection of boots, ties, balls and other paraphernalia that only a die-hard fan will appreciate. Various tours of the grounds can be arranged through Gateway to Newlands (☎/fax 686 2151, e gatenew@mweb.co.za).

Complementing the sporting theme of the area is the adjacent **Ohlsson's Cape Breweries (Map 11, #9)** (☎ 685 7511, e valen cia.africa@sabreweries.com, 3 Main Rd, Newlands). Free guided tours are available (minimum eight people). They are held at 10am and 2pm and last around two hours.

Newlands train station is next to the cricket ground (exit east). To reach the rugby stadium, museum and brewery you'll need to exit on the west side of the station and walk around five minutes north along Sport Pienaar Rd to Boundary Rd.

If you're driving, take the M3 from the city, take the UCT exit, turn left at the T-intersection and travel along Woolsack Dr.

KIRSTENBOSCH BOTANICAL GARDENS (Map 11, # 13)

These gardens (☎ 762 9120, W www.nbi .ac.za, Rhodes Dr, Bishopscourt; adult/child R15/10; open 8am-7pm Sept-Mar,

8am-6pm Apr-Aug) are among the most beautiful in the world. They have an incomparable site on the eastern side of Table Mountain, overlooking False Bay and the Cape Flats. The 36-hectare landscaped section seems to merge almost imperceptibly with the 492 hectares of *fynbos* (fine bush) vegetation cloaking the mountain slopes.

The main entrance at the Newlands end of the gardens is where you'll find plenty of parking, the information centre, an excellent souvenir shop and the **conservatory** (open 9am-5pm daily). Further along Rhodes Dr is the Ryecroft Gate entrance, the first you'll come to if you approach the gardens from Constantia. There's a good restaurant and a food court (see Kirstenbosch Botanical Gardens in the Places to Eat chapter). Call to find out about guided walks, or hire the My Guide electronic gizmo (R30) to receive recorded information about the various plants you'll pass on the three signposted circular walks.

Apart from a portion of that famous hedge planted by Van Riebeeck back in 1660, some magnificent oaks, and the Moreton Bay fig and camphor trees planted by Cecil Rhodes, the gardens are devoted almost exclusively to indigenous plants. About 9000 of Southern Africa's 22,000 plant species are grown here. You'll find a fragrance garden that has been elevated so you can more easily sample the scents of the plants; a Braille Trail; a kopje (hill) that has been planted with pelargoniums; a sculpture garden; and a section for plants used for *muti* (medicine) by sangomas (traditional African healers).

The atmosphere-controlled conservatory displays plant communities from a variety of terrains, the most interesting of which is the Namaqualand and Kalahari section, with baobabs, quiver trees and others. There is always something flowering but the gardens are at their best between mid-August and mid-October. The **Sunday afternoon concerts** (admission R25 including entry to the gardens) from December to March are a Cape Town institution.

If you're driving from the city centre, the turn-off to the gardens is on the right at the intersection of Union Ave (the M3) and Rhodes Ave (the M63).

A Rikki from the City Bowl to the gardens costs R50 for the first four people and R10 for each extra person. Alternatively, walk down from the top of Table Mountain. This could be done in three hours by someone of moderate fitness, but make sure you have a map and are prepared for a sudden change in weather. The trails are well marked, and steep in places, but the way to the gardens from the cableway and vice versa is not signposted.

TOKAI ARBORETUM (Map 11, #23)

If you're wine tasting in the Constantia area, or driving down to False Bay, you may want to swing by this pleasant wooded area, a favourite spot for picnics and walks. The Tokai Arboretum is a historic planting of some 150 different trees begun in 1885 by Joseph Storr Lister, the conservator of forests for the Cape Colony. There's a pleasant cafe here where you can pick up a map for the walk to Elephant's Eye Cave, the forest's best walk. The 6km zig-zag path is fairly steep and offers little shade as you climb higher up Constantiaberg, so bring a hat and water.

To reach the forest from the city centre, follow the M3 towards Muizenberg and take the Retreat and Tokai exit.

RONDEVLEI NATURE RESERVE (Map 11)

Situated at Zeekoevlei, 24km south-east of Cape Town, this small nature reserve (☎ 706 2404, Fisherman's Walk Rd, Zeekoevlei; adult/child R5/3; open 7.30am-5pm daily Mar-Nov, 7.30am-7pm Mon-Fri Dec-Feb, 7.30-am-7pm Sat & Sun Dec-Feb) encompasses a picturesque wetlands protecting native marsh and dune vegetation. Hippos lived in this area 300 years ago and were reintroduced to the reserve in 1981. It's a favourite spot for bird-watchers (see the boxed text 'Birdlife on the Cape' in the Facts about Cape Town chapter). Facilities include an environmental education centre, a waterside trail, two viewing towers and hides.

Boat trips and camping are also possible; contact the reserve for details.

ATLANTIC COAST (Map 11)

The Atlantic coast of the Cape Peninsula has some of the most spectacular coastal scenery in the world. The beaches include the trendiest on the Cape, with the emphasis on sunbaking. Although it's possible to shelter from the summer south-easterlies, the water comes straight from the Antarctic and swimming is rather exhilarating.

Shared taxis regularly run along Main Rd to the end of Regent Rd in Sea Point (Map 16). Golden Arrow buses follow the same route, then continue on to Victoria Rd and down to Hout Bay. After that, you're on your own. If you plan to drive down to Clifton and Camps Bay in summer be prepared to search a while for a parking space, especially at the weekend.

Bloubergstrand (Map 1)

Twenty five kilometres north of the city on Table Bay, Bloubergstrand was the site of the 1806 battle that resulted in the second British occupation of the Cape. This is also the spot with the most dramatic (and most photographed) view of Table Mountain – you know, the one with wildflowers and sand dunes in the foreground, surf, and, across the bay, the cloud-capped mountain ramparts looming over the city.

This is a booming area for antiseptic new suburbs, but the village of Bloubergstrand itself is attractive enough, with picnic areas, some long, uncrowded, windy stretches of sand, and a good pub, the Blue Peter (see Bars & Pubs in the Entertainment chapter). This is windsurfer territory but there are also opportunities for some surfing, best with a moderate north-easterly wind, a small swell and an incoming tide.

You'll need a car to get here. Take the R27 north from the N1.

The Docks (Map 12)

Overwhelmingly industrial are the Duncan and Ben Schoeman docks. Constructed from the mid-1930s as part of the foreshore reclamation project, the busy docks also

From Signal Hill, a Table Mountain tableau

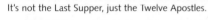

It's not the Last Supper, just the Twelve Apostles.

Got a Lion's Head for heights?

The delicate colours of Table Mountain sandstone appear to change throughout the day.

Top: A visit to the townships needn't be a hairy experience. Join an organised tour to see Imizamo Yethu near Hout Bay, the home of this barbershop. **Middle:** Barbed wire, a symbol of the horror of Robben Island prison, has been appropriated by the maker of this radio. **Bottom:** It's wall-to-wall good times at Oak Lodge, once a commune, now a hostel, decorated with murals.

SIMON RICHMOND

support a healthy yacht-building industry. You'll see plenty of yachts moored at the **Royal Cape Yacht Club (Map 12, #13)** *(☎ 421 1354)* and in the nearby harbour for small craft.

There are a few interesting places to eat here, and yachties might be able to talk their way into the dining room at the yacht club.

To get here, drive towards the sea on Adderley and Heerengracht Sts. Go under the freeway and turn right onto Duncan Rd at the T-intersection. You have to go through the customs checkpoint, but it's rarely staffed.

Green Point & Mouille Point (Map 14)

The next outcrop of land west of the Waterfront is Green Point, a largely undeveloped area of reclaimed land with a stadium, a golf course and a large Sunday market. As well as being the name of the actual point, Green Point is the name of a suburb similar in style and facilities to neighbouring Sea Point.

Right on the coast near Green Point is Mouille Point, which is an oddly isolated little residential area.

The coast is too rocky for swimming, but Mouille Point is an atmospheric place for a stroll on a stormy day and provides clear views of Robben Island.

The lighthouse in the area used to house a booming foghorn that could be heard all over town.

Sea Point (Map 16)

Separated from the City Bowl by Signal Hill, densely populated Sea Point is a bustling residential suburb with numerous multistorey apartment buildings fringing the coast. Main and Regent Rds are lined with restaurants, cafes and shops.

There's a pleasant promenade running from Mouille Point's lighthouse down to the Sea Point Pavilion, a favourite spot for joggers, in-line skaters and strollers. The coast itself is rocky and swimming is dangerous, although there are a couple of rock pools. At the north end, **Graaff's Pool (Map 16, #16)** is for men only and is generally favoured by

nudists. Just south of here is **Milton's Pool (Map 16, #20)**, which also has a stretch of beach.

The best place to swim is **Sea Point Pavilion (Map 16, #25)** *(Beach Rd; adult/child R6/3; open 7am-6.45pm Oct-April, 8.30am-5pm May-Sept)*, a huge outdoor pool complex that gets very busy on hot summer days. The pools are always at least 10°C warmer than the ocean.

A number of reefs produce good waves for surfing. Solly's and Boat Bay near the Sea Point Pavilion have lefts and rights that work on a south-east wind. Further along the beach towards Mouille Point there are a number of left reefs.

Clifton (Map 12)

A suburb along from Sea Point are the four linked beaches at Clifton, accessible by steps from Victoria Rd. They might be the trendiest beaches on the Cape, almost always sheltered from the wind, but the water is still cold. If you care about these things, No 1 and No 2 beaches are for models and confirmed narcissists, No 3 is the gay beach, and No 4 is for families. Although vendors hawk drinks and ice creams along the beach, there are no shops down here, so bring your own food if you're out for a day of sunbaking.

Camps Bay (Map 12)

With the spectacular Twelve Apostles of Table Mountain as a backdrop, and soft, white sand, Camps Bay has one of the most beautiful beaches in the world. That it is within 15 minutes of the city centre also makes it very popular, particularly on weekends. The beach is often windy, and again the water is decidedly on the cool side. There are no life-savers and the surf is strong, so take care if you do swim.

Accommodation possibilities here are generally upmarket and you'll have to tough it out for a restaurant or cafe table with a view along Victoria Rd, particularly at the height of summer. The atmosphere, though, is seductive, and you should make sure you see the sunset from here at least once during your stay.

Finding a Windless Beach

As a resident of Cape Town and as a surfer, I realise how difficult it must be for visitors to deal with the excessive winds we get down here. To help you avoid the winds, here are some tips that even Capetonians may not know:

- It's possible to get away from almost any wind if you know where to go. The weather bureau does not give accurate indicators of wind direction or speed, even though its forecasts are the city's main source of weather information.
- If the wind is a northerly or north-easterly (mainly from April to September), head to the Bloubergstrand area. This is away from the cloud and rain that is experienced closer to Table Mountain. The beaches are also more pleasant here because the wind is off-shore and cooling, rather than chilly.
- During the westerlies (from November to April), go to the coastal area between Muizenberg and Simon's Town. The mountains by the coast shield this region from the worst of the wind.
- If the wind is a southerly or south-westerly (throughout the summer), head for Llandudno and Sandy Bay. Sandy Bay in particular is shielded by the Sentinel (the tall mountain to the south), and can be gloriously warm when everywhere else is miserable. The city centre and the Waterfront are also windless during the southerlies and south-westerlies.
- The most famous wind, the Cape doctor, gets lifted by Table Mountain, so beaches on the western seaboard such as Camps Bay and Llandudno are protected.
- Surprisingly, Kalk Bay is protected from the Cape doctor. A 'bubble' seems to form against the mountain and creates an area of calm, while just down the road in Fish Hoek, the wind howls onshore.
- The general rule is to look for the most expensive neighbourhoods, as they are located where the least wind is experienced.

Red Ceglowski

Llandudno & Sandy Bay (Map 11)

Although it's only 18km away, Llandudno seems completely removed from Cape Town, let alone Africa. It's a small, exclusive seaside village clinging to steep slopes above a sheltered beach. It has no shops. The remains of the tanker *Romelia*, which was wrecked in 1977, lie off Sunset Rocks. There's surfing on the beach breaks (mostly rights), best at high tide with a small swell and a south-easterly wind.

You'll need to head to Llandudno if you want to get to Sandy Bay, Cape Town's nudist beach and gay stamping ground. It is a particularly beautiful stretch of sand and there's no pressure to take your clothes off if you don't want to.

Like many such beaches, it has no direct access roads. From the M6, turn towards Llandudno, keep to the left at forks, and head towards the sea until you reach the Sunset Rocks parking area. The beach is roughly a 15-minute walk to the south. Waves here are best at low tide with a south-easterly wind.

Hout Bay (Map 2)

Hout Bay nestles behind the almost vertical Sentinel and the steep slopes of Chapman's Peak. Inland from the 1km stretch of white sand, there's a fast-growing satellite town that still manages to retain something of its village atmosphere. There's also the township of Imizamo Yethu, also known as Mandela Park, in which it's possible to do a walking tour (see Organised Tours in the Getting Around chapter).

The main information centre **(Map 2, #3)** (☎ 790 3270) on Andrews Rd is open from 9am to 5.30pm Monday to Friday and 9am to 1pm Saturday. Also useful is the Accommodation Cafe **(Map 2, #4)** (☎ 790 0198), Candlewood Centre, Victoria Dr, open 7am to 7pm daily, where you can get information and make accommodation bookings for the area.

Although increasingly given over to tourism, the harbour still functions and the southern arm of the bay is an important fishing port and processing centre. From here

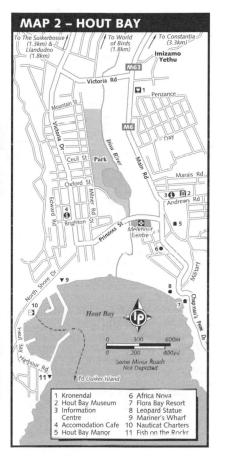

MAP 2 – HOUT BAY

To The Suikerbossie (1.3km) & Llandudno (1.8km)
To World of Birds (1.8km)
To Constantia (3.3km)
Imizamo Yethu

Victoria Rd
Penzance
Mountain St
Day
Cecil St
Park
Marais Rd
Oxford St
Andrews Rd
Edward Rd
Brighton St
Princess St
Melkbout Centre
North Shore Dr
Hout Bay
To Duiker Island
Hout Bay Harbour Rd
Some Minor Roads Not Depicted
Chapman's Peak Dr

0   300   600m
0   300   800yd

1 Kronendal
2 Hout Bay Museum
3 Information Centre
4 Accomodation Cafe
5 Hout Bay Manor
6 Africa Nova
7 Flora Bay Resort
8 Leopard Statue
9 Mariner's Wharf
10 Nauticat Charters
11 Fish on the Rocks

end of the drive is a bronze **leopard statue** (Map 2, #8). It has been sitting there since 1963 and is a reminder of the wildlife that once roamed the area's forests (which have also largely vanished).

The small **Hout Bay Museum (Map 2, #2)** (☎ 790 3270, 4 Andrews Rd; adult/child R2/1; open 10am-12.30pm & 2pm-4.30pm Tues-Sat) has displays on local history and organises guided walks at the weekend for R6 per person.

World of Birds (☎ 790 2730, W www.worldofbirds.org.za, Valley Rd; adult/child R28/23; open 9am-5pm daily) is South Africa's largest aviary, with 330 species of birds. Although caging birds is not an attractive idea, a real effort has been made to make the aviaries large and natural.

Noordhoek & Kommetjie (Map 11)

In the shadow of Chapman's Peak, Noordhoek has a 5km stretch of magnificent beach, favoured by surfers and horse riders. It tends to be windy, and dangerous for swimmers. The Hoek, as it is known to surfers, is an excellent right beach break at the northern end that can hold large waves (only at low tide); it's best with a south-easterly wind. Noordhoek has a caravan park and a tiny rustic shopping and dining complex.

Kommetjie (also known as 'Kom') is an equally small, quiet and isolated crayfishing village, with precious few tourist facilities. It is, however, the focal point for **surfing** on the Cape, offering an assortment of reefs that hold a very big swell. Outer Kommetjie is a left point out from the lighthouse. Inner Kommetjie is a more protected smaller left with lots of kelp (only at high tide). They both work best with a south-easterly or south-westerly wind.

Since the closure of Chapman's Peak Drive, the best way to these small beachside communities, some 30km south of the city centre, is via the False Bay communities of Fish Hoek and Simon's Town.

FALSE BAY (Map 1)

The beaches on False Bay, to the south-east of the city, are not quite as scenically

Nauticat Charters (Map 2, #10) (☎ 790 7278) runs daily cruises, including one-hour trips (adult/child R35/15) to Duiker Island, also known as Seal Island because of its colony of Cape fur seals. The sunset trips (R75) include snoek and champagne.

Hout Bay is the start of the truncated (for the time being) **Chapman's Peak Drive**, one of the most spectacular stretches of coastal road in the world. Dangerous rock slides have closed the road about 2km south of Hout Bay, but coming up here is still worthwhile for the views back across the bay. Perched on a rock near the Hout Bay

spectacular (or as trendy) as those on the Atlantic side, but the water is often 5°C or more warmer, and can reach 20°C in summer. This makes swimming far more pleasant. Suburban development along the coast is more intense, presumably because of the train line, which runs all the way through to Simon's Town, the most interesting single destination besides the Cape of Good Hope Nature Reserve.

The train is the best way to get here; the line hugs the coast from Muizenberg to the terminus at Simon's Town and offers spectacular views. It's reasonably safe as long as you travel first class and during the peak times. Consider hopping off at the fishing village of Kalk Bay, a delightful destination in its own right.

On the eastern side of False Bay (Map 1), you'll need a car to reach Strand and Gordon's Bay, each a cross between a satellite suburb and a beach resort. They're nothing particularly special, but do have great views back to the Cape and are themselves in the shadow of the spectacular Hottentots Hollandberge range. There's a superb stretch of coastal road that rivals Chapman's Peak Drive, with a great caravan park and a couple of spots where you can get access to the beach (the surf can be very dangerous for swimmers). For more information on this side of False Bay, see Overberg in the Excursions chapter.

During October and November, False Bay is a favourite haunt of whales and their calves: Southern right whales, humpback whales and bryde (pronounced '**bree**-dah') whales are the most commonly sighted. They often come quite close to the shore.

Muizenberg (Map 3)

Unless the sun is shining, Muizenberg can be pretty bleak, but when the sun's out, you can escape the run-down waterfront for a broad white beach that shelves gently and is generally safer than most of the peninsula beaches. It's a popular surfing spot, too.

There's a very pleasant coastal walk from Muizenberg's handsome station to the more upmarket suburb of **St James**. At both communities' beaches you'll see the much-

photographed, colourfully painted Victorian bathing huts. Unfortunately, they are let by the season – you can't hire one for the day. The St James tidal pool (Map 3, #8) is safe for children.

To see Cape Town's best collection of antique playthings, visit the **Muizenberg Toy Museum (Map 3, #3)** (☎ *788 1569, 8 Beach Rd, Muizenberg; adult/child R5/3; open 10am-4pm Tues-Sun).*

Also worth a look is the **Natale Labia Museum (Map 3, #6)** (☎ *788 4106, 192 Main Rd, Muizenberg; adult/child R3/free; open 10am-5pm Tues-Sun)*, a charming Venetian-style mansion and a satellite of the South African National Gallery with a lovely cafe.

If you have more time, pop into the pretty cottage that once belonged to Cecil Rhodes, now the **Rhodes Cottage Museum (Map 3, #7)** (☎ *788 1816, Main Rd, St James; admission by donation; 9.30am-4.30pm Mon-Sat, 10.30am-4.30pm Sun)*. Here you can find out more about the founder of De Beers, who died here in 1902 (see the boxed text 'Cecil Rhodes: Empire Builder' earlier in this chapter).

Kalk Bay (Map 3)

Kalk Bay (Kalkbaai), named after the kilns that in the 17th century produced lime from seashells for painting buildings, is a busy fishing harbour with a lively daily fish market (Map 3, #18). The swimming here is good, and to the north of the harbour there's an excellent left reef break (best with a west to north-westerly wind).

With plenty of dining options and a row of quirky antiques and craft shops, Kalk Bay is a charming pit stop en route to Simon's Town, or a lazy-day destination in its own right. For the more energetic there are also plenty of trails up into the mountains of the Silvermine Nature Reserve, now part of the Cape Peninsula National Park.

Clovelly & Fish Hoek (Map 11)

Both these suburbs have wide, safe beaches but are less attractive than their neighbours. From Kalk Bay south there are numerous grottoes and caves that were occupied by humans aeons ago. **Jager's Walk** at the

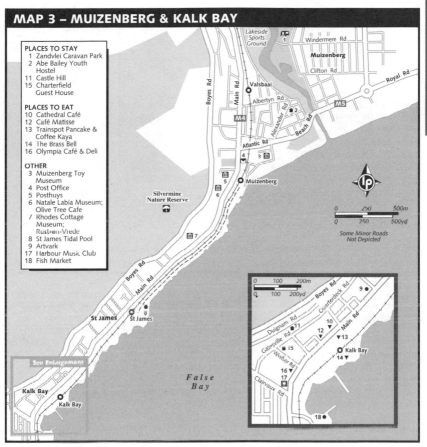

MAP 3 – MUIZENBERG & KALK BAY

PLACES TO STAY
1 Zandvlei Caravan Park
2 Abe Bailey Youth
   Hostel
11 Castle Hill
15 Charterfield
   Guest House

PLACES TO EAT
10 Cathedral Café
12 Café Matisse
13 Trainspot Pancake &
   Coffee Kaya
14 The Brass Bell
16 Olympia Café & Deli

OTHER
3 Muizenberg Toy
   Museum
4 Post Office
5 Posthuys
6 Natale Labia Museum;
   Olive Tree Cafe
7 Rhodes Cottage
   Museum;
   Rust-en-Vrede
8 St James Tidal Pool
9 Artvark
17 Harbour Music Club
18 Fish Market

0   250   500m
0   250   500yd

*Some Minor Roads
Not Depicted*

*False
Bay*

---

southern end of the beach at Fish Hoek provides a pleasant stroll to Sunny Cove, also on the train line. You could walk the remaining 5km from here along an unpaved road to Simon's Town.

Simon's Town (Map 4)

Most people come to Simon's Town just to see the penguins at Boulders Beach. Linger longer and you'll discover an attractive, historic town that's the nation's third-oldest European settlement.

Simon's Town (Simonstad), named after governor Simon Van Der Stel, was the VOC's winter anchorage from 1741 and became a naval base for the British in 1814. It has remained one ever since, the frigates now joined by pleasure boats that depart for spectacular trips to Cape Point. St George's St, the main thoroughfare, is lined with preserved Victorian buildings and there's an intriguing Muslim side to the town that is slowly being revived.

Information (including information on walking tours) and accommodation bookings are available at the helpful Simon's Town Publicity Association **(Map 4, #11)** (☎ 786 2436) at 111 St George's St next to the

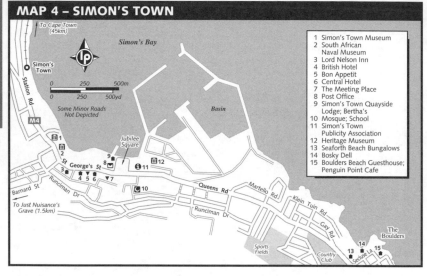

MAP 4 – SIMON'S TOWN

To Cape Town (45km)

Simon's Bay

Simon's Town

Station Rd

M4

Some Minor Roads Not Depicted

Jubilee Square

Basin

St George's St

Runciman Dr

Barnard St

To Just Nuisance's Grave (1.5km)

Queens Rd

Martello Rd

Klein Tuin Rd

Runciman Dr

Gay Rd

The Boulders

Sports Fields

Country Club

Seaforth La

1 Simon's Town Museum
2 South African Naval Museum
3 Lord Nelson Inn
4 British Hotel
5 Bon Appetit
6 Central Hotel
7 The Meeting Place
8 Post Office
9 Simon's Town Quayside Lodge; Bertha's
10 Mosque; School
11 Simon's Town Publicity Association
12 Heritage Museum
13 Seaforth Beach Bungalows
14 Bosky Dell
15 Boulders Beach Guesthouse; Penguin Point Cafe

Jubilee Square marina development. It's open from 9.30am to 5pm daily.

The **Heritage Museum (Map 4, #12)** (☎ 786 2302) in Almay House on King George Way, 100m from the publicity association, is the town's most interesting museum. It includes displays on the Cape Muslim community of over 7000 people forcibly removed during the apartheid era, and is enthusiastically curated by Zainab Davidson, whose family was kicked out in 1975. Nearby Alfred Lane leads to the handsome mosque and attached school **(Map 4, #10)**, built in 1926.

The rambling **Simon's Town Museum (Map 4, #1)** (☎ 786 3046, St George's St; adult/child R5/2; open 9am-4pm Mon-Fri, 10am-4pm Sat, 11am-4pm Sun) is about 600m south of the train station. Based in the old governor's residency (1777), its extensive exhibits trace the history of the town and port, and include a display on Just Nuisance, the Great Dane that was adopted as a navy mascot in WWII, and whose grave above the town makes for a healthy walk.

Next door is the **South African Naval Museum (Map 4, #2)** (☎ 787 4635, St George's St; admission free; open 10am-

4pm daily). Definitely one for naval nuts, it nonetheless has plenty of interesting exhibits, including a mock submarine in which to play out boyish adventure fantasies.

For boat trips contact **Sweet Sunshine Boat Charters** (☎ 082 575 5655), which operates a 42-foot catamaran from the jetty at Jubilee Square. Four-hour trips to Cape Point are R140; 1½-hour False Bay cruises cost R60.

For detailed information on trains to and from Simon's Town, see the Getting Around chapter.

Boulders (Map 11)

As its name suggests, Boulders, about 3km from Simon's Town, is an area with a number of large boulders and small sandy coves. Within the area is Boulders Beach. The sea is calm and shallow in the coves, so Boulders is popular with families and can get extremely crowded, especially on holidays and weekends.

Boulders Beach is part of the **Cape Peninsula National Park** (☎ 786 2329, W www.cpnp.co.za; open 8am-6.30pm daily). The beach is home to a colony of 3000 African penguins. Delightful as they are, the penguins are also pretty stinky, which may put you off spending too long paddling with them. Admission to the penguin colony costs R10/5 for adults/children.

There are two entrances to the penguins' protected area. The first, as you come along Queens Rd (the continuation of St George's St) from Simon's Town, is at the end of Seaforth Rd; the second is at Bellevue Rd, where you'll also find accommodation and places to eat. You can observe the penguins from the boardwalk at Foxy Beach, but at Boulders Beach you can get in the water with them.

The penguin colony has only been here since the mid-1980s; nobody knows why the birds came and they may just as easily take off again. They may look pretty healthy, but the African penguin (formerly called the jackass penguin) is an endangered species susceptible to avian malaria and pollution (see the boxed text 'Saving the African Penguin' earlier in this chapter).

Rikkis (☎ 786 2136) meet all trains to Simon's Town and go to Boulders.

CAPE OF GOOD HOPE NATURE RESERVE (Map 11)

Truly awesome scenery, some fantastic walks and deserted beaches, plus the chance to spot wildlife including bonteboks, elands and zebras, are what a visit to this nature reserve (☎ 780 9204; R20 per person, minimum R40 per car; open 7am-6pm Oct-Mar, 7am-5pm Apr-Sept) is all about. If you come on one of the many tours that whip into the reserve, now part of the Cape Peninsula National Park, pause at the tourist centre, walk to Cape Point and back, and then zip out again, you'll not even have seen the half of it. If possible, hire a car and take your time to explore the reserve the way it should be: on foot.

If the weather is good – or even if it isn't – you can easily spend at least a day here. It's particularly beautiful in spring, when the wildflowers are in bloom. There are a number of picnic spots; there's also a restaurant but it's generally packed with tour-bus crowds.

It's not a difficult walk, but if you're feeling lazy a **funicular railway** (adult R22/8 return, R15/6 one way) runs up beside the restaurant to the souvenir kiosk next to the old lighthouse (1860). The old lighthouse was too often obscured by mist and fog, so a new lighthouse was built at Dias Point in 1919, reached by a thrilling walkway along the rocks; if the winds are howling, as they often are, the old lighthouse is likely to be as far as you'll feel safe in going.

Pick up a map at the entrance gate if you intend to go walking, but bear in mind that there is minimal shade in the park and that the weather can change quickly.

There are some excellent beaches, usually deserted. This can make them dangerous if you get into difficulties in the water, so take care. One of the best beaches for swimming or walking is **Platboom Beach (Map 11, #28)**. **Maclear Beach (Map 11, #30)**, near the main car park, is good for walks or diving but is too rocky for enjoyable swimming. Further down towards Cape Point is beautiful **Dias Beach (Map 11, #29)**. Access is on foot from the car park.

On the False Bay side, the small but pretty beach at **Buffels Bay** offers safe swimming.

The only public transport to the Cape is with Rikkis (for details, see the Getting

Don't Feed the Baboons!

There are signs all over Cape Point warning you not to feed the baboons. This isn't just some mean-spirited official stricture designed to keep baboons from developing a taste for potato crisps and chocolate. One group told us about the time they stopped and opened the car windows to take photos of baboons: 'The next thing we knew, the baboons were in the car and we were out of the car. It took about half an hour before they were satisfied that they'd thoroughly trashed the interior, and we drove back to the rental agency in a car full of baboon shit'.

Nature Reserve 95

...man

...sion of the *Flying* ...hat the ghost of this ...e for eternity because ...s captain bet his soul ...ie Cape in a storm. In the spooky equino...al sea mists it doesn't seem too unlikely that the ancient square-rigger with its doomed crew might appear. In fact, the *Flying Dutchman* is 'sighted' more often near the Cape Peninsula than anywhere else in the world.

The Cape has a fearsome reputation for wrecking ships. Part of the reason is the fast-flowing current a few kilometres offshore. Ships that avoid the current by sailing between it and the coast are at risk if one of the area's violent storms sweeps in. And there's a good chance one will – the Cape of Good Hope was originally called the Cape of Storms. If the wind is blowing in the opposite direction to the current, freak waves can develop. Add to this scenario a panicky crew claiming to see a ghost ship flying before the wind, and there's a good chance the ship will come to grief.

Around chapter), which run from Simon's Town (accessible by train) and cost R65 per hour.

Numerous tour companies include Cape Point on their itineraries; try the Baz Bus (see the Getting There & Away chapter). Both Day Trippers and Downhill Adventures are recommended because they offer the chance to cycle within the park (see Organised Tours in the Getting Around chapter). Much better, though, is to hire a car for the day, so you can explore the rest of the peninsula.

CAPE FLATS (Map 11)

For the majority of Capetonians, home is in one of the townships sprawling across the shifting sands of the Cape Flats. These are rife with crime and poverty, their dusty, litter-strewn streets alive with people and wandering livestock. Most white locals, and many coloureds too, wouldn't dream of visiting here and will advise you not to either. Don't listen.

If you've toured any other Third-World hellhole, what you'll see here will come as little surprise. What is shocking is that it can exist in close proximity to such wealth and apparent indifference, and that the vast majority of residents should show visitors such courtesy and friendliness.

Taking a tour – the only way of safely travelling here besides making friends with and being accompanied by a resident – is one of the most illuminating and life-affirming things you can do while in Cape Town. Most half-day itineraries are similar. After starting in the Bo-Kaap for a brief discussion of Cape Town's colonial history, you'll move on to the District Six Museum, then be driven to the Cape Flats to visit some or all of the following townships: Langa, Guguletu, Crossroads and Khayelitsha. Tour guides are generally flexible in where they go, and respond to the wishes of the group. The following are possible stops (for detailed information on companies that offer tours, see Organised Tours in the Getting Around chapter).

In Langa, the **Guga S'Thebe arts and cultural centre** (☎ 082 746 0246) is brilliantly decorated with ceramic murals.

In Guguletu, the **Sivuyile Tourism Centre** (☎ 637 8449, W *www.sivuyile.co.za; open 8am-5pm Mon-Fri, 8am-2pm Sat, 9am-1pm Sun*) has a photographic display on the townships, artists at work and a good gift shop. It's inside the local technical college, where you'll also find the creative Uncedo Pottery Project.

The **Philani Nutrition Centre** (☎ 387 5124, W *philani.snowball.co.za*) has its printing project in Crossroads. A community-based health and nutrition organisation, it has been going since 1980 and now has six projects running in the townships, including a weaving factory in Khayelitsha's Site C. Women are taught how to feed their families adequately on a low budget, and the creche and various projects enable them to earn an income through weaving rugs and wall hangings, making paper, printing and other

The Townships

Cape Town's townships played a major role in the struggle against apartheid (see Racism Rules in the Facts about Cape Town chapter). Langa, meaning 'sun', was established in 1927 and is South Africa's oldest planned township. The type of dormitory accommodation that would become common for migrant labourers was first built here.

Until the pass laws were abolished, such hostels were for men only. They lived in basic units, each accommodating 16 men, who shared one shower, one toilet and one small kitchen. Tiny bedrooms each housed up to three men. After the pass laws were abolished, most men brought their families to live with them (earlier, those who didn't have a job outside the Homelands were not allowed to leave). So each unit became home to up to 16 families, each room sleeping up to three families.

It's no wonder that people moved out and built shacks, joining the hundreds of thousands of others who had come without work and set up home in communities such as Nyanga (literally 'moon'), the second formal township, which sprouted the famous shanty town of Crossroads, now a township in its own right. Guguletu (Our Pride) was set up in 1962, while Khayelitsha (New Home) has boomed from being a squatter settlement home to those cleared out of Crossroads into South Africa's third-largest township, with a population estimated at 1.8 million.

The infrastructure has certainly improved since 1994, with the rows of concrete Reconstruction and Development Program (RDP) houses being the most visible example. But vast squatter camps, with a communal standpipe for water and a toilet shared among scores of people in the best of circumstances, still remain and are expanding all the time.

crafts. Philani goods are available from many shops around the Cape.

Rosie's Soup Kitchen (☎ 448 0903) is run by a wonderful woman who serves some 600 meals a day to the poor at 60 cents a plate. **Golden** is a talented bloke who together with his family makes beautiful flowers from scrap tins.

If you want to climb what locals refer to as Khayelitsha's Table Mountain then head to the **Tygerberg Tourism Facility**. An impressive wooden staircase leads to the top of this sand hill, which is the highest point in the townships, and provides a sweeping view of the surroundings, particularly at sunset.

ACTIVITIES
Camel Riding

At Kommetjie you can climb aboard one of four camels tethered together for a lope along the beach. Contact **Cape Camel Rides** (☎ 789 1711) for details.

Canoeing & Rafting

As a day trip the Breede River, 100km east of Cape Town, is the only canoeing and rafting option, and then a seasonal one. One reputable operator is **Felix Unite** (☎ 693 6433).

Cycling

A variety of cycling trips and adventures is available from **Downhill Adventures (Map 13, #79)** (☎ 422 0388, W www.downhilladventures.co.za, Orange St, Gardens). Try a thrilling mountain-bike ride down from the lower cable car station on Table Mountain (R200), or ride through the Constantia winelands and the Cape of Good Hope Nature Reserve (R295).

Day Trippers (☎/fax 531 3274, W www daytrippers.co.za) also runs trips that include cycling.

The **Cape Argus cycle tour** (W www.cycletour.co.za) around the peninsula is held in the second week of March and is the largest bicycle race in the world, with more than 30,000 entries each year.

If you just want to hire a bicycle, contact Downhill Adventures or **Le Africa Express (Map 16, #3)** (☎ 439 0901, 16A Main Rd, Three Anchor Bay).

Diving

Cape Town offers a number of excellent shore and boat dives. Corals, kelp beds, wrecks, caves, drop-offs, seals and a wide variety of fish are some of the attractions.

The best time is from June to November, when the water on the False Bay side is warmer and visibility is greater.

Table Bay Diving at **Waterfront Adventures (Map 14, #37)** (*☎ 419 8822, Waterfront*) is an accredited dive school with a solid reputation. A boat dive costs R130, a shore dive R60, and an open-water course R1350. Equipment hire is also available.

For information on diving with sharks, see Two Oceans Aquarium earlier in this chapter.

Golf

Golf courses are dotted around Cape Town, and some are superb. Many welcome visitors (but you should book).

Milnerton Golf Club (*☎ 434 7808*), north of the City Bowl along the R27, has a magnificent position overlooking Table Bay with great views of Table Mountain. Wind can be a problem, though. More sheltered is **Erinvale Country Estate** (*☎ 847 1144*), a course designed by Gary Player and located in the lee of the Helderberg mountains around 35km east of the city centre; take the N2 and turn off at Somerset West.

If you just want to practise your swing, the **River Club (Map 17, #2)** (*☎ 448 6117, Observatory Rd, Observatory*) has a driving range and offers lessons.

Hiking & Mountain-Climbing

Apart from the hundreds of hikes on Table Mountain, there are some fantastic hikes around the peninsula, including to the peak of Lion's Head (start from the road at the top of Kloof Nek; it involves a little climbing but there are chains on the rocks) and in the Cape of Good Hope Nature Reserve.

It is important to be properly equipped with warm clothing, a map and a compass. Numerous books and maps give details, including Mike Lundy's *Best Walks in the Cape Peninsula*.

Cape Union Mart (see the Shopping chapter) has a hiking club that runs a weekly schedule of walks around the peninsula; inquire at any of its stores. Serious climbers can contact the **Mountain Club of South Africa (Map 15, #41)** (*☎ 465 3412, 97 Hatfield St*).

Details of guided city walks are available from Cape Town Tourism. For information on a walking tour of the City Bowl, see the special section 'Cape Town Architecture'.

Horse Riding

Sleepy Hollow Horse Riding (*☎ 789 2341, ☎ 083 261 0104*) offers rides along Noordhoek beach and through the countryside.

Mont Rochelle Equestrian Centre (Map 10) (*☎ 083 300 4368, fax 021-876 2363*) in Franschhoek offers horseback tours of various wineries and estates for R70 per hour.

In Stellenbosch, the wine estate **Spier (Map 9, #21)** (*☎ 809 1100, fax 809 1134, W www.spier.co.za*) offers horse riding along with wine tasting and a host of other options.

@Lighthouse Farm Lodge (Map 11, #4) (*☎/fax 447 9177, e msm@mweb.co.za, Violet Bldg, Oude Molen Village, Alexandria Rd, Mowbray*) also offers horse riding. The cost is R40 per hour, and there's a trail running up to the Rhodes Memorial.

Ice-Skating

One of the few good reasons to head out to the GrandWest Casino in Milnerton is to take advantage of its **ice rink (Map 11, #1)** (*☎ 535 2260; admission R20 including skate hire*).

Kayaking

Real Cape Adventures (*☎ 790 5611, ☎ 082 556 2520, W www.seakayak.co.za*) runs a variety of kayaking trips around the Cape and further afield for paddlers of all levels. Simon's Town and Kalk Bay are good spots and tend to be less buffeted by wind than the Atlantic coast.

Surfing & Sand-Boarding

The Cape Peninsula has fantastic surfing possibilities – from gentle shore breaks ideal for beginners to 3m-plus monsters for experts only. There are breaks that work on virtually any combination of wind, tide and swell direction (for tips on choosing one, see the boxed text 'Finding a Windless Beach' earlier in this chapter).

In general, the best surf is along the Atlantic side, and there is a string of breaks

Cape Town Adrenaline

Cape Town offers a raft of activities that together constitute an outdoor-thrill-seeker's charter. With Table Mountain on hand, obviously walking and rock climbing are popular, but if it's adventure you're after, you won't have to look far for some operator who'll be quick to take your money. Among the most heart-pumping activities we've come across are the following:

Abseiling off Table Mountain

Don't even think of tackling this unless you've got a head (and a stomach) for heights, but otherwise we guarantee this 112m shimmy down a rope – the world's highest abseil – will give you a huge adrenaline rush. Take your time, because the views are breathtaking. Contact Abseil Africa at **Adventure Village (Map 13, #85)** (☎ 424 1580, 229B Long St, City Bowl).

Kloofing in Kamikaze Canyon

This is just one of the kloofs (cliffs or gorges) near Cape Town in which you can go kloofing (called canyoning elsewhere). This sport, which entails climbing, hiking, swimming and jumping, is great fun, but can be dangerous (so check out operators' credentials carefully before signing up). Two long-running operators are Adventure Village and **Day Trippers** (☎/fax 531 3274, W www.daytrippers.co.za). On the Adventure Village tour the high jumps into pools are optional, but on the Day Trippers tour there's one 15m jump that you cannot avoid. The cost for a day trip is around R400.

Gliding down to La Med

On a day when the winds are not too strong, look up while you're lounging at Camps Bay beach, or having a beer at La Med at the Glen Country Club in Clifton, and you might see a paraglider heading towards you. Launch sites on Table Mountain, Lion's Head and Signal Hill are popular and it's possible for the total novice to arrange a tandem flight. The **South African Hang Gliding and Paragliding Association** (☎ 011-805 5429, W www.paragliding.co.za) can provide names of operators, and plenty of schools offer courses for beginners. Try **Paragliding Cape Town** (☎ 082 727 6584) or **Ferdinand's Tours & Adventures** (☎ 465 8550). A tandem flight will cost around R550.

Skydiving over Table Bay

Given the shaky rand, this is one of the cheapest places for you to learn to skydive or do a tandem dive. The view over Table Bay and the peninsula alone makes it worth it. Adventure Village can put you in contact with reliable operators. **Delta 200 Flying School** (☎ 082 800 6290) is based about 20km north of the city centre in Melkbosstrand. All up a dive will cost around R800.

THINGS TO SEE & DO

from Bloubergstrand through to the Cape of Good Hope. Most of these breaks work best in south-easterly conditions. The water can be freezing (as low as 8°C) so a steamer wet suit and booties are required.

On False Bay, head to Muizenberg and Kalk Bay. The waves here tend to be less demanding in terms of size and temperature (up to 20°C), and work best in north-westerlies. There's a daily surf report on Radio Good Hope at 7.15am.

Downhill Adventures (Map 13, #79) *(☎ 422 0388,* W *www.downhilladventures .co.za, Orange St, Gardens)* runs a surf school with introductory courses for R395; you're guaranteed to be standing on the board within a day. If getting wet isn't your style, then try the sand-boarding trip (R395), a variation on snowboarding, on the dunes north of Cape Town.

Surf Centre (Map 13, #114) *(☎ 423 7853, 45 Castle St, City Bowl)* has a good stock of wetsuits and boards for sale or rental. So does **Extreme Sports Shack (Map 13, #65)** *(☎ 426 0294,* e *extremesports@worldon line.co.za, 220 Long St, City Bowl).*

Windsurfing

With all that summer wind it's hardly surprising that the Cape coast is a favourite spot for windsurfers. Blouebergstrand **(Map 1)** is a popular location, as is the lagoon in Langebaan **(Map 1)**, further north. In Langebaan you'll find **Cape Sport Centre** *(☎ 022-772 1114,* W *www.capesport .co.za)*, which can provide tuition and gear.

CAPE TOWN ARCHITECTURE

From the venerable 17th-century Castle of Good Hope to the late-20th-century redevelopment of the Victoria & Alfred Waterfront, Cape Town's wealth of interesting architecture is one of its most attractive features. Although the city has been extensively developed, much that would have been destroyed elsewhere has been preserved, and a walking tour of Cape Town's City Bowl is a great way to get a feel for the different periods of history through which the city has developed.

Dutch Colonial Architecture Built between 1666 and 1679, the **Castle of Good Hope (Map 13)** is frequently cited as South Africa's oldest surviving colonial structure. This pentagonal fort has been changed over the centuries. The entrance used to be on what is now Strand St, facing directly onto the sea, which once lapped at the walls (land reclamation has since pushed the water a good kilometre away).

Jan Van Riebeeck's vegetable garden, forerunner of the **Company's Gardens (Map 13)**, actually predates the castle by 14 years. The first incarnation of the **Slave Lodge (Map 13, #49)** at the gardens' northern end was built in 1660 as a single-storey building to house up to 500 wretched souls. This building was substantially changed under later British administrations.

Out at Muizenberg on False Bay is the thatched and white-washed **Posthuys (Map 3, #5)**, which dates from 1673. The building's rustic style is still echoed along the Western Cape coast, particularly in fishing villages such as Arniston and Paternoster (see the Excursions chapter).

Similarly, the more ornate style of Cape Dutch architecture started in Cape Town and spread out around the colony. Governor Simon Van Der Stel built his quintessential manor house, **Groot Constantia (Map 11, #19)**, in 1692, thus establishing the prototype for other glorious estates to follow in the Winelands further inland. **Vergelegen (Map 9)**, near Somerset West, dates from 1699, while **Boschendal (Map 10)**, between Franschhoek and Stellenbosch, dates from 1685. These and a whole road of reconstructed beauties in **Tulbagh (Map 1)** are all worth seeing. (For details, see the Excursions chapter and the special section 'Cape Wineries'.)

Inset: Clock tower, V&A Waterfront (Photo detail by Richard I'Anson)

Right: Groot Constantia (Photo by Simon Richmond)

In the city centre, the best place to get an idea of what Cape Town looked like during the 18th century is to take a stroll through the Bo-Kaap. Blot out the more modern pastel paint jobs and you'll notice flat roofs instead of gables, and a lack of shutters on the outside of the windows. These features are the result of building regulations instituted by the Dutch East India Company (Vereenigde Oost-Indische Compagnie, or VOC) in the wake of fires that swept the city.

On Strand St, the fancy facade of the late-18th-century **Koopmans de Wet House (Map 13, #112)** is attributed to Louis Thibault, who, as the VOC's lieutenant of engineers, was responsible for the design of most of Cape Town's public buildings in this period. Thibault also had a hand in the handsome **Rust-en-Vreugd (Map 15, #33)**, which dates from 1778, famous for its delicately carved rococo fanlight above the main door and its double balconies and portico.

Bordering the Company's Gardens is the lovely **Tuynhuis (Map 13, #94)**, dating from 1700; you can see the VOC monogram on the building's pediment. Now the official residence of the republic's president (thus off limits to visitors), the building was altered during the British administration of the 19th century.

British Colonial Architecture

British governor Lord Charles Somerset made the biggest impact on the architectural look of Cape Town during his 1814–26 tenure. (It was he who ordered the restyling of the Tuynhuis to bring it into line with Regency tastes for verandas and front gardens.)

Built around 1840, the two-storey brick **Bertram House (Map 15, #16)**, at the southern end of Government Ave, is an example of late Georgian style.

As the British Empire reached its zenith in the late 19th century, Cape Town boomed and a whole slew of monumental buildings was erected. Walk down Adderley St and through the Company's Gardens and you'll pass the 1880 **Standard Bank (Map 13, #124)** with its pediment, dome and soaring columns; the 1884 **Houses of Parliament (Map 13, #96)**, outside which stands a

Above: Parliament (Photo by Simon Richmond)

marble statue (1890) of Queen Victoria herself; and the Byzantine-influenced **Old Synagogue (Map 15, #40)** dating from 1862 (the neighbouring and much more baroque Great Synagogue with its twin towers dates from 1905).

Long St is where you can see Victorian Cape Town at its most appealing, with the wrought-iron balconies and varying facades of shops and buildings such as the **Long St Baths (Map 13, #80)**, while in the salubrious suburbs of Tamboerskloof and Oranjezicht on the slopes of Table Mountain many mansions of that era still survive.

Cecil John Rhodes, prime minister of the Cape Colony from 1890 to 1896, commissioned a young English architect, Herbert Baker, to build his home, **Groote Schuur (Map 12, #23)**, in Rondebosch in 1898, thus kicking off the style known as Cape Dutch Revival. In 1902 Baker designed **Rust-en-Vrede (Map 3, #7)**, Rhodes' thatched cottage by the sea in Muizenberg, just in time for the mining magnate to die in it. It now houses the Rhodes Cottage Museum.

As the Victorian era came to a close, Cape Town's grandest public building, the **Old Town Hall (Map 13, #130)**, rose on the south-west side of Grand Parade in 1905; it was from the

Above: Old Town Hall (Photo by Simon Richmond)

balcony here that Nelson Mandela made his first public address as a free man in 1990.

20th-Century Architecture Edwardian Cape Town is best represented by the **Centre for the Book (Map 13, #90)**, which opened in 1913 as the headquarters of the now-defunct University of Good Hope. More recently it has become an annexe of the National Library of South Africa, and gained some notoriety as the venue for the inquiry into cricket match-fixing in 2000.

Fine examples of Art-Deco architecture can be seen along St George's Mall and around **Greenmarket Square**: Shell House, now the Holiday Inn **(Map 13, #34)**, dates from 1929. Opposite the main post office, on Darling St, is the handsome **Mutual Building (Map 13, #133)** of 1940, the continent's first skyscraper, decorated with friezes and frescoes, all with South African themes.

There was little architectural development in Cape Town during the apartheid era. Examples of rationalist architecture include **Artscape (Map 13, #107)** and the adjoining **Civic Centre (Map 13, #109)** on the foreshore, which display the obsession with concrete that was typical of international modernism (we would call it concrete brutalism at its worst).

The less said about the total lack of planning or official architectural concern for the townships probably the better, although it is worth mentioning the tremendous ingenuity and resilience that residents show in creating livable homes from scrap. A visit to the townships today reveals colourfully painted shacks and murals, homes and churches made from shipping crates, and more recent imaginative structures such as the Guga S'Thebe arts and cultural centre in Langa.

For the vast majority of visitors, though, contemporary Capetonian architecture is summed up in the re-development of the **Victoria & Alfred (V&A) Waterfront (Map 14)**. Say what you like about this (and many people do): In comparison with the florid bombast of the more recent GrandWest Casino **(Map 11, #1)** and the gargantuan Canal Walk shopping centre **(Map 11, #2)** in the northern suburbs, the Waterfront increasingly looks a model of restraint and thoughtful integration of the old and the new.

Cape Dutch Style Drive around South Africa for just a short time and you'll realise how pervasive the Cape Dutch style of architecture is. The style began to emerge in the late 17th century. Thanks to Britain's wars with France, the British turned to the Cape for wine, so the burghers prospered and, during the 18th and 19th centuries, were able to build many of the impressive estates that can be seen today. The building materials were brick and plenty of plaster and wood (often teak), and reeds were used to thatch the roof.

The main features of a Cape Dutch manor are the stoep (a raised platform, the equivalent of a veranda) with seats at each end, the large central hall running the length of the house, and the main rooms symmetrically arranged on either side of the hall. Above the front entrance is the gable, the most obvious feature, and there are usually

Above Left: Typical Cape Dutch style (Photo by Manfred Gottschalk)

A self-guided walking tour of the City Bowl is the best way to get a feel for the area's eclectic architecture (you won't need 10 legs or platform shoes).

Flea market and Old Town Hall, City Bowl, Cape Town

University of Stellenbosch

Burgerhuis, Stellenbosch

Rhodes Memorial, Cape Town

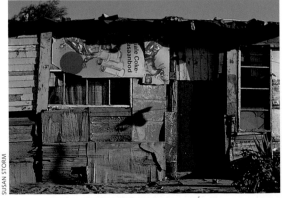

Crossroads township shanty, Cape Town

less elaborate gables at each end. The house is covered by a steep thatched roof and is invariably painted white.

The front gable, which extends up above the roof line and almost always contains a dormer window, shows the influence of 18th-century Dutch styles. The large ground-floor windows have solid shutters. The graceful plaster scrolls of the gable are sometimes reflected in the curved moulding above the front door (above which is a fanlight, sometimes with elaborate woodwork). Sometimes the doorway shows neoclassical features such as Doric pilasters or a simple pediment.

Inside, the rooms are large and simply decorated. The main hall is often divided by a louvred wooden screen, which is thought to have derived from similar screens the Dutch would have seen in the East Indies. Above the ceilings many houses had a *brandsolder*, a layer of clay or brick to protect the house if the thatching caught fire. The roof space was used for storage, if at all.

For more information there are several books available, the most useful of which is Phillida Brooke Simons' *Cape Dutch Houses & Other Old Favourites*.

Right: Lioness Gateway, Castle of Good Hope (Photo by Simon Richmond)

City Bowl Walking Tour

The following walk around the City Bowl **(Map 13)** could take the best part of a day, depending on the stops you make, although it is only about 6km long. For information on the many museums and galleries you will pass, see Museums & Galleries in the Things to See & Do chapter.

The **Castle of Good Hope** is an appropriate place to start. Immediately to the west is Grand Parade, the former military parade and public execution ground, which is now home to a lively market every Wednesday and Saturday. Jan Van Riebeeck's original mud-walled fort was here, too, and you can see its position outlined in red at the Plein St end of the Parade.

The impressive **Old Town Hall (Map 13, #130)**, on the south-west side of the parade, has been superseded by the hideous Civic Centre towards the foreshore.

Castle of
Good Hope •

Old Town Hall •

Walk up Buitenkant St towards the **District Six Museum (Map 13, #139)**, turn right onto Albertus St, then turn right again at Corporation St to reach Mostert St and its continuation, Spin St. On the traffic island beside pretty Church Square, look down to see the circular plaque marking the tree from where slaves were once sold.

In front of you is the **Groote Kerk (Map 13, #48)** *(admission free; open 10am-2pm daily)*, the mother church for the Dutch Reformed Church (Nederduitse Gereformeerde Kerk, or NG Kerk). The first church on the site was built in 1704, but only parts of this remain, most of the current building dating from 1841. A number of early notables have tombs inside and the mammoth organ and ornate Burmese teak pulpit are well worth seeing.

Adjacent to the Groote Kerk is the Slave Lodge, which was once a brothel and now houses the **Cultural History Museum (Map 13, #49)**. Opposite, at the end of Wale St, is **St George's Cathedral (Map 13, #50)**, designed by Herbert Baker in 1897. This was Archbishop Desmond Tutu's cathedral (lunch-time concerts are held here from 1pm to 1.50pm).

Turn right into St George's Mall, then take the second left onto Longmarket St, and you'll emerge on cobbled **Greenmarket Square**, created as a farmers' market in the early 18th century. The **Old Town House (Map 13, #40)**, which dates from 1761, has a balcony overlooking the bustling square, which is now filled Monday to Saturday with a colourful crafts and souvenir market. Note the fine Art-Deco architecture of the building opposite, on the Shortmarket St side of the square.

At the Old Town House turn left onto Burg St and then right into Church St, which is lined with good art and antiques shops. The pedestrian section has a flea market specialising in antiques and bric-a-brac. At the junction with Long St turn right, and pause at the **South African Missionary Meeting House Museum (Map 13, #20)** (☎ 423 6755, 40 Long St; admission free; open 9am-4pm Mon-Fri), also known as the Sendinggestig Museum, built in 1802. Its interior is plain but quite handsome, the focus, as always, being the wooden pulpit.

At the junction with Strand St turn right to view **Koopmans de Wet House (Map 13, #112)** (☎ 424 2473, 35 Strand St; adult/child R5/2; open 9.30am-4.30pm Tues-Sat), a classic example of a Cape Dutch townhouse and furnished with 18th- and early-19th-century antiques. It's an atmospheric place with ancient vines growing in the courtyard and floorboards that squeak just as they probably did during the times of Marie Koopmans de Wet, the socialite owner after whom the house is named.

Head north-west along Strand St towards Buitengracht St, passing on the right-hand side the magnificent old **Lutheran Church (Map 13, #6)** (98 Strand St; admission free; open 10am-2pm Mon-Fri). Converted from a barn in 1780, it also has a striking pulpit, perhaps the best created by the master German sculptor Anton Anreith, whose work can also be seen in Groote Kerk and at Groot Constantia. The parsonage next door, Martin Melck Huis, is now the **Gold of Africa**

District Six
Museum

Groote Kerk

Cultural History
Museum

St George's
Cathedral

Greenmarket
Square

Old Town House

South African
Missionary
Meeting House
Museum

Koopmans de
Wet House

Lutheran Church

Gold of Africa
Museum

Museum (Map 13, #7) (☎ 423 7083, 96 Strand St; adult/child R5/2; open 9am-5pm Mon-Sat).

Turn left onto Buitengracht St and walk to Van Riebeeck Square. On the Bree St side of this parking lot is **St Stephen's Church (Map 13, #19)**, built in 1799, originally the African Theatre and later a school for freed slaves before it became a church in 1839. Immediately behind you is **Heritage Square**, a beautiful collection of Cape Georgian and Victorian buildings saved from the wrecking ball in 1996 and since transformed into the city's trendiest enclave of restaurants, bars, shops, and the Cape Heritage Hotel, as well as an operational blacksmith's.

Cross Buitengracht St and head uphill along Longmarket St to enter the heart of the preserved Cape Muslim quarter, better known as the **Bo-Kaap**. The steep streets (some of which are still cobbled) are lined with 18th-century flat-roofed houses and with mosques. Residents of the area are still predominantly Muslim. The Bo-Kaap area is well worth exploring in its own right (although take care to do it in daytime since the narrow deserted streets are not safe at night). Chiappini and Rose Sts contain the prettiest houses, many of which have been spruced up with pastel paint. (If you've got the legs for it, hike all the way up Longmarket St to witness the firing of the Noon Gun on Signal Hill.) There's the interesting **Bo-Kaap Museum (Map 13, #17)** on Wale St and the **Auwal Mosque (Map 13, #28)**, the oldest in Cape Town, on Dorp St. One of the best ways to see Bo-Kaap is on a guided tour (see Organised Tours in the Getting Around chapter). Listen out while you're walking for the horn tooted by the mobile fishmonger doing the rounds.

From the Bo-Kaap Museum, head south-east down Wale St, cross Buitengracht St again and return to the upper end of Long St. Turn right and follow Long St until it joins with Orange St. The **Long St Baths (Map 13, #80)** on the corner are still in operation. Turn left into Orange St, and left again into Grey's Pass, which takes you past the excellent **South African Museum & Planetarium (Map 15, #30)**.

From here, you enter the top end of the **Company's Gardens**. An exceedingly pleasant place to stroll or relax, the surviving six hectares of Van Riebeeck's original 18-hectare vegetable garden once provided fresh produce for the VOC's ships. As sources of supply were diversified, the garden was gradually changed to a superb pleasure garden, with a fine collection of botanical species from South Africa and the rest of the world.

Among the museums and grand buildings that surround the gardens is **Bertram House (Map 15, #16)** (☎ 424 9381, Cnr Orange St & Government Ave; adult/child R5/2; open 9.30am-4.30pm Tues-Sat). A couple of other things to keep an eye out for are statues designed by Herbert Baker, including the **Delville Wood Memorial (Map 15, #29)**, honouring South African soldiers who fell during WWI, and the statue of **Cecil Rhodes (Map 13, #93)**, hand held high and pointing north in his vainglorious imperialist dream of an empire from the Cape to Cairo. There's also the Gardens Restaurant **(Map 13, #92)** in case you fancy a reviving cuppa or something more substantial.

Margin notes:
St Stephen's Church
Heritage Square
Bo-Kaap
Bo-Kaap Museum
Auwal Mosque
Long St Baths
South African Museum & Planetarium
Company's Gardens
Bertram House
Delville Wood Memorial
Cecil Rhodes statue

Exit the gardens along Government Ave (where you're likely to spot scurrying squirrels) onto Adderley St, named after a British parliamentarian and historically regarded as Cape Town's main street. Until 1849, the street was named Heerengracht, after a canal of the same name in Amsterdam. (A waterway did once run down here from Government Ave to the sea, but it's long since been built over.) Heading towards the train station you'll pass Trafalgar Square, a covered alley next to the hideous Golden Acre Centre, where flower sellers gather.

Just past the station, where Adderley St again becomes Heerengracht, are the **statues (Map 13, #104)** of those who started it all back in 1652, Jan Van Riebeeck and his wife Maria De La Queillerie.

● Van Riebeeck
statues

◀ **Finish**

Left: Housing at the base of Table Mountain (Photo by Richard I'Anson)

Places to Stay

Cape Town's range of accommodation is impressive at all levels, with backpackers and those in search of a characterful guesthouse especially well catered for.

If there's somewhere you particularly want to stay, plan ahead, especially during school holidays from mid-December to the end of January and at Easter – prices can double and many places are fully booked. Also consider location. For example, if you plan to hit the beaches, then suburbs along the Atlantic or False Bay coast will make better sense than, say, Gardens or City Bowl. If you have transport, then anywhere is OK, but remember to inquire about the parking options when making a booking.

Rates at many places fluctuate according to demand, and it's always worthwhile asking about special deals. For longer stays rates are definitely negotiable.

ACCOMMODATION AGENCIES

Cape Town Tourism (see Tourist Offices in the Facts for the Visitor chapter) runs an accommodation booking service and some-times has special deals. Like any agency, it will only recommend its members.

The Bed 'n' Breakfast organisation (☎ 683 3505, fax 683 5159, W www.bnb .co.za) has a number of members around the Cape Peninsula. Most rooms are in large, luxurious suburban houses, often with swimming pools. Self-catering flats and cottages are also available. Advance booking is preferred and prices start at around R100/150 per person in low/high season. You can pay a lot more than this.

For self-catering places, try the Accommodation Shop (☎ 439 1234, fax 434 2238, W www.accommodationshop.co.za); Cape Holiday Homes (☎ 419 0430, fax 422 0306, e info@capehomes.co.za); and A–Z Accommodations (☎ 551 2785, W www.a-zholi dayhomes.co.za).

For information on consistently excellent places to stay covering a wide range of budgets, consult the various booklets produced by the Portfolio Collection (☎ 011-880 3414, fax 788 4802, W www.portfolio collection.com), Box 52350, Saxonwold, Johannesburg 2132.

Accommodation Prices

There's one annoying thing to watch out for in accommodation advertising. You might see a hotel boasting that rooms cost R190: It usually means R190 *per person* in a twin or double room. A single room might cost R290. When we quote the cost of a double room we give the full price, not the per-person price.

Most rooms have a private bathroom; if this isn't the case and there are communal bathrooms we list a price for rooms 'with shared bathroom'. Also note that many places automatically include breakfast in their tariff; if this is the case we quote prices for B&B. If dinner is also part of the package, we quote prices for DB&B, and if all meals are thrown in as standard, the price quoted is for full board.

PLACES TO STAY – BUDGET
Camping

To stay at any of Cape Town's caravan parks you will need your own transport.

Zandvlei Caravan Park (☎ 788 5215, fax 788 5250, The Row, Muizenberg) **Map 3, #1** Camp sites R50-90 depending on season, chalet from R200. On the edge of Zandvlei lagoon and within walking distance of the beach. From Valsbaai train station walk east along Albertyn Rd, cross the bridge, turn left, then turn left again onto The Row.

Chapman's Peak Caravan Park (☎/fax 789 1225, Noordhoek Main Rd, Noordhoek) **Map 11, #24** Camp sites from R66. This place is handy for Atlantic surf beaches, but a longer journey to and from the city now that Chapman's Peak Dr is closed.

Miller's Point Caravan Park (☎/fax 786 1142, e millerspoint@xsinet.co.za,

Miller's Point Rd) **Map 11, #27** Camp sites R50-90 depending on season. Head 8km south of Simon's Town towards Cape Point to reach this caravan park on a small private beach with just 12 sites. It doesn't always accept tents.

Several central hostels have tent space, including Ashanti Lodge, The Hip Hop and @Lighthouse Farm Lodge (see Hostels, following, for details).

Hostels

Competition between the city's many hostels is fierce and most places offer a raft of inducements including free airport pick-ups and meals. It's impossible for us to list all the options, so what follows is a selection of the better places we've come across.

Unless otherwise indicated, you can assume that the hostels mentioned here have private rooms (usually with shared bathrooms) as well as dorm beds (for which you'll be paying around R55), but you can't assume that any will be vacant when you arrive. Book ahead.

City Bowl *The Backpack* (☎ 423 4530, fax 423 0065, W www.backpackers.co.za, 74 New Church St) **Map 13, #76** Dorm beds from R60, singles/doubles from R120/160. Grand-daddy of the non-HI (non–Hostelling International) hostels in Cape Town, still among the best (and certainly one of the cleanest), and constantly making improvements. The attached Africa Travel Centre is one of the most clued up (see Travel Agencies in the Facts for the Visitor chapter).

Zebra Crossing (☎/fax 422 1265, e zeb racrossing@intekom.co.za, 82 New Church St) **Map 13, #77** Dorm beds R40, singles/doubles R100/150. Smaller, quieter, more personal and slightly cheaper than most. There's a piano to tinkle in the lounge and a peaceful atmosphere.

Long St Backpackers (☎ 423 0615, fax 423 1842, e longstpb@mweb.co.za, 209 Long St) **Map 13, #86** Dorm beds R45, singles/doubles R70/120. First of the Long St hostels and still standing out from the pack. In a block of 14 small flats, with four

beds and a bathroom in each, arranged around a leafy, quiet courtyard.

Overseas Visitors' Club (☎ 424 6800, fax 423 4870, 230 Long St, W www.ovc.co.za) **Map 13, #71** Dorm beds R50. Only dorms are available in this nice old building, with high-quality facilities and a pub-like bar. This place is missing that rowdy backpacker atmosphere, which could be a bonus; there is a 10% discount for HI members.

Train Lodge (☎ 418 4890, fax 418 5848, W www.trainlodge.co.za, Old Marine Dr) **Map 13, #127** Dorm beds/singles/doubles all R50. When busy this novel hostel (the rooms are in stationary trains) charges more for singles and doubles – otherwise it's a bargain, although you could end up spending more on nonshared taxis to get safely back to this deserted part of town late at night.

Gardens & Oranjezicht *Oak Lodge* (☎ 465 6182, fax 465 6308, 21 Breda St, Gardens) **Map 15, #46** Dorm beds R55, doubles R160-180. A hippy air still pervades this one-time commune, now the most chilled hostel in Cape Town. It's taken over nearly all the flats in the attached block, which represent a great long-term accommodation option with their own kitchens and bathrooms (in low season you could stay here for R1000 a week).

Ashanti Lodge (☎ 423 8721, fax 423 8790, e ashanti@iafrica.com, 11 Hof St, Gardens) **Map 15, #13** Camping R40 per person, dorm beds R55, doubles R140, doubles B&B from R180. Book well ahead to get into this super-popular party hostel in a big and brightly painted old house. For something quieter opt for the excellent B&B rooms in a separate National Monument house down the road. There is a 10% discount for HI members.

Cloudbreak (☎ 461 6892, fax 461 1458, e cloudbrk@gem.co.za, 219 Buitenkant St, Oranjezicht) **Map 15, #47** Dorm beds R50, singles/doubles R130/150. Friendly little place with a student vibe and popular with surfers. It's recently taken over another house nearby at 18 Vredehoek Ave and has garage space for four vehicles.

Green Point *St John's Waterfront Lodge*
(☎ *439 1404, fax 439 1424,* W *www.nis*
.za/stjohns, 6 Braemar Rd) **Map 14, #18**
Dorm beds R60, doubles R150/180 with
shared/private bathroom. Close to the Waterfront and not too far from the city, this often-
recommended hostel is a large, relaxed and
friendly place with very good facilities,
including a large garden and two pools.

The Hip Hop (☎ *439 2104, fax 439*
8688, e *hiphop@cis.co.za, 11 Vesperdene*
Rd) **Map 14, #16** Camping R30 per person,
dorm beds R50, doubles R140. There are
mainly dorm beds on offer at this nicely
decorated old house with a garden and a
larger pool than most. There's a free beer
on check-in.

The Big Blue (☎ *439 0807, fax 439 8068,*
e *big.blue@mweb.co.za, 7 Vesperdene Rd)*
Map 14, #17 Dorm beds R40, doubles
R120/140 with shared/private bathroom.
The dorm beds are a bit cramped but this
relatively new kid on the block makes all
the right moves otherwise.

Atlantic Coast *Carnaby the Backpacker*
(☎ *439 7410, fax 439 1222,* W *www.carnaby*
backpacker.co.za, 219 Main Rd, Three
Anchor Bay) **Map 16, #1** Dorm beds R55,
singles/doubles from R125/175. This rambling old hotel converted into a rather funky
backpacker place has one of the better pools
and a happening bar. Most rooms have their
own bathroom and TV.

Aardvark Backpackers (☎ *434 4172, fax*
439 3813, e *aardbp@mweb.co.za, 319*
Main Rd, Sea Point) **Map 16, #18** Dorm
beds R60, doubles R222. In a wing of the
Lion's Head Lodge (see Places to Stay –
Mid-Range later in this chapter) and sharing
its facilities, this hostel has dorms in converted flats. There's a useful travel centre. A
10% discount is available for HI members.

Stan Halt Youth Hostel (☎/fax *438 9037,*
e *stanh@new.co.za, The Glen, Camps Bay)*
Map 12, #3 Dorm beds R40 for HI members, R45 for nonmembers. This place has
only dorms; they are in the one-time stables
of the Round House hunting lodge, which is
a National Monument. At the time of research there was a question mark hanging

over its future; its closure would be a great
shame since it's in a serene location, surrounded by trees, with sea views to die for.
Unless you have transport there's a steep
15-minute walk to the nearest shops and
restaurants in Camps Bay, but it's still worth
considering as a place to kick back. If you're
coming by public transport, the easiest way
is to take a shared taxi to the top of Kloof
Nek, then walk down Kloof Rd towards
Camps Bay.

Observatory & Pinelands These suburbs, favourites with students at the nearby
university, are a long way from the city centre and the Waterfront – by Cape Town standards, anyway. That said, the area is only a
few minutes from the city by car or train,
and has good nightlife and places to eat.

Green Elephant (☎ *448 6359, fax 448*
0510, e *greenelephant@iafrica.com, 57*
Milton Rd) **Map 17, #4** Dorm beds R55,
singles/doubles/triples B&B R150/180/195.
In the heart of this student neighbourhood,
and split over two houses, the Green Elephant is spacious and generally quiet, with a
tree-climbing dog for entertainment. A simple
breakfast is included in the rates.

@Lighthouse Farm Lodge (☎/fax *447*
9177, e *msm@mweb.co.za, Violet Bldg,*
Oude Molen Village, Alexandria Rd, Mow-
bray) **Map 11, #4** Camping R15 per person,
dorm beds R30, doubles R110. An old hospital set in spacious grounds has been
turned into one of the city's more original
and most relaxing locations for a hostel.
This is the nicer of the two hostels on the
grounds. There's also horse riding (R40 per
hour), with a trail running up to the Rhodes
Memorial, an organic permaculture farm,
and the *Sunshine Cafe*, which has live jazz
on Friday and Saturday nights. A dubious-
sounding African village is planned, as are
a pool and a vegetarian restaurant. It's best
if you have your own transport, but otherwise it's within walking distance of
Pinelands train station, and there's good
security around the complex.

False Bay *Abe Bailey Youth Hostel* (☎/fax
788 2301, 11 Maynard Rd, Muizenberg)

Map 3, #2 Dorm beds R45, doubles R100. It's pretty basic, but a friendly reception and a short walk to the beach, plus proximity to Valsbaai train station, make this a reasonable choice if you're looking for a quiet, cheap place away from the hustle of downtown Cape Town.

Seaforth Beach Bungalows (☎ 786 1463, 082 848 6106, Queens Rd, Simon's Town) Map 4, #13 Dorm beds R50, doubles R150. This is the closest budget accommodation to Boulders Beach, just a three-minute walk from those famous penguins. Self-catering units are also available.

Guesthouses

St Paul's B&B Guest House (☎ 423 4429, fax 423 1580, 182 Bree St) Map 13, #72 Singles/doubles with shared bathroom B&B R120/200. One of the best budget places, with neat rooms and a quiet courtyard – and Long St is a trice away.

Travellers Inn (☎ 424 9272, fax 424 9278, 208 Long St) Map 13, #68 Singles/doubles B&B from R90/120. In one of the old wrought-iron decorated buildings, this inn has character, but the front rooms can suffer from street noise. Breakfast is a make-it-yourself affair.

Conifer Lodge (☎ 465 6052, fax 465 6051, 6 Scott St, Gardens) Map 15, #44 Doubles B&B from R170-200. Nice if small rooms, in a good location within walking distance of the Company's Gardens.

Ambleside Guesthouse (☎ 465 2503, fax 465 3814, 11 Forest Rd, Oranjezicht) Map 15, #52 Singles/doubles B&B from R150/240. Ambleside is not as flash as some of its neighbours, but it has a kitchen for self-catering and pleasant, clean rooms. The owner offers guided walks on the mountain for around R150.

Hotels

Hotel Formule 1 (☎ 418 4664, Ⓦ www.hotelformule1.co.za, Between Jan Smuts St & Hammerschlag Way, Foreshore) Map 13, #108 Singles/doubles/triples all R165. Clean but soulless budget chain hotel, in a tricky-to-find location immediately east of the Artscape complex.

Check Inn (☎ 439 4444, 155 Main Rd, Green Point) Map 14, #6 Singles/doubles/triples R170. This budget hotel in the Formule 1 mode offers air-con rooms, a double bed with a single bunk bed above, and a private shower. Its location, midway between Green Point and Sea Point, is in its favour.

PLACES TO STAY – MID-RANGE
B&Bs & Guesthouses

There are many mid-range B&Bs and guesthouses – the following is just a small sample. For more options, see the special section 'Gay & Lesbian Cape Town'.

Gardens & Oranjezicht *Belmont House* (☎ 461 5417, fax 461 6642, Ⓔ capeguest@mweb.co.za, 10 Belmont Ave, Oranjezicht) Map 15, #49 Doubles B&B from R130. In a residential area, the rooms in this smart guesthouse are small, but nicely decorated. There is a kitchen for guests' use.

Underberg Guesthouse (☎ 426 2262, fax 424 4059, Ⓦ www.underbergguesthouse.co.za, Cnr Carstens St & Tamboerskloof Rd) Map 15, #1 Singles/doubles B&B from R230/350. This completely unmissable pink Victorian mansion is a bit twee but very well run.

Waterkant & Green Point *The Lodge* (☎/fax 421 1106, 49 Napier St, Waterkant) Map 14, #67 Doubles B&B from R200. A bargain given how ritzy this area has become, this is a great guesthouse run by a friendly British guy, and it's very handy for clubbing in the gay district.

Dungarvin House (☎/fax 434 0677, Ⓔ kom@mweb.co.za, 163 Main Rd, Green Point) Map 14, #5 Singles/doubles B&B from R160/220 to R330/480 in high season. An elegant and child-friendly B&B in a restored Victorian mansion.

Sea Point *Ashby Manor Guesthouse* (☎ 434 1879, fax 439 3572, 242 High Level Rd) Map 16, #35 Singles/doubles from R170/200. This rambling old Victorian house is on the slopes of Signal Hill above Sea Point. All rooms have a fridge and hand basin and there's a kitchen.

Villa Rosa (☎ 434 2768, fax 434 3526, W www.villa-rosa.com, 277 High Level Rd) **Map 16, #24** Singles/doubles from R215/310. Tastefully decorated rooms with huge bathrooms, some with fireplaces, in a nice old house.

Olaf's Guest House, (☎ 439 8943, 24 Wisbeach Rd) **Map 16, #15** Singles/doubles B&B R460/610. This gorgeous place has eight individually decorated rooms and a plunge pool in the front garden. German is spoken here.

Kalk Bay *Charterfield Guest House* (☎ 788 3793, fax 788 8674, e info@chartfield .co.za, 30 Gateseville Rd) **Map 3, #15** Doubles B&B from R160. Good-value place with sweeping views of False Bay; handy for Kalk Bay train station and shops.

Castle Hill (☎ 788 2554, fax 788 3843, e theinn@mweb.co.za, 37 Gatesville Rd) **Map 3, #11** Singles/doubles B&B from R230/350. Some of the charming rooms in this renovated Edwardian home overlook the bay and all are decorated with works by local artists.

Simon's Town *Boulders Beach Guesthouse* (☎ 786 1758, fax 786 1825, e boulders@ iafrica.com, 4 Boulders Place, Boulders Beach) **Map 4, #15** Singles/doubles B&B from R270/450, self-catering units R650. Close by the penguin colony, this smart guesthouse also has a range of good-sized self-catering units and a pleasant cafe with an outdoor deck.

Bosky Dell (☎ 786 3906, fax 786 1830, e bosky@new.co.za, 5 Grant Ave, Boulders Beach) **Map 4, #14** B&B from R200 per person. Bosky Dell offers pretty whitewashed cottages with lovely beach views.

Khayelitsha (Map 11) Of the four B&Bs listed here, only Vicky's is in an original shack; the other three are in brick buildings in the more developed parts of the township.

Kopanong (☎/fax 361 2084, e kopanong @xsinet.co.za, Site C-329 Velani Crescent, Khayelitsha) Singles/doubles B&B R190/300. The most upmarket option, Kopanong is run by Thope Lekau, who's also a registered

guide and experienced development worker. Two stylishly decorated rooms, one with private bathroom, are available. A three-course dinner is R70.

Majoro's B&B (☎ 361 3412, fax 364 9660, mobile ☎ 072 170 6175, 69 Helena Crescent, Graceland, Khayelitsha) B&B R150 per person. Run by the friendly Maria Maile, this B&B in a quiet part of Khayelitsha has a homely feel. Dinner, available on request, costs R30 to R60 and there's safe parking should you choose to drive here.

Malebo's (☎ 361 2391, 083-475 1125, 18 Mississippi Way, Graceland, Khayelitsha) B&B R150 per person. Lydia Masoleng is the proprietor of this modern, spacious home with three rooms for guests. The welcome is warm and dinner is available for R50.

Vicky's (☎ 387 4422, W www.enkosi.com, Site C-685A, Khayelitsha) DB&B R150 per person. The dynamic Vicky Ntozini fully deserves all the rave reviews we've received about her. To call her delightful B&B (designed by her resourceful husband Piksteel) a shack would be a grave disservice, especially considering Vicky and Piksteel have probably by now added their dreamed-for second storey. Apart from Vicky's bountiful hospitality, there's the added bonus of Cape Town's other *Waterfront*, a long-running and lively shebeen, right across the road.

Hotels

Many mid-range hotels were built in the 1960s and show their age, but practically all are clean and perfectly good places to stay if you don't fancy a B&B or guesthouse.

City Bowl *Tudor Hotel* (☎ 424 1335, fax 423 1198, e tudorhotel@iafrica.com, Greenmarket Square) **Map 13, #41** Singles/doubles B&B from R195/295. Cosy little hotel with a central location. It could do with renovation but it's OK. Parking is available nearby (at a price).

Metropole Hotel (☎ 423 6363, fax 423 6370, 38 Long St) **Map 13, #21** Dorm beds R70, singles/doubles from R130/170. An attractive older-style hotel with a wood-panelled interior, an antique elevator and a few six-bed dorms. Prices are good given the degree of comfort offered, but the more expensive rooms have rather cheesy decor.

Parliament Hotel (☎ *461 6710, fax 461 6740,* e *reservations@parliamenthotel .co.za, 9 Barrack St)* **Map 13, #136** Singles/doubles B&B R220/280. One of the best inexpensive central hotels, with spotless rooms and a cafe.

The Townhouse, (☎ *465 7050, fax 465 3891,* e *hotel@townhouse.co.za, 60 Corporation St)* **Map 13, #135** Singles/doubles R369/562. Great service and high standards are on offer at this often-recommended four-star hotel. The rates rise only slightly in summer. Ask for a room with a view of the mountain.

Days Inn (☎ *422 0030, fax 422 0090,* e *ctydays@new.co.za, 101 Buitengracht St)* **Map 13, #27** Singles/doubles both R395. Not much cop from the outside, but inside the stylishly decorated rooms are fair value. Underground parking is available.

Gardens *Cape Gardens Lodge* (☎ *432 1260, fax 423 2088,* e *info@capegardens lodge.com, 88 Queen Victoria St)* **Map 15, #28** Singles/doubles/triples B&B from R270/360/450. This good mid-range hotel has a great location next to the Company's Gardens. The rooms with views of Table Mountain are more expensive.

iKhaya Guest Lodge (☎ *461 8880, fax 461 8889,* w *www.ikhayalodge.co.za, Dunkley Square)* **Map 15, #42** Singles/doubles B&B from R395/590, singles/doubles self-catering R630/840. You'll find bags of African style at this excellent option in the trendy media district. The luxurious lofts are worth checking out, especially for the views across to Lion's Head.

The Fritz Hotel (☎ *480 9000, fax 480 9090,* w *www.fritzhotel.co.za, 1 Faure St)* **Map 15, #19** Singles/doubles B&B R350/ 400. The rooms look as though they've been art-directed with their tasteful mix of Art-Deco, 1950s and modern furnishings. No wonder it's a favourite with media types doing business in the area.

Waterfront & Green Point *City Lodge* (☎ *419 9450, fax 419 0460,* e *clva.resv@*

citylodge.co.za, Cnr Dock Rd & Alfred St) **Map 14, #61** Singles/doubles R398/560, Fri-Sun rate for doubles R398. A chain hotel offering one of the area's better deals.

Victoria Junction (☎ *419 8800, fax 419 8200,* e *vicjunct@icon.co.za, Cnr Somerset St & Ebenezer Rd, Green Point)* **Map 14, #58** Singles/doubles R450/550. Arty loft-style boutique hotel that's part of the Protea chain. It's popular, so book ahead.

Breakwater Lodge (☎ *406 1911, fax 406 1070,* e *brkwater@fortesking-hotel.co.za, Portswood Rd, Waterfront)* **Map 14, #22** Singles/doubles from R210/250. Professional operation in a restored jail right next to the Waterfront. The rooms aren't bad but the cheapest ones are small and have a shower rather than a bath.

Claridges B&B Hotel (☎ *434 1171, fax 434 6650,* e *cheerin@new.co.za, 47 Main Rd, Green Point)* **Map 14, #14** Singles/doubles B&B R130/200. Great location for this old-fashioned but quite acceptable hotel, which is cheaper for long stays. The staff are friendly, there's a small pool, the rooms have TVs and big bathrooms (but no phones) and there's a huge buffet breakfast.

Atlantic Coast *Winchester Mansions Hotel* (☎ *434 2351, fax 434 0215,* w *www .winchester.co.za, 221 Beach Rd, Sea Point)* **Map 16, #14** Singles/doubles from R490/ 630 low season, R710/925 high season. Cape Dutch–style beauty on the seafront. You'll pay more for the sea views, but the courtyard with a fountain is lovely too. Sunday brunch with live jazz is held from 11am to 2pm for R85.

The Ritz (☎ *439 6010, fax 439 1848,* e *gkhotels@iafrica.com, Cnr Main & Camberwell Rds, Sea Point)* **Map 16, #5** Singles/doubles from R270. Tower block with a revolving restaurant on top. Most of the nicely decorated rooms have great views. Parking is R16 per day and there's a pool.

Lion's Head Lodge (☎ *434 4163,* w *www.lions-head-lodge.co.za, 319 Main Rd, Sea Point)* **Map 16, #18** Doubles from R280, 2-person flats from R310. The rates at this good budget hotel fall if you stay longer than one night. It has a reasonable-size pool and a bar, and does three-course Sunday lunches for R30.

Hout Bay Manor (☎ *790 0116, fax 790 0118,* [W] *www.houtbaymanor.co.za, Baviaanskloof Rd, Hout Bay)* **Map 2, #5** Singles/doubles from R395/590. The original building at this small luxury hotel dates from 1871 and has recently been renovated. The rooms are big and attractively furnished.

Monkey Valley Beach Nature Resort (☎ *789 1391, fax 789 1143, Mountain Rd, Noordhoek)* **Map 11, #26** Singles/doubles B&B from R270/540. An imaginatively designed small resort with rustic cabins shaded by a milkwood forest. It offers plenty of activities, but with Noordhoek's splendid beach moments away you might not need any other distraction.

Simon's Town *Lord Nelson Inn* (☎ *786 1386, fax 786 1009, 58 St George's St)* **Map 4, #3** Singles/doubles B&B from R240/310. Above a small, old-fashioned pub, this is a pleasant, refurbished place, with plain but smart rooms. Some overlook the sea (which is largely obscured by a shed in the naval dockyards) but suffer traffic noise.

Simon's Town Quayside Lodge (☎ *786 3838, fax 786 2241,* [e] *info@quayside.co.za, Off Jubilee Square, St George's St)* **Map 4, #9** Singles/doubles B&B from R450/615. The more expensive rooms here face the water, but all are quite pleasant and comfortable.

Self-Catering
For agencies that specialise in arranging fully furnished houses and flats, see Accommodation Agencies earlier in this chapter.

Gardens *Gardens Centre Holiday Flats* (☎ *461 8000, fax 461 5588, Mill St)* **Map 15, #45** 2-person apartments from R240. Modern, well-furnished single-bedroom flats above the Gardens Centre shopping mall. The views are good. Rates vary widely according to the season, but include free undercover parking.

Cape Mews Cottages (☎ *423 8190, fax 426 1795,* [e] *capeswiss@fortesking-hotels.co.za, Nicol St)* **Map 15, #6** Cottages from

R620. Stylish one- or two-bed cottages with small patios and BBQ areas, just around the corner from the trendy Kloof St bars.

Waterkant & Green Point *Harbour View Cottages* (☎ *422 2721, fax 426 5088,* [e] *reservations@hvc.co.za,* [W] *www.village andlife.com, Waterkant)* **Map 14, #70** Singles/doubles B&B from R290/380, 2-person flats from R550. The hotel has a plunge pool and all rooms have glossy-magazine-style furnishings. If you want breakfast, it's taken at the nearby Village Cafe.

Fawlty Towers (☎ *439 7671, fax 1075, Upper Portswood Rd, Green Point)* **Map 14, #15** Dorm beds R50, 2-bed flats R400/600 in low/high season. The budget flats here sleep four or seven people. Nothing fancy, but they're in a convenient location with a small pool and braai area.

Atlantic Coast *The Place on the Bay* (☎ *438 7060, fax 438 2504,* [W] *www.theplaceonthebay .co.za, Cnr Fairways & Victoria Rds, Camps Bay)* **Map 12, #6** Singles/doubles from R330/550. These are smart, modern self-catering flats but the rates can soar in peak season. The same management runs the nearby *Fairways* **(Map 12, #7)**, a classy hotel in the Victorian mould, where singles/doubles cost from R195/385.

Flora Bay Resort (☎*/fax 790 1650, Chapman's Peak Dr, Hout Bay)* **Map 2, #7** 2-person flats from R300. There are 27 different self-catering units, all sea-facing, at this complex, which has its own beach.

Simon's Town *British Hotel* (☎*/fax 786 2214,* [e] *british-hotel@iafrica.com, 90 St George's St)* **Map 4, #4** Flats for 2/3/4 people from R200/450/500. Huge rooms and amazingly spacious bathrooms are on offer at these grand self-catering apartments, which are set around a lovely courtyard.

Central Hotel (☎*/fax 786 3775,* [e] *centralhotel@intekom.co.za, 96 St George's St)* **Map 4, #6** Singles/doubles R175/250. B&B is available at this characterful renovated hotel, although all the six top-notch flats are self-catering. It has a three-bed cottage nearby for rent too.

PLACES TO STAY – TOP END
Guesthouses

De Waterkant Lodge & Cottages (℡/*fax 419 1097, 20 Loader St*) **Map 14, #69** B&B from R700 per person. Choose either the beautifully restored lodge, discreetly located in the heart of the Waterkant, with its magnificent roof-top views, or one of the exemplary self-catering cottages, each individually decorated with top-quality art and antiques.

Villa Belmonte (℡ *462 1576, fax 462 1579,* W *www.villabelmontehotel.co.za, 33 Belmont Ave, Oranjezicht*) **Map 15, #50** Singles/doubles B&B R670/890. Ornate and luxurious Italianate villa with huge pool and excellent facilities.

Table Mountain Lodge (℡ *423 0042, fax 423 4983,* W *www.tablemountainlodge .co.za, 10a Tamboerskloof Rd, Tamboerskloof*) **Map 15, #3** Singles/doubles B&B from R435/540. Classy place with a tiny pool and a Scottish-theme bar.

Leeuwenvoet House (℡ *424 1133, fax 424 0495,* W *www.leeuwenvoet.co.za, 93 New Church St, Gardens*) **Map 15, #4** Singles/doubles B&B from R285/330. Pronounced Loo-en-foot, this is one of the most stylish of the area's upmarket B&Bs and has luxuriously decorated rooms.

Montague House (℡ *424 7337, fax 426 0423,* e *montague@mweb.co.za, 18 Leeuwenhof Rd, Higgovale*) **Map 12, #2** Singles/doubles B&B from R650/850. The plays of Shakespeare inspired the design of the rooms at this delightful and luxurious guesthouse. It offers great views, a good pool and king-size four-poster beds.

Hotels

City Bowl *Cape Heritage Hotel* (℡ *424 4646, fax 424 4949,* W *www.capeheritage .co.za, 90 Bree St*) **Map 13, #13** Singles/doubles from R570/780. This delightful five-star boutique hotel is part of the Heritage Square redevelopment. Each room is individually decorated in elegant style. A favourite with politicians when they visit town.

Cape Sun Hotel (℡ *488 5100, fax 423 8875,* W *www.interconti.com, Strand St*) **Map 13, #116** Doubles from R1265. The rooms are nicely furnished, but this shiny multistorey hotel with a swimming pool, a fitness centre and several restaurants is now beginning to look oh-so-'80s.

The Cullinan (℡ *418 6920, fax 418 3559,* e *intmktg@southernsun.com, 1 Cullinan St*) **Map 14, #78** Singles/doubles R555/800. A reasonable deal, if you can stand the Greek-temple-on-steroids architecture. The rooms are less OTT and the views impressive.

Gardens *Mount Nelson Hotel* (℡ *483 1000, fax 423 1060,* W *www.mountnelson hotel.orient-express.com, 76 Orange St*) **Map 15, #15** Doubles from R2640. Surrounded by seven acres of grounds and dating from 1899, the 'Nellie' feels like the last bastion of the British Empire. The rooms are on the chintzy side but full of character. Even if you don't stay, drop by for afternoon tea or a meal (see Gardens in the Places to Eat chapter).

Waterfront *The Cape Grace* (℡ *410 7100, 419 7622,* W *www.capegrace.com, West Quay*) **Map 14, #56** Doubles B&B from R1990. More like an exclusive yet amiable club than a hotel. There's understated luxury in most rooms (go for the ones facing Table Mountain), and kids under 12 get to stay for free.

Victoria & Alfred Hotel (℡ *419 6677, fax 419 8955,* e *res@v-and-a.co.za*) **Map 14, #53** Singles/doubles from R925/R1440. Smart place with the cheaper rooms facing the Waterfront rather than towards the mountain. Guests can use the facilities of the nearby Virgin Active gym in Green Point.

The Table Bay (℡ *406 5000, fax 406 5767, Quay 6*) **Map 14, #33** Doubles from R1500. The biggest of the Waterfront's upmarket hotels, with 329 smartly decorated rooms, including ones for the disabled. The facilities include a business centre, a gym, a decent-size pool, and a glitzy lobby.

Portswood Square Hotel (℡ *418 3281, fax 419 7570,* W *www.legacyhotels.co.za, Portswood Rd*) **Map 14, #43** Singles/doubles R915/1160. On the Green Point side of the Waterfront, this is the slightly cheaper sibling of *The Commodore* next door. Like its neighbour it has a pleasing nautical theme, and guests are welcome to use all the facilities of both hotels.

Atlantic Coast *The Bay Hotel (☎ 438 4444, fax 438 4455, Victoria Rd, Camps Bay)* **Map 12, #8** Singles/doubles from R670/920 in low season, minimum R1410 in high season. This hang-out for the well-heeled is just a stone's toss from the beach. The sea-view rooms, which are all very comfy, naturally attract a premium price.

Protea Hotel President (☎ 434 8111, fax 434 9991, e sales@president.co.za, Alexander Rd, Bantry Bay) **Map 16, #34** Doubles B&B from R805. Fine hotel with brightly decorated rooms, and lovely sea views from the pool and the dining area.

Ellerman House (☎ 439 9182, 434 7257, W www.ellerman.co.za, 180 Kloof Rd, Bantry Bay) **Map 16, #38** Doubles B&B from R2400. Unsurpassed luxury at this ultraexclusive landmark overlooking the Atlantic. Rates include airport transfers, breakfast, laundry, all drinks (save vintage wine and champagne) and secretarial services.

Southern Suburbs *Vineyard Hotel (☎ 683 3044, fax 683 3365, W www.vineyard.co.za, Colinston Rd, Newlands)* **Map 11, #11** Singles/doubles from R595/835. Excellent value for what you get, and handy for both Kirstenbosch Botanical Gardens and the cricket. It's worth visiting for tea in the lounge and a stroll in the lovely gardens.

*Constantia Uitsig (☎ 794 6500, fax 794 7605, W www.constantiauitsig.co.za, Spaan-*schemat River Rd, Constantia)* **Map 11, #21** Singles/doubles from R920/1320. A suitably exclusive and salubrious hotel with two top-notch restaurants to choose from.

Alphen (☎ 794 5011, fax 794 5710, W www.alphen.co.za, Peter Cloete Ave, Hohenhot) **Map 11, #16** Singles/doubles B&B from R720/940. The Alphen is a National Monument Cape Dutch manor, shaded by old oak trees. There's a swimming pool, a restaurant and a bar, and prices are reasonable. The area has quite a few cycling routes.

LONG-TERM RENTALS

Blencathra (☎ 424 9571, e cwykeham @mweb.co.za, Cnr De Hoop & Cambridge Aves, Tamboerskloof) **Map 12, #1** Dorm beds from R50, singles from R100. There are only a few rooms at this delightful family home, high on Tamboerskloof's slopes overlooking the City Bowl, but they're great ones and often booked up for months in advance.

The Lodge (☎/fax 448 6536, e thelodge @mweb.co.za, 36 Milton Rd, Observatory) **Map 17, #3** Dorm beds from R40, doubles from R90. There's a one-month minimum stay here; the lady who runs it has five houses in the area and the double rooms are all a good size and well maintained. The dorms have three or four beds.

Most hostels and some cheaper hotels, such as Claridges B&B Hotel in Green Point, will do deals with long-term guests. For other long-term rental options, contact the organisations listed under Accommodation Agencies near the beginning of this chapter.

PLACES TO STAY

Places to Eat

Cape Town has an impressive cosmopolitan dining scene. There's a wide variety of cuisines available, and the quality of the ingredients is high. You shouldn't miss the opportunity to sample some traditional Cape Malay food, and there are some good African restaurants, too.

The one disappointment, given Cape Town's history as the 'Tavern of the Seas', is a lack of adventurousness and a depressing similarity in many restaurants' menus. Still you'd be hard pressed to have a bad meal, and given the favourable exchange rate, it's a challenge to blow your budget, even at the fanciest of places.

Capetonians seem to have an insatiable appetite for new restaurants. One place may be the hit of the season, but dead a month later, patrons having moved on to the next hot spot. Intelligent operators keep up by closing shop every so often, having a make-over, then reopening under a new name, hopefully to renewed acclaim. So don't be surprised if some of the places listed here aren't there, or aren't quite what you expected.

This said, there are some honourable long troupers and reliable areas for finding a good feed. To browse the options head for Long St, Kloof St, the Waterfront and the Main Rd restaurant strips of Green Point and Sea Point, and to Lower Main Rd in Observatory. For meals with sea views, Camps Bay, Hout Bay, Kalk Bay and Simon's Town are the go. Heritage Square in the City Bowl is one of the current trendy spots, sporting no fewer than five fancy restaurants, as is the gay Waterkant gay district.

For options other than those listed in this chapter, see the special section 'Gay & Lesbian Cape Town', and Bars & Pubs in the Entertainment chapter. For details of restaurant guides, see Books in the Facts for the Visitor chapter.

FOOD

Apart from the home-grown dishes of Cape Malay and Afrikaner cuisine, you'll find a world of cooking here, from Turkish and Middle Eastern to Chinese, Japanese and Indian. Some of the Italian restaurants, in particular, are excellent, and there's also

---

Cape Malay Cuisine

Although some will undoubtedly find it overly stodgy and sweet, the unique Cape Malay cuisine (along with its close cousin Afrikaner cuisine) is well worth trying. This intriguing mix of Malay and Dutch styles originated in the earliest days of European settlement and marries pungent spices with local produce.

The Cape Malay dish you'll come across most often is bobotie, a kind of shepherd's pie made with lightly curried mince topped with savoury egg custard, and usually served on a bed of turmeric-flavoured rice with a side dab of chutney. There is a variety of bredies (pot stews of meat or fish, and vegetables); one unusual example is *waterblommetjie bredie*, a mutton dish with faintly peppery water-hyacinth flowers and white wine. Plenty of recipes make use of game; some include venison, which will be some type of buck.

For dessert there are *malva* pudding, a delicious sponge traditionally made with apricot jam and vinegar, and the very similar brandy pudding (note that true Cape Malay cuisine – which is strongly associated with the Muslim community – contains no alcohol).

Among the places to sample this type of food are Biesmiellah and the Noon Gun Tearoom & Restaurant in Bo-Kaap, and Jonkerhuis at Groot Constantia (not to be confused with the Jonkershuis Restaurant at the Spier wine estate near Stellenbosch, which offers a fine Cape Malay buffet).

a mouth-watering range of delis, often with attached cafes.

As you'd expect in a city by the water, seafood is plentiful. In many places you'll see 'line fish' advertised – this means the catch of the day. Meaty local fish such as kingklip and snoek are often served; search out the freshest specimens at the Waterfront, Kalk Bay (which has a marvellous fish market) and Hout Bay.

Restaurants serving African dishes, most of which don't originate in South Africa, are becoming more popular – try a meal at the exceptional Africa Café or the lively Mama Africa, both in the City Bowl. For a slightly less touristy experience, head out to one of the growing number of places serving food in the Cape Flats. You'll find here that the staple for most blacks is rice or mealie (maize) meal, often served with a fatty stew. It isn't especially appetising, but it's cheap. The same goes for the sheep's heads, or *smilies*, that you'll see being boiled up and served on the streets.

Traditional Afrikaner cuisine shows its Voortrekker heritage in foods such as biltong (the deliciously moreish dried meat) and rusks, perfect for those long journeys into the hinterland. Boerewors (farmers' sausage) is the traditional sausage, and must be 90% meat, of which 30% can be fat.

Fast-food lovers will not be disappointed. Among the local chains are Steers for burgers, and Spur for steaks and a salad bar. The internationally known Nandos, which purveys spicy Portuguese-style chicken, is one of the tastier fast-food options.

Prices are remarkably consistent. For lunch, between R20 and R30 is typical, while for dinner, R60 for a main dish is the upper limit in all but a handful of places, with R40 being the norm.

DRINKS

It's OK to drink the tap water. There are plenty of good local fruit juices, and international soft-drink brands are sold everywhere. Note that cans of fizzy drink are called cool drinks.

Draught beers are served in large (500mL) or small (250mL) glasses. Usually you will be sold lager-style beer in cans or *dumpies* (small bottles) for around R8. Black Label and Castle are popular brands but Amstel and Carlsberg are also good. Look out for Mitchell's and Birkenhead's beers, which come from a couple of small breweries. Windhoek beer, brewed in Namibia, is made with strictly natural ingredients. The alcohol content of beer is around 5%, stronger than UK or US beer. Even Castle Lite has 4% alcohol.

Most restaurants are licensed but some allow you to bring your own wine for little or no corkage charge. Call ahead to check the restaurant's policy. Many have long wine lists and stock a few varieties in 250mL bottles, handy if you want to try a few wines or are eating alone. A few low-alcohol wines are available, and they aren't bad. For more information on wine, see the special section 'Cape Wineries'.

CITY BOWL
Self-Catering
Atlas Trading Company (☎ 423 4361, 94 Wale St, Bo-Kaap) **Map 13, #18** Open 8am-5.15pm Mon-Thur, 8am-12.15pm & 2pm-5.15pm Fri, 8.30am-1pm Sat. Atlas provides the Cape Muslim community with over 100 different herbs and spices. It's a wonderfully atmospheric place and the proprietors will happily share some local recipes with you.

Wellington Fruit Growers (☎ 461 7160, 96 Darling St) **Map 13, #132** Open 8am-5pm Mon-Fri, 8am-1pm Sat. A Cape Town institution, this long, narrow shop sells a huge range of nuts, dried and glacé fruit, deli items, tinned foods and *lots* of lollies (sweets or candy).

Morris's **(Map 13, #82)** *(265 Long St)*, which has been in business since 1959, is one of the best places for biltong and boerewors.

Cafes & Snack Bars
You'll have no problem finding takeaway food or a cheap cafe in the city centre on weekdays during business hours, but this is generally not the best area to be wandering around late at night or at the weekend (particularly on Sunday), when it's practically deserted.

Great Picnic Spots

If ever a city was made for picnics it's Cape Town. Pre-prepared picnics can be enjoyed at the Boschendal, Spier and Vergelegen wine estates (see the special section 'Cape Wineries'), but you must book in advance. Otherwise, for provisions, check the large and cheap *Pick 'n' Pay* supermarkets first – you'll find branches at the Waterfront, Gardens Centre, Sea Point and Camp's Bay. They're all open daily. Some branches of *Woolworths*, South Africa's version of the UK's Marks & Spencer, also sell a good but pricey range of high-quality foods. You'll find them again at the Waterfront, on Adderley St in the City Bowl and at the Cavendish Square shopping centre in Claremont.

For specialist products check out the excellent delis, such as Gionvanni's Deli World in Green Point, Melissa's in Gardens, Atlas Trading Company in the Bo-Kaap district, and Wellington Fruit Growers in the City Bowl (see the reviews for details).

So fill up your basket and head to one of these choice spots:

Clifton
Take your pick from beaches one to four and arrive close to sunset. Remember to bring candles for the ultimate romantic experience.

Lion's Head
Another sunset spectacular. Hike up this hill with your picnic on a full-moon night to enjoy the spectacular view by moonlight.

Kirstenbosch Botanical Gardens
A Sunday afternoon institution, particularly during the summer months when you can enjoy a concert on those verdant rolling lawns.

Buitenverwachting
The Constantia estate on which to enjoy a prepacked picnic (R60). Book on ☎ 794 1012.

Tokai Forest
Tranquil and soulful, this shady forest is close by the arboretum, which has a good cafe, and is handy for walks up the mountain.

Bloubergstrand
Enjoy the postcard-perfect views of Table Mountain from this northern beach strip.

There are several cafes around Greenmarket Square that are great for people-watching. Check out *Le Petit Paris* **(Map 13, #37)** *(36 Shortmarket St)* or *Cycles* **(Map 13, #34)** on the terrace outside the Holiday Inn Greenmarket Square, which are good for a beer. The *Ivy Garden Restaurant* (see Restaurants following) serves snacks and drinks in front of the Old Town House.

Cafe Mozart *(☎ 424 3774, 37 Church St)* **Map 13, #43** Open 7am-3pm Mon-Fri, 8am-1pm Sat. This deservedly popular cafe has tables spilling out onto the street and fine bistro-style food.

Gardens Restaurant *(☎ 423 2919, Company's Gardens)* **Map 13, #92** Mains around R30. Open 8am-5pm daily. Licensed and with a large menu, this cafe and restaurant, with outdoor tables shaded by the trees, does everything from breakfast (R20 to R27) to bobotie (a traditional Cape Malay dish with curried mince, egg custard and rice).

Off Moroka Cafe Africaine *(☎ 422 1129, 120 Adderley St)* **Map 13, #47** Breakfast from R14, lunch R25-30. Open 6.30am-9pm Mon-Thur, 6.30am-midnight Fri, 8.30am-midnight Sat. Pleasant and gay-friendly place to sample some fairly genuine African food and listen to tapes of African music. It's decorated with the work (for sale) of local artists.

D6 Snack Bar *(☎ 082 970 7217, 104-106 Darling St)* **Map 13, #140** Mains R20. Open 10am-9pm Mon-Fri, noon-9pm Sat. This small cafe, bar and takeaway is on the fringes of the old District Six. It does a Friday-night special of Afrikaner food for R20 including a free beer.

Long St has a plethora of options. One of the cheapest sit-down lunch-time feeds (around R16) can be had at the *Pan African Kitchen* **(Map 13, #32)** in the Pan African Market (for details see the Shopping chapter), where the balcony cafe provides a bird's-eye view of the passing parade. Also check out the following Long St places.

Shambala *(☎ 426 5452, 134 Long St)* **Map 13, #51** Mains R25. Open 9am-9pm Mon-Fri, 9am-4pm Sat. Blissed-out holistic cafe and shop serving a mean range of smoothies and delicious vegetarian food.

Sooz Baguette Bar (☎ 423 3246, 150 Long St) **Map 13, #57** Sandwiches from R15. Open 7.30am-4.30pm Mon-Fri. Make up your own sandwich from the range of ingredients or go for one of the hotpots.

Mr Pickwick's (☎ 424 2696, 158 Long St) **Map 13, #61** Mains around R20. Open 8am-1am Mon-Thur, 8am-4am Fri & Sat. This licensed, deli-style cafe stays open very late for good snacks and meals. Try the foot-long rolls. The place to recuperate after a night out clubbing.

Diablo Bar Tapas (☎ 426 5484, 224B Long St) **Map 13, #69** Mains from R10. Open 11am-midnight Mon-Sat, 5pm-11pm Sun. Offers a good range of reasonably authentic tapas and a relaxed atmosphere.

Lola's (☎ 423 0885, 228 Long St) **Map 13, #70** Open 8am-midnight daily. Funky vegetarian cafe serving interesting food, with street tables and a gay-friendly vibe.

Long St Cafe (☎ 424 2464, 255 Long St) **Map 13, #83** Mains around R30. Open 9.30am-1am Mon-Sat, 5pm-1am Sun. A spacious, appealing cafe and bar with big windows to catch all the street action.

Restaurants

Bukhara (☎ 424 0000, 33 Church St) **Map 13, #45** Mains around R40. Open noon-3pm Mon-Sat, 6.30pm-11pm daily. This Indian restaurant is everyone's favourite. Spicy, tasty food in a stylish setting.

Primi Piatti (☎ 424 7466, 52 Shortmarket St) **Map 13, #36** Mains R35. Open 7am-11pm daily. Hyperactive modern Italian cafe serving up yummy pizzas and enormous salads. It has branches at the Waterfront and on Victoria Rd, Camps Bay.

Ivy Garden Restaurant (☎ 423 2360, Old Town House, Greenmarket Square) **Map 13, #40** Mains R40. Open 10am-5pm Mon-Fri, 10am-4pm Sat. Delightful courtyard restaurant serving a range of snacks and full meals including a platter of four Cape specialities for R60. For something truly wicked, try the brandy pudding (R17).

Five Flies (☎ 424 4442, 14-16 Keerom St) **Map 13, #55** Two courses R77.50, three courses R95.70. Open noon-3pm Mon-Fri, 7pm-11pm Mon-Sat. This atmospheric fine restaurant in the restored Dutch Club building (1752) offers inventive contemporary cooking.

Biesmiellah (☎ 423 0850, Wale St) **Map 13, #16** Mains R40. Open noon-11pm Mon-Sat. The authentic Cape Malay and Indian food at this Bo-Kaap institution is all halal and no alcohol is served.

Noon Gun Tearoom & Restaurant (☎ 424 0529, 273 Longmarket St, Signal Hill) **Map 14, #20** Mains R45. Open 10am-10pm Mon-Sat. After witnessing the noon blast of the cannon, slip into this pretty restaurant with a great view. It serves Cape Malay dishes such as bobotie and can get busy with tour groups.

Murco's African Place (☎ 423 5412, 15 Rose Lane, Bo-Kaap) **Map 13, #2** Mains R40. Open noon-late daily. Marco's serves a range of dishes from around the continent, including local specialities such as samp (maize) and beans. It also has live music.

Africa Café (☎ 422 0221, 108 Shortmarket St) **Map 13, #15** Meals R95. Open 6.30pm-11pm Mon-Sat. Our favourite of the Heritage Square restaurants. Fantastic decor and the best place in Cape Town to sample a range of African food. No fewer than 15 different dishes make up the pan-continental feast and you can have as much as you like of each.

Other good options on Heritage Square, both upmarket, are *Savoy Cabbage* (Map 13, #10) (☎ 423 2626) and *...and Lemon* (Map 13, #14) (☎ 423 4873).

Mesopotamia (☎ 424 4664, Cnr Long & Church Sts) **Map 13, #42** Mains R40-50. Open 7pm-11pm Mon-Sat. Kurdish restaurant dabbling in all things Ottoman, with kilims on the walls, and floor cushions around low copper salver tables. Serves excellent meze and has belly dancing Friday and Saturday from around 9pm.

Mama Africa (☎ 426 1017, 178 Long St) **Map 13, #62** Mains R40-60. The buzzing atmosphere here, fuelled by the swinging African bands playing nightly, outpaces the variable food, which includes a tourist-pleasing range of game and African dishes. Bookings are essential at weekends unless you want to perch at the bar.

Mexican Kitchen (☎ *423 1541, 13 Bloem St*) **Map 13, #66** Buffet lunch R27.50, dinner R38.50. Open 10am-11pm daily. Offers authentic Mexican dishes and a relaxed vibe. The buffet is great value.

Kennedy's (☎ *424 1212, 251 Long St*) **Map 13, #84** Mains R60-70. Open noon-3pm Mon-Fri, 7pm-11pm Mon-Sat. This stylish restaurant, which has a hint of 1930s glamour, serves some interesting dishes using local produce such as springbok, ostrich and crocodile. There are a cigar lounge and bar and good live jazz music from around 9.30pm nightly.

Anapurna (☎ *418 9020, 1st floor, Seeff House, 42 Hans Strijdom Ave*) **Map 14, #77** Mains R40-60. Open 12.30pm-3pm & 6pm-10.30pm Sun-Fri, 6pm-10.30pm Sat. Excellent North Indian cuisine served in a handsome airy setting.

Col' Cacchio (☎ *419 4848, Seeff House, 42 Hans Strijdom Ave*) **Map 14, #77** Mains R35. Open noon-2.30pm & 6.30pm-11pm Mon-Fri, 6.30pm-11pm Sat & Sun. Poor service, but great pizza with a delicious range of toppings.

De Waterblommetjie (☎ *461 4895, Castle of Good Hope*) **Map 13, #128** Mains R50. Open 7pm-11pm Tues-Sun. This sophisticated restaurant in the old pump house beside the castle walls specialises in modern interpretations of Cape Malay dishes.

The Famous Butchers Grill (**Map 13, #27**) (☎ *422 0880, 101 Buitengracht St*) is a celebrated steak house at Days Inn.

GARDENS
Self-Catering
Fields Health Store (☎ *423 9587, 84 Kloof St*) **Map 15, #9** Open 8am-7pm Mon-Fri, Sat 9.30am-4pm. Long-established health-food store, with a vine-covered courtyard where you can grab a snack.

Cafes & Snack Bars
The ***Gardens Centre*** (**Map 15, #45**) has a good range of cafes for breakfast, lunch or a snack.

Mount Nelson Hotel (☎ *483 1000, fax 423 1060,* **W** *www.mountnelsonhotel.orient-express.com, 76 Orange St*) **Map 15, #15**

For sheer indulgence, the hotel serves a delicious afternoon tea (R65) from 2.30pm to 5.30pm daily.

Naked on Kloof (☎ *424 4748, 51 Kloof St*) **Map 15, #20** Mains R20. Open 9am-11pm daily. Breezy deli-cafe specialising in fab-tasting wraps (a variety of fillings rolled up in lavash bread) and freshly squeezed fruit juices. Fully deserves its rave reviews.

Cafe Bardeli (☎ *423 4444, Longkloof Studios, Darter St, Gardens*) **Map 15, #21** Mains R20-30. Open 9am-1am Mon-Sat. Cafe Bardeli is in the recycled Longkloof Studios building off Kloof St (near the corner of Rheede St). It's not quite as trendy as it once was, but still a reliable place to be seen with the beautiful people and eat decently too. Sunday night opening is planned and occasionally there's live music. The kitchen closes at midnight.

Melissa's (☎ *424 5540, 94 Kloof St*) **Map 15, #7** Buffet R55 per kilogram. Open 7.30am-8pm Mon-Fri, 8am-8pm Sat & Sun. Getting a seat at this super-popular deli can be tricky, so perhaps plan a takeaway. It's a serve-yourself buffet with price worked out on weight. (There's another branch on the corner of Kildare and Main Rds in Newlands.)

Restaurants
Maria's (☎ *461 8887, 31 Barnet St*) **Map 15, #43** Mains R40. Open 11.30am-11pm Mon-Fri, 5.30pm-11pm Sat & Sun. Small friendly taverna facing Dunkley Square, offering a decent range of Greek dishes.

Café Riteve (☎ *465 1594, 88 Hatfield St*) **Map 15, #40** Mains R25. Open 9.30am-5pm Mon-Wed, 9.30am-10pm Thur & Sun, 9.30am-3pm Fri. Everything from bagels to crumbed hake is on offer at this contemporary bistro in the grounds of the South African Jewish Museum. All the food is kosher, and the cafe hosts regular live music, plays and comedy shows in the evenings (from R55 for meal and show).

Nelson's Eye (☎ *423 2601, 9 Hof St*) **Map 15, #14** Mains around R80. Open 11.30am-2pm Mon-Fri, 6.30pm-10.30pm daily. This darkly atmospheric steak house, serving prime meat with some delicious sauces, may not be the cheapest but it's among the best.

Rozenhof *(☎ 424 1968, 18 Kloof St)* **Map 15, #23** Mains R50. One of the area's longest-running restaurants. Dishes such as cheese souffle and crispy roast duck have become legendary.

Heading uphill, the seafood chain restaurant ***Ocean Basket*** **(Map 15, #18)** *(☎ 422 0322, Kloof St)* and the pizzeria ***Peasants*** **(Map 15, #7)** *(☎ 424 3445, 96 Kloof St)* are reliable and inexpensive.

The Happy Wok *(☎ 424 2423, 62A Kloof St)* **Map 15, #5** Mains R30. Open 5.30pm-10.30pm daily. Come here for cheap pan-Asian food. If it's made in a wok (and sometimes if it isn't, as with the Japanese dishes), then you can get it here.

Cafe Dharma *(☎ 422 0909, 68 Kloof St)* **Map 15, #8** Mains R60. Open 7pm-1.30am Mon-Sat. The Café del Mar set comes to Cape Town at this so-stylish-it-hurts restaurant and DJ bar. The food, by the way, is fusion.

Cafe Paradiso *(☎ 423 8653, 110 Kloof St)* **Map 15, #12** Mains R30-40. Open 10am-midnight Mon-Fri, 9am-midnight Sat & Sun. Fashionable but informal up market cafe, serving the standard range of Mediterranean-inspired dishes. The outdoor tables are a nice place to sip a drink and watch Kloof St go by.

WATERFRONT

Despite its convenience and lively atmosphere – especially on balmy nights – the Waterfront's restaurants and cafes fare poorly in comparison with their more interesting, and generally lower priced, brethren in town. This is just as you'd expect for what is in essence a giant tourist trap.

This said, with scores of options catering to all budgets, there are some decent places here. The Waterfront's information kiosk **(Map 14, #29)** and visitor centre **(Map 14, #45)** have a sizable booklet listing them all. As well as the franchises, such as ***St Elmo's*** (pizza and pasta), ***Spur*** (mainly steaks) and the ubiquitous ***Hard Rock Cafe***, there are some local spin-offs too, including ***Caffé San Marco*** **(Map 14, #35)** *(☎ 418 5434,*

Victoria Wharf) and the Greek takeaway ***Ari's Souvlaki*** **(Map 14, #35)** *(☎ 418 5544, Victoria Wharf)*, both siblings of the Sea Point institutions.

For drinks and snacks, other favourite cafes are ***Mugg & Bean*** **(Map 14, #31)** *(☎ 419 6451)* and ***Zerban's*** *(☎ 425 3431)*, both on the ground floor of the Victoria Wharf mall. For cheap fish and chips, head to the takeaway ***Fisherman's Choice*** **(Map 14, #38)** facing Quay Four; there are tables here but everyone has to queue to be served.

Den Anker *(☎ 419 0249, Pierhead)* **Map 14, #50** Mains R45-65. Open 11am-11pm daily. Charming setting and a great range of authentic Belgian beers with which to wash down a menu heavy on mussels and other seafood.

Musselcracker Restaurant *(☎ 419 4300, Upper level, Victoria Wharf)* **Map 14, #35** Open 12.30pm-2.30pm & 6.30pm-11pm daily. Buffet lunch R75, dinner R95. This blow-out seafood buffet packs them in nightly. Booking advised.

Quay 4 *(☎ 419 2000, Quay Four, Pierhead)* **Map 14, #39** Mains R30-40. Open noon-10.30pm daily, closed for lunch Sat. Right by the water, this pricey seafood brasserie is unbelievably popular, which means you could wait a while for your food.

Quay West *(☎ 418 0520, The Cape Grace, West Quay)* **Map 14, #56** Mains R60-70. Can't afford to stay at one of Cape Town's most exclusive hotels? So come for its buffet breakfast (R69) or for a dinner of delights such as Cape Malay crayfish.

For other Waterfront dining options see Ferryman's Freehouse and The Sports Cafe under Bars & Pubs, and Green Dolphin under Live Music, all in the Entertainment chapter.

WATERKANT & GREEN POINT

While the main restaurant strips of Waterkant and Green Point are safe, the stretch of Main Rd linking them is where prostitutes ply their trade; you might feel more comfortable catching a cab or shared taxi for the short distance between the two areas.

Anatoli *(☎ 419 2501, 24 Napier St)* **Map 14, #63** Cold/hot meze from R10.50/12.50. Open Tues-Sun. Anatoli has been here for years and with good reason: The delicious meze brought round on enormous wooden trays make a great meal.

Vasco da Gama Tavern (☎ 425 2157, 3 Alfred St) **Map 14, #62** Mains R25. Open 11.30am-8pm (last food order) Mon-Sat. Munch on excellent seafood, including Mozambique prawns and Portuguese sardines while old blokes argue the toss at the other end of the laminated bar.

The Restaurant (☎ 419 2921, 51A Somerset St) **Map 14, #60** Mains R70-80. Open 6.30pm-10.30pm Mon-Sat. The modern South African cuisine is on the pricey side (especially if you indulge in the wine selections), but exceptionally tasty and well presented.

Beluga (☎ 418 2948, The Foundry, Prestwich St) **Map 14, #57** Mains R40-50. Open noon-3pm Mon-Sat, 6pm-11pm daily. Chic warehouse where the smart set dines. There's Beluga caviar on the menu at R400 a pop, but there are plenty of cheaper dishes and a pleasant cafe too.

Serendipity (☎ 433 0158, 47 Main Rd) **Map 14, #14** Mains R40-50. Open 6pm-10pm daily. It's moved out of Long St, but still scatters rose petals on the floor and dares to mix ingredients such as gorgonzola and lychees, or chocolate and rosemary. A romantic original.

0932 (☎ 439 6306, 79 Main Rd) **Map 14, #12** Mains R50. Open noon-11.30pm Mon-Thurs, noon-midnight Fri-Sat, noon-10.30pm Sun. The trendier of Cape Town's two Belgian-beer restaurants is a bit pretentious, but it's a cool place to hang out and the two-course deal for R50 from noon to 7pm isn't bad.

News Café (☎ 434 6196, 83 Main Rd) **Map 14, #11** Mains R20-40. Open 7.30am-2pm Mon-Fri, 9am-2am Sat & Sun. At the other end of the revamped Exhibition Building from 0932, this buzzy cafe-bar is a good spot for a substantial snack or a bistro-type meal.

Mario's (☎ 439 6644, 89 Main Rd) **Map 14, #10** Mains R30-40. Open noon-2.30pm Tues-Fri & Sun, 6.45pm-10.30pm Tues-Sun. Long-established Italian restaurant, where customer praise is scribbled all over

the walls and ceiling. Perfect pasta and an extensive list of daily specials.

Go Mama Go (☎ 439 4918, 105 Main Rd) **Map 14, #9** Mains R25-35. Open noon-3pm & 6.30pm-10pm Mon-Sat. Conveyor-belt sushi comes to Cape Town, with plates ranging from R10 to R20. Other Japanese dishes are available and it's all very postmodern. (There's another branch, *Mama Yama*, just off Greenmarket Square.)

Gionvanni's Deli World (☎ 434 6983, 103 Main Rd) **Map 14, #8** Open 8.30am-9pm daily. We'll stick our neck out and award this 'top deli' status – it's not as big as its rivals, but it's bursting with energy and flavoursome products. The staff will make up any sandwich you fancy from all their provisions. If you can't wait to eat, there's a small cafe.

Newport Market & Deli (☎ 439 1538, 47 Beach Rd, Mouille Point) **Map 14, #2** Mains R25. Open 8am-8pm daily. An appealing deli and cafe in a quiet spot overlooking Mouille Point's rocky beach. Good for a coffee, sandwich or salad.

Theo's (☎ 439 3494, 163 Beach Rd, Mouille Point) **Map 14, #3** Mains R50. Open noon-2.30pm Sun-Fri, 6pm-10.30pm daily. The meat is matured specially on the premises at this award-winning steakhouse. It also does good seafood, and it's not too expensive. (There's a branch on Victoria Rd in Camps Bay.)

SEA POINT

There are dozens of places to eat along Main and Regent Rds, between the suburb of Mouille Point and the Bantry Bay end of Sea Point.

Self-Catering

Joubert & Monty's Meat Boutique (**Map 16, #31**) *(53 Regent Rd, Sea Point)* is great for biltong and boerewors.

Cafes & Snack Bars

Reise's Deli (☎ 434 3465, 267 Main Rd) **Map 16, #22** Mains R15-30. Open 8.30am-7pm daily. This authentic deli has kerbside tables and good snacks (but we found the gefilte fish not as good as grandma makes).

Atlantic Express (☎ *439 3038, 1B Regent Rd)* **Map 16, #27** Mains R18-28. Open 8am-midnight daily. Not quite an alternative to the *Blue Train,* but this cafe in a converted Pullman rail carriage serves some good light meals including Cape Malay dishes.

Kauai (☎ *434 7645, Cnr Regent & Clarens Rds)* **Map 16, #28** This slick Hawaiian franchise operation offers a wide range of smoothies (starting at R8), juices and healthy sandwiches. (There are other branches at 39A Long St and SRG House, 1 Mostert St, in the city centre.)

New York Bagels (☎ *439 7523, 51 Regent Rd)* **Map 16, #30** Mains R10-20. Open 7am-11pm daily. As well as the deli there's the airy multilevel cafe next door where you wander around various stalls to choose a mix 'n' match meal of, say, a hot-beef-on-rye sarnie followed by a spicy stir-fry. You can buy alcohol here too.

Restaurants

Maz Japanese Cuisine (☎ *439 1806, Adelphi Centre, 127 Main Rd)* **Map 16, #9** Mains R30-40. Open 10.30am-9.30pm Mon-Sat. This reasonably priced sushi bar is generally packed so you might have to go with a takeaway.

San Marco (☎ *434 1469, 92 Main Rd)* **Map 16, #8** Mains R40-60. Open noon-2.30pm Sun only, 6pm-10.30pm Wed-Mon. San Marco is considered one of the country's top restaurants, which is pretty much on the mark. Try the amazing ostrich *carpaccio* (raw ostrich meat), as well as the great pasta. The gelateria, open from 10am to 11.30pm, has delicious takeaway gelati.

Mr Chan's (☎ *439 2239, 178A Main Rd)* **Map 16, #21** Mains R40, set menu R62. Open noon-2pm & 6pm-10.30pm daily. Serves dishes from all over China.

La Perla (☎ *439 9538, Beach Rd)* **Map 16, #29** Mains from R45. Open noon-11.30pm daily. This stylish Italian restaurant with terrace seating and a comfy bar is one of the few decent seaside options in this area. It serves some 30-plus pastas.

Ari's Souvlaki (☎ *439 6683, 83A Regent Rd)* **Map 16, #33** Mains R20. Open 10am-midnight daily. Meze, shwarma and felafel

(R15) are on offer at this Greek institution. It's nothing fancy but it's honest.

CAMPS BAY

Because Camps Bay is one of the hot spots for sundowners (drinks at sunset), you'd be well advised to book ahead for anywhere with a view. If you haven't booked, a stroll along the beach, followed by a beer and dinner at one of the pavement tables fronting Victoria Rd, is a genuine pleasure.

The Sandbar (☎ *438 8336, 31 Victoria Rd)* **Map 12, #5** Mains R22-30. Open 10am-9.30pm daily. Good sandwiches and light meals are the deal at this laid-back cafe with street tables.

Blues (☎ *438 2040, The Promenade, Victoria Rd)* **Map 12, #8** Mains from R40. Open noon-midnight daily. Casual dining in the 'Californian tradition', which means the menu has something to please practically everyone. Book well ahead if you want a window seat.

Dizzy Jazz (☎ *438 2686, 41 The Drive)* **Map 12, #9** Mains R50-60. Cover charge R10-20 at night. Open noon-3pm & 6pm-1am daily. Dizzy's specialises in seafood platters, but many people come here for the live music, which ranges from country to jazz and blues.

The Codfather (☎ *438 0782, 37 The Drive)* **Map 12, #9** Mains R40. Open noon-3pm & 6pm-11pm Mon-Fri, noon-midnight Sat. Set back from the main drag but still with a decent beach view is this sophisticated seafood restaurant with a conveyor-belt sushi bar (plates from R6 to R20).

HOUT BAY & NOORDHOEK

Until Champman's Peak Dr is fixed you'll have to take the long way round the peninsula to drive between these neighbouring Atlantic Coast suburbs. Among Hout Bay's several takeaway fish-and-chip places is *Fish on the Rocks* **(Map 2, #11)**, open from 10.30am to 8.15pm daily, in a prime spot right at the end of Hout Bay Harbour Rd.

Mariner's Wharf (☎ *790 1100, Hout Bay Harbour)* **Map 2, #9** Mains R50. Open 9am-10pm daily. This harbour-side complex has several options. In the upmarket Wharfside

Grill, the waiters are dressed as sailors to match the sea-salt decor. The cheaper deal is at the takeaway downstairs.

The Suikerbossie *(☎ 790 1450, 1 Victoria Dr, Hout Bay)* **Map 11, #14** Mains from R30. Open 9am-4.30pm Tues-Sun. There's a lovely tea garden at this large house (often used for functions so call ahead), which has been in business since the 1930s. The Sunday carvery (R79) is very popular. The Suikerbossie is tucked away at the top of the hill before you descend to Hout Bay from the north.

The Red Herring *(☎ 789 1783, Cnr Beach & Pine Rds, Noordhoek)* **Map 11, #25** Mains from R20. Open noon-3pm & 7pm-10pm Tues-Sun. Pizzas, salads and sandwiches are offered in a peaceful, rustic setting. There's a view of the beach from the roof terrace. The pub here is open from 11am until late Tuesday to Sunday, and from 5pm until late on Monday.

WOODSTOCK & OBSERVATORY

Emily's Bistro *(☎ 448 2366, 77 Roodebloem Rd, Woodstock)* **Map 12, #14** 3-course set menu R120. Open 12.30pm-2.30pm Tues-Fri, 7pm-10.30pm Mon-Sat. Think zebra stripes, purple walls, grand pianos and big flower displays and you get the general campy picture. The food is as creative as the decor.

Along Lower Main Rd in Observatory it's wall-to-wall restaurants, cafes and bars. There's little to choose between the following casual places, with menus slanted towards the tastes and budgets of the resident student population.

Obz Café **(Map 17, #8)** *(115 Lower Main Rd)* is a trendy long-runner; ***Café Whatever*** **(Map 17, #9)** *(☎ 448 9129, 90 Lower Main Rd)* is a more laid-back bistro; ***A Fu Chinese*** **(Map 17, #8)** *(☎ 447 1811, 109 Main Rd)* is a cheap Chinese cafe; ***The Wholefood Store*** **(Map 17, #16)** *(☎ 447 7375, 73 Lower Main Rd)* is your average vegetarian and vegan pit stop; the new ***Green Mamba Cafe*** **(Map 17, #14)** *(☎ 447 2165, 64 Lower Main Rd)* offers up African food; and ***Café Ganesh*** **(Map 17, #14)** *(☎ 448 3435, 38B Trill Rd)*, a classic funky

student hang-out, dishes out felafel, roti, curries and the like.

More restaurant options include the cheerful ***Pancho's Mexican Kitchen*** **(Map 17, #8)** *(☎ 447 4854, 127 Lower Main Rd)*; ***Senhõra Sardine*** **(Map 17, #15)** *(☎ 448 1979, Cnr Trill & Lower Main Rds)*, serving Portuguese dishes; and ***Diva*** **(Map 17, #11)** *(☎ 448 0282, 88 Lower Main Rd)*, a highly rated Italian restaurant with faded Venetian-style decor.

SOUTHERN SUBURBS

Rhodes Memorial Restaurant *(☎ 689 9151, Groote Schuur Estate, Rondebosch)* **Map 12, #20** Snacks from R15. Open 9am-5pm daily. This is a fantastic spot for afternoon tea, on the side of Devil's Peak and right behind the memorial – the scones are just enormous.

The Fat Cactus *(☎ 689 9970, 55 Durban Rd, Mowbray)* **Map 12, #17** Mains R40. Open 9am-11pm Mon-Fri, 6pm-11pm Sat. Fajitas, burritos, and nachos are on the menu at this casual, fun Mexican cafe-bar. The combo platter is big enough for two people to share.

The Gardener's Cottage *(☎ 689 3158, 31 Newlands Ave, Newlands)* **Map 11, #10** Mains R20. Open 8am-4.30pm Tues-Fri, 8.30am-4.30pm Sat & Sun. This cute cafe and tea garden is in the grounds of the Montebello craft studios (see the Shopping chapter).

The Miller's Plate *(☎ 685 6233, Josephine Mill, Boundary Rd, Newlands)* **Map 11, #9** Mains R20-30. Open 8.30am-4pm Sun-Fri. Set amid bamboo, palms and Japanese maple trees, this very pleasant cafe is in the Josephine Mill next to the rugby ground. It does a three-course roast lunch on Sunday for R40.

Cavendish Square shopping centre **(Map 11, #11)** has several good cafes, including ***Seattle Coffee Company*** on the lower ground floor and ***Mugg & Bean*** on the ground floor. There's also a ***food court*** located on the upper level. The international restaurant ***Scoozi!*** *(☎ 683 5458)* does a meal-and-movie deal every night except Sunday for R55.

KIRSTENBOSCH BOTANICAL GARDENS

Kirstenbosch has a couple of dining options in case you forgot that picnic basket.

Fynbos Food Court Map 11, #13 Buffet breakfast R30, lunch R45. Open 9am-5pm daily. This self-service restaurant offers light meals and takeaways, including beer and wine, in a pleasant setting.

Silver Tree (☎ 762 9585) Map 11, #13 Mains around R55. Open 11.30am-3pm & 6.30pm-10pm daily. This is *the* a la carte restaurant, with crisp white tablecloths. Call about the monthly food and wine evenings.

CONSTANTIA

Thaifoon (☎ 794 0022, Groot Constantia Rd) Map 11, #17 Mains R25-40. Open noon-2.30 Sun-Fri, 6pm-10pm daily. This exotic basement restaurant in the cluster of places at the entrance to the Groot Constantia estate offers Thai food, including recipes using ostrich.

Jonkerhuis (☎ 794 4255, Groot Constantia) Map 11, #19 Mains R40. Open 9am-11pm Tues-Sat, 9am-5pm Sun & Mon. Jonkerhuis specialises in traditional Cape dishes such as bobotie and bredies (pot stews of meat or fish, and vegetables). Its Cape brandy tart (R25) is a tea-time treat. Pity the poor waiters who have to dress in 17th-century slave costumes. On the same estate, *The Tavern Restaurant* (☎ 794 1144) serves continental food.

Spaanschemat River Café (☎ 794 3010, Spaanschemat River Rd) Map 11, #21 Mains R35-50. Open 8am-4pm daily. Next to the wine shop at the entrance to the Constantia Uitsig estate, this relaxed restaurant is good value and serves huge portions; the club sandwiches are the business and the desserts are divine.

La Colombe (☎ 794 2390, Constantia Uitsig, Spaanschemat River Rd) Map 11, #21 Mains R75. Open 12.30pm-2pm & 7.30pm-9pm daily. The menu – all written in French – changes daily at this light and relaxed Provençale-style restaurant.

Buitenverwachting (☎ 794 3522, Klein Constantia Rd) Map 11, #19 Mains R84-98. Open noon-1.30pm Tues-Fri, 7pm-9pm

Tues-Sat. Elegant furnishing and blissful views across the vines to the mountain add to the epicurean delights on offer here.

Peddlars on the Bend (☎ 794 7747, Spaanschemat River Rd) Map 11, #20 Mains R35. Open noon-11pm daily. If you don't fancy all that highfalutin wine-estate fodder, the hearty dishes such as chicken-and-leek pie and *eisbein* (pork knuckle) served at this lively pub should suit you fine.

For details of the wineries in this area, see Constantia in the special section 'Cape Wineries'.

KALK BAY

Kalk Bay's Main Rd runneth over with cafes; good ones include the reliable *Cathedral Café* (Map 3, #10) (64 Main Rd) and *Trainspot Pancake & Coffee Kaya* (Map 3, #13), a funky alfresco joint next to the station.

The Brass Bell (☎ 788 5455) Map 3, #14 There are several options at this Cape Town institution between the train station and the sea. The formal restaurant serves everything from breakfast to dinner. There's an oriental-food section, an alfresco pizzeria and, of course, the bar. Fish braais are held on the terrace on Sunday from 6.30pm.

Café Matisse (☎ 788 1123, 76 Main Rd) Map 3, #12 Mains R25-30. Open 8.30am-11pm daily. Eclectic decor and candles at night enhance the atmosphere at this bistro, which serves pizzas and a good meze plate.

Olympia Café & Deli (☎ 788 6396, 134 Main Rd) Map 3, #16 Mains R20. Open 7am-6pm Tues & Wed, 7am-9pm Thur-Sat, 7am-2pm Sun. Local artists display their work at this relaxed, rustic cafe, which is renowned for its breakfasts and pastries.

SIMON'S TOWN

Bon Appetit (☎ 786 2412, 90 St George's St) Map 4, #5 Mains R50. Open noon-2pm & 6.30pm-10pm Tues-Sun. This stylish French bistro is one of the best on the peninsula.

Bertha's (☎ 786 2138, 1 Wharf Rd) Map 4, #9 Mains R35. Open 8am-10pm daily. Right by the harbour, Bertha's serves a good variety of dishes. Service is friendly and the mood relaxed.

The Meeting Place (☎ *786 1986, 98 St George's St)* **Map 4, #7** Mains R20-25. Open 9am-6pm Sun-Wed, 9am-9pm Thur-Sat. The balcony overlooks the street and harbour at this trendy deli-cafe, a foodie's delight.

Apart from the cluster of places near the Simon's Town marina, there's also the good *Penguin Point Cafe* **(Map 4, #15)** at Boulders Beach.

CAPE FLATS

You need to be on a tour or with a private guide to visit these places.

Gugu le Afrika (☎ *364 3395, 8 Lwandle Rd, Khayelitsha)* Mains around R15. Open 8.30am-4.30pm Mon-Fri. Gugu is a catering training centre but is still a professional operation, with a full menu of very reasonably priced Western and African dishes. Check out the fabric-printing and design workshop next door.

Lelapa (*49 Harlem Ave, Langa)* is used on the Township Music Tour run by Our Pride Tours (see Township Tours in the Getting Around chapter). The host Sheila is well travelled and a great cook.

Masande Restaurant (☎ *371 7173)* is in the same Crossroads complex as the Philani Flagship Printing Project. The name means 'let us prosper'. You can try traditional dishes such as samp and beans with stew; pap (maize porridge) and tripe; and *umvubo* (sour milk and mealie meal), as well as home-brewed beer.

PLACES TO EAT

Entertainment

If you're up for a good time (or a 'jol' as they say in South Africa), the old 'Tavern of the Seas' is still a dab hand at beguiling rands from locals and visiting foreigners alike. The city has such a good atmosphere (especially in summer) that many people put in some very long nights bar-hopping and clubbing.

As well as the more commercial venues there's a range of informal places that come and go. Some started out as private parties that were just too good to stop. Among the hottest tickets in town for those interested in dance are the monthly Vortex trance parties (see Clubs later in this chapter), while *everyone* wants to party at the Mother City Queer Projects bash each December (see the special section 'Gay & Lesbian Cape Town').

It's not all about drinking and dancing. Cape Town has a decent range of cinemas and theatres, while music spans the gamut from classical to rock via jazz and marimba. Free live music is a feature of the Waterfront, in particular. Attending the inaugural concert of the revitalised Cape Town Philharmonic Orchestra, which played splendidly alongside a multiracial choir, was a highlight of our last research trip.

It's sad to say, though, that such examples of entertainment harmony are rare in Cape Town, since bars and clubs where blacks, coloureds and whites happily rub shoulders are few and far between. And practically the only way you're going to safely explore the nightlife of the Cape Flats is on a tour, such as that offered by Our Pride Tours (see Organised Tours in the Getting Around chapter).

INFORMATION
The weekly arts guide in the *Mail & Guardian* is excellent, and the daily *Cape Argus* has an entertainment section. The monthly magazines *Cape Review* and *SA Citylife* are also good for listings – both are available at CNA shops and other bookstores, as well as at the Cape Town Tourism office.

Highlights

- Enjoy Cape Town's wealth of music, from the marimba of the township shebeens to classical concerts at Artscape.

- Dance the night away at one of Long St's many clubs or the monthly Vortex trance parties.

- Learn traditional African drumming at the Drum Cafe.

- Experience local theatre at Gauloises Warehouse and the Baxter Theatre.

- Cheer along with the sports-mad crowds at Newlands' cricket and rugby grounds.

Computicket (☎ 918 8910, W www.computicket.com), a computerised booking agency, has practically *every* seat for *every* theatre, cinema and sports venue on its system. You can be shown the available seats and get your ticket on the spot. There are outlets in the Golden Acre Centre (Map 13, #119), in the Gardens Centre (Map 15, #45), at the Waterfront (Map 14, #29), in Sea Point's Adelphi Centre (Map 16, #12) and in many other places.

BARS & PUBS
Wednesday, Friday and Saturday are the biggest nights in the bars and clubs. The upper (south-west) ends of Long and Kloof Sts and the gay Waterkant district are incredibly lively all night long on summer weekends, as is the Waterfront. Try not to miss out on a night at the Drum Cafe (see Live Music later), which is a great place for a drink even if you choose not to join a session of drumming.

City Bowl
Fireman's Arms (☎ 419 1513, 25 Mechau St) Map 14, #75 Dating from 1906, and one of the few old pubs left in town, the Fireman's is a great place to come watch a

rugby match on the big-screen TV, grab some seriously tasty pizza or a cheap bar meal or just down a lazy pint or two.

The Carriage (☎ *419 6484, 77 Dock Rd, Foreshore)* **Map 14, #76** This convivial British-style pub has live music on Fridays. If your car needs a wash, rock up on Monday or Tuesday for lunch and have it done for free.

The Square All Bar None (☎ *082 416 4106, 36 Shortmarket St)* **Map 13, #39** Pavement cafe and modern bar and dance venue just off Greenmarket Square, playing a range of music, including '70s to '90s retro tracks on Thursday.

Pa Na Na Souk Bar (☎ *423 4889, Heritage Square)* **Map 13, #12** Sybaritic bar with balconies overlooking the Heritage Square's restored courtyard.

The Purple Turtle (☎ *423 6194, Cnr Long & Shortmarket Sts)* **Map 13, #33** Cape Town's grunge and Goth centre. Dress up in black and wear purple make-up to feel at home. It's worth checking out for its alternative-music gigs too.

Jo'burg (☎ *422 0241, 218 Long St)* **Map 13, #69** Long St's coolest hang-out, with occasional live music. Check out the groovy Perspex light sculptures decorating the walls.

Gardens

Stag's Head Hotel (☎ *465 4918, 71 Hope St)* **Map 15, #38** The ground-floor bar has a motley assortment of locals staring morosely into their beers, while in the rear there's a younger crowd. The real action happens upstairs, with plenty of pool tables, pinball machines and loud music (sometimes live).

The Perseverance Tavern (☎ *461 2440, 83 Buitenkant St)* **Map 15, #34** Cecil Rhodes called this pioneering pub his local. The flickering candles in the dim interior still give it plenty of atmosphere and the simple meals (mains around R30) aren't too bad.

Dros (☎ *423 6800, 22 Kloof St)* **Map 15, #22** An unfortunate choice of name for this otherwise quite acceptable chain pub-restaurant (the letters in the name actually stand for AWOL – absent without leave – in Afrikaans).

While on Kloof St, check out the trendy twosome *Cafe Bardeli* **(Map 15, #21)** and *Cafe Dharma* **(Map 15, #8)**. Also try *Cafe Camissa* **(Map 15, #9)**, which has good live music on Wednesdays and Sundays, and the local branch of reggae bar *Cool Runnings* **(Map 15, #11)**.

The Shed (☎ *461 5892, 43-45 De Villiers St)* **Map 15, #35** Part of the complex of venues on the edge of District Six, this happening bar and pool hall packs an interesting crowd. Next door is the laid-back *Blue Lizard Internet Café* **(Map 15, #35)**.

Waterfront & Green Point

Bascule Bar **(Map 14, #56)** at the Cape Grace hotel is the sophisticated option and specialises in whisky. If you're feeling flush go for the 50-year-old Glenfiddich, just R15,200 a tot.

Ferryman's Freehouse (☎ *419 7748, East Pier Rd)* **Map 14, #40** Adjoining Mitchell's Waterfront Brewery, this relaxed pub-restaurant serves a variety of freshly brewed beers and good-value meals (around R30 for a meal).

The Sports Cafe (☎ *419 5558, Upper level, Victoria Wharf)* **Map 14, #34** All the sports action on big-screen TVs and a chance to catch overseas games on live satellite broadcasts. There are plenty of burgers and snacky options to go with the amber nectar.

Chilli 'n' Lime (☎ *498 4668, 23 Somerset St)* **Map 14, #66** There's a range of events at this ever-lively, mainly straight bar and club in the heart of the gay district.

Andy Cap's (☎ *434 0593, 47 Main Rd)* **Map 14, #13** Small, British-style pub serving cheap pizza, decorated with a collection of, you guessed it, caps. Good for a quiet tipple.

Buena Vista Social Café (☎ *433 0610, Exhibition Bldg, 81 Main Rd)* **Map 14, #12** This places takes its inspiration from the famous CD of Cuban music. A tapas menu supplements the mix of cigars, Bacardi and Cokes, and beautiful people.

Atlantic Coast

La Med (☎ *438 5600, Glen Country Club, Clifton)* **Map 12, #4** One of the choice places to be at sunset in summer, although essentially it's just a bar with lots of outdoor tables and a good view. Food is of the steak roll (R30) variety. The entrance, along Victoria Rd on the way to Clifton from Camps Bay, is easily passed.

Baraza (☎ 438 1758, *Victoria Rd, Camps Bay*) **Map 12, #8** Wine and cocktail bar with a killer view (you may have to kill to be able to admire it from one of the hotly contested cane chairs).

Kronendal (☎ 790 4011, *869 Main Rd, Hout Bay*) **Map 2, #1** Three ales and a lager are brewed in this pub-restaurant with a Cape Dutch exterior. It serves meals and has live jazz on Saturday afternoons.

Woodstock

89 Woodstock (☎ 447 0982, *89 Roodebloem Rd, Woodstock*) **Map 12, #15** Open 6pm-late Tues-Sun. Sip your drink in this relaxed pub under the gaze of a wall-size mural of Stravinsky and various classics by Tretchikoff, Cape Town's internationally known painter of lounge-music icons.

Don Pedro's (☎ 447 4493, *113 Roodebloem Rd, Woodstock*) **Map 12, #16** Long-time favourite with white liberals for a boozy late night out; now popular with the yuppies moving into the area.

Observatory

Cool Runnings (☎ 448 7656, *96 Station St, Observatory*) **Map 17, #5** Sand has been dumped outside this chain reggae bar to create that beach-side feel, carried through in the island-hut decor. It's a fun hang-out, with another branch on Kloof St (minus the beach).

Rolling Stones (☎ 448 9461, *94 Lower Main Rd*) **Map 17, #10** Open noon-3am daily. Otherwise known as Stones, this giant pool bar has a long balcony, a great spot from which to observe the comings and goings of Lower Main Rd. There's also a branch at 166A Long St.

A Touch of Madness (☎ 448 2266, *42 Trill Rd, Observatory*) **Map 17, #13** You could hardly swing a cat in this wackily decorated bar-bistro, but it still manages to have plenty of cosy corners.

The Curve Bar at the Bijoux (☎ 448 0183, *178 Lower Main Rd, Observatory*) **Map 17, #1** It's at the dodgy end of Observatory, but safe enough to venture to when there's a club night on (for which you'll pay around R20 admission). The decor comprises cool industrial style in an old converted cinema space.

Newlands

The Foresters' Arms (☎ 689 5949, *52 Newlands Ave, Newlands*) **Map 11, #10** Mains R30. Open 10am-11pm Mon-Sat, 9am-4pm Sun. This big mock-Tudor pub, affectionately known as Forries, is more than 120 years old; it offers a convivial atmosphere and good pub meals.

Barristers (☎ 674 1792, *Cnr Kildare Rd & Main St, Newlands*) **Map 11, #10** Mains around R40. The long-time favourite of Newlands' rugger buggers has had an upgrade and offers a more sophisticated atmosphere for dining as well as drinking.

Bloubergstrand

The Blue Peter (☎ 554 1956, *Popham St*) Mains R25. Open 10am-11pm daily. The thing to do here is grab a beer, order a pizza and plonk yourself on the grass outside to enjoy the classic view of Table Mountain and Robben Island.

CLUBS

Cape Town's club scene is on something of a roll with top overseas DJs, including Pete Tong and Judge Jules, increasingly jetting in to play alongside local hotshots such as Krushed 'n' Sorted. Keep your ear to the ground for special events, such as the *Vortex trance parties* (☎ 794 4032). The main backpacker hostels should know when these monthly out-of-town overnight raves are happening and can often arrange transport.

At clubs, expect to pay a cover charge of between R10 and R30 depending on the night and the event. Most places don't get going until after 11pm. For more dance clubs, including the very hot 55 and the perennial favourite Bronx, see the special section 'Gay & Lesbian Cape Town'.

City Bowl

Long St is the epicentre of the city's club scene.

The Jet Lounge *(☎ 424 8831, 74 Long St)* **Map 13, #25** Slick venue offering house, funk and disco beats. There's a pre-club bar downstairs.

Long Beach *(☎ 422 1368, 94 Long St)* **Map 13, #53** The beach on the roof conjures up memories of partying in Ibiza or Goa.

169 on Long *(☎ 426 1107, 169 Long St)* **Map 13, #154** Open 6pm-late Fri & Sat only. One of the few Long St venues where you're guaranteed to party with more blacks and coloureds than whites. The funky music, often live R&B, is probably what accounts for it.

The Lounge *(☎ 424 7636, 194 Long St)* **Map 13, #64** Drum-and-bass or jungle provide the background for that cool drink on the long iron-lace balcony.

Rhythm Divine *(☎ 0861 400 500, 156 Long St)* **Map 13, #60** Plenty of different parties to attend at this happening venue with two sizeable dance floors and a pool room.

Coffee Lounge *(☎ 424 6784, 76 Church St)* **Map 13, #29** Old-time artist Tretchikoff again features big in this funky four-storey club and bar, which serves up an eclectic range of events.

The Fez *(☎ 423 1456, 38 Hout St)* **Map 13, #23** City-centre hot spot, with queues out the door at weekends (although given Capetonians' fickle nature it could well have gone off the boil by now).

Rhodes House *(☎ 424 8844, 60 Queen Victoria St)* **Map 13, #91** Admission R50. Come party with the glam set at this imaginative and beautiful venue. Wildly expensive but generally worth it.

Elsewhere

The Jam *(☎ 465 2106, 43 De Villiers St)* **Map 15, #35** This popular club often has live music and sets by visiting DJs. It's part of the same complex as The Shed (see Bars & Pubs).

Club Galaxy *(☎ 637 9132, College Rd, Ryelands Estate, Athlone)* **Map 11, #8** Open 9pm-3am Thurs-Sat. A younger crowd haunts this long-time Cape Flats favourite

where you can get down to R&B and live bands. On Thursday, women get in for free until 11pm.

Dockside *(☎ 552 2030, Century City, Century City Blvd, Milnerton)* **Map 11, #3** Women can get in for free every Wednesday before 11pm at this mega club beside the mammoth Canal Walk shopping centre. International DJs occasionally grace the decks but they'd have to be pretty special to tempt you out here otherwise.

CINEMAS

Cape Town has plenty of cinemas (including one excellent art-house venue) showing all the latest international releases, and hosts several film festivals each year. See the local press for a full rundown of cinemas and the films they are showing.

Labia *(☎ 424 5927, 68 Orange St, Gardens)* **Map 15, #17** Admission R15/18 day/evening. This is the best cinema for 'mainstream alternative' films. It is named after the old Italian ambassador and local philanthropist Count Labia.

IMAX Theatre *(☎ 419 7365, Waterfront)* **Map 14, #26** Adults/children R34/20. Shows 10am-9pm daily. For huge-screen entertainment.

For commercial films, there are ***Nu Metro cineplexes*** *(☎ 086 110 0220)* at the Waterfront **(Map 14, #28)** and the Canal Walk shopping centre **(Map 11, #2)**. *Cinema Nouveau* shows a slightly classier range of movies at Cavendish Square **(Map 11, #11)** *(☎ 683 4063)* and the Waterfront **(Map 14, #28)** *(☎ 425 8222)*. Tickets at both these venues are R25, half-price on Tuesdays. It pays to book in advance, especially for the Waterfront cinemas, which are very popular.

THEATRE

Major drama productions are staged at Artscape (see Live Music following).

Gauloises Warehouse *(☎ 421 0777, 6 Dixon Rd)* **Map 14, #66** This place specialises in cutting-edge and local theatre – it's where *Shopping and Fucking*, the hit London play, had its Cape Town premiere.

Baxter Theatre *(☎ 685 7880, Main Rd, Rondebosch)* **Map 12, #22** A wide range of theatre from kids' shows to Zulu dance spectaculars is on offer here at three different venues including the Concert Hall and the Sanlam Studio Theatre.

Little Theatre (☎ 480 7129, UCT Hiddingh Campus, Orange St, Gardens) **Map 15, #25** Productions of the University of Cape Town's drama department are staged here.

Independent Armchair Theatre (☎ 447 1514, 135 Lower Main Rd, Observatory) **Map 17, #7** This is the Sunday night home of the Cape Comedy Collective, a witty bunch of comedians who do the rounds of other venues, including the GrandWest Casino and Galaxy night club. The venue also has an eclectic range of other events, including Japanese animated movies on Monday nights, and band gigs.

Theatre on the Bay (☎ 438 3301, 1 Link St, Camps Bay) **Map 12, #11** As you'd expect of a venue in this well-heeled suburb, the program is far from adventurous, but perhaps worth a look if you fancy a conventional play or a one-person show

Comedy Warehouse (☎ 425 2175, 22 Somerset Rd, Green Point) **Map 14, #59** This new venue, as its name suggests, offers various comedy and live music shows.

AMUSEMENT PARK

Ratanga Junction (☎ 550 8504, Century City, Milnerton) **Map 11, #3** Adult/child R69/39 including rides, admission only R29, Open 10am-5pm Sun-Tues, Thur & Fri, 10am-6pm Sat. This big amusement park with an African theme is next to the enormous Canal Walk shopping centre, around 5km north of the city centre along the N1. For a 90-second adrenaline rush the 100km/h Cobra is recommended. You'll need a car to get out here, as you will also for the nearby casino.

CASINO

GrandWest Casino (☎ 505 7174, W www .grandwest.co.za, Old Goodwood showgrounds, Milnerton) **Map 11, #1** Apparently this overblown Disneyland of gambling was inspired by Cape Town's architectural heritage, the old post office serving as the model

for the florid facade. It took US$20 million in revenue in its first three months, making it a huge success (or a huge tragedy for the thousands of impoverished gamblers and their families). Still you might want to come here for its state-of-the-art cinema complex, food court, Olympic-sized ice rink, kids' theme park and music shows.

LIVE MUSIC

At times it seems as if Cape Town is pounding to a perpetual beat. The opportunities to catch musical performances are wide and varied, spanning everything from acapella buskers at the Waterfront or in Greenmarket Square to thumping African funk at Mama Africa or Marco's African Place (see the Places to Eat chapter).

Classical

Artscape (☎ 421 7695, W www.artscape .co.za, 1-10 DF Malan St, Foreshore) **Map 13, #107** The old Nico performing arts complex is home to the Cape Town Philharmonic Orchestra. You can catch regular classical concerts as well as ballet, opera and theatre. Every March the Cape philharmonic performs a proms program in the Old Town Hall. Note that walking around this area at night is not recommended and you'll need to book ahead for a nonshared taxi since there are none to be found on the streets.

Bands

Drum Cafe (☎ 461 1305, W www.drum cafe.co.za, 32 Glynn St, Gardens) **Map 15, #37** Admission R30, drum hire R20. Every Monday, Wednesday, Friday and Saturday from 9pm there are drumming workshops or live bands or both at this funky hang-out; Wednesday's facilitated drum circle is a blast – don't miss it. Check the cafe's Web site for details of events, lessons and kids' workshops.

The Jam (☎ 465 2106, W www.thejam .co.za, 43 De Villiers St, District Six) **Map 15, #35** Open from 9pm Tue-Sat. Top SA bands belt their stuff out here.

Cafe Camissa (☎ 424 2289, 80 Kloof St) **Map 15, #9** This groovy little cafe-bar with

Musical Notes

Cape Town is one of the world's jazz capitals and home to some internationally known musicians, including Dollar Brand (Abdullah Ibrahim), and the trio of Robbie Jansen, Basil 'Manneberg' Coetzee and Winston 'Ngozi' Mankunku. All these musicians occasionally play in town (your best chance of catching them will be at a jazz festival). Up-and-coming locals to watch out for include the guitarist Jimmy Dludlu, pianist Paul Hanmer and singer Judith Spehuma.

Techno, trance and jungle have all found their way from the mixing boards of London to Cape Town dance clubs. Here you can also tune in to *kwaito*, the local dance-music sensation that's a mix of mbaqanga jive, hip-hop, house and ragga. The music of local singing superstar Brenda Fassie now includes a strong kwaito flavour. Hip-hop is also big, with Moodphase 5ive one of the better groups around mixing the genre with soul.

The popularity of black music with white audiences extends to live music – look out for concerts by Fetish, Valiant Swart and the Blues Broers (pronounced brews – it's slang for brother), an immensely popular five-piece Afrikaner blues band. Hot rock bands include Stellenbosch's Springbok Nude Girls, Sugar Drive and Boo!.

---

a gay-friendly, studenty vibe hosts live world music on Wednesday and Sunday (R10).

River Club (☎ 448 6117, Observatory Rd, Observatory) **Map 17, #2** This is a good place to catch local bands and performers, although it's gone more upmarket and mainstream than in the past. It hosts a folk-music club every Monday.

Harbour Music Club (☎ 789 1021, The Troubadour, 17 Johns Rd, Kalk Bay) **Map 3, #17** A platform for aspiring musos. There's live music from Wednesday to Sunday, with Wednesday a good night to drop by and pay R15 to check out four different acts.

Jazz

Jazz offered (and still offers) one of the few opportunities for South Africans of all races to interact as equals. Some excellent jazz is played in Cape Town and while there are few permanent venues, many places occasionally have jazz – check the papers for details.

Visiting a township jazz club is an unforgettable experience, but you are strongly advised not to go alone. Companies such as Our Pride Tours (see Organised Tours in the Getting Around chapter) arrange good township music tours that include a visit to the famous **Duma's Falling Leaves** (☎ 426 4260) in Guguletu.

The two-day *North Sea Jazz Festival* (**W** *www.nsjfcapetown.co.za*) is held during the end of March, often at the Good Hope Centre **(Map 13, #141)** on Darling St in the City Bowl. Bands and artists at the 2001 event included Randy Crawford, St Germain and the Brand New Heavies as well as local superstar Hugh Masekela.

Green Dolphin (☎ *421 7471,* **W** *www .greendolphin.co.za, Waterfront*) **Map 14, #51** Cover charge R20. Open noon–midnight daily. This upmarket jazz venue serves decent food and has live bands every evening from 8pm. If you don't mind an obstructed view, the cover charge is R15. The nearby *Quay 4* (see Waterfront in the Places to Eat chapter) sometimes has local bands and musos performing.

Gignet Theatre Café (☎ *424 1064,* **W** *www.gignet.co.za, 67-69 Buitengracht St, City Bowl*) **Map 13, #11** Open from 7.30pm Wed-Mon. This new supper club and jazz venue in the city centre is part of the Heritage Square revival.

Dizzy Jazz (☎ *438 2686, 41 The Drive, Camps Bay*) **Map 12, #9** Just off Victoria Rd in Camps Bay, this restaurant and music venue is open daily until very late. It has live jazz on Friday and Saturday and other types of music the rest of the week.

West End (☎ *637 9132, Cine 400 Bldg, College Rd, Ryelands*) **Map 11, #7** One of Cape Town's top jazz venues, West End attracts international stars. You'll need to drive here but there's plenty of security Thursday is R&B night.

Hanover St Jazz Club (☎ *418 8966, GrandWest Casino, Goodwood*) **Map 11, #1** A well-stocked bar and top acts are the draw at this classy venue out at the new casino.

SPECTATOR SPORTS

Capetonians are just as mad about sport as other South Africans. Big international rugby and cricket matches and high-profile local soccer fixtures aside, the city's most glamorous sporting event is the J&B Met horse race, held the first Saturday of February at Kenilworth Racecourse **(Map 11, #12)**.

After Cape Town's failed bid for the 2004 Olympics, it came as a bitter blow for South Africa to narrowly miss out on the chance to host the 2006 soccer World Cup. In 2003, though, the cricket World Cup is scheduled to be played in the country.

Soccer

Supported by over 50% of the country (as opposed to 10% support for rugby), soccer really is the national game these days. The national squad is known as 'Bafana Bafana' (literally 'Boys Boys', meaning 'Our Lads') and major teams in the local competition include the Kaiser Chiefs and the Orlando Pirates (known as Bucs, as in Buccaneers), both from the Johannesburg (Jo'burg) area. It was these two teams that were playing when 43 fans died in a crush at Jo'burg's Ellis Park Stadium in April 2001.

Professional games are played between August and May with teams competing in the Premier Soccer League and the knockout Rothman's Cup.

The main local squads are Santos, based at Athlone Stadium **(Map 11, #6)**; Hellenic at Green Point Stadium **(Map 14)**; and Ajax Cape Town (affiliated with Ajax Amsterdam) at Newlands Rugby Stadium **(Map 11, #9)**. Tickets for league matches cost around R15 and can be booked at Computicket outlets (see Information earlier in this chapter).

Rugby

The game of rugby (union, not league) is traditionally the Afrikaners' sport, although the 1995 World Cup, hosted and won by South Africa, saw the entire population go rugby mad. Since then, cross-race support for the game has waned somewhat in the face of efforts to introduce greater balance in the ethnic composition of teams.

The most popular games to watch are those of the Super 12 tournament, in which four teams each from South Africa, Australia and New Zealand compete between late February and the end of May. If you're in town when one of these is on it's worth getting a ticket, as it would be for any international match.

Important games are played at *Newlands Rugby Stadium* (☎ *689 4921*) **(Map 11, #9)**, one of South African rugby's shrines and home of the Stormers. Tickets for Super 12 games cost R75 in seats, R30 in the stands. Tickets for international matches cost around R250.

Cricket

Cricket fans tend to be English-speaking South Africans, but for a while after South Africa's return to international sport in the 1992 World Cup, cricket occupied centre stage. The game was the first of the 'whites only' sports to wholeheartedly adopt a non-racial attitude, and development programs in the townships are now beginning to pay

dividends. Cape Town's second test ground opened in the township of Langa in 2000.

The sport suffered a setback, however, in 2000 when Hansie Cronje, the youngest captain in South Africa's cricketing history, admitted taking bribes of over US$100,000 to rig matches, and was banned for life.

Important games are played at the *Newlands cricket ground* (☎ 674 4146) **(Map 11, #9)**, which vies with Australia's Adelaide Oval for the title of the world's prettiest cricket ground. Tickets cost around R30 for local matches, and from R90 to R160 for international matches.

RICHARD I'ANSON

MANFRED GOTTSCHALK

RICHARD I'ANSON

The designer boutiques, luxurious accommodation and cosmopolitan atmosphere tell only part of the story: Much of the charm of the Victoria & Alfred Waterfront lies in its role as a working harbour.

Top: What do Tinky Winky, Brad Pitt and John Travolta have in common? Ask the folk at Amsterdam Guest House, home to this fabulous mural. **Bottom:** Rainbow nation: Since the 1994 election, South Africa has become the only nation in the world to enshrine gay and lesbian rights in its constitution.

GAY & LESBIAN CAPE TOWN

For some time Cape Town has been setting out its stall as Africa's premier gay destination. Well, what's a sexy, style-obsessed girl with an adventurous outdoor streak and a taste for the finer things in life – wine, song, a good beach – to do?

Some would argue that Johannesburg (Jo'burg) has a larger gay scene: It was home to the nation's first Gay Pride parade in 1990, an annual event that's still going strong. But who – other than a gold-digger, perhaps – would want to mush up their make-up in the republic's crime capital when they could be sunning themselves at the beach by day, and partying in the trendy Waterkant by night?

It wasn't always this way. In the early days of the Cape Colony, homosexual men were drowned in the harbour. The fate of the colony's lesbians isn't recorded (an early example, perhaps, of the lower profile of the lesbian community).

An open gay and lesbian community was a far-from-prominent feature of the apartheid years, although a few brave souls, such as Pieter-Dirk Uys, used their left-of-centre position to criticise the government (see the boxed text 'South Africa's Gay Icon'). The repressive state was unsupportive of gay activists (the police in particular were known for their brutality), but generally its violent attentions were focused elsewhere. When political freedom for the country's black majority began to become reality in the early 1990s it was taken for granted that gay rights would also be protected under the new constitution.

Today, South Africa has the only constitution in the world that guarantees freedom of sexual choice. Despite this the National Coalition for Gay and Lesbian Equality (☎ 011-487 3810, ✉ carrie@ncgle.co.za) still has plenty to lobby the government for. Same-sex marriages are not legally recognised, there isn't an equal age of consent, and the Sexual Offences Act doesn't recognise male rape.

Locals will tell you the level of 'tolerance' and acceptance of gays and lesbians across South Africa is surprisingly high, something we're not about to contradict. Still, outside the cities and a handful of small, mainly tourism-focused towns, homosexuality remains, if not taboo, pretty much frowned upon in black, white and coloured communities. Even in Cape Town there was a public rumpus when an international delegation of gay travel agents visited in 2001, causing the local Christian and Muslim communities to band together to denounce the promotion of the city as a gay destination.

But elements of gay cultures have long permeated straight Cape Town. Take 'moffie', the local derogatory term for a homosexual – this is the Afrikaans word for glove and is also the word used for the leader of a performance troupe in the Cape Minstrel Carnival (see Special Events in the Facts for the Visitor chapter). These leaders wear gloves and are often gay, hence moffie's alternative meaning. South African

Inset: Photo detail by Simon Richmond

137

South Africa's Gay Icon

Cape Town has several high-profile gay characters, but queen of the crop is without doubt actor and writer Pieter-Dirk Uys, whose alter ego Evita Bezuidenhout is the republic's very own Dame Edna Everage – she likes to be known as 'the most famous white woman in Africa'. Evita holds forth in the long-running show *Tannie Evita Praat Kaktus (Aunty Evita Talks Cactus)*, a readily understandable and very funny mixture of English and Afrikaans covering a variety of pertinent topics, not least her own role in the end of apartheid and the process of reconciliation.

Evita, who has had her own TV chat show and has perfume and wine named after her, is not the only character in Uys's repertoire. Bambi Kellerman is Evita's rather disreputable younger sister; Ouma Ossewanie Kakebenia Poggenpoel her outspoken 100-year-old mother; and Ms Nowell Fine a liberal, loud-mouthed *kugel* (Jewish woman). It's not all role-playing as Uys steps out as himself to front shows on racism *(Dekaffirnated)* and AIDS *(For Facts Sake)*.

Having been embraced by the establishment, and even introduced to the real queen, Elizabeth II, on her visit to Cape Town, Uys performs these shows regularly at his wonderfully kitsch theatre in Darling (see the Excursions chapter) and most Mondays at On Broadway (see Entertainment later). For details, check the Web site W www.evita.co.za.

MICK WELDON

gays have now reclaimed moffie as a word to use among themselves, in much the same way that many gays have appropriated 'queer' in an effort to repudiate its negative connotations.

Gay Capetonians have also developed their own code language, called Gail, in which women's names stand in for certain words. For example, a Cilla is a cigarette; Nadia means no; Wendy, white; Priscilla, police; and Bula, beautiful. Gail was apparently developed in the 1950s by the gay hairdressers of Sea Point, who wanted to gossip among themselves without their clients cottoning on. So if you hear someone talking about Dora in a bar, you'll know they're after a drink (they could also be calling someone a drunk!).

The Lesbian Scene

Cape Town's lesbian scene is pretty low profile. One leading light is Brenda (☎ 083 250 1195), who hosts monthly parties. Another good contact is Michelle Petring (☎ 082 359 4343), who runs Rainbow Trade (W www.rainbowtrade.co.za), a company supplying gay-pride goods and souvenirs; you'll sometimes find her and her colourful products outside Cafe Manhattan, where a women's night is held on the last Thursday of every month (see Places to Eat later).

The lesbian community comes out in force every February for Out in Africa (W www.oia.co.za), the gay-and-lesbian film festival, which shows off a rather good selection of international as well as local queer cinema. And in December everyone fights for tickets for the Mother City Queer Projects party.

Where to Go

The Waterkant (Map 14), the city's self-proclaimed gay village, is a compact grid of streets that will take you all of 10 minutes to wander around. There are also small gay scenes in Sea Point (Map 16), around the northern end of Long St (Map 13), and around the northern end of Kloof St (Map 13).

The beaches to head for are Clifton No 3 (Map 12), Camps Bay (Map 12) and Sandy Bay (Map 11), the clothing-optional stretch of sand discreetly located a walk away from Llandudno Bay (for details, see Llandudno & Sandy Bay in the Things to See & Do chapter).

Further afield, consider visiting Darling, which is home to Evita se Peron, the cabaret theatre of Pieter-Dirk Uys (see Darling in the Excursions chapter). In the Winelands, Franschhoek is a particularly divine place to spend a lazy few days swanning around wineries and some of the Cape's top restaurants.

Heading down the coast there are a couple of gay guesthouses around Hermanus, the whale-watching hot spot. Further afield, Knysna, about 500km east of Cape Town, has made its mark as the gayest resort town on South Africa's Garden Route. In 2001 it hosted the Pink Loerie Carnival (W www.gaymay.co.za), four huge days of gay-and-lesbian partying, shows and a street parade, set to become an annual event. (For detailed information on Knysna and the Garden Route, see Lonely Planet's *South Africa, Lesotho & Swaziland*).

Information

The useful *Pink Map* is updated annually and available from Cape Town Tourism and most places listed here. Like the similarly ubiquitous *Cape Gay Guide* booklet it's free but contains only information on businesses that have paid for the advertising.

Both the local listings magazine *Cape Review* and the national glossy *SA Citylife* include gay listings. The Web site W www.gaynet capetown.co.za teams up with the *Cape Argus* newspaper on the last Thursday of the month to publish a what's- on guide.

The monthly newspaper *Exit* (☎ 011-622 2275, W www.exit.co.za) is South Africa's longest-running gay publication. The glossy magazine *Outright* is about as insubstantial as overseas gay lifestyle magazines in the same niche. Its lesbian equivalent *Womyn* is more imaginative and visually stylish: All are available at CNA and Exclusive bookstores.

For general information on the gay scene across South Africa check GaySA (W www.GaySouthAfrica.org.za), which has links to other useful sites.

On the HIV/AIDS and counselling front, Cape Town's Triangle Project (☎ 448 3812, e triangle@icon.co.za), 41 Salt River Rd, Salt River, is one of the leading support organisations, offering legal advice and a range of education programs.

Wanderlust Women's Travel (☎ 683 9215, fax 671 2639, e info @wanderlustwomen.co.za, W www.wanderlustwomen.co.za) can organise accommodation bookings, transport and all sorts of tours, including adventure, cultural and environmental tours. The women who run it cater for all women, while being 'particularly attuned to the needs of their lesbian sisters'.

Africa Outing (☎ 671 4028, fax 683 7377, W www.afouting.com), 5 Alcyone Rd, Claremont, is run by two experienced and knowledgeable guys who can arrange pretty much whatever type of vacation you want in South Africa, including safaris. They also offer car hire and book flights.

Your Friend in Travel **(Map 16, #4)** (☎ 434 2382) is a gay-run tour company and travel agent operating out of the Atlantic Tourist Information Centre (W www.capetowntravel.co.za) at 242 Main Rd, Three Anchor Bay. It handles hire of all kinds of vehicles from helicopters to jet skis, and can organised rentals and an executive butler service.

Places to Stay

Amsterdam Guest House (☎ 461 8236, fax 461 5575, W www.amster dam.co.za, 19 Forest Rd, Oranjezicht) **Map 15, #51** Singles/doubles B&B from R345/445. Exclusively gay male and very friendly. The wacky mural beside the pool showing Brad Pitt and a Teletubby is alone worth a look. There's a range of rooms, all pretty comfortable with good facilities. Rates are a third less out of season.

Parker Cottage (☎/fax 424 6445, 🕸 www.parkercottage.co.za, 3 Carstens St, Tamboerskloof) **Map 15, #2** Singles/doubles B&B from R250/350. There are eight individually decorated double rooms at this elegant Victorian mansion, handy for the trendy restaurants and bars of Kloof and Long Sts.

Verona Lodge (☎/fax 434 9477, 🕸 www.veronalodge.co.za, 11 Richmond Rd, Three Anchor Bay) **Map 14, #4** Singles/doubles B&B R210/320 low season, R320/450 high season. Not exclusively gay, this quiet, homely residence is run by an older couple, John and Malcolm. You can eat breakfast in the pretty back garden.

Britford House (☎/fax 439 0257, 🕸 www.safarinow.com/go/Brit fordHouse, 15 Oliver Rd, Sea Point) **Map 16, #19** Singles/doubles B&B from R280/340. A few short steps from Sea Point's promenade is this gorgeous Victorian villa with a plunge pool and antique furnishings. All rooms have a TV and most are nonsmoking. Book early – it's popular.

65 Kloof (☎/fax 434 0815, 65 Kloof Rd, Sea Point) **Map 16, #36** Singles/doubles B&B from R150/350 low season, R200/400 high season. Each of the seven rooms in this spacious, stylish and exclusively gay male B&B is decorated differently. There's a reasonably large pool and guests can use the kitchen.

Bantry Bay Bed & Breakfast (☎ 439 1067, fax 439 7439, 🕸 www .bantrybaybandb.co.za, 103 Kloof Rd, Bantry Bay) **Map 16, #37** Doubles B&B R300/450 low/high season, self-catering cottage R500/300 high/low season. This sweet, brightly painted B&B has a stunning view of the coast, a private garden that runs up the hill and bags of style. It's not exclusively gay, but owner André is as camp as they come and great fun.

Clarence House (☎ 683 0307, fax 683 0255, 🕸 www.chchouse.co.za, 6 Obelisk Rd, Claremont) **Map 11, #11** Singles/doubles B&B from R280/380. An angel in sequined pants hangs above the bar at this otherwise camp-free luxurious guesthouse in the leafy southern suburbs. Safe parking, dinner and lunch on request, satellite TV and great views of Table Mountain are among its several virtues.

Apart from the places listed here, there are several popular gay-friendly options in the Places to Stay chapter, including Harbour View Cottages, The Lodge and Victoria Junction in the Wakerkant, and The Fritz Hotel in Gardens. Wanderlust Women's Travel can arrange accommodation for women (see Information earlier in this section).

Places to Eat

Cafe Manhattan (☎ 421 6666, 🕸 www.manhattan.co.za, 74 Waterkant St, Waterkant) **Map 14, #71** Mains R40-50. Open noon-1am Mon-Thur, noon-2am Fri & Sat, 6pm-1am Sun. This convivial, long-running bar and restaurant is better recommended as a bar. Still, the restaurant area is relaxed, with a straight and gay clientele and a menu that will suit the undemanding. There are outdoor tables, and the place occasionally hosts women-only nights.

Robert's Café & Cigar Bar (☎ 425 2478, 72 Waterkant St, Waterkant) **Map 14, #73** Mains R40. Open 12.30pm-midnight Mon-Fri, 6.30pm-midnight Sat & Sun. Steaks are the speciality but all the food comes in giant portions and is well presented. Indulge in the delicious 'telephone pudding', made from a recipe Robert's mum phoned in.

The Village Cafe (☎ 421 0632, 159 Waterkant St, Waterkant) **Map 14, #68** Mains R25. Open 7.30am-6.30pm Mon, Tue & Thur, 7.30am-10pm Wed, Fri & Sat, 7.30am-3.30pm Sun. Delightful cafe in the heart of the Waterkant, with outdoor tables from which to take in the passing parade, and a good deli section for takeaways.

Gorgeous (☎ 424 4554, 210 Loop St, City Bowl) **Map 13, #74** Mains R50-60. Open 11.30-2.30pm Tues-Fri, 6pm-11pm Tues-Sun. Who could resist a restaurant where they answer the phone 'Hello, Gorgeous'? Run by Capetonian theatre identity Peter Hayes, Gorgeous has fabulous decor and tasty cuisine that features lots of local ingredients. The menus also features disposable cameras (R80) to capture the moment.

Priscilla's (☎ 422 2378, 196 Loop St, City Bowl) **Map 13, #73** Mains from R30. Open 4pm-midnight Mon-Thur, 5pm-1am Fri & Sat. Despite the movie-alluding name, the decor is straight, the place spacious and the vibe friendly to all comers. Food is of the steak and seafood variety.

L'Orient (☎ 439 6572, 50 Main Rd, Sea Point) **Map 16, #6** Mains R35-60. Open 6.30pm-10.30pm Mon-Sat. L'Orient serves Malaysian and Indonesian dishes. Try the spicy prawn soup for flavours you might have been missing in South Africa.

Café Erté (☎ 434 6624, 265A Main Rd, Sea Point) **Map 16, #7** Snacks R25. Open 11am-4am daily. Vibey cafe with Internet terminals. Chilled hang-out for the late-night clubbing set; popular with lesbians.

Bloemers Kosteater (☎ 448 0256, 85 Roodebloem Rd, Woodstock) **Map 12, #15** Mains R30. Open 7pm-10.30pm Mon-Sat. If you had an Afrikaner *ooma* (granny) the food served here would be the sort of thing she'd cook. The menu is in Afrikaans (but the staff will translate) at this characterful, gay-friendly place.

Lola's, Off Moroka Café Africaine, De Waterblommetjie and Olympia Café & Deli, all described in the Places to Eat chapter, have gay management.

Entertainment

Clubs & Bars **Bronx** (☎ 419 9219, Cnr Somerset & Napier Sts, Waterkant) **Map 14, #65** Open 8pm-very late daily. The city's premier gay bar is a lively place that has them dancing until dawn (and singing karaoke on Monday). The main bar is on the corner, while from the courtyard you can also enter two other dance spaces, **Angels** and **Detour**.

On Broadway (☎ *418 8338*, W *www.onbroadway.co.za*, *21 Somerset St, Waterkant)* **Map 14, #66** This cabaret supper venue is popular with all Capetonians, so book ahead. The dynamic drag duo Mince are great performers, and on Mondays Pieter-Dirk Uys takes to the stage (see the boxed text 'South Africa's Gay Icon').

55 (☎ *425 2739*, *Cnr Somerset & Napier Sts, Waterkant)* **Map 14, #64** Admission after 11pm R10. Diagonally opposite Bronx, this is the hot dance spot of the moment. Lots of dark spaces and a wraparound balcony for watching the dance-floor action.

Bar Code (☎ *421 5305*, *16 Hudson St, Waterkant)* **Map 14, #74** Open 9pm-late Tues-Sun. Admission R15. Get your leather and latex out for the Mother City's only leather bar. In the courtyard you can grab some air away from the pounding disco beat, and there's pool. Admission includes a beer.

Rosie's (*125A Vos St, Waterkant)* **Map 14, #72** Open 4pm-late Mon-Fri, 1pm-late Sat & Sun. The two tables in this small, chic pool bar have red rather than green baize. It's R2 a game and there's a braai on Sundays.

A Touch of Madness, 89 Woodstock and Cafe Camissa, all listed in the Entertainment chapter, are gay-friendly.

Mother City Queer Projects

This costume party is the closest Cape Town comes to a no holds-barred Mardi Gras event. It's been held each December since 1994 when 2000 people turned up for the first theme party, the Locker Room Project. Organised as a tribute to a deceased lover by 'party architect' André Vorster (who really is an architect), the bash followed in the tradition of Mexico's Festival of the Dead and was such a raging hit that it has become a firm fixture on the city's events calendar.

Each year the party gets bigger and bigger – in 2000, the Toy Box extravaganza took over the massive Good Hope Centre and hosted some 7000 revellers. Tickets (R100) can be bought, usually from the start of December, at Ticketweb outlets (☎ 003 140 0500, 082 140 0500, W www.ticketweb.co.za). For more details see the MCQP Web site (W www.mcqp.co.za).

Shopping

WHAT TO BUY

Craft from across South Africa and the rest of the continent is available in Cape Town, but few pieces are actually made here. Traditional Zulu or Ndebele crafts, for example, are brought from other areas of the country and have hefty mark-ups. If you're going to travel around South Africa you might want to just browse Cape Town's more upmarket craft shops to get an idea of quality and prices, then buy in the areas of the country where they were made and are likely to be cheaper.

Along with items associated with traditional cultures, there is a lot of craft generated for the tourist trade, with some quality items among the dross. It's a matter of looking through the many informal stalls set up around the city. You'll find clusters of them beside the Cape Town train station in the City Bowl **(Map 13)**, on the seaside road to Hout Bay **(Map 11)** and on the M65 at Scarborough near the Cape of Good Hope Nature Reserve **(Map 11)**.

If you're looking for gifts but don't want tacky tourist stuff, consider some township-produced crafts, which are products of poverty plus ingenuity. Items such as picture frames, hats and simple toys made from recycled drink or oil cans are genuine artefacts from a vibrant culture (well, they were until recently – some are now made for the trade).

Cape Town has troves of antiques and collectibles for sale, often at reasonable prices. The local art is also excellent and often reasonably priced.

WHERE TO SHOP
Shopping Centres

Big shopping complexes, such as the Waterfront and Canal Walk, are proving hugely popular with Capetonians. Thankfully, the city centre's shops have not been entirely abandoned (at least not during the week) and you can still find most things you need without trekking out to the suburbs.

Shopping Hours

Most shops, particularly those in the City Bowl area, are open from 9am to 5pm Monday to Friday and 9am to 1pm on Saturday. If opening hours are not given in the listings in this chapter you can assume these hours apply. Shopping centres keep longer hours: Check out the Waterfront, Cavendish Square and Canal Walk centres, which are open daily.

Golden Acre Centre (Adderley St) **Map 13, #119** This dated shopping complex is connected to St George's Mall by underground arcades and is an interesting place to explore for bargains, although its long corridors can get a bit spooky and should certainly be avoided in the evening and on weekends.

Gardens Centre (Orange St, Gardens) **Map 15, #45** The most central shopping complex. It's handy for the backpacker hostels and has good cafes and bookshops, a Pick 'n' Pay supermarket, a Flight Centre and a Cape Union Mart camping supplies shop.

Victoria Wharf Shopping Centre (☎ 418 2369, Waterfront) **Map 14** One of the best places to shop close to the city centre. It has plenty of parking. You'll find branches of all the major stores and supermarkets here, plus some good speciality shops for gifts and souvenirs.

Cavendish Square (☎ 674 3050, Cavendish St, Claremont) **Map 11, #11** One of Cape Town's most stylish shopping centres with branches of all the top stores plus restaurants, a food court and a multiplex cinema. There's plenty of parking on site and it's close to Claremont train station on the Simon's Town line.

Canal Walk (☎ 555 4444, Ⓦ www.canal walk.co.za, Ratanga Junction, Century City, Milnerton) **Map 11, #2** It brags of being the largest mall in Africa with some 450 shops and 50-odd restaurants, but once you've been swallowed up inside this gargantuan place you could be anywhere in the Westernised world. The food court is so big that acrobatics shows are often held over the diners. Drive here along the N1.

Markets
There are craft markets in Greenmarket Square **(Map 13)** Monday to Saturday and beside Green Point Stadium **(Map 14)** on Sunday. The market at Grand Parade **(Map 13)** on Wednesday and Saturday doesn't sell much of interest to visitors, but it's much livelier than the others, with people scrambling for bargains, mainly clothing.

24-Hour Shops
After hours it can be difficult to find vital bits and pieces like milk and cigarettes. There are a few *7-Eleven* shops, with one on Main Rd in Sea Point **(Map 16, #10)** open 24 hours. Many petrol stations are open 24 hours and most stock basic necessities.

Bookshops
The main mass-market bookshop and newsagent is *CNA*, with numerous shops around the city.

Exclusive Books (☎ 419 0905, Victoria Wharf, Waterfront) **Map 14, #30** Open 9am-10.30pm Mon-Thurs, 9am-11pm Fri & Sat, 10am-9pm Sun. An excellent range including some books in French. There's a branch at the Cavendish Square shopping centre **(Map 11, #11)** in Claremont.

Travellers Bookshop (☎ 425 6880, Victoria Wharf, Waterfront) **Map 14, #28** Open 9am-9pm daily. This shop stocks all the books you might need on destinations all over the world, and has a good range of volumes on Cape Town and South Africa.

Clarke's (☎ 423 5739, W www.clarkes books.co.za, 211 Long St, City Bowl) **Map 13, #88** An unsurpassed range of books on South Africa and the continent, and a great second-hand and antiquarian section. If you can't find it here it's unlikely to be found at the many other second-hand bookstores along Long St (although there's no harm in browsing).

Ulrich Naumann's (☎ 423 7832, 15-19 Burg St, City Bowl) **Map 13, #115** This is the best place to come for German-language books.

Crafts & Souvenirs
Along St George's Mall you'll find some very good (as well as some very ordinary) art by township artists. Some of the artists are quite well known but prefer to sell directly to the public rather than pay commission to a gallery. You can pay over R200 for a print but some are worth it.

The *Red Shed Craft Workshop* **(Map 14, #27)**, part of Victoria Wharf at the Waterfront, is a permanent market of craft shops where you may catch some artists at work; don't expect any bargains on prices though.

On Monday and Thursday *Khayelitsha Craft Market* at St Michael's church is a great place to look for interesting souvenirs, and you can be sure that your money goes directly to the people who need it most. (For more information, call Matanzina on ☎ 361 2904.)

Montebello (☎ 685 6445, 31 Newlands Ave, Newlands) **Map 11, #10** Open 9am-5pm daily. This development project aims to promote good local design and create jobs in the craft industry. On weekdays you can visit the artists' studios. There's an outlet in the city beneath Cape Town Tourism **(Map 13, #113)**.

Pan African Market (☎ 424 2957, W pan afr icanmarket.co.za, 76 Long St, City Bowl) **Map 13, #32** Open 9am-5pm Mon-Fri, 9am-3pm Sat. A microcosm of the continent with a bewildering range of art and craft packed into its three floors.

African Image (☎ 423 8385, Cnr Church & Burg Sts, City Bowl) **Map 13, #46** Fab range of new and old craft and artefacts, at reasonable prices. You'll find a lot of township crafts here. The branch at Victoria Wharf in the Waterfront **(Map 14, #32)** stocks a more upmarket range.

Clementina Ceramics & Fine Art (☎ 462 5226, W www.clementina.co.za, 31 Breda St, Oranjezicht) **Map 15, #48** The Cape Town branch of the Paarl-based ceramics studio specialises in distinctive homewares.

Crafts of the Region

For decades, African art was dismissed by European colonisers as 'mere craft', as distinct from 'art'. Be prepared to surrender this artificial Western distinction as you root around the craft shops and markets of Cape Town. The following are a few things to look out for:

Pottery

The master potters of the Venda people, who live in the north-eastern corner of Northern Province, are all women. Their hand-fashioned pots come in 10 different sizes and designs. Each one has a different function: cooking, serving food or liquids, or storage. The pots, which feature brightly coloured geometric designs, are more ornamental than functional.

More modern, but equally distinctive, ceramics are those designed by the Clementina Van Der Walt studio. The main studio is in Paarl (see the Excursions chapter), but the products are available in Cape Town too (see Crafts & Souvenirs in this chapter).

Beadwork

Zulu beadwork is now mainly used for decoration, and sometimes in traditional ceremonies. It takes many forms, from the small, square *umgexo*, which is widely available and makes a good gift, to the more elaborate *umbelenja*, a short skirt or tasselled belt worn by girls from puberty until they are married. *Amadavathi* (bead anklets) are worn by men and women.

Beads are also traditionally used as a means of communication, especially as love letters. Messages are 'spelled out' by the colour and arrangement of the beads. For example, red symbolises passion or anger; black, difficulties or night; blue, yearning; white or pale blue, pure love; brown, disgust or despondency; and green, peace or bliss.

There have always been ambiguities in this system. For example, a 'letter' predominantly red and black could be promising a night of passion or it could mean that the sender was annoyed.

Basketwork

Zulu handwoven baskets, although created in a variety of styles and colours, almost always have a function. The raw materials vary depending on seasonal availability – a basket could be woven from various grasses, palm fronds, bark, even telephone wire.

Two designs predominate: the triangle, which denotes the male, and the diamond, which denotes the female. Two triangular shapes above one another in an hourglass form indicate that the male owner of the basket is married; similarly, two diamonds so arranged mean the female owner of the basket is married.

Township Crafts

New and imaginative types of crafts have sprung up in the townships, borrowing from old traditions but using materials that are readily available. For example, old soft-drink cans and food tins are used to make hats, picture frames and toy cars and planes, while wire and metal bottle tops are used for bags and vases.

Complex wirework sculptures and mixed-media paintings and collages are common. Printing and rug-making are also taking off – the Philani Nutrition Centre's projects in the Cape Flats townships are a good example (for details, see Cape Flats in the Things to See & Do chapter).

Woodwork

Venda woodcarvings are also popular. Traditionally, woodcarving was a men-only occupation, but these days expert female woodcarvers can be found. A number of local woods are used, including *mudzwin*, *mutango* and *musimbiri*. Carved items include bowls, spoons, trays, pots, walking sticks, chains attached to calabashs, and knobkerries (sticks with a round knob at one end, used as clubs or missiles).

Mnandi Textiles & Design (☎ 447 6814, 90 Station St, Observatory) **Map 17, #6** Sells cloth and clothing printed with everything from ANC election posters to animals and traditional African patterns.

Africa Nova (☎ 790 4454, Main Rd, Hout Bay) **Map 2, #6** Open 9am-5pm Mon-Fri, 10am-2pm Sat & Sun. A tasteful and colourful collection of more contemporary African textiles, art and craft.

Antiques & Art

In the City Bowl, Church St and Long St in particular are worth a browse. There's a small market daily along the pedestrianised section of Church St between Long and Burg Sts, and this is where you'll also find several interesting commercial galleries.

Metropolitan Gallery (☎ 424 7436, 35 Church St, City Bowl) **Map 13, #44** Exhibition space for the nonprofit Association for Visual Arts (AVA), which shows some very interesting work by local artists.

Everard Read (☎ 418 4527, 3 Portswood Rd, Waterfront) **Map 14, #42** Open 9am-6pm Mon-Sat. The top gallery for contemporary South African art, Everard Read is well worth a browse. At the time of research there was another branch in the Old Port Captain's Office **(Map 14, #47)**, also at the Waterfront.

The Junk Shop (☎ 424 0706, 206 Long St, City Bowl) **Map 13, #67** Intriguing junk spanning the eras with some decent bits and bobs for those prepared to dig.

Hotchi-Witchi (☎ 082 955 0054, 90 Kloof St, Gardens) **Map 15, #10** Antiques and bric-a-brac shop specialising in old cameras and kewpie dolls!

Artvark (☎ 788 5584, 48 Main Rd, Kalk Bay) **Map 3, #9** Open 10am-6pm daily. One of several shops in Kalk Bay specialising in local artists' paintings, pottery and crafts.

Jewellery

Afrogem (☎ 424 8048, 64 New Church St, City Bowl) **Map 13, #75** Open 8.30am-5pm Mon-Sat. Produces jewellery and other items from semiprecious stones, gold and silver. You can call in and see how it's done on a free guided tour.

The Bead Shop (☎ 423 4687, 207 Long St, City Bowl) **Map 13, #87** For an enormous range of beads, some in African designs, check out this long-running store, which also stocks ethnic jewellery.

Music

The African Music Store (☎ 426 0857, 90a Long St, City Bowl) **Map 13, #31** The knowledgeable staff here can advise you on the big selection of local music.

Look & Listen (☎ 683 1810, Cavendish Square, Claremont) **Map 11, #11** This CD and video megastore has an impressive range and some discount prices. There's also a branch at Canal Walk **(Map 11, #2)**.

Wine & Tobacco

Cape wines are of an extremely high quality and very cheap by international standards. It's worth considering having a few cases shipped home, although you will almost certainly have to pay duty. All wineries can arrange shipping. (For more information, see the special section 'Cape Wineries'.)

Vaughan Johnson's Wine & Cigar Shop (☎ 419 2121, **e** vjohnson@mweb.co.za, Dock Rd, Waterfront) **Map 14, #41** Open 9am-6pm Mon-Fri, 10am-5pm Sat & Sun. It stocks practically every wine you could wish to buy (plus a few more) and is open, unlike most wine sellers, on Sunday.

Sturk's Tobacconists (☎ 423 3928, 54 Shortmarket St, City Bowl) **Map 13, #35** Established in 1793, this is the place to pick up a cigar to enjoy at one of Cape Town's several cigar bars.

Camping Gear

Cape Union Mart has branches at shop 142 at the Waterfront (☎ 419 0019) **(Map 14, #30)**; on the corner of Mostert and Corporation Sts in the City Bowl **(Map 13, #134)** (☎ 464 5800); and in the Gardens Centre (☎ 461 9678) **(Map 15, #45)**.

Excursions

Highlights

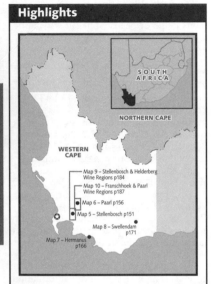

- Sample the wines at the estates around Stellenbosch, Helderberg, Franschhoek and Paarl.
- Drive along spectacular mountain roads such as the Bainskloof Pass.
- Hike the Boesmanskloof Trail from Die Galg to Greyton.
- Spot whales and dolphins along the coast near Hermanus.
- Search for San rock art in the Cederberg Wilderness Area.
- Slip back in time at the Karoo train stop of Matjiesfontein.

Cape Town has plenty to keep most visitors occupied, but you really shouldn't miss out on seeing some of the surrounding area too. Western Cape province has some truly beautiful scenery and interesting old towns, some tucked away in wine country first planted with vines over three centuries ago. For the semidesert landscapes typical of large chunks of South Africa you'll have to travel further afield, although it's quite possible to get a glimpse of the Karoo on a two- or three-day trip.

You'll need at least three days spare if you want to travel to and from the Garden Route, which starts around 400km south-east of Cape Town. (For details of the Garden Route and the rest of the country, see Lonely Planet's *South Africa, Lesotho & Swaziland*.)

Winelands

The Boland (meaning 'Upland'), as the wine-producing country around Stellenbosch is known, is the loveliest of South Africa's several wine-producing areas. The vineyards form a patchwork in the fertile valleys, and dramatic mountain ranges shoot up to over 1500m. The Franschhoek and Bainskloof Passes that cross them are among the most spectacular in the country (see the boxed text 'Great Mountain Passes' later in this chapter).

Stellenbosch is the area's most interesting and lively town, Franschhoek has the best location and dining scene, and Paarl is a busy commercial centre with plenty to see. All three are historically important and attractive, and promote routes around the surrounding wineries (see the special section 'Cape Wineries').

It is possible to see Stellenbosch and Paarl on day trips from Cape Town, but Stellenbosch is the easiest to get around if you don't have a car. To do justice to the region and to visit the many wineries, you'll need wheels – bicycle wheels will do.

STELLENBOSCH
☎ 021 • postcode 7600 • pop 184,000
Established on the banks of the Eerste River by Governor Van Der Stel in 1679, Stellenbosch is the second-oldest town (after Cape Town) in South Africa, and one of the best preserved. The town is full of architectural

gems (Cape Dutch, Georgian and Victorian) and is shaded by enormous oak trees. There are several interesting museums, not least the Village Museum, which is spread across four buildings representing the different periods in the town's history.

The Afrikaans-language University of Stellenbosch, established in 1918, continues to play an important role in Afrikaner politics and culture. It has over 17,000 students, which means the town's nightlife can get wild during term time – visit in February during the Venster Versiering festival and you'll see what we mean!

Orientation & Information

The train station is a short walk west of the centre. The train line effectively forms the western boundary of the town, and the Eerste River, the southern. Dorp St, which runs roughly parallel to the river, is the old town's main street and is lined with numerous fine old buildings. The commercial centre lies between Dorp St and the university to the east of the Braak, the old town square.

The Stellenbosch Publicity Association (Map 5, #24) (☎ 883 3584, W www.istellen bosch.org.za), 36 Market St, is open from 8am to 6pm Monday to Friday, 9am to 5pm Saturday and 9.30am to 4.30pm Sunday. The staff are extremely helpful. Pick up the excellent free brochure *Discover Stellenbosch on Foot*, with a walking-tour map and information on many of the historic buildings (also available in French and German); and *Stellenbosch & Its Wine Route*, which includes details of many nearby wineries. You'll also find an Internet cafe here. Guided walks leave from the publicity association at 10am and 3pm. They cost R30 per person (minimum three people).

There's a Rennies Travel foreign exchange office (Map 5, #26) on Bird St.

The Bookshop (Map 5, #30) (☎ 886 9277) and Ex Libris (Map 5, #30) (☎ 886 6871), both on Andringa St, are good bookshops.

Village Museum (Map 5, #33)

The Village Museum *(Dorp Museum; ☎ 887 2902, 18 Ryneveld St; adult/child R10/5; open 9.30am-5pm Mon-Sat, 2pm-5pm Sun)*

is a group of carefully restored and period-furnished houses dating from 1709 to 1850. The main entrance on Ryneveld St leads into the oldest of the buildings, the Schreuderhuis. The whole block bounded by Ryneveld, Plein, Drostdy and Church Sts is occupied by the museum, and includes most of the buildings and some charming gardens. Grosvenor House is on the other side of Drostdy St.

Toy & Miniature Museum (Map 5, #23)

This museum *(☎ 887 2937, Cnr Market & Herte Sts; adult/child R5/1; open 9.30am-5pm Mon-Sat, 2pm-5pm Sun, closed Sun May-Aug)*, behind the publicity association in another historic building, is a delightful surprise. Many of the miniatures are amazingly detailed, highlights being a model railway set, and houses made entirely of icing sugar – ask the guide to point out some of the best pieces.

The Braak

At the north end of the Braak (the old town square), an open stretch of grass, you'll find the neo-gothic St Mary's on the Braak Church (Map 5, #16), completed in 1852. To the west is the VOC Kruithuis (Map 5, #21) *(admission free; open 9.30am-1pm Mon-Fri)*, built in 1777 to store the town's weapons and gunpowder and now housing a small military museum. On the north-west corner is the Burgerhuis (Map 5, #15), also known as Fick House, a fine example of late-18th-century Cape Dutch style. Most of this building is now occupied by Historical Homes of South Africa, an organisation established to preserve important architecture.

Rembrandt Van Rijn Art Gallery (Map 5, #48)

This small gallery *(☎ 886 4340, Dorp St; admission free; open 9am-12.45pm & 2pm-5pm Mon-Fri, 10am-1pm & 2pm-5pm Sat)* has some fine examples of 20th-century South African art, including paintings by Irma Stern and incredibly lifelike sculptures by Anton Van Wouw; even if the art doesn't interest you, it's worth visiting to see the house, which was built in 1783.

Activities

There are lots of walks in the Stellenbosch area – ask the publicity association about maps and permits for the **Vineyard Hiking Trail (Map 9)**.

Jonkershoek (☎ 889 1568) is a small nature reserve within a timber plantation that offers walking and biking trails; entry is R10 per car, R5 for walkers and cyclists.

Bicycles can be rented from Stumble Inn (see Places to Stay).

Special Events

The Oude Libertas Amphitheatre (☎ 918 8950, **W** www.oudelibertas.co.za) holds a performing arts festival between January and March.

The Van Der Stel Festival in late September and early October is a celebration of local music, art, food and wine.

Places to Stay

Hostels *Stumble Inn* (☎/fax 887 4049, 12 Market St, www.jump.to/stumble)* **Map 5, #42** Camping R30 per person, dorm beds R50, doubles R150. In two old houses, one with a small pool, the other with a pleasant garden, this place has a lively atmosphere. The well-travelled owners are a good source of information. They also rent bicycles for R50 per day, and run Easy Rider Wine Tours (see Organised Tours in the Getting There & Away chapter).

Hillbillies Haven (☎/fax 887 9905, 24 Dennesig St)* **Map 5, #8** Dorm beds R55, singles/doubles R75/R90. Less of a backpacker scene and more a family home in a quiet area, Hillbillies Haven is within easy walking distance of the town centre. The rooms are clean and reasonably spacious.

Backpackers Inn (☎ 887 2020, fax 887 2010, **e** bacpac1@global.co.za, 1st floor, De Wett Centre)* **Map 5, #29** Dorm beds R50, singles/doubles R120/160. This rather plain hostel has a central location. It's recently been taken over by the folks from Stumble Inn, so expect some upgrading. The entrance is just off Church St.

B&Bs, Guesthouses & Hotels The publicity association can provide you with a booklet that lists the many B&Bs. Prices start at R90 per person near the town centre,

---

Stellenbosch Walking Tour (Map 5)

Start at the publicity association on Market St and head north-west to the Braak, the old town square, where you'll find several old buildings, including the VOC Kruithuis, an 18th-century powder magazine.

Cross the Braak and turn left (north) up Bird St, right onto Beyers St, left onto Andringa St and right onto Victoria St. Follow Victoria St and you'll come to the University of Stellenbosch. This pretty campus is crammed full of Cape Dutch buildings, as befits the country's (and thus the world's) leading Afrikaans university.

Find your way back to Victoria St and head west until you come to Neethling St. Turn right, walk past the Botanical Gardens to the junction with Van Riebeeck St, turn right again (some of the fine old homes around here offer accommodation) and continue to Ryneveld St, on the edge of the town centre. Turn left down Ryneveld St to visit the Village Museum.

Follow Ryneveld St south onto Dorp St, one of Stellenbosch's oldest and most impressive streets, then turn right. Continue down Dorp to the Rembrandt Van Rijn Art Gallery (outside which you'll see a giant wine press) and turn left to cross the Eerste River; the willow-shaded De Oewer (see Places to Eat) is a good spot to revive.

Retrace your steps across the bridge back to Dorp St, cross over and turn up Market St to return to where you started. On the way back you'll pass the elegant 18th-century Van Der Bijlhuis, now occupied by an architect's office.

MAP 5 – STELLENBOSCH

PLACES TO STAY
- 8 Hillbillies Haven
- 29 Backpackers Inn
- 31 D'Ouwe Werf
- 38 Stellenbosch Hotel; Jan Cats Brasserie
- 40 De Oude Meul
- 41 De Goue Druif
- 42 Stumble Inn

PLACES TO EAT
- 2 Studentesentrum; Brollocks
- 3 The Workshop
- 4 Fusion Café
- 19 Decameron Italian Restaurant
- 27 Mugg & Bean
- 28 Wijnhuis
- 32 Spice Cafe
- 35 Java Cafe
- 36 De Soete Inval
- 39 Coastal Catch
- 45 The Blue Orange
- 49 De Oewer
- 50 De Volkskombuis

OTHER
- 1 Hospital
- 5 Bohemia
- 6 Minibus Taxis
- 7 Caltex Petrol Station
- 9 Simonsberg Cheese Factory
- 10 Bergkelder
- 11 Tollies; Fandangos
- 12 Club 8tease Fever
- 13 Dros
- 14 The Terrace
- 15 Burgerhuis (Fick House)
- 16 St Mary's on the Braak Church
- 17 Shopping Mall
- 18 Botanical Gardens
- 20 Post Office
- 21 VOC Kruithuis
- 22 Van Der Bijlhuis
- 23 Toy & Miniature Museum
- 24 Stellenbosch Publicity Association
- 25 Minibus Taxis
- 26 Rennies Travel
- 30 The Bookshop; Ex Libris
- 33 Village Museum (Dorp Museum)
- 34 Grosvenor House
- 37 Moto
- 43 De Akker; The Hidden Cellar
- 44 Oom Samie se Winkel
- 46 BP Petrol Station & 24-Hour Shop
- 47 De Kelder
- 48 Rembrandt Van Rijn Art Gallery

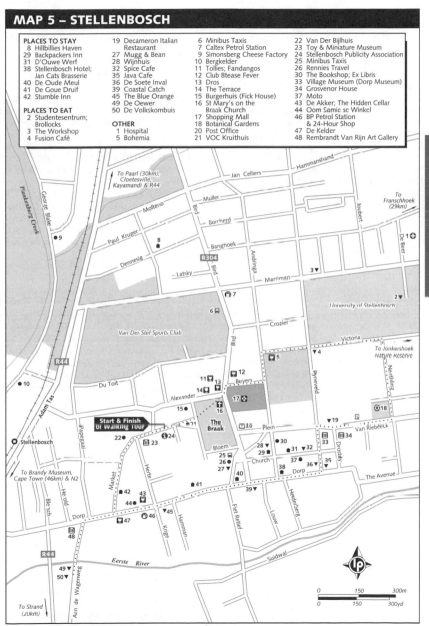

EXCURSIONS

R70 in suburban areas, and R110 on nearby farms (less for self-catering cottages). You might have to press the staff to tell you about the very cheapest places.

Wilfra Court (☎/fax 889 6091, 16 Hine St, Cloetsville) Singles/doubles B&B R110/220. Readers have recommended this place. It's a fair way from the town centre, but friendly, and interesting because it's run by the local mayor and his wife, who are a coloured couple. They only have two rooms, so book ahead and get them to give you directions.

De Oude Meul (☎ 887 7085, fax 883 9549, W www.deoudemeul.snowball.co.za, 10a Mill St) Map 5, #40 Singles/doubles B&B R175/225. Above an antiques shop in the centre of town, the accommodation here is very reasonable for the price (which is even lower in winter). Some of the rooms have balconies.

De Goue Druif (☎ 883 3555, 110 Dorp St) Map 5, #41 Singles/doubles B&B from R200/360. This rambling old Cape Dutch home offers comfortable and individually decorated rooms.

Stellenbosch Hotel (☎ 887 3644, fax 887 3673, W www.stellenbosch.co.za/hotel, Cnr Dorp & Andringa Sts) Map 5, #38 Singles/ doubles R340/490. A rather idiosyncratic but comfortable country hotel. Some of the rooms have four-poster beds and Victorian styling. A section dating from 1743 houses the *Jan Cats Brasserie*, an OK place to drink but not to eat.

D'Ouwe Werf (☎ 887 4608, fax 887 4646, W www.ouwewerf.com, 30 Church St) Map 5, #31 Singles/doubles B&B from R570/840. This appealing, old-style hotel dating back to 1802 has a pool and a good restaurant – it's well worth dropping by the shady courtyard for lunch. The more expensive rooms are furnished with lovely antiques.

For details of the luxurious Lanzerac hotel, see the special section 'Cape Wineries'.

Places to Eat

There's no shortage of places to eat and drink, and several of the nearby vineyards have restaurants too (see the special section 'Cape Wineries').

Cafes & Snack Bars For a range of reasonably cheap snacks and meals check out the *Studentesentrum* (Student Centre) **(Map 5, #2)** at the university.

Coastal Catch (☎ 887 9550, 137 Dorp St) Map 5, #39 Mains R20-25. Open 11am-9pm daily. Come here for high-quality fish and chips. It's mainly takeaway, but there are a few tables if you want to eat here.

Mugg & Bean (☎ 883 2972, Muel St) Map 5, #27 Open 7am-11pm daily. This reputable chain cafe is a good choice for breakfast with bagels, huge muffins, and self-service bottomless cups of coffee for R5.50.

The Blue Orange (☎ 887 2052, 77-79 Dorp St) Map 5, #45 Open 8am-5pm Mon-Sat, 9am-5pm Sun. A pleasant cafe with attached farm shop serving hearty breakfasts. Its shaded veranda is a good spot to relax with a book.

Java Cafe (☎ 887 6261, 2C Ryneveld St) Map 5, #35 Open 8.30am-11pm daily. Surprisingly high-quality food is served at this simple Internet cafe (access R10 per half hour). It has a quiet courtyard, too.

Spice Cafe (☎ 883 8480, 34 Church St) Map 5, #32 Mains around R22, self-serve buffet R35. Open 9am-5pm Mon-Fri, 9am-2pm Sat, 10pm-2am Sun. Gourmet sandwiches (and the buffet) are offered at this brightly painted house with a courtyard shaded by a peppercorn tree.

Restaurants *The Workshop (☎ 887 9985, 34 Merriman St)* Map 5, #3 Mains R40. Open 10.30am-1.30am Mon-Sat. The roomy bistro-restaurant serving good-value fusion cuisine is upstairs; the buzzy bar is downstairs. Popular with students from the nearby university.

De Soete Inval (☎ 886 4842, 5 Ryneveld St) Map 5, #36 Mains R30-40. Open 9am-10pm daily. Known primarily for its choice of 30 different pancakes, this cheerful place also does a fine Indonesian *rystafel* (rice with many dishes). Buy six dishes for R50, or a half portion for R35.

Wijnhuis (☎ 887 7196, Andringa St) Map 5, #28 Mains R40-50. Open 10am-late daily. A stylish option with both indoor and

Divine sights: **Top left:** Noor Islam mosque, Simon's Town **Top right:** Dutch Reformed church, Stellenbosch **Bottom:** Assembly of God church, Khayelitsha

RICHARD I'ANSON

SIMON RICHMOND

RICHARD I'ANSON

SIMON RICHMOND

Cape wineries uncorked: Pack a picnic blanket and a corkscrew and head for the vines. **Clockwise from top:** Groot Constantia; La Couronne; Groot Constantia; Vergelegen outdoor dining areas, an extensive menu and an even longer wine list. Few wines are available by the glass, but a tasting of six wines costs R15.

De Volkskombuis (☎ *887 2121, Aan de Wagenweg)* **Map 5, #50** Mains R50. Open noon-2.30pm daily, 7pm-9pm Mon-Sat. This place specialises in traditional Cape Malay cuisine and is favoured by locals, not just tourists. The building was designed by Sir Herbert Baker and the terrace looks across fields to Stellenboschberge. The Cape country sampler (R45) consists of four traditional specialities. Booking is advisable.

De Oewer (☎ *886 5431, Aan de Wagenweg)* **Map 5, #49** Mains R30. Open noon-3pm daily, 7pm-10pm Mon-Sat. Next to De Volkskombuis, with an open-air section shaded by willow trees beside the river. The light menu is typified by dishes such as haloumi cheese salad with figs (R18).

Decameron Italian Restaurant (☎ *883 3331, 50 Plein St)* **Map 5, #19** Mains R40-50. Open 10am-midnight daily. Considered by many to be the town's best Italian restaurant, Decameron is good for a quick pizza (from R30) or a full meal, and has outdoor seating for those balmy evenings.

Fusion Café (☎ *883 8593, 3 Victoria Rd)* **Map 5, #4** Mains R25-60. Open 9am-3.30pm & 6pm-late Mon-Sat. Funky joint with a cooler-than-thou vibe, serving everything from a full breakfast (R27) to Thai-style springbok, and duck breast with gooseberry chutney.

Entertainment

Stellenbosch has a lively nightlife, geared towards the tastes of the university students. It's generally safe to walk around the town centre at night, so a pub crawl is certainly on the cards (if you're staying at the Stumble Inn one you'll probably find one organised anyway). All the places listed are open daily till very late.

Dros **(Map 5, #13)**, *The Terrace* **(Map 5, #14)** and *Tollies* **(Map 5, #11)**, clustered together in the complex just off Bird St and north of the Braak, are among the liveliest bars; you can eat at them all, but that's not what most of the patrons have in mind. If you're looking for a slightly more sophisticated option try *Fandangos* **(Map 5, #11)**, which is a cocktail bar and Internet cafe in the same complex.

Bohemia **(Map 5, #5)** (☎ *882 8375, Cnr Andringa & Victoria Sts)* has live music and the novelty of hubble-bubble pipes with a range of different tobaccos to choose from.

De Kelder **(Map 5, #47)** (☎ *883 3797, 63 Dorp St)* is a reasonably pleasant restaurant, bar and beer garden, popular with German backpackers for some reason.

De Akker **(Map 5, #43)** (☎ *883 3512, 90 Dorp St)* is a classic student drinking hole, with pub meals from under R20. Upstairs is the *Hidden Cellar*, where bands occasionally play.

At the time of research *Club 8tease Fever* **(Map 5, #12)** on Bird St, upstairs in the shopping centre opposite Dros, was the dance club of choice. *Brollocks* **(Map 5, #2)** in the Studentesentrum is notorious for its wet-T-shirt antics.

Shopping

Bergkelder (☎ *809 8492, George Blake St)* **Map 5, #10** Open 8am-5pm Mon-Fri, 9am-1pm Sat. Drop by here for an introduction to the area's many wines. A slide show, a cellar tour and tastings of up to 12 wines costs R10. You pour your own tastings, so take it easy or it might be your last stop for the day! The Bergkelder is a short walk from the train station; tours are held at 10am, 10.30am (in German) and 3pm.

Simonsberg cheese factory (☎ *809 1017, 9 Stoffel Smit St)* **Map 5, #9** Open 9am-5pm Mon-Fri, 9am-12.30pm Fri. Up the road from the Bergkelder, this factory's free tastings are very popular with hungry backpackers and it sells inexpensive cheese.

Oom Samie se Winkel (Uncle Sammy's Shop; ☎ *887 0797, 84 Dorp St)* **Map 5, #44** Open 9am-5pm daily. This is a tourist trap, but it's still worth visiting for its amazing range of goods, from high kitsch to genuine antiques and everything in between.

Getting There & Away

Metro trains run the 46km between Cape Town and Stellenbosch; 1st-/economy-class tickets cost R9.50/5.50 and the trip takes about an hour. For inquiries, call Stellenbosch station (☎ 808 1111). To be safe, travel in the middle of the day and not at weekends.

Most of the buses running to Cape Town are the long-distance services, which charge high prices for this short sector and do not take bookings.

Backpacker Bus (☎ 082 809 9185, e bpackbus@mweb.co.za) runs trips from Cape Town to Stellenbosch (R90).

A shared taxi to Paarl is about R10 but you'll probably have to change taxis en route.

Getting Around

With largely flat countryside (unless you try to cross Franschhoek Pass), this is good cycling territory. Bicycles can be hired from Stumble Inn and Hillbillies Haven. Mopeds are available from Moto (☎ 887 9965), at 42 Ryneveld St, for R170 a day.

Tazzis (☎ 887 2203) runs its tiny vans here, like the Rikkis in Cape Town, and R5 (sharing) will get you just about anywhere in town.

FRANSCHHOEK

☎ 021 • postcode 7690

The toughest decision you'll have to make in Franschhoek is where to eat. This booming village, nestling in one of the loveliest settings in the Cape, has so many fine restaurants and wineries that you could find yourself lingering here longer than you expected to – not a bad thing since Franschhoek is a good base from which to visit both Stellenbosch and Paarl as long as you have transport. (For more on wineries in the area, see the special section 'Cape Wineries'.)

Wining and dining apart, there's an interesting museum commemorating the 200 French Huguenots who settled in the region in the 17th century, as well as some decent walks in the surrounding mountains and plenty of galleries and designer shops to mop up any spare cash.

Orientation & Information

The town is clustered around Huguenot St. At the eastern end it reaches a T-junction, with the Huguenot Memorial Museum in front. Turn left here for the spectacular Franschhoek Pass.

Franschhoek Vallée Tourisme (☎ 876 3603, W www.franschhoek.org.za) is in a small building on the main street. The staff can provide a map of the area's scenic walks and issue permits (R10) for walks in nearby forestry areas, as well as book accommodation. From September to March it's open 8.30am to 6pm Monday to Friday, 9am to 5pm Saturday and 10am to 5pm Sunday. Call for opening hours in other months.

Internet access is available at the Stationery Shop, Bordeaux St, which is open from 9am to 5pm daily and charges R10 per 30 minutes.

Huguenot Memorial Museum

This engrossing museum (☎ 876 2532, Malherbe St; adult/child R4/1; open 9am-5pm Mon-Sat, 2pm-5pm Sun) celebrates South Africa's Huguenots and houses the genealogical records of their descendants plus some hefty Cape Dutch furniture. Behind the main complex is a pleasant cafe; in front is the **Huguenot Monument** (adult/child R3/1; open 9am-5pm daily); and across the road is the annexe with displays on the Anglo-Boer War and natural history, plus a souvenir shop.

Places to Stay

The cheapest B&Bs cost around R150 per double, but prices drop if you stay out of town. For details of winery accommodation, see the special section 'Cape Wineries'.

The Cottage (☎ 876 2392, e thecottage@sholtz.wcape.school.za, 55 Huguenot St) Singles/doubles B&B R150/260. Just the one cottage, sleeping two or four at a pinch, but it's a beauty. Private and quiet, it's a few minutes' walk from the village centre – and very good value.

Ballon Rouge (☎ 876 2651, fax 876 3743, e info@ballon-rouge.co.za, 7 Reservoir St East) Singles/doubles B&B R230/360. All the quality rooms at this small hotel open onto the veranda and there's a pool and a restaurant.

Auberge Bligny (☎ 876 3767, 28 Van Wyk St) Singles/doubles B&B R290/390. Once a

Victorian homestead, this centrally located guesthouse has seven pleasant, comfortable rooms and a small pool.

Reeden Lodge *(☎/fax 876 3174, ⓔ reeden @telekomsa.net, End of Fabriek St)* Self-catering cottages from R125 per person. The well-equipped cottages on this farm, about 10 minutes' walk from town, sleep four to six people. They're good if you've got kids because there are sheep, a tree house and lots of space.

La Cabrière Country House *(☎ 876 4780, fax 876 3852, Ⓦ www.lacabriere.co.za, Middagkrans Rd)* Doubles B&B R750. A refreshing break from all that Cape Dutch architecture, this modern boutique guesthouse has just four sumptuously decorated rooms and very personal service.

Le Quartier Français *(☎ 876 2151, fax 876 3105, 16 Huguenot Rd)* Doubles from R1210, doubles DB&B R1800. One of the best places to stay in the Winelands. Set around a leafy courtyard and pool, the guest rooms are very large, with fireplaces, huge beds and stylish decor.

Places to Eat
Franschhoek is so small that it's easy to stroll around and see what appeals. Good cheaper places along Huguenot St include **Gideon's Famous Pancake House** at No 50 and **Cafe Rendezvous Bistro** in the Oude Stallen Centre at No 19, but if ever there was a place to splash out on a meal it's here.

Topsi & Company *(☎ 876 2952, 7 Reservoir St)* Mains R50-60. Open 12.30pm-3pm & 7.30pm-10pm Thurs-Mon. Our favourite in a heavily contested field. Quirky and very relaxed, with the chefs popping out from the open kitchen to serve the totally delicious food. BYO wine.

Le Quartier Français *(☎ 876 2248, 16 Huguenot Rd)* Mains R60-70. Open noon-2.30 & 7pm-9pm daily. This highly acclaimed restaurant is neither pompous nor ridiculously expensive. It opens onto a cottage garden with views of the surrounding mountains. If the restaurant is beyond your budget, try the hotel's bar, which does lighter meals for around R30.

Haute Cabrière *(☎ 876 3688, Franschhoek Pass Rd)* Mains R60-80. Open noon-3pm daily, 7pm-9pm Wed-Mon. A dramatic dining space in a cellar cut into the mountain side. An intriguing menu, with items available as either starters or mains, to match the winery's best vintages.

La Petite Ferme *(☎ 876 3016, Franschhoek Pass Rd)* Open noon-4pm daily. Come here for the romantic views, the boutique wines and the smoked, deboned salmon trout, the delicately flavoured signature dish. A shorter menu is available from 3pm to 4pm. (If you feel like staying overnight, there are a few double suites for R750 including breakfast.) Bookings are absolutely essential.

Getting There & Away
The best way to reach Franschhoek is in your own vehicle; there's no public transport. If you take a shared taxi from either Stellenbosch or Paarl you'll have to change along the way – when you get in, ask the driver where.

PAARL
☎ 021 • postcode 7646 • pop 154,000

Less touristy and more spread out than Stellenbosch, Paarl is a large commercial centre surrounded by mountains and vineyards on the banks of the Berg River. There are several vineyards and wineries within the sprawling town limits, including the huge Kooperatieve Wijnbouwers Vereeniging, better known as the KWV (for more information, see the special section 'Cape Wineries').

Paarl is not really a town to tour on foot, but there is still quite a lot to see and do. There are great walks in the Paarl Mountain Nature Reserve, some excellent Cape Dutch architecture and significant monuments to Afrikaner culture.

The surrounding valley was settled by Europeans in the 1680s, and Paarl was established in 1720. It became a centre for wagon-building, but the town is most famous for its important role in the development and recognition of Afrikaans as a language in its own right.

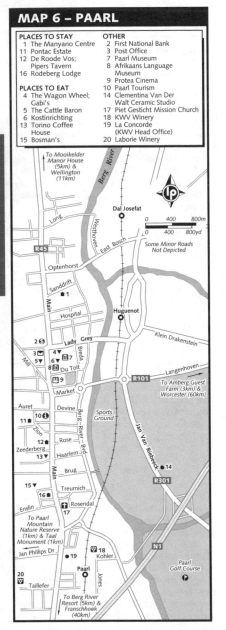

MAP 6 – PAARL

PLACES TO STAY
1 The Manyano Centre
11 Pontac Estate
12 De Roode Vos;
   Pipers Tavern
16 Rodeberg Lodge

PLACES TO EAT
4 The Wagon Wheel;
   Gabi's
5 The Cattle Baron
6 Kostinrichting
13 Torino Coffee
   House
15 Bosman's

OTHER
2 First National Bank
3 Post Office
7 Paarl Museum
8 Afrikaans Language
   Museum
9 Protea Cinema
10 Paarl Tourism
14 Clementina Van Der
   Walt Ceramic Studio
17 Piet Gesticht Mission Church
18 KWV Winery
19 La Concorde
   (KWV Head Office)
20 Laborie Winery

Orientation & Information

Main St runs 11km along the entire length of the town, parallel to the Berg River and the railway line. It's shaded by oaks and jacarandas and is lined with many historic buildings. The busy commercial centre is around Lady Grey St.

Paarl Tourism **(Map 6, #10)** (☎ 872 3829, Ⓦ www.paarlonline.com) at 216 Main St, on the corner of Auret St, has information on the whole region. The staff are particularly helpful for arranging accommodation. The office is open from 9am to 5pm Monday to Friday, 9am to 1pm Saturday and 10am to 1pm Sunday.

Paarl Museum (Map 6, #7)

Apart from the local wineries, the most interesting place to visit is the Paarl Museum (☎ 863 2537, 303 Main St; adult/child R5/free; open 10am-5pm Mon-Fri). Housed in the Old Parsonage (Oude Pastorie) built in 1714, this collection of Cape Dutch antiques and relics of Huguenot and early Afrikaner culture is fascinating. There's a bookcase modelled on King Solomon's temple, and there are displays on the road to reconciliation and the old mosques of the local Muslim community.

Paarl Mountain Nature Reserve

The three giant granite domes that dominate this popular reserve and loom over the town on its western side apparently glisten like pearls if they are caught by the sun after a fall of rain – hence 'Paarl'. The reserve has mountain *fynbos* (literally 'fine bush', a type of vegetation) and a particularly large number of proteas. The cultivated wildflower garden in the middle is a nice spot for a picnic, and there are numerous walks with excellent views over the valley.

Access is from the 11km-long Jan Phillips Drive, which skirts the eastern edge of the reserve. The picnic ground is about 4km from Main St. A map showing walking trails is available from Paarl Tourism.

While up this way you could also visit the **Taal Monument** (adult/child R5/2; open 9am-5pm daily), the giant needlelike edifice that commemorates the Afrikaans language.

On a clear day there are stunning views from here as far as Cape Town.

Afrikaans Language Museum (Map 6, #8)

Of marginal interest is the Afrikaans Language Museum *(Afrikaans Taal Museum; ☎ 8721 3441, Pastorie Ave; adult/child R2/1; open 9am-1pm & 2pm-5pm Mon-Fri)*. The birth of Afrikaans is chronicled in the former home of Gideon Malherbe, the meeting place for the Association of True Afrikaners and the birthplace of the first Afrikaans newspaper. The house has been painstakingly restored.

Places to Stay

Berg River Resort (☎ 863 1650, fax 863 2583) Camping for up to 6 people from R60, double chalets from R200. Beside the Berg River, this attractive municipal park has a swimming pool, canoes, trampolines and a cafe. It's 5km from Paarl towards Franschhoek on the R45.

Amberg Guest Farm (☎/fax 862 0982, e amberg@mweb.co.za) Dorm beds R45, singles/doubles B&B from R200/300, self-catering cottages from R240. These well-equipped cottages and the farmhouse with a pool command a spectacular view across the valley. The amiable hosts also run the Swiss-style *Amberg Country Kitchen*, serving Swiss specialities. They will pick you up in town for a small fee; the farm is on the R101 along Du Toitskloof Pass.

The Manyano Centre (☎ 872 2537, fax 872 2568, e manyanocentre@cci.org.za, Sanddrift St) **Map 6, #1** Dorm beds R35. An enormous accommodation complex with spartan three-bed dorms; you'll need to bring a sleeping bag. Call in advance, especially on weekends, when it fills up with groups. The Manyano Centre is closer to Huguenot train station than to the main Paarl station.

De Roode Vos (☎/fax 872 5912, 152 Main St) **Map 6, #12** Singles/doubles B&B R120/190. This, one of Paarl's cheaper guesthouses, offers homely if unspectacular lodgings. The reliable bistro *Pipers Tavern* is next door.

Rodeberg Lodge (☎ 863 3202, fax 863 3203, e rodeberg@ctm-web.co.za) **Map 6, #16** Singles/doubles B&B R190/300. This guesthouse has good rooms (some with air-con and TV), sensibly located away from the busy main road. The hosts are friendly and breakfast is taken in the conservatory, which opens onto a leafy garden.

Pontac Estate (☎ 872 0445, fax 872 0460, e pontac@iafrica.com, 16 Zion St) **Map 6, #11** Singles/doubles B&B from R275/400. This small, stylish Victorian-era hotel commands a good view of the valley and is centrally located. The rooms are comfortable and there's one self-catering cottage.

Mooikelder Manor House (☎ 863 8491, fax 863 8361, Noorder Paarl). Singles/doubles B&B from R330/540. Around 5km north of the town centre along the R45 is this elegant homestead, once occupied by Cecil Rhodes. The management is friendly and the facilities are excellent.

For details on staying at Laborie winery, see the special section 'Cape Wineries'.

Places to Eat

Several of the local vineyards have restaurants or do picnic lunches and they are among the best places to eat (for details, see the special section 'Cape Wineries'). In town, steak is the dominant cuisine.

The Wagon Wheel (☎ 872 5265, 57 Lady Grey St) **Map 6, #4** Mains R50. Open noon-2pm Tues-Fri, 6pm-late Tues-Sat. More than your average steak joint, this cosy wood-panelled restaurant has won many awards and packs them in nightly; next door the same management has added *Gabi's* (open evenings only), a continental-style cafe-bar.

The Cattle Baron (☎ 872 2000, 3 Gymnasium St) **Map 6, #5** Mains R60. Open noon-3.30pm Mon-Fri & Sun, 5.30pm-11.30pm daily. This branch of the upmarket steakhouse chain has a lively atmosphere and a reasonable selection of local wines.

Kostinrichting (☎ 871 1353, 19 Pastorie Ave) **Map 6, #6** Mains R30. Open 8am-4pm Mon-Fri, 8am-1pm Sat. Pleasant cafe, good for a snack or light meal, in a Victorian-era

EXCURSIONS

building that once was a school. A craft shop is attached.

Torino Coffee House (☎ *872 5967, 130 Main St)* **Map 6, #13** Open 9am-5.30pm Tues-Sun. This elegant restored building has a courtyard out the back. Breakfast starts at R17.50, while sandwiches go for R20. There's a very tempting chocolate shop next door.

Bosman's (☎ *863 2727, The Grande Roche, Plantasie St)* **Map 6, #15** Mains R100. Open 7pm-9pm daily. Outrageously expensive (for South Africa) but undoubtedly classy, with chandeliers inside, flickering candles outside on the veranda and a wine list that runs to over 50 pages! A four-course set menu is R218.

Shopping
Clementina Van Der Walt Ceramic Studio (☎ *872 7514,* W *www.clementina.co.za, Parys Farm, Van Riebeeck Dr)* **Map 6, #14** Open 9am-5pm Mon-Fri, 9am-4pm Sat, 10am-4pm Sun. This is the showroom and production site for one of South Africa's most appealing and colourful ranges of pottery. The adjoining gallery displays arts and crafts from all over Africa. Van Riebeeck Dr is the R301.

Getting There & Away
Several long-distance bus services come through Paarl, but the fare from Cape Town is R85, so consider taking the cheaper Metro trains. These run between Cape Town and Paarl roughly every hour Monday to Friday and less frequently at weekends. An economy-/1st-class ticket costs about R6/12 and the trip takes about 1¼ hours. Take care to travel on trains during the busy part of the day since robberies have been reported.

You can travel by train from Paarl to Stellenbosch if you take a Cape Town–bound train and change at Muldersvlei.

Getting Around
If you don't have your own transport, then your only option for getting around Paarl, apart from walking, is to call a taxi: Try Paarl Radio Taxis on ☎ 872 5671.

AROUND PAARL
Bainskloof Pass
This is one of the country's great mountain passes, with a superb caravan park halfway along. (For more information on Bainskloof Pass, see the boxed text 'Great Mountain Passes'.)

Tweede Tol Caravan Park & Camp Site (☎ *021-945 4570)* Camping R46 for up to 6 people, plus R5 per vehicle. Gates open 7.30am-6pm mid-Sept–end May. This camping ground, in a wonderful spot at the head of the pass, is surrounded by magnificent fynbos. There are swimming holes nearby. Firewood is available for sale, and there are braai facilities on site.

The camp is a good base if you plan to tackle the walks in the area. For these you'll need to buy a permit (R29), available from the Cape Nature Conservation desk at Cape Town Tourism (for contact details, see Tourist Offices in the Facts for the Visitor chapter).

The **Patatskloof Trail** is a long day-walk that begins and ends at the ***Oasis Tea Room***, which is open from 8.30am to 6pm Thursday to Sunday, on the road leading up to the pass from Wellington. You can make it an overnight walk by arranging to stay in a cave on the trail; for more information, call ☎ 021-873 4231.

Breede River Valley

North-east of the Winelands on the western fringes of the Little Karoo is an intensively cultivated and mountainous area known as the Breede River Valley after the river that cuts through it.

Europeans settled here early in the 18th century, but the area did not really take off until passes were pushed through the mountains in the 19th century (see the boxed text 'Great Mountain Passes').

Since the opening of the 4km Huguenot Toll Tunnel east of Paarl, towns such as Robertson and Montagu are more quickly accessible from Cape Town (the drive takes about two hours), although using the tunnel means missing the wonderful views from Du Toitskloof Pass.

Great Mountain Passes

One of the pleasures of touring Western Cape by car is the opportunity to drive through some awesome mountain passes, many of which were constructed in the 19th century by Andrew Bain and his son Thomas.

Bainskloof Pass (Map 1) is named after the elder Bain, who completed it in 1852. Other than having its surface tarred, the road has not been altered since it was built and is now a National Monument. It's a magical drive that would be even better experienced by bicycle. To reach the pass take the R301 from Wellington, about 11km from Paarl.

Du Toitskloof Pass (CT08), between Paarl and Worcester, is the longer and more scenic route between these two towns, now connected by the Huguenot Toll Tunnel for those in a hurry.

An interesting route back to Cape Town from Citrusdal is to traverse the **Middleburg Pass (Map 1)**, which takes you up on a gravel road into the high Cederberg plateau and a narrow valley completely walled by raw, rock hills with rich mineral colouring. Further on, the floor of the valley spreads out and is irrigated so it's usually emerald green, with a patchwork of orchards. About 20km north of Ceres you hit a sealed road, eventually emerging at the 1000m-high **Gydo Pass (Map 1)** overlooking the Ceres Valley, where the world seems to drop away at your feet.

Continue through Ceres and you'll hit **Mitchell's Pass (Map 1)** immediately following the Breede River. The first settlers dismantled their wagons and carried them over the mountain but in 1765 a local farmer built a track along the river. From 1846 to 1848 Andrew Bain constructed a proper road, which became the main route onto the South African plateau to the north. The pass has recently been rebuilt to highway standards but you can still enjoy the views and appreciate what a remarkable engineer Bain was.

EXCURSIONS

TULBAGH

☎ 023 • postcode 6820 • pop 31,000

Overshadowed by the dramatic Witsenberg range, Tulbagh is one of the most complete examples of 18th- and 19th-century Cape Dutch villages in South Africa. Many of the buildings were substantially rebuilt after an earthquake in 1969, but thanks to the painstaking restoration, the town doesn't feel in the least bit fake.

The Tulbagh Valley was first settled in 1699, although most of Tulbagh's surviving buildings date from the first half of the 19th century. The village began to take shape after the construction of a church in 1743. It was here, on the outer rim of the settled European areas, that early Boer families would bring their children out of the wilderness to be baptised.

Church St, the famous street in which every building has been declared a National Monument, runs parallel to the town's main thoroughfare, Van Der Stel St. A visitor's first port of call should be the tourist information centre (☎ 230 1348, W www.tulbagh.com) at 14 Church St, which also has a cafe and accommodation.

Church St aside, there are several wineries to visit in the area, and the mountains offer ample hiking opportunities.

Oude Kerk Volksmuseum

The Oude Kerk Volksmuseum (*Old Church Folk Museum*; ☎ 230 1041, Church St; adult/child R5/2; open 9am-5pm Mon-Fri, 9am-4pm Sat, 11am-4pm Sun) is a mildly interesting museum complex made up of three buildings. Start at No 4, which includes a photographic history of Church St covering the earthquake and reconstruction; then visit the beautiful Oude Kerk itself (1743). At No 22, you'll find a reconstructed dwelling from the 18th century.

The Old Drostdy Museum

A sweet surprise is available in the atmospheric wine cellar of The Old Drostdy Museum (☎ 230 0203; admission free; open

10am-12.30pm & 2pm-4.50pm Mon-Sat, 2.30-4.50pm Sun). The former official landdrost's residence, dating from 1806, is well furnished with appropriate antiques and an odd collection of gramophones. It's 3km north of the town centre along Van Der Stel St.

Places to Stay & Eat
There are plenty of accommodation options, including cottages on farms; inquire at the tourist information centre.

***Kliprivier Park Resort** (☎/fax 230 0506)* Camp sites from R70, chalet doubles from R180. This is quite a pleasant resort on the edge of town (1km north of the centre along Van Der Stel St), offering reasonable chalets and caravan sites.

***Oude Kerk Kombuis** (☎ 230 0428, 14 Church St)* Singles/doubles with shared bathroom B&B R100/200. The best-value option along Church St has only a couple of pleasant rooms so it's best to book ahead.

***The Wagon Shed** (☎ 230 0107, 16 Church St)* Singles/doubles B&B R150/ 270. A plunge pool and an interesting gallery are attached to this guesthouse, which has a more contemporary style than some of the twee Cape Dutch homes.

***De Oude Herberg** (☎/fax 230 0260, 6 Church St)* Singles/doubles B&B R200/ 350. A guesthouse since 1885 (although not continuously), this very friendly and pleasant place has a plunge pool; its *restaurant* is open to nonguests from 9am to 3.30pm and 7.30pm to 10.30pm (bookings essential for dinner).

***Paddagang Restaurant** (☎ 230 0242, 23 Church St)* Mains R50. Open 7.45am-5pm daily, 7pm-9.15pm Wed & Fri. The town's most famous restaurant, in a beautiful old homestead with a vine-shaded courtyard, serves snacks and light meals. A full breakfast is R29; at night one of the big steaks is the best bet.

***Reader's Restaurant** (☎ 230 0087, 12 Church St)* Mains R35-40. Open 12.30pm-2.30pm & 7pm-10pm Wed-Mon. A good choice. The menu changes daily but you can expect food as varied as beef teriyaki and the Cape Malay dish bobotie (a kind of

shepherd's pie made with lightly curried mince topped with savoury egg custard, usually served on a bed of turmeric-flavoured rice with a side dab of chutney).

***Forties** (☎ 230 0567, 40 Church St)* Open 7pm-late Wed-Sun. The bar at this lively pub retains authentic earthquake damage. There might be a braai going on the veranda some nights.

Getting There & Away
The most convenient way of getting here is by car: Take the N1 from Cape Town to Paarl, then drive to Wellington and over the Bainskloof Pass. Once in Tulbagh if you keep going along Van Der Stel St past the Old Drostdy Museum you'll come to a dead end at the head of the valley (overlooked by the mountains of the Groot Winterhoek Wilderness Area).

Shared taxis leave from the 'location' (township) on the hill just outside town, but you might find one at Tulbagh Toyota (the Shell petrol station) on the main street.

An interesting way to visit Tulbagh is to take one of the train trips organised by Mike and Rachel Barry (see Organised Tours in the Getting Around chapter).

WORCESTER
☎ 023 • postcode 6850 • pop 134,000
A service centre for the rich farmland of the Breede River Valley, Worcester is a large and fairly nondescript place that needn't detain you longer than it takes to visit its farm museum and botanic gardens.

Most of the town lies to the south of the N1. There are some impressive old buildings near and around the edge of Church Square (off High St). The tourism bureau (☎ 348 2795), 23 Baring St, is on the east side of Church Square. It's open from 8am to 4.30pm Monday to Friday and 8.30am to 12.30pm Saturday.

Kleinplasie Farm Museum
This excellent farm museum (☎ 342 2225; adult/child R12/5; open 9am-4.30pm Mon-Sat, 10.30am-4.30pm Sun) takes you from a Trekboers' hut, to a complete, functioning 18th-century farm complex.

It's a 'live' museum, meaning there are people wandering around in period clothes and rolling tobacco, making soap, operating a smithy, milling wheat, spinning wool and so on. Visit in the morning when you can see activities such as the baking of bread. The place is fascinating and can easily absorb a couple of hours. A miniature train runs around the complex, leaving hourly.

At the museum shop you can sample (with caution) and buy various flavours of the 60%-proof *witblitz* (white lightning), a traditional Boer spirit distilled from fruit. To get the full taste first inhale, then sip and roll the liquor around your mouth before swallowing. Finally exhale.

Next door is the Kleinplasie Winery where you can sample less potent libations.

The museum is 1km from the town centre on the road to Robertson.

Karoo National Botanic Garden

This is an outstanding garden (☎ 347 0785; *adult/child R9/5; open 8am-4pm daily*) that includes 140 hectares of natural semidesert vegetation (with both Karoo and fynbos elements) and 10 hectares of landscaped garden. Labels will help you to identify some of the extraordinary indigenous plants.

There is something to see at any time of the year; bulb plants flower in autumn, the aloes flower in winter and the annuals flower in spring. There's also a collection of weird stone plants and other succulents.

The garden is about 1km north of the N1 and 2.5km from the centre of town.

KWV Brandy Cellar

This modern cellar and brandy distillery (☎ 342 0255, *Cnr Church & Smith Sts; open 8am-4.30pm Mon-Fri*) isn't as famous as the one in Paarl (see the special section 'Cape Wineries'), but it is the largest of its kind in the world under one roof. Hour-long tours in English are held at 2pm and cost R13.

Places to Stay & Eat

Wykeham Lodge B&B (☎ 347 3467, *fax 347 6776*, [e] *wykehamlodge@telkomsa.net, 168 Church St*) Singles/doubles B&B R190/300. If you do choose to stay in town,

this is one of the best guesthouses. In a thatched building dating from 1835, the rooms have wooden beams and floors and face onto a quiet courtyard.

Kleinplasie Country Chalets (☎ 347 0091) Doubles R200. These chalets are convenient for the Kleinplasie Farm Museum, which is next door.

Kleinplasie Restaurant (☎ 347 5118) Mains R35. Open 9am-4.30pm Mon-Sat, 10.30am-4.30pm Sun. Traditional Cape Malay and Afrikaner dishes such as bobotie and chicken pie are on offer; there's some outdoor seating as well.

St Geran's (☎ 342 2800, *48 Church St*) Mains around R35. Open noon-3pm & 7pm-10pm Mon-Sat. This popular steakhouse in the town centre also does some seafood and chicken dishes.

Getting There & Away

All long-distance buses stop at the Shell Ultracity petrol station. From Cape Town, the cheapest fare is R95 with Translux.

The daily *Trans Karoo* between Cape Town and Johannesburg (Jo'burg) stops here. So does the *Southern Cross* between Cape Town and Oudtshoorn, heading east on Friday evening and west early on Monday morning. The extremely circuitous *Trans Oranje* to Durban also stops here.

Of the several shared-taxi companies in town, WUTA Taxis stops near the corner of Tulbagh and Barry Sts, near the train station. The daily shared taxi to the Belville area of Cape Town (R30) leaves sometime after 6am and there are less regular but usually daily shared taxis to Robertson (R15) and to Ashton (R18), the town at the bottom of the pass that runs up to Montagu. Another place to find shared taxis is near the corner of Grey and Durban Sts.

ROBERTSON

☎ 023 • postcode 6705 • pop 35,000

Robertson, the centre of one of the largest wine-growing areas in the country, and famous for its horse studs, is a prosperous but dull place. There's little reason to stay overnight here with McGregor and Montagu both a short drive away.

The helpful tourism bureau (☎ 626 4437, W www.robertson.org.za) is on the corner of Piet Retief and Swellendam Sts, opposite the Dutch Reformed church. It's open from 9am to 1pm and 2pm to 5pm Monday to Friday.

Things to See & Do
The **museum** (☎ 626 3681, 50 Paul Kruger St; admission free; open 9am-noon Mon-Sat), a few blocks north-east of the church, has a notable collection of lace. Occasionally, tea is occasionally served in the garden.

If you're up here to explore the countryside, it's worth inquiring at the tourism bureau about the two-day Dassieshoek and Avangieskop **hiking trails** that take you into the mountains above Robertson.

Places to Stay & Eat
The information centre can tell you about B&Bs and self-catering farm cottages starting at around R70 per person.

Grand Hotel (☎ 626 3272, fax 626 1158, 68 Barry St) Singles/doubles B&B R195/310. The rooms, a couple with balconies, are of better quality than the foyer would suggest. The same management runs the adjacent **Travel Lodge** (Singles/doubles B&B R130/240) and guests are free to use the hotel's facilities, including **Simone's Grill Room & Restaurant** and the pool.

Branewynsdraai (☎ 626 3202, 1 Kromhout St) Mains R50. Open noon-3pm & 6pm-9pm Mon-Sat. Near the Shell petrol station on Voortrekker St, this pleasant restaurant specialises in local dishes and wines to complement them.

Getting There & Away
Translux buses from Cape Town stop here (R95) en route to Port Elizabeth via Oudtshoorn and Knysna.

The weekly Southern Cross train between Cape Town and Oudtshoorn also stops here.

Shared taxis running between Cape Town (R40 from Robertson) and Oudtshoorn (R110 from Robertson) stop at the Shell petrol station on the corner of Voortrekker and John Sts. These taxis also run through Montagu (R20). A shared taxi to McGregor costs R7 but service is infrequent.

McGREGOR
☎ 023 • postcode 6780
The tranquil village of McGregor feels as though it got stuck in the mid-19th century, when most of the buildings along its one major thoroughfare, Voortrekker St, were built. Thatched cottages, many turned into B&Bs and self-catering units, are surrounded by orchards, vegetable gardens and vineyards; there are some 30 wineries within half an hour's drive.

The tourism bureau (☎ 625 1954, W www.mcgregor.org.za) is about halfway along Voortrekker St (there are no street numbers) and is open from 9am to 5pm Monday to Friday and 10am to 1pm Saturday.

Things to See & Do
McGregor has become a place of retreat and, with the magnificent Riviersonderendberge range on its doorstep, a base for hiking. The highly recommended Boesmanskloof Trail starts near here (see the boxed text).

Villagers Coffee Shop (see Places to Stay & Eat) rents bicycles for R15 per hour or R45 per day.

Vrolijkheid Nature Reserve, between Robertson and McGregor, has an 18km circular walking trail and bird hides with about 150 species to see. At the south end of Voortrekker St you'll find the **Krans Nature Reserve** with more walks; the staff at the tourism bureau can provide details.

Places to Stay & Eat
The tourism bureau has a full list of accommodation (including B&Bs from R100 per person per night) but doesn't take bookings.

McGregor Camp Ground (☎ 625 1754, Church St) is not a camp site, but a dormitory building that you can hire out for a minimum of R240 – which might work out if there's a crowd of you.

Temenos Country Retreat (☎ 625 1871, e temenos@lando.co.za, Bree St) Singles/doubles R180/250. The individually designed cottages are set in spacious gardens and open to all comers (except children under 12), not just those on retreat. It's a peaceful place, with a decent lap pool, nooks for quiet contemplation and a coffee shop.

Boesmanskloof Trail

The best reason to come to McGregor is to hike the Boesmanskloof Trail to Greyton, roughly 14km through the spectacular fynbos-clad Riviersonderendberge range. The trail actually starts at Die Galg, about 15km south of McGregor; you'll need your own transport to get here or you can arrange a transfer with the folks at Whipstock Farm (see Places to Stay & Eat). The car park at Die Galg is a safe enough place to leave your car and there's basic dorm accommodation at the trail head: For details, contact the Vrolijkheid Nature Reserve.

If you don't fancy the full hike, go for a six-hour round trip to the lovely Oak Falls, roughly 6km from Die Galg, where you can cool off with a swim in the tannin-stained waters. To hike the whole trail takes between four and six hours, making an overnight stay in Greyton the preferred option; many people then hike back to Die Galg. It's slightly easier walking from McGregor to Greyton than in the opposite direction. At the start of the trail you'll see signs of a long-abandoned project to construct a pass across the range.

Permits are issued by the Vrolijkheid Nature Reserve (☎ 023-625 1621, fax 625 1674, Private Bag X614, Robertson). The cost is R13 for entry, plus R20 for each day of walking. It's best to book in advance, especially for the weekends and during the holidays, since only 50 people a day are allowed on the trail. The office is on the road from Robertson to McGregor. Permits are also available from Greyton Municipal Offices (☎ 028-254 9620).

McGregor B&B (☎/fax 625 1656, *Voortrekker St)* Doubles B&B from R250. There's one slightly more expensive self-catering unit at this B&B, which has large gardens, a small pool and a tiny 'Irish' pub.

Old Mill Lodge (☎ 625 1841, fax 625 1941, Smit St) Singles/doubles DB&B from R285/470. A clutch of modern cottages, tastefully and comfortably decorated, surround the old mill and its outhouses at the south end of the village. It's a beautiful spot, and in case you feel active there's a swimming pool and nearby fishing. This is the only place in McGregor open to nonguests for dinner (R77 for three courses) so it's just as well that the food is excellent.

McGregor Country Cottages (☎ 625 1816, fax 625 1840, [e] mcgregorcottages @mcgregor.org.au, Voortrekker St) Cottages from R250 per double. This complex of seven pretty cottages, at the north end of the village, is beside an apricot orchard. The cottages, three of which are wheelchair accessible, are fully equipped and terrific value.

Whipstock Farm (☎/fax 625 1733, [e] whipstock@netactive.co.za) Singles/ doubles DB&B R170/340. Serenely located and tastefully decorated accommodation in

a variety of buildings, some historic, plus fine food. The friendly hosts can organise transfers to and from the Boesmanskloof Trail. The farm is 7km from McGregor towards the mountains on a dirt road.

Villagers Coffee Shop (☎ 625 1915, *Voortrekker St)* Mains R20. Open 9.30am-5pm Mon-Fri, 9.30am-1pm Sat. This convivial country store offers light meals and a refreshing range of home-made fruit juices.

Getting There & Away

Getting to and from McGregor is easiest if you have your own transport. Otherwise, you'll need to catch a bus, train or shared taxi to Robertson, then take a shared taxi (R7) to McGregor; service is infrequent.

GREYTON & GENADENDAL
☎ 028 • postcode 7233

Although they are officially part of the Overberg region, we've included Greyton and the neighbouring village of Genadendal here because of their link to McGregor via the Boesmanskloof Trail.

Greyton

Even locals admit that the whitewashed, thatched cottages of Greyton, a village much more twee and polished than McGregor, are a bit artificial.

Greyton's tourist office (☎ 254 9414), on the village's main road, is open from 10am to noon and 2.30pm to 4.30pm Monday to Saturday.

Greyton comes into its own is as a base for **hiking** in the Riviersonderendberge range, which rises in Gothic majesty immediately to the village's north. Apart from the Boesmanskloof Trail, the area has several shorter walks.

Genadendal

As pleasant as Greyton is, it needs to be seen in conjunction with the old Morovian mission of Genadendal, 3km to the west, whose well-preserved historic buildings couldn't be more authentic. The oldest mission station in South Africa, Genadendal was founded in 1738 and for a brief time was the largest settlement in the colony after Cape Town.

The tourist centre (☎ 251 8291) is open from 8.30am to 5pm Monday to Friday and 10am to 1pm Saturday. There's a cafe here selling home-made bread and interesting souvenirs including Khoi-style pottery (many of the villagers are descended from the Khoi).

Entering the village from the R406, head down Main Rd until you arrive at the cluster of National Monuments around Church Square. The **Moravian church** is a handsome, simply decorated building. The village's fascinating history is documented in the excellent **Mission Museum** *(☎ 251 8582; adult/child R7/2; open 9am-1pm & 2pm-5pm Mon-Thurs, 9am-3.30pm Fri, 9am-1pm Sat)*, based in what was South Africa's first teacher-training college. Elsewhere in this historic precinct you can see one of the oldest printing presses in the country, still in operation today, and a water mill.

The two-day **Genadendal Trail**, a 25.3km circular route that begins and ends at Genadendal's Moravian church, is for the serious hiker. For more details, pick up the Cape Nature Conservation leaflet from the tourist centre.

Places to Stay & Eat

For its size, Greyton has a wide range of accommodation and plenty of places to eat. The following are among the best.

Toad Hall (☎ 083 425 2472, Main Rd) Singles/doubles R90/180. Greyton's cheapest option has large rooms, named after characters from *The Wind in the Willows*, with private bathrooms but no breakfast.

High Hopes B&B (☎/fax 254 9898, 89 Main Rd) Doubles B&B from R330. It's not the cheapest place to stay but certainly one of the nicest, with tastefully furnished rooms, lovely gardens and a well-stocked library. Prices for singles are negotiable and afternoon tea is thrown in for all guests. It's convenient for hikers because it's the B&B closest to the start of the Boesmanskloof Trail.

Guinea Fowl (☎ 254 9550, fax 254 9653, W longreyton.co.za, Cnr DS Botha & Oak Sts) Singles/doubles B&B R165/330. Comfortable and quiet, this guesthouse has a pool for summer, a log fire for winter, and good breakfasts year round.

Posthaus Guesthouse (☎ 254 9995, fax 254 9920, Main Rd) Doubles B&B from R400. Based around a pretty garden, the gimmick here is the naming of rooms after Beatrix Potter characters (we told you this was a twee place). The associated English-style pub *The Ball & Bass* is a cosy place for a drink or a meal.

Greyton Lodge (☎ 254 9876, fax 254 9672, e greytonlodge@kingsley.co.za, 46 Main Rd) Singles/doubles B&B R315/550. A pair of stocks and rampant lion statues flank the entrance to this upmarket hotel in the old police station. There's a pool and a reasonably priced but unadventurous *bistro*, open from 7pm to 9pm daily.

The Oak & Vigne Cafe (☎ 254 9037, DS Botha St) Mains R20. Open 8am-6pm Mon-Sat, 8am-5pm Sun. Evidence of the creeping yuppification of Greyton is this trendy deli, art gallery and cafe, which is a fine place to grab a snack and chill out watching the world go by.

Rosie's Restaurant (☎ 254 9640, 2 High St) Mains R35. Open 6.30pm-late Tues-Sun. The house specialities are pizzas from the wood-fired oven (which are delicious and huge) and steaks.

Getting There & Away

If you're not hiking in from McGregor, the only way to Greyton and Genadendal is with your own transport. From Cape Town follow the N2 to just before Caledon and then take the R406. From Robertson take the R317 south to the N2 at Stormsvlei then head west to Riviersonderend to connect with the R406.

Overberg

The Overberg (its name literally means 'Over the Mountains') is the region south and west of the Franschhoekberge range, and south of the Wemmershoekberge and Rivier-sonderendberge ranges, which, along with the Breede River Valley, form a natural barrier.

Coming from Cape Town, the R44 from Strand, towards Hermanus around Cape Hangklip, is a thrilling coastal drive, in the same class as the now curtailed Chapman's Peak Drive. The first major stop is Hermanus, famous for the whales that frequent its shores (although it's so famous now that you might well choose to do your whale-watching at a less crowded location along the coast).

If you're looking for somewhere quiet to hang out, both the miraculously undeveloped fishing village of Arniston and De Hoop Nature Reserve will fit the bill. The best all-round base for the area is Swellendam, a historic and attractive town beneath the impressive Langeberge mountains.

BETTY'S BAY

☎ 28

The best bit of the drive along the R44 from Cape Town is between Gordon's Bay and Kleinmond. Along the way consider pausing at Betty's Bay, a small, scattered holiday village just east of Cape Hangklip. Here you'll find the **Harold Porter National Botanical Gardens** *(☎ 272 9311; adult/child R5/free; open 8am-4.30pm Mon-Fri, 8am-5pm Sat & Sun)*, which protect some of the surrounding

fynbos, and are definitely worth visiting. There are paths through the area and, at the entrance, tearooms and a formal garden where you can picnic. There's also a colony of African penguins at Stony Point.

Buçaco Sud *(☎/fax 272 9750, W www .bucacosud.co.za, Clarence Dr)* Singles/doubles B&B from R145. We've received plenty of readers' recommendations for this Mediterranean-style B&B with sea views. The facilities are excellent and the hosts gay-friendly.

KLEINMOND

☎ 28

Kleinmond is not particularly attractive, but it does have a wild and beautiful beach, reliable swells for surfers and some good accommodation choices.

Palmiet Caravan Park *(☎ 271 4050)* Camping R34.50/R60.75 in low/high season. On the beach on the western side of town, this is the most attractive camping option.

Roots Rock Backpackers *(☎/fax 271 5139, ⓔ kaybee90@hotmail.com, Harbour Rd)* Dorm beds R45, doubles R140. This small, rustic place faces the sea, close by a cluster of shops and cafes.

The Beach House *(☎ 271 3130, fax 271 4022, W www.relais.co.za, Sandown Bay)* Singles/doubles B&B from R415/640. The most upmarket choice overlooks the town's best beach. It has prettily decorated rooms in pastel shades.

HERMANUS

☎ 028 • postcode 7200 • pop 31,000

Within day-tripping distance of Cape Town (122km), Hermanus was originally a fishing village and still retains vestiges of its heritage, including a small museum at the old harbour. It's best known now as a place to view whales.

There are some great beaches, most west of the town centre. Rocky hills, vaguely reminiscent of Scotland, surround the town, and there are good walks and a nature reserve protecting some of the prolific fynbos. The pleasant town centre, easily negotiated on foot and east of the new harbour, is well endowed with restaurants and shops. Be

MAP 7 – HERMANUS

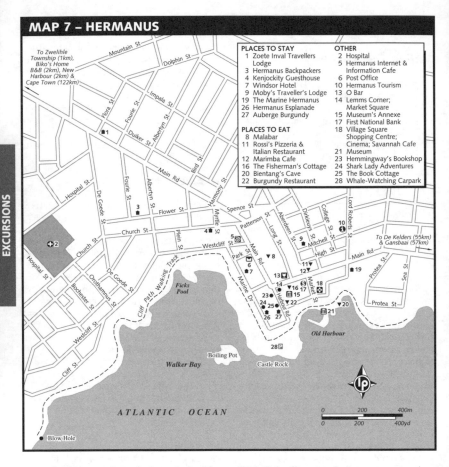

PLACES TO STAY
1 Zoete Inval Travellers
   Lodge
3 Hermanus Backpackers
4 Kenjockity Guesthouse
7 Windsor Hotel
9 Moby's Traveller's Lodge
19 The Marine Hermanus
26 Hermanus Esplanade
27 Auberge Burgundy

PLACES TO EAT
8 Malabar
11 Rossi's Pizzeria &
    Italian Restaurant
12 Marimba Cafe
16 The Fisherman's Cottage
20 Bientang's Cave
22 Burgundy Restaurant

OTHER
2 Hospital
5 Hermanus Internet &
   Information Cafe
6 Post Office
10 Hermanus Tourism
13 O Bar
14 Lemms Corner;
    Market Square
15 Museum's Annexe
17 First National Bank
18 Village Square
    Shopping Centre;
    Cinema; Savannah Cafe
21 Museum
23 Hemmingway's Bookshop
24 Shark Lady Adventures
25 The Book Cottage
28 Whale-Watching Carpark

warned: Hermanus is packed out during the school holidays in December and January.

Information

Hermanus Tourism **(Map 7, #10)** (☎ 312 2629, **W** www.hermanus.co.za) at the Old Station Building, Mitchell St, is helpful and has a large supply of information about the area including walks and drives in the surrounding hills. Short tours of the local Zwelihle township can also be arranged. It's open from 9am to 5pm Monday to Saturday.

Hermanus Internet & Information Cafe **(Map 7, #5)** in the Waterkant Building,

Main Rd, offers speedy Internet connections (R10 for 15 minutes).

The Book Cottage **(Map 7, #25)** (☎ 313 0834, 10 Harbour Rd) sells travel guides and other new books. Hemmingway's Bookshop **(Map 7, #23)** (☎ 312 2739), at 4 Main Rd, has an extensive collection of second-hand volumes.

Markets

There's a small market daily at Lemms Corner **(Map 7, #14)**, in the Market Square off Main Rd; on Saturday a craft market is held there, too.

Old Harbour

The old harbour clings to the cliffs in front of the town centre; here you'll find a small and generally uninteresting **museum (Map 7, #21)** *(☎ 312 1475; adult/child R2/1; open 9am-1pm & 2pm-5pm Mon-Sat, noon-4pm Sun)* and a display of old fishing boats. The museum's annexe **(Map 7, #15)**, in the old schoolhouse on the Market Square, displays some evocative old photographs of the town and its fishermen.

Shark-Diving

Although all the boats depart from Gansbaai, some 35km along the coast, diving in cages to view great white sharks is heavily promoted in Hermanus, and several operators are based here. There's no doubting the activity's popularity, but it's also controversial. Operators use bait to attract the sharks to the cage, which means these killer fish are being trained to associate humans with food. It's not a pleasant scenario, especially if you're a surfer.

Most operators require you to have an internationally recognised diving qualification to take part, although some allow snorkellers into the cage. Brian McFarlane (☎ 312 2766, **W** www.hermanusinfo.co.za/greatwhite) is one experienced operator. His trips last six hours and cost around R600. Another good choice is Shark Lady Adventures (☎/fax 313 1415). The shark lady herself, Kim Maclean, has been running trips for 10 years; they cost around R700.

Places to Stay

There's been an explosion of places to stay in Hermanus over the last few years, but in the holiday season the town can still be bursting at the seams, so take care to book ahead. Hermanus Tourism can help you find a place to stay. Agencies such as Whale Route Accommodation (☎ 316 1682) and the Hermanus Accommodation Centre (☎ 313 0004) arrange house rentals and book other accommodation.

Hostels *Zoete Inval Travellers Lodge (☎/fax 312 1242,* **e** *zoetein@hermanus .co.za, 23 Main Rd)* **Map 7, #1** Dorm beds R45, singles/doubles R120/150. More a

---

Watching the Whales

Between June and November, southern right whales *(Eubalaena australis)* come to Walker Bay to calve. There can be up to 70 whales in the bay at once. South Africa was a whaling nation until 1976, and this species was hunted to the verge of extinction, but its numbers are now recovering. Humpback whales *(Megaptera novaeangliae)* are also sometimes seen.

Whales often come very close to shore and there are some excellent vantage points from the cliff paths that run from one end of Hermanus to the other. The best places are Castle Rock, Kraal Rock and Sievers Point. There's a telescope on the cliff top above the old harbour.

It's only recently that the people of Hermanus bothered to tell the outside world that the whales were regular visitors. They took them for granted. Now, however, the whales' tourism potential has been recognised and just about every business in town has adopted a whale logo. There's a whale-spotting hotline (☎ 0800 22 8222) and a whale crier, who walks around town blowing on a kelp horn and carrying a blackboard that shows where whales have been recently sighted. A whale festival is held in late September or early October.

Despite all this hoopla, viewing of whales from boats is strictly regulated. No boat-viewing is allowed in the bay and jet skis are banned. There are only two boat-viewing operators licensed to operate in the seas outside the bay: Southern Right Charters (☎ 082 353 0550) and Hawston Fishers (☎ 082 396 8931). They charge around R250 for a one- to two-hour trip.

Although Hermanus is the best-known whale-watching site, whales can be seen all the way from False Bay (Cape Town) to Plettenberg Bay and beyond. The west coast also gets its share. Check out **W** www.cape-whaleroute.co.za for more information.

guesthouse than a backpacker hostel, this is one of the friendliest places we've come across, with nicely furnished rooms and good amenities.

Hermanus Backpackers (☎ *312 4293, fax 313 2727,* e *moobag@mweb.co.za, 26 Flower St)* **Map 7, #3** Dorm beds B&B R50, singles/doubles B&B R85/140. A smashing place with clued-up staff, great decor and great facilities, including a bar and small pool.

Moby's Traveller's Lodge (☎ *313 2361, fax 312 3519,* e *moby@hermanus.co.za)* **Map 7, #9** Dorm beds B&B R50, singles/doubles B&B 125/150. We visited the day it moved into new premises, but this converted hotel, with a pool, bar and central location, looks as though it might shape up to be a popular place.

Shark Lady Adventures (☎/*fax 313 1415, 61 Marine Dr)* **Map 7, #24** R100 per person. What the shark lady offers is not exactly a hostel, but it's good shared accommodation.

B&Bs, Guesthouses & Self-Catering If all the B&Bs in Hermanus are full, you might want to try those further down the coast at De Kelders or Gansbaai.

Kenjockity Guesthouse (☎/*fax 312 1772,* e *kenjock@hermanus.co.za, 15 Church St)* **Map 7, #4** Singles/doubles with shared bathroom R125/250. This guesthouse, the first in Hermanus, has a nice atmosphere and fair-sized rooms. More expensive rooms with private bathrooms are available. You'll pay more in December.

Biko's Home B&B (☎ *312 2776,* e *princessbiko@wam.co.za, 106 Zwelihle St)* Singles/doubles B&B R100/200. Run by Princess Biko, this cosy B&B will give you an insight into township life and hospitality. Princess has only two rooms but will make you feel at home and will cook dinner too for an extra R50.

Hermanus Esplanade (☎ *312 3610, fax 313 1125,* e *clarkbro@hermanus.co.za, 63 Marine Dr)* **Map 7, #3** Apartments from R250. These are standard self-catering apartments, but some overlook the sea; the lowest rates actually cover the whale-watching season from May to October.

Auberge Burgundy (☎ *313 1202, fax 313 1204,* e *auberge@hermanus.co.za, 16 Harbour Rd)* **Map 7, #27** Doubles B&B from R640. This is a wonderful place, built in the style of a Provençal villa, with fine facilities and a personal touch. If there are six of you, consider splashing out on the penthouse (R1450). The same management runs the excellent *Burgundy Restaurant*, across the road.

Hotels *Windsor Hotel* (☎ *312 3727, fax 312 2181,* w *www.windsor-hotel.com, 49 Marine Dr)* **Map 7, #7** Singles/doubles B&B from R250/350 low season, R350/450 high season. Naturally, you'll want one of the more expensive sea-facing rooms at this characterful old hotel with a new wing; from some you might be able to see whales without even leaving your bed.

The Marine Hermanus (☎ *313 1000, fax 313 0160,* w *www.marine-hermanus.co.za, Marine Dr)* **Map 7, #19** Doubles from R1195. This superbly renovated hotel is the last word in comfort and has an ideal sea-facing spot and a couple of good restaurants. Check for marginally cheaper midweek and weekend deals.

Places to Eat

There's no shortage of places to eat in Hermanus, with new places opening all the time.

Burgundy Restaurant (☎ *312 2800, Marine Dr)* **Map 7, #22** Mains around R50. Open 10am-4.30pm daily, 7pm-9.30pm Mon-Sat. Booking is essential at one of the most acclaimed and popular restaurants in the province. It's in a pair of cottages, which are the oldest buildings in town (1875), with a garden and sea views.

The Fisherman's Cottage (☎ *312 3642, Lemms Cnr)* **Map 7, #16** Mains R30. Open noon-3pm, 6.30pm-10pm Tues-Sun. Good cheap seafood is on the menu at this cute restaurant in a whitewashed cottage draped with fishing nets.

Marimba Cafe (☎ *312 2148, 108D Main Rd)* **Map 7, #12** Mains R35. Open 7pm-10pm daily. The lively atmosphere matches the eclectic menu at this restaurant where you can eat traditional African dishes.

Malabar (Shop 3, Long St Arcade) **Map 7, #8** Mains R35. Open 6.30pm-late daily. Curries are the go at this cosy spot.

Rossi's Pizzeria & Italian Restaurant (☎ 312 2848, 10 High St) **Map 7, #11** Mains around R30. Open 6.30pm-late daily. A long-running operation with a pleasant and relaxed atmosphere.

Savannah Cafe (☎ 312 4259, Village Theatre, Marine Dr) **Map 7, #18** Mains around R20. Open 9am-5pm Mon-Fri, 8am-8pm Sat & Sun. Good for lunch or a snack, this place overlooks the beach and is convenient for the cinema next door.

Bientang's Cave (☎ 312 3454, Marine Dr) **Map 7, #20** Mains R40. Open 11am-5pm daily. Beside the water, between the museum and the Marine Hermanus Hotel, this really *is* a seaside cave, containing a good but pricey restaurant. Try the fish dishes and the pizza.

Entertainment
O Bar **(Map 7, #13)** *(121 Main Rd)*, a stylish DJ bar, is *the* late-night place to party on the weekends. For other times there are pool tables and an open fire. Entry costs R10 on Friday and Saturday.

Getting There & Away
Backpacker Bus (☎ 082 809 9185, [e] bpack bus@mweb.co.za) runs charter trips from Cape Town to Hermanus (R120), but there are no regular bus services.

You might find a shared taxi running to Bellville (Cape Town), but not daily – inquire at Hermanus Tourism.

Most of Cape Town's main operators of organised tours offer day trips to Hermanus, particularly in whale-watching season. For their contact details, see Organised Tours in the Getting Around chapter.

AROUND HERMANUS
There are several walks and drives in the hills behind the town – Hermanus Tourism has maps. The 1400-hectare **Fernkloof Nature Reserve** is worth visiting, particularly if you are interested in fynbos.

If you want to see whales in a much less commercialised environment, head south

from Hermanus to the sleepy village of **De Kelders**. Next along is **Gansbaai**, an unprepossessing fishing town that is riding the wave of interest in shark-diving (see Shark-Diving under Hermanus earlier). If this is not your bag, then the nearby **Dyer Island**, where the sharks hang out, also hosts colonies of African penguins and seals; regular boat trips are available.

Grootbos Private Nature Reserve (☎ 028-384 0381, fax 384 0552, [e] grootbos@her manus.co.za) Singles/doubles DB&B R1700/ 2200. This beautifully designed award-winning property, covering 1000 hectares, is the best place to stay in the Overberg. It's about 50km south-east of Hermanus, and about 5km out of Gansbaai. The rates cover all activities, including guided nature walks, horse rides and mountain-bike rides.

On the unsealed inland route between Gansbaai and Cape Agulhas is **Elim**, a picturesque but poor Moravian mission village founded in 1824.

BREDASDORP
☎ 028
Rolling wheat and sheep country surround the town of Bredasdorp, through which you'll have to pass to reach Cape Agulhas by tarred road. You'll find the friendly Suidpunt Tourism Bureau (☎ 424 2584, [W] www.suid punttourism.co.za) in the Dowling Building on Dr Jansen St.

CAPE AGULHAS
☎ 028
Welcome to the southernmost point of Africa. On stormy days the low, shattered rocks and dramatic crashing seas seem very atmospheric.

Otherwise Cape Agulhas isn't especially impressive and there's little reason to linger longer than it takes to peek at the nearby **lighthouse** *(☎ 435 6222; adult/child R5/2; open 9am-4.15pm Mon-Sat, 9am-2pm Sun)*, built in 1848 and the second-oldest in South Africa.

If you're feeling peckish or you want to shelter from those storms, the *tearoom (☎ 435 7506)* at the lighthouse isn't bad; it serves reasonably priced meals and snacks.

EXCURSIONS

ARNISTON

Arniston, in a dramatic, windswept setting, is a charming, undeveloped village named after the vessel wrecked off its treacherous coast in 1815, with the loss of 344 lives. Its Afrikaans name, Waenhuiskrans (Wagon-House Cliff), comes from the enormous cavern eroded into the cliffs around 1km south from the village.

Things to See & Do

John Midgely at Southwinds (see Places to Stay) runs a 4WD eco-trip to see both the scant remains of the *Arniston* (it's practically covered by sand) and the cave. The trip is a fine way to get a feel for this rugged coast washed by a beguilingly sapphire-blue ocean. It costs R50 and takes two hours.

Otherwise, Arniston's main draw is the rustic fishing community of **Kassiesbaai**, established in 1820 and notable for its whitewashed thatched cottages. The cottages are very photogenic, but their inhabitants are very poor.

Places to Stay & Eat

South of Africa Backpackers' Resort (☎ 445 9240, fax 445 9254, Ⓦ www.south ofafrica.co.za) Singles/doubles/triples B&B R95/150/180. This is part of Die Herberg resort, and shares all its amenities, including gym, large pool, sauna and two full-size billiard tables. The neighbouring military test site gives a clue as to why such a salubrious hotel was built here and it's possible you'll still rub shoulders with soldiers over the full buffet breakfast. The resort is signposted off the R316, 2km outside of Arniston.

Arniston Seaside Cottages (☎ 445 9772, fax 445 9125) Singles/doubles R225/300. In the village, most of these well-equipped self-catering cottages are thatched and some have sea views.

Southwinds (☎/fax 445 9303, Ⓔ south winds@kingsley.co.za, First Ave) Singles/ doubles B&B R220/350. There's a friendly welcome at this B&B, a short stroll from the beach. It has comfortable, nicely furnished rooms.

Arniston Hotel (☎ 445 9000, fax 445 9633) Singles/doubles B&B from R425/650. The Arniston is a luxurious hotel facing the sea. Upgrades of some rooms are planned, as is a change of location for the fine *restaurant* to a pair of new cottages to be built behind the hotel. Light meals (R13.50 to R30) are served during the day in the classy ocean-view bar.

Die Waenhuis (☎ 445 9797, Dupreez St) Mains from R40. Arniston's only other dining option, serving a good range of dishes, is tucked away behind the Arniston Centre general store.

Getting There & Away

Arniston is another place you'll really need a car to reach, although you could try your luck with a shared taxi from Bredasdorp – inquire at the tourism bureau there.

DE HOOP NATURE RESERVE
☎ 028

This is one of Cape Nature Conservation's best reserves (☎ 542 1126, Ⓔ dehoopinfo@ sdm.dorea.co.za; admission R6; open 7am-6pm daily). Its 36,000 hectares, plus 5km out to sea, include lonely stretches of beach, dunes and rocky cliffs from where you can spot whales. Other fauna includes the Cape mountain zebra, the bontebok and a wealth of birdlife.

There are various hikes, a multiday mountain-bike trail, for which bookings should be made in advance, and good snorkelling along the coast. Since the reserve is east of Cape Agulhas, the water is reasonably warm. Camping here costs R46, and four-person cottages start at R180 (bring your own bedding, kitchen utensils and food).

The reserve is about 260km from Cape Town, and the final 50km from either Bredasdorp or Swellendam is along gravel roads. The only access to the reserve is via Wydgeleë on the Bredasdorp to Malgas road. A manually operated pont (pontoon ferry) operates at Malgas on the Breede River between dawn and dusk. The village of Ouplaas, 15km away, is the nearest place to buy fuel and supplies.

SWELLENDAM

☎ 028 • postcode 6740 • pop 33,200

Swellendam is an historic and attractive town dotted with old oaks and surrounded by rolling wheat country and mountains. It makes a great base for exploring the Overberg and the Little Karoo. It's also a handy stop between Cape Town and the Garden Route, and even if you don't have your own wheels there's the chance to walk in indigenous forest quite close to town.

The town backs up against a spectacular ridge, part of the 1600m-high Langeberge range. The distinctive square-topped outcrop is known locally as 12 O'Clock Rock because at noon the sun appears very close to the rock, making it impossible for anyone in town to see what is going on up there. You can walk up and back in a day. A permit costs R12 and is obtainable from the Nature Conservation Department (☎ 514 1410) at the entrance to the Marloth Nature Reserve, 3km north of Swellendam, or from Swellendam Backpackers.

History

Swellendam dates from 1746 and is the third-oldest magistracy in South Africa. The swift expansion by independent farmers and traders beyond the Cape Peninsula meant that by the 1740s they had drifted beyond the control of the VOC's authorities at Stellenbosch. As a result, Swellendam was established as the seat of a landdrost, an official representative of the colony's governor who acted as local administrator, tax collector and magistrate. The residence of a landdrost was known as a *drostdy* and included his office and courtroom as well as his family's living quarters. The Swellendam drostdy is now the centrepiece of a fine museum complex.

Information

The Swellendam Tourism Bureau (Map 8, #14) (☎/fax 514 2770, W www.swellen dam.org.za) is in the old mission, or Oefeninghuis, on Voortrek St (the main street). It is open from 9am to 5pm Monday to Friday,

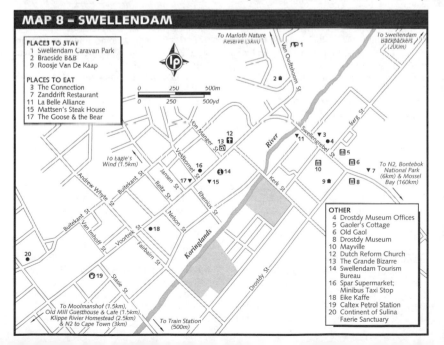

MAP 8 – SWELLENDAM

PLACES TO STAY
1 Swellendam Caravan Park
2 Braeside B&B
9 Roosje Van De Kaap

PLACES TO EAT
3 The Connection
7 Zanddrift Restaurant
11 La Belle Alliance
15 Mattsen's Steak House
17 The Goose & the Bear

To Marloth Nature Reserve (3km)
To Swellendam Backpackers (200m)

To Eagle's Wind (1.5km)

To N2, Bontebok National Park (6km) & Mossel Bay (160km)

To Moolmanshof (1.5km),
Old Mill Guesthouse & Cafe (1.5km),
Klippe Rivier Homestead (2.5km)
& N2 to Cape Town (3km)

To Train Station (500m)

OTHER
4 Drostdy Museum Offices
5 Gaoler's Cottage
6 Old Gaol
8 Drostdy Museum
10 Mayville
12 Dutch Reform Church
13 The Grande Bizarre
14 Swellendam Tourism Bureau
16 Spar Supermarket; Minibus Taxi Stop
18 Eike Kaffe
19 Caltex Petrol Station
20 Continent of Sulina Faerie Sanctuary

EXCURSIONS

and 9am to 12.30pm Saturday. Note the twin clocks, one of which is permanently set at 12.15pm. This was once the time of the daily church service; illiterate townspeople only had to match the working clock with the painted one to know when their presence was required.

If you're interested in architecture or history, pick up a copy of the brochure *Swellendam Treasures* (R5), which details scores of interesting buildings around town. Also inquire at the bureau about guided walks.

The cheapest Internet connection in town is at the Grande Bizarre **(Map 8, #13)**, an art and antiques gallery and cafe at 17 Voortrek St, charging R15 per half-hour.

Drostdy Museum
The centrepiece of the excellent Drostdy Museum **(Map 8, #8)** *(☎ 514 1138, 18 Swellengrebel St; adult/child R10/1; open 9am-4.45pm Mon-Fri, 10am-3.45pm Sat & Sun)* is the beautiful drostdy itself, which dates from 1746. The ticket also covers entrance to the Old Gaol **(Map 8, #6)**, where you'll find some of the original administrative buildings, the gaoler's cottage **(Map 8, #5)** and a water mill; and to Mayville **(Map 8, #10)**, a residence dating back to 1853, with a formal Victorian garden.

Continent of Sulina Faerie Sanctuary (Map 8, #20)
The self-styled Continent of Sulina Faerie Sanctuary *(☎ 514 1786, 37 Buitekant St; admission R2; open 9am-5pm Fri-Sun)* is a charming attraction which the owners claim draws even more visitors than the Drostdy Museum. Surrounding this backstreet home is an enchanted-garden trail peppered with fairy statues; inside some 20 artists display their tiny sculptures and fairy creations. Kids of all ages will love it.

Activities
For permits to walk in Marloth Nature Reserve in the Langeberge range, 3km north of town, contact the **Nature Conservation Department** *(☎ 514 1410)* at the entrance to the reserve, during business hours. There

are day, overnight and week-long hikes, and accommodation is available.

Two Feathers Horse Trails *(☎ 082 494 8279,* e *mwleepip@iafrica.com)* offers one-hour rides for R85 and caters for inexperienced as well as experienced riders (but doesn't offer hard hats). Overnight rides can be arranged too.

Swellendam Outdoor Adventures *(☎ 514 2648)*, based at Swellendam Backpackers, offers day trips to places including Cape Agulhas and De Hoop Nature Reserve (both R150), and activities such as canoeing and gliding. It, and guesthouses in town, can also arrange sunset cruises on a double-decker wooden raft on the lake near the Buffeljachts Dam in the Langeberge range. The cost is R60.

Places to Stay
There are so many excellent B&Bs and guesthouses in and around Swellendam that you can afford to ignore the town's one overpriced hotel.

Swellendam Caravan Park (☎ 514 2705, fax 514 2694, Glen Barry Rd) **Map 8, #1** Camp sites R62, single/double cottages from R155/167. Tucked under the mountains and surrounded by trees, this caravan park is a 10-minute walk from town.

Swellendam Backpackers (☎ 514 2648, fax 514 1249, e *backpack@dorea.co.za, 5 Lichtenstein St)* Camp sites R30, dorm beds R45, doubles R130. Set on a huge plot of land, with its own river, this is an excellent hostel with enthusiastic management. The Baz Bus will drop you directly outside.

Braeside B&B (☎ 514 3325, fax 514 1899, w *www.braeside4u.homestead.com, 13 Van Outdtshoorn Rd)* **Map 8, #2** Singles/doubles B&B from R175/250. Gracious Cape Edwardian home with fantastic views and really knowledgeable, friendly hosts.

Roosje Van De Kaap (☎/fax 514 3001, e *roosje@dorea.co.za, 5 Drostdy St)* **Map 8, #9** Singles/doubles B&B R200/300. This is a friendly little guesthouse in a converted old stable with a small pool. The excellent *restaurant* serves some Cape Malay dishes and wood-fired-oven pizzas; mains cost around R40. It's open to nonguests but bookings are essential.

Moolmanshof (☎ 514 3258, fax 514 2384, W *www.moolmanshof.homestead.com, 217 Voortrek St)* Singles/doubles B&B from R250/320. This place, around 2km from the town centre, is a gem. The house dates from 1798 and is furnished with period furniture; it's set in lovely gardens.

Old Mill Guesthouse (☎ 514 2790, fax 514 1292, W *www.oldmill.co.za, 241 Voortrek St)* Doubles B&B R260/200 in high/low season. It's just the one tiny but cute cottage behind the antiques and craft shop and pleasant *cafe* of the same name.

Eagle's Wind (☎/fax 514 3797, e *mwlee pip@iafrica.com)* Full board R225 per person. Tired of all that Cape Dutch architecture? Then this encampment of tepees (each sleeping two people on twin futons) in a stunning setting could be your thing. It's part of a holistic centre that also offers workshops and other activities; to get here, head 2km north-west of the centre down a dirt road from the golf course.

Klippe Rivier Homestead (☎ 514 3341, fax 514 3337, e *krh@sdm.dorea.co.za)* Doubles B&B R900. Three kilometres south-west of town, there are six beautifully decorated guest suites in this luxurious homestead dating from 1820. The top-notch three-course dinner (R120) is available to nonguests if the dining room is not full, but you'll need to book.

Places to Eat

Mattsen's Steak House (☎ 514 2715, 44 Voortrek St) **Map 8, #15** Mains R35-50. Open 11am-3pm daily, 6pm-late Mon-Sat. Mattsen's is popular for its steaks, seafood and pizzas. Light meals and snacks are available during the day.

The Goose & the Bear (☎ 514 3101, 35 Voortrek St) **Map 8, #17** Mains R25. Open 11.30am-2am Mon-Sat, 7pm-midnight Sun. Standard pub meals and the occasional braai are the deal at this convivial bar.

Zanddrift Restaurant (☎ 514 1789, 132 Swellengrebel St) **Map 8, #7** Mains R45. Open 8.30am-4.30pm. Breakfast (available all day) is a must, consisting of a huge plat-ter of omelette, ham, pate, fruit and so on. Other dishes depend on what's available that day. The restaurant adjoins the museum and is in a building that dates from 1757.

La Belle Alliance (☎ 514 2252, 1 Swellengrebel St) **Map 8, #11** Mains R35. Open 8am-5pm daily. This appealing tea-room in an old masonic lodge has shaded outdoor tables beside the Koringlands River. It's a good spot for an inexpensive snack.

The Connection (☎ 514 1988, 10-12 Swellengrebel St) **Map 8, #3** Mains R50. Open 10am-10pm Thurs-Tues. The home-cooked favourites here are similar to those at Zanddrift: highly recommended.

Getting There & Away

All three major bus companies plus the Baz Bus pass through Swellendam on their runs between Cape Town and Port Elizabeth. Eike Kaffe **(Map 8, #18)** at 108 Voortrek St is the Intercape agent.

The weekly *Southern Cross* train between Cape Town and Oudtshoorn stops here.

For information on shared taxis check at the stop **(Map 8, #16)** behind the Spar supermarket on Voortrek St. The daily ser-vice to Cape Town is about R90, and to Mossel Bay R70.

BONTEBOK NATIONAL PARK
☎ 028

Some 6km south of Swellendam is Bonte-bok National Park *(☎ 514 2735; adult/child R8/4)*. This small chunk of land has been set aside to ensure the preservation of the en-dangered bontebok, an antelope with un-usual markings which once roamed the region in large numbers.

As a national park, Bontebok doesn't offer much competition to Kruger et al, but as a place to relax it's hard to beat. The park falls within the coastal fynbos area, so the vege-tation is interesting, and it's on the Breede River where swimming is possible. In addi-tion to the bontebok, the rhebok, grysbok, duiker, red hartebeest and Cape mountain zebra are present. Birdlife is abundant.

Camping costs R65 for two people. Six-person 'chalavans' are R150 for two people, plus R20 per extra person.

West Coast & Swartland

Although these areas are popular with Capetonians seeking a break, few overseas visitors head north of Cape Town up the West Coast and through the area known as the Swartland (Black Land). Those who do are likely to find the rugged, desolate Cederberg Wilderness Area and the West Coast National Park more appealing than the lacklustre resorts and fishing towns of the coast.

The prettiest coastal village is Paternoster, while inland the country town of Darling, home of a South African entertainment icon, is worth a stop.

Most public transport through this area travels from Cape Town north along the N7, either going all the way to Springbok and Namibia or leaving the N7 and heading through Calvinia to Upington in Northern Cape province. Getting to the coastal towns west of the N7 isn't easy if you don't have a car.

DARLING
☎ 022

Some 70km north of Cape Town is the sleepy country town of Darling, which was recently catapulted to fame by the presence of Evita Bezuidenhout, the alter ego of actor and satirist Pieter-Dirk Uys (see the boxed text 'South Africa's Gay Icon' in the special section 'Gay & Lesbian Cape Town').

Things to See & Do
Shows featuring Uys' cast of characters run every Friday, Saturday and Sunday at **Evita se Perron** (☎ 492 2851, **W** www.evita .co.za). Although Uys performs partly in Afrikaans, there's much for English-speaking audiences to enjoy, and his shows are frequently hilarious and thought-provoking. The splendidly kitsch theatre-restaurant, in a converted station building next to the railway line, is well worth visiting in its own right. Tickets to the shows cost R65 per person.

Across the road from the theatre is a reasonable **craft market** (open 10am-4pm Thurs-Sun) where you can buy souvenirs.

The typically cluttered **museum** (☎ 492 3361, Cnr Pastorie & Hill Sts; admission free; open 10am-1pm & 2pm-4pm daily) is worth a browse (it doubles as the town's tourist information centre).

While in the area you could also visit the poor Moravian mission village of **Marme**, 20km south of Darling, or the coastal resort of **Yzerfontein** 15km west. This holiday village has some dramatic views over a rugged, rocky coastline, and a left point for surfers that works on south-easterly winds and moderate south-westerly swells.

Places to Stay & Eat
Darling is so close to Cape Town there's no pressing need to stay overnight, although there are some very nice guesthouses.

Darling Guest House (☎ 492 3062, 22 Pastorie St) Singles/doubles B&B R175/ 270. This is an elegant and imaginatively decorated place.

Parrot's Guest House (☎ 492 3430, 19 Long St) Singles/doubles B&B from R180/300. The upmarket choice, with a lovely garden, a small pool and a good cafe.

Through the Looking Glass (☎ 492 2858, 19 Main Rd) Open 9.30am-4.30pm Mon-Fri, 10am-3pm Sat. This arty cafe offers Internet access.

You can eat at Evita se Perron; at show-times traditional Afrikaans food such as chicken pie and bobotie is available for around R40.

Getting There & Away
Drive up the R27 from Cape Town and look for the signs. It's worth inquiring about the occasional Sunday excursions here on the Spier steam train (☎ 021-419 5222). The 2½-hour trip includes a picnic lunch and entry to the show at Evita se Perron.

WEST COAST NATIONAL PARK
☎ 022

The West Coast National Park (☎ 772 2144; admission R9-18; open 7am-7pm daily) covers around 18,000 hectares and extends north from Yzerfontein to just short of Langebaan. It's made up of a peculiar mix of semi-independent zones, some of which are leased (rather than owned) by the national park authorities.

The park protects wetlands of international significance and important seabird breeding colonies. In summer it hosts enormous numbers of migratory wading birds. Numerically, the dominant species is the delicate-looking curlew sandpiper (which migrates north from the sub-Antarctic in huge flocks). Flamingos, Cape gannets, crowned cormorants, numerous gull species and African black oystercatchers are also to be found among the hordes. The offshore islands are home to colonies of African penguins.

The vegetation is predominantly *sandveld*, made up of stunted bushes, sedges and many flowering annuals and succulents. There are some coastal fynbos species in the east, and the park is famous for its wildflower display, usually between August and October. Several large mammals can be seen in the part of the park known as the Postberg section (open August to September), including wildebeests, bonteboks, elands and various small antelopes

About 120km from Cape Town and 7km south of Langebaan, the park is clearly signposted and can easily be visited on a day trip from the city. The park's roads are dirt and can be quite heavily corrugated. A return trip along the length of the park is more than 80km, so allow yourself plenty of time.

LANGEBAAN
☎ 022

Poor development spoils Langebaan, which otherwise has a rather beautiful location, overlooking the aquamarine Langebaan Lagoon. It's a good place for sailing and windsurfing.

The tourist information centre (☎ 772 1515, W www.langebaaninfo.com), in the same building as the West Coast National Park office at the end of Hoof St, is open 9am to 5pm Monday to Friday, 9am to 12.30pm Saturday and 9am to noon Sunday.

Places to Stay & Eat
None of the three *caravan parks* run by the local municipality allows tents. This is to avoid rowdy parties of locals, so if you don't look like trouble you might be able to persuade the manager to let you camp.

Oliphantskop Farm Inn (☎/fax 772 2326) Dorm beds R65, singles/doubles B&B R109/218, 4-person self-catering cottage R220. Across the road from the Mykonos resort complex, around 3km from the centre of Langebaan, this friendly and attractive place offers accommodation at backpacker rates, and has a reputation for good food.

Windstone Backpackers (☎ 766 1645, fax 766 1038, W www.windstone.co.za) Camp sites R35 per person, dorm beds R55, doubles R160-180. This one's a long way from Langebaan and the sea, though the facilities are quite good and include an indoor pool. The place is also a boarding kennel for cats and dogs, and an equestrian centre. It's near Langeenheid train station on the R45.

The Farmhouse (☎ 772 2062, fax 722 1980, W www.thefarmhouselangebaan .co.za, 5 Egret St) Singles/doubles B&B from R400/540. Langebaan's best hotel has a good location overlooking the bay, comfortable rooms and a classy *restaurant*.

Die Strandloper (☎ 772 2490) All-you-can-eat deal R95. Open for lunch Wed, Sat & Sun, dinner Wed-Sun. This rustic open-air seafood restaurant and bar is on the beach, outside of town on the way to the Mykonos resort. Call ahead to check it's open.

Very similar is *Boesmanland Farm Kitchen (☎ 772 1564)* in the Mykonos resort, where you'll also find *Bouzouki*, a Greek restaurant by the marina.

Getting There & Away
You might be able to get to Langebaan on the West Coast Shuttle (☎ 083 556 1777), which operates a rather pricey minibus service (R60 one way) from Cape Town to the Club Mykonos resort and casino in Langebaan.

The Seaplane Company (☎ 0800 006, 878, W www.seaplane.co.za) operates a seaplane shuttle service between Cape Town's Waterfront and Club Mykonos.

No other form of public transport runs to Langebaan.

PATERNOSTER
☎ 022

The sleepy fishing village of Paternoster is 15km from the missable inland town of Vredenburg. It's an attractive, low-key kind of place with a clutch of simple whitewashed homes where local fishing families live – and which are becoming highly desired as holiday houses for wealthy Capetonians.

The surrounding countryside is attractive, the rolling hills scattered with strange granite outcrops. The **Columbine Nature Reserve**, 3km past the town, protects 263 hectares of coastal fynbos around Cape Columbine. Further north along the coast is the village of **St Helena Bay**, with a lovely sheltered stretch of water, but no real beach.

Tietiesbaai (☎ 752 1718) Camp sites R20. This small, basic camping and caravan park near Cape Columbine has 10 sites.

Ahoy! Guesthouse (☎/fax 752 2725) Singles/doubles B&B from R160/250, 6-person self-catering cottage R400. Around the corner from the general store, this is the nicest accommodation in Paternoster, and offers comfortably furnished rooms.

Paternoster Hotel (☎/fax 022-752 2703, **e** *paternosterhotel@webnet.co.za)* Singles/doubles B&B from R130/260. This rough-edged, quirky country hotel, virtually on the beach front, is a popular venue for people interested in fishing. Its fish and crayfish braais are famous. We warn you: The bar is a feminist's nightmare.

Voorstrandt Restaurant (☎ 752 2038, Strandloperweg) Mains R35-50. Open 10am-10pm daily. You can hop from this designer red-and-green-painted beach shack right onto the sand. Seafood is the speciality. It's an excellent spot to watch sunset over a beer.

OLIFANTS RIVER VALLEY

The scenery changes dramatically at the Piekenaarskloof Pass; coming north on the N7 you suddenly overlook the intensively cultivated Olifants River Valley. The elephants that explorer Jan Danckaert came upon in 1660, and which gave their name to the area, have long gone.

Today the river provides irrigation for hectares of grapevines and orange trees, which are beautifully maintained by a huge labour force. The comfortable bungalows of the white farmers are surrounded by green and leafy gardens, masking them from the shanties.

On the valley floor are some acclaimed wineries and co-ops, which specialise in white wine. The eastern side is largely bounded by the spectacular Cederberg range, which is protected by the extensive Cederberg Wilderness Area. Citrusdal and Clanwilliam, to the south and north of the wilderness area, are the two main towns in the region.

As an alternative route to the N7, there's a spectacular partly tarred road (the R303) between Citrusdal and Ceres (see the boxed text 'Great Mountain Passes' earlier in this chapter).

CEDERBERG WILDERNESS AREA
☎ 027

The Cederberg is a rugged area of valleys and peaks extending roughly north-south for 100km from north to south between Citrusdal and Vanrhynsdorp. A good proportion is protected by the 71,000-hectare Cederberg Wilderness Area, which is administered by Cape Nature Conservation. The highest peak is Sneeuberg (2028m), and the area is famous for its weathered sandstone formations, which sometimes take bizarre shapes. San art can be found on the rocks and in some of the area's caves.

The area is also famous for its plant life, which is predominantly mountain fynbos. Spring is the best time to see the wildflowers, although there's plenty of interest at other times of the year. The vegetation varies with altitude but includes the Clanwilliam cedar (which gives the region its name) and the rare snowball protea. There are small populations of baboons, rheboks, klipspringers and grysboks; predators include the caracal, the Cape fox, the honey

EXCURSIONS

badger and the leopard, which is rarely seen.

Orientation & Information

The Cederberg is divided into three excellent hiking areas of around 24,000 hectares. Each has a network of trails, but this is a genuine wilderness area with an unusual ethos: You are *encouraged* to leave the trails and little information on routes is available. It's up to you to survive on your own. Similarly, you probably won't be given directions to the area's rock art. Work out for yourself where the San are likely to have lived.

There is a buffer zone of conserved land between the wilderness area and the farmland, and here more intrusive activities such as mountain-biking are allowed.

There's no real season for walking; from May to the end of September expect rain and possibly snow. From December to April there's likely to be very little water.

A permit is required if you want to walk, and the number of visitors per hiking area is limited to 50 people. The maximum group size is 12 and, for safety, the minimum size is three adults. Maps (R14) are available at the Algeria Camping Ground and the chief nature conservator's office (☎ 027-482 2812), Private Bag X6, Citrusdal 7340.

To be certain you'll get a permit, apply well in advance. Outside school holidays and weekends, there is a chance you'll be able to get on the spot, but you should definitely phone before arriving to make sure. Permits must be booked through the chief nature conservator or through the Cape Nature Conservation office in Cape Town (for contact details, see Tourist Offices in the Facts for the Visitor chapter). Bookings open on 1 February for the March to June period; 1 June for July to October; and 1 October for November to February. The cost is R12 per person per day, plus the park entry charge of R5.

The entrance to the Algeria Camping Ground closes at 4.30pm (9pm on Friday). You won't be allowed in if you arrive late. Permits have to be collected during office hours, so if you're arriving on Friday evening, you'll need to make arrangements.

For information on guided hikes in the area, contact Reinhardt Slabber at Gekko Backpackers Lodge near Citrusdal (see Citrusdal later).

Places to Stay

You'll need to book either of the following camp sites in the same way that you book hiking. There are basic huts for hikers in the wilderness area and a couple of better-equipped cottages.

Algeria Camping Ground (☎ 027-482 2812) Camping from R46 for a six-person site. These are exceptional grounds in a beautiful, shaded site alongside the Rondegat River, which is the headwaters of the Olifants River. There are swimming holes and lovely spots for picnicking beside the river. Day visitors (not allowed during peak periods) are charged R12.

Kliphuis State Forest camping ground (☎ 027-482 2812) Camp sites from R46. Nestling in the forest, near the Pakhuis Pass on the R364, about 15km north-east of Clanwilliam, this is another excellent camping ground. Surrounded by rock walls and cut by a fresh mountain stream, facilities are fairly spartan but there are toilets, showers and water.

Getting There & Away

The Cederberg range is about 200km from Cape Town, accessible from Citrusdal and the N7.

There are several roads into Algeria Camping Ground, and they all offer magnificent views. Algeria is signposted from the N7, from where it's about 20 minutes' drive (there's an amazing collection of plants, including proteas, along the side of the road).

There are some dusty but interesting back roads that run south-east through the hamlet of Cederberg (where you can buy fuel and stay in huts for about R100) and south to Ceres.

Public transport into Algeria is non-existent; walking from Citrusdal, the nearest town, will take about two days.

Ferdinand's Tours & Adventures runs weekend trips from Cape Town to the

Cederberg for around R650 (for contact details, see Organised Tours in the Getting Around chapter).

CITRUSDAL
☎ 022 • postcode 7340

The small town of Citrusdal is a good base for exploring the Cederberg – both the wilderness area and the equally interesting surrounding mountains. Wildflower season is from August to September, and the displays can be spectacular. This is also one of the best times for hiking.

The tourism bureau (☎ 921 3210), at 39 Voortrekker St, can help you find accommodation in the area and provide information on the local mountain-biking and hiking trails. It's open from 8am to 5pm Monday to Friday and 8am to 1pm Saturday.

If the tourism bureau is closed, head on over to Craig Royston (☎ 921 2963), on Modderfontein Farm, open from 8am to 5pm daily. This large old farm building, 2km out of Citrusdal off the N7, houses a cafe, a shop and a small museum. It hasn't been renovated to within an inch of its life, and the old shop is where farm workers still buy their supplies. It's a welcome relief after all those squeaky-clean tourist ventures. There are excellent light meals for around R25 and you can sample (and buy) local wines. It's also a good place to come for information, and it holds monthly cabaret evenings in Afrikaans.

Places to Stay & Eat
Drop Zone (☎ 921 3747, fax 921 3467, Voortrekker St) Dorm beds R50. The simple accommodation above this African-style cafe on the main road comes with a light breakfast. The shower is made from an old oil drum.

Gekko Backpackers Lodge (☎ 921 3353, W home.mweb.co.za/vi/vism) Dorm beds R50, cottage from R200 for 2 people. Here you'll find fine backpacker accommodation on a farm with a river pool and San rock-art trails within its extensive grounds. Hiking packages are available. The lodge is 17.5km from Citrusdal towards Clanwilliam on the N7.

Cedarberg Lodge (☎ 921 2221, fax 921 2704, W www.cedarberglodge.co.za, Voortrekker St) Singles/doubles from R115/150. This reasonable hotel is not far from the tourism bureau. All rooms have air-con, TV and en-suite bathrooms, and there are a sizable pool and a restaurant.

Staalwater (☎ 921 3337) 6-person cottage R80 per person. This self-catering cottage has a serene location 12km from town, on the road to the Baths health spa.

The Baths (☎ 921 3609, fax 921 3988, e baths@kingsley.co.za) Camp sites R30 per person, doubles R120, chalets from R180. About 18km from Citrusdal, this health spa with two outdoor pools in a pretty, wooded gorge is a good place to relax for a few days. Accommodation options range from camp sites and fairly inexpensive apartments to chalets (all of which cost more on weekends). If you call ahead, you can arrange a pick-up from the bus stop on the highway. The baths themselves are open to day visitors during the week (adult/child R15/7.50).

Patrick's Restaurant (☎ 921 3062, 77 Voortrekker St) Mains R40-50. Open noon-2.30pm Tues-Fri, 7pm-11pm Mon-Thurs, 7pm-midnight Fri & Sat. The best, and practically the only, place for dinner in town. It offers good steaks and, for some reason, pizzas with banana topping.

Uitspan Cafe (☎ 921 3273, 39 Voortrekker St) Mains R30. Open 8am-5pm Mon-Fri, 8am-1pm Sat. This bright cafe next to the tourism bureau does sandwiches, salads and cakes.

Getting There & Away
Intercape buses stop at the petrol station on the N7 outside town; from Cape Town the fare is R120. Shared taxis to Cape Town and north to Clanwilliam stop at the Caltex service station in town.

There's an excellent scenic road (the R303) over Middelburg Pass into the Koue (Cold) Bokkeveld and a beautiful valley on the other side, which is topped only by the Gydo Pass and the view over the Ceres Valley (see the boxed text 'Great Mountain Passes' earlier in this chapter).

Karoo

MATJIESFONTEIN
☎ 023

One of the most fascinating places in the Karoo, Matjiesfontein (pronounced '**my**-keys-fontein') is a small railway siding around a grand hotel that has remained virtually unchanged for 100 years. If you're passing this way, you should certainly pause to look around, or better still stay overnight.

The developer of the hotel and the surrounding hamlet was one Jimmy Logan, a Scot whose rise through Cape society was so swift that by the age of 36 he was not only a member of parliament, but also running every railway refreshment room between the Cape and Bulawayo (Zimbabwe). Matjiesfontein was his home base, and the hotel and other accommodation, together with the climate (the air has been likened to dry champagne), attracted wealthy people looking for a health resort.

Things to See & Do
As well as the attractive old buildings, which include a church, a court house, and a post office and general store, there's a fascinating **museum** *(admission R3; open 8am-5pm Tue, Thurs, Sat & Sun, 8.30am-5.30pm Mon, Wed & Fri)*. Located in the train station, it's a right old jumble sale, containing everything from trophy heads to a collection of commodes.

Places to Stay & Eat
The Lord Milner Hotel (☎ 551 3011, fax 551 3020, W www.matjiesfontein.com) Singles/doubles B&B from R240/380, 6-person cottage R400. This classic period piece has bags of old-world charm, with a range of comfortable rooms and atmospheric reception areas. Have a look at the swimming pool in the gardens at the back. The hotel's dining room, with waitresses in bobbin-lace caps, is surprisingly reasonably priced and has silver service to boot. It's open from 7pm to 9pm daily; mains cost R40.

The same people run *The Losieshuis*, excellent-value accommodation in converted cottages next to the hotel; singles/doubles cost R170/260.

For a snack try the *Coffee Shop*, open 9am to 5pm daily, and for a drink nip into *The Laird's Arms*, an authentic Victorian boozer.

Getting There & Away
Matjiesfontein is just off the N1, 240km from Cape Town. A night in the hotel would be worth a stopover on the *Trans Karoo* train trip between Jo'burg and Cape Town, although 24 hours here might be a bit long unless you have a good book. Alternatively, take the train from Cape Town (arriving at 2.46pm), stay the night and catch the 8.25am train back again next day. It's a 5½-hour trip.

The *Blue Train* pauses here for an hour, with travellers being given a tour of town on the double-decker London bus that stands outside the station.

CAPE WINERIES

It was Stellenbosch in the 1970s that first pro-moted a 'wine route', an idea that has since been enthusiastically taken up by 13 other parts of the country. Stellenbosch's wine route remains the largest, covering some 80 wineries; if you lump in the nearby areas of Franschhoek, Helderberg and Paarl, you're looking at over 160 wineries within a day's drive of Cape Town.

Several wineries are capitalising on the industry's popularity by adding on restaurants, accommodation (much of it luxurious) and other attractions. Of these, we've selected some of the more notable ones, as well as vineyards that are renowned for their fine wines. For more information, the bible is the annual *John Platter's South African Wine Guide*.

History

'Today, praise be the Lord, wine was pressed for the first time from Cape grapes.'

Jan Van Riebeeck, 2 February 1659

Although the founder of the Cape Colony, Jan Van Riebeeck, had planted vines and made wine himself, it was not until the arrival of Governor Simon Van Der Stel in 1679 that wine making began in earnest. Van Der Stel created Groot Constantia, the superb estate on the flanks of Table Mountain, and passed on his wine-making skills to the burghers settling around Stellenbosch.

Between 1688 and 1690, some 200 Huguenots arrived in the country. They were granted land in the region, particularly around Franschhoek, and although only a few had wine-making experience, they gave the infant industry fresh impetus.

For a long time, Cape wines other than those produced at Groot Constantia were not in great demand and most grapes ended up in brandy. But the industry received a boost in the early 19th century as war between Britain and France meant more South African wine was imported into the UK.

Apartheid-era sanctions and the power of the Kooperatieve Wijn-bouwers Vereeniging (KWV), the cooperative formed in 1918 to control minimum prices, production areas and quota limits, didn't exactly en-courage innovation, and hampered the industry. However, since 1992 KWV, now a private company, has relinquished some of its influence.

Many new and progressive wine makers are leading South Africa's re-emergence onto the world market. New wine-producing areas are being established away from the hotter inland areas, in particular in the cooler coastal areas east of Cape Town around Mossel Bay, Walker Bay and Elgin.

Inset: Photo detail by Olivier Cirendini

Workers' Wines Since the first vines were planted, the infamous 'tot' system has been in use in the Winelands, whereby the wages of some labourers – mainly poor coloureds – are paid partly in wine. The consequences, socially and physiologically, have been disastrous.

Balancing this is the recent emergence of workers' cooperative wineries. Fair Valley **(Map 10, #7)**, one of the first such empowerment initiatives, is a 17-hectare farm next to Fairview. It's still developing its own vineyards but has already produced three seasons of chenin blanc (sold through the UK wine chain Oddbins) made with grapes bought in from Fairview.

Up the road, north of Paarl, is Nelson's Creek **(Map 10, #1)** (☎ 021-863 8453), where the owner has donated part of the estate to his workers to produce their own wines. Under the label New Beginnings, these wines – a classic dry red, a rosé and a dry white – are being sold in the UK, the Netherlands and Japan. And at the Backsberg estate **(Map 10, #11)** (☎ 021-875 5141), south-west of Paarl, the Freedom Road wine (a sauvignon blanc) helps fund a workers' housing project.

Other worker empowerment wines to look out for include Thandi (☎ 021-859 0605) from the Elgin area, available at Tesco in the UK, and Tukulu (☎ 021-808 7911) from the Darling area, a highly successful operation run by Carmen Stevens, a coloured woman, and getting rave reviews for its pinotage and chenin blanc.

Wines

The most common variety of white wine is chenin blanc, or *steen*. In the last decade or so, more fashionable varieties such as chardonnay and sauvignon blanc have been planted on a wide scale. Other widely planted whites include colombard, semillon, crouchen blanc (known as Cape riesling) and various sweet muscats. Table whites, especially chardonnay, once tended to be heavily oaked and high in alcohol, but lighter, more fruity whites are now in the ascendancy.

Older, more robust red varieties such as shiraz, cabernet sauvignon and the Cape's own pinotage (a cross between pinot noir and hermitage or shiraz which produces a very bold wine) are being challenged by lighter blends of cabernet sauvignon, merlot, shiraz and cabernet franc, making a style closer to Bordeaux styles. The reds attracting the highest prices are cabernet sauvignon and the Bordeaux-style blends.

The Worcester region is the country's leading producer of fortified wines, including port, brandy and South Africa's own hanepoot. This dessert wine is made from the Mediterranean grape variety known as muscat of Alexandria to produce a strong, sweet and suitably high-alcohol tipple for the domestic market. In Worcester you'll also find the KWV Brandy Cellar, the largest in the world and the final stop on the Brandy Route, which runs from Van Ryn Brandy Cellar **(Map 9, #20)** (☎ 021-881 3875) at Vlottenburg, 8km south-west of Stellenbosch. For more information contact the South African Brandy Foundation (☎ 021-886 6381, Ⓦ www.sabrandy.co.za).

Wine Regions

Constantia Constantia is the oldest of South Africa's wine-growing regions. Groot Constantia, the original estate established by Simon Van Der Stel in 1685, was divided up after his death in 1712, so today you can also visit Buitenverwachtig and Klein Constantia. One more winery, Steenberg Vineyards (which also makes wine for the nearby Constantia Uitsig estate), completes the Constantia wine route.

If you're short of time, head for Groot Constantia, which is among the grandest vineyards and homesteads in the Cape. A delightful way to spend a day, though, is to take Downhill Adventures' cycling tour of this lush area (see Cycling in the Things to See & Do chapter).

For details of places to eat in the area, see Constantia in the Places to Eat chapter.

Groot Constantia (☎ 021-794 5128, W *www.grootconstantia.com, Groot Constantia Rd, High Constantia*) **Map 11, #19** Tastings (R12) & sales 10am-4.30pm daily. Although it's a bit of a tourist trap, Groot Constantia is also a superb example of Cape Dutch architecture, and embodies the gracious lifestyle the wealthy Dutch created in their adopted country. In the 18th century, Constantia wines were exported around the world and were highly acclaimed. The beautifully restored homestead is now a museum and appropriately furnished; take a look at the tiny slave quarters beneath the main building. Admission to the museum costs R8/2 for adults/children. The Cloete Cellar, the estate's original wine cellar, now houses old carriages and a display of storage vessels. Tours of the modern cellar run at least twice daily at 11am and 3pm; you need to book. Concerts are held occasionally in the Bertrams Cellar tasting room. Avoid visiting on a weekend as it can get very crowded.

Buitenverwachtig (☎ 021-794 5190, e *buiten@pixie.co.za, Klein Constantia Rd*) **Map 11, #19** Tastings (free) & sales 9am-5pm Mon-Fri, 9am-1pm Sat. The name means 'beyond expectations', which is certainly the feeling one gets on visiting this estate set on 100 hectares. For R60 per person you can enjoy a picnic lunch in front of the 1786 manor house; to book, call ☎ 794 1012. The internationally renowned Christine claret usually sells out on 18 September, the day of its release each year. Chardonnay and Rhine riesling are among the good whites produced here. The estate is known to offer good working and living conditions for its employees.

Klein Constantia (☎ 021-794 5188, W *www.kleinconstantia.com, Klein Constantia Rd*) **Map 11, #18** Tastings (free) & sales 9am-5pm Mon-Fri, 9am-1pm Sat. This small winery, part of the original Constantia estate, is famous for its Vin de Constance, a deliciously sweet muscat wine which was Napoleon's solace on St Helena and which one of Jane Austen's heroines recommended for having the power to heal 'a disappointed heart'. We can't guarantee that, but we can say that while Klein Constantia doesn't offer any of the frills and bonuses of other wineries, it's still worth visiting for its excellent tasting room and informative displays. At the estate's entrance, pause to look at the *karamat* (saint's tomb) of Sheik Abdurachman Matebe Shah; he was buried in 1661.

Constantia Uitsig (*☎ 021-794 1810*, W *www.constantiauitsig.co.za, Spaanschemat River Rd*) **Map 11, #21** Tastings (free) & sales 9am-5pm Mon-Sat. The wine on sale here is actually made at the nearby Steenberg Vineyards, and you can also taste wines from some 60 other estates. It's one for foodies since it boasts several excellent restaurants (see La Colombe in the Places to Eat chapter) and a luxurious hotel (see Constantia Uitsig in the Places to Stay chapter).

Steenberg Vineyards (*☎ 021-713 2211*, W *www.steenberghotel .com, Steenberg Rd*) **Map 11, #22** Tastings (free) & sales 9am-4.30pm Mon-Fri, Sept-Feb only 9am-1pm Sat. The oldest Cape wine estate after Constantia, Steenberg began life as Swaaneweide (Feeding Place of the Swans) in 1682. Its merlot, sauvignon blanc reserve and semillon are the wines to go for. Today the estate encompasses a five-star country hotel in the original restored manor house, and an 18-hole golf course.

Stellenbosch For details of wineries in this area not listed here, contact the Wine Route Office (*☎ 021-886 4310*), or the Stellenbosch Publicity Association (see Stellenbosch in the Excursions chapter).

Blaauwklippen (*☎ 021-880 0133*, e *mail@blaauwklippen.com*) **Map 9, #23** Tastings (R10) & sales 9am-4.45pm Mon-Fri, 9am-4pm Sat. This rustic 300-year-old estate has several fine Cape Dutch buildings. Cellar tours are by appointment only and lunch is available; call for exact times for lunch, which change according to the season. Klaauwklippen is on the R44 towards Somerset West.

Delaire (*☎ 021-885 1756*, e *delaire@iafrica.com*) **Map 9, #13** Tastings (R10) & sales 10am-5pm Mon-Sat, 10am-4pm Sun. Come for the view from this small, friendly winery on the Helshoogte Pass. There's wheelchair access to its restaurant, and picnics are available in season (bookings essential). It's on the R310 towards Franschhoek.

Hartenberg Estate (*☎ 021-882 2541*, e *hartenberg@cybertrade .co.za*) **Map 9, #11** Tastings (free) & sales 9am-5pm Mon-Fri, 9am-3pm Sat. Founded in 1692, this estate produces many award winning wines (partly because it has its own microclimate), particularly merlot, cabernet sauvignon and shiraz. Lunch is available from noon to 2pm (bookings essential). The estate is 10km north-west of Stellenbosch, off Bottelary Rd.

Lanzerac (*☎ 021-887 1132, fax 887 2310*, W *www.lanzerac.co.za, Jonkershoek Valley*) **Map 9, #15** Tastings (R15) & sales 10am-4pm Mon-Fri, 10am-2pm Sat. Singles/doubles B&B from R850/1240 in low season, R1475/1990 in high season. Stellenbosch's most luxurious hotel also produces very good merlot and quaffable chardonnay and cabernet sauvignon. Facilities at the 300-year-old manor house include several pools and restaurants.

Morgenhof (*☎ 021-889 5510*, W *www.morgenhof.com*) **Map 9, #9** Tastings (R10) & sales 9am-6pm Mon-Fri & 10am-5pm Sat & Sun

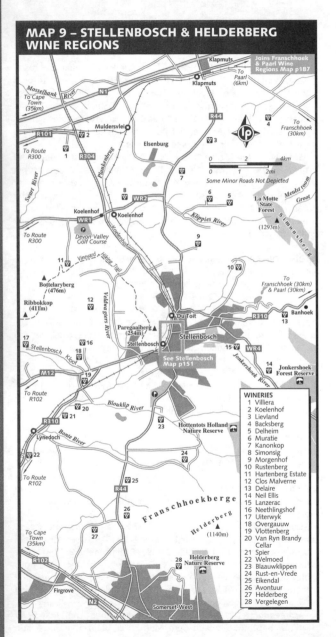

MAP 9 – STELLENBOSCH & HELDERBERG WINE REGIONS

WINERIES
1 Villiera
2 Koelenhof
3 Lievland
4 Backsberg
5 Delheim
6 Muratie
7 Kanonkop
8 Simonsig
9 Morgenhof
10 Rustenberg
11 Hartenberg Estate
12 Clos Malverne
13 Delaire
14 Neil Ellis
15 Lanzerac
16 Neethlingshof
17 Uiterwyk
18 Overgauuw
19 Vlottenberg
20 Van Ryn Brandy Cellar
21 Spier
22 Welmoed
23 Blaauwklippen
24 Rust-en-Vrede
25 Eikendal
26 Avontuur
27 Helderberg
28 Vergelegen

Nov-Apr, 9am-4.30pm Mon-Fri & 10am-3pm Sat & Sun May-Oct. This old estate, on the slopes of Simonsberg on the R44 towards Paarl, has fine architecture. Light lunches are available, and the coffee shop serves breakfast from 9am to noon daily.

Spier (☎ *021-809 1100, fax 809 1134,* **W** *www.spier.co.za)* **Map 9, #21** Tastings (R12) & sales 9am-5pm daily. Doubles from R950. There's something for everyone at this mega-estate: a good Cape Malay–style hotel; steam-train trips from Cape Town (☎ 021-419 5222); horse riding; a performing arts centre; beautifully restored Cape Dutch buildings; and a wide range of dining options. The only aspect we're unsure about is the cheetah park, where listless animals pose for photos with tourists. Its wines are nothing to shout about, but you can try lots of other vineyards' wines. Check out the annual arts festival, which runs from January to March and is as good a reason for coming here as any. Spier is off the R310 towards Cape Town.

Helderberg This area around Somerset West, 20km south of Stellenbosch, has some 20 wineries, including Vergelegen, arguably the most beautiful estate in the Cape.

Vergelegen (☎ *021-847 1334,* **W** *www.vergelegen.co.za, Lourensford Rd, Somerset West)* **Map 9, #28** Admission R10. Tastings (R5) & sales 9.30am-4pm daily Nov-Apr, 9.30am-4pm Mon-Sat May-Oct. Although you have to pay an entrance fee, it's well worth it to visit this lovely estate where vines were first planted by Simon Van Der Stel's son Willem in 1700. The buildings and elegant grounds with ravishing mountain views have a stately-home feel to them; cellar tours are available for R10. On the dining front you can choose from a picnic hamper (R140 for two; bookings essential), the upmarket Lady Phillips Restaurant (bookings essential), and the casual Rose Terrace.

Franschhoek Many of Franschhoek's wineries are within walking distance of the town centre, but to reach Boschendal, on the R310 towards Stellenbosch, you'll need transport. Call Vignerons de Franschhoek (☎ 021-876 3062) for information on other wineries in the area.

Boschendal (☎ *021-870 4210,* **W** *www.boschendal.com, Pniel Rd, Groote Drakenstein)* **Map 10, #14** Manor house open daily 9.30am-5pm. Admission R6. Tastings (R6) & sales 8.30am-4.30pm Mon-Fri & 8.30am-12.30pm Sat May-Oct, 8.30am-4.30pm Mon-Sat Nov-Apr, 9.30am-12.30pm Sun Dec-Jan. Tucked beneath some awesome mountains, this is a classic Winelands estate, with great architecture, food and wine. The blow-out buffet lunch (R125) in the main restaurant is mainly a group affair. Far nicer, especially in fine weather, is Le Café (open 10am to 5pm daily), with seating inside and outside the converted slave quarters. Also very popular are the Le Pique Nique hampers (R62.50 per person, for a minimum of two) served under parasols on the lawn from mid-October to the end of April (bookings essential on ☎ 870 4274). Note that the wine-tasting area is at the opposite end of the estate from the manor house and restaurants.

Cabrière Estate (☎ *021-876 2630,* W *www.cabriere.co.za, Berg St)* **Map 10, #24** Tastings (R15) 11am & 3pm Mon-Fri, 11am Sat. Sales 9.30am-4.30pm Mon-Fri, 11am-2pm Sat. The tastings here include two sparkling wines and one of each type from the vineyard's range of excellent brandies and white, red and dessert wines. At the Saturday session, stand by for proprietor Achim Von Arnim's party trick of slicing open a bottle of bubbly with a sabre (this session costs an extra R5 and includes a cellar tour). For information on the estate's Haute Cabrière restaurant, see Franschhoek in the Excursions chapter.

Chamonix (☎ *021-876 2498, 876 2498 for guest cottages, fax 876 3237,* W *www.chamonix.co.za, Uitkyk St)* **Map 10, #18** Tastings (R10) & sales 9.30am-4.30pm daily. 4-bed cottages from R120 per person. The tasting room is in a converted blacksmith's, and there's a range of schnapps and mineral waters to try too. Cellar tours are available at 11am and 2pm by appointment. The pretty La Maison de Chamonix restaurant is open for lunch daily and for dinner on Friday; mains cost from R30 to R60. The good-value self-catering cottages (☎ 876 2498) are in the midst of the vineyards.

La Couronne (☎ *021-876 2770, fax 876 3788,* W *www.lacouronne hotel.co.za, Robertsvlei Rd)* **Map 10, #25** Tastings (R5) & sales 10am-4pm Tues-Sun. Doubles B&B from R1300. It's all gilt-edged luxury at this boutique hotel, restaurant and winery with a magnificent view across the valley. The Ménage à Trois Bordeaux blend gets high marks. The restaurant is open daily for lunch and dinner; the menu changes regularly and mains cost around R60.

Mont Rochelle (☎ *021-876 3000,* e *montrochelle@wine.co.za)* **Map 10, #23** Tastings (R5) & sales 11am-5pm Mon-Sat, 11am-1pm Sun. Another vineyard in a beautiful location, this one offers great wines and good-value picnic baskets (R40 per person for two people), or soup and bread by a roaring fire in winter. Cellar tours are conducted at 11am, 12.30pm & 3pm Monday to Friday (R5). For details about horseback tours of this and other nearby estates, contact Mont Rochelle Equestrian Centre (☎ 083 300 4368, fax 021-876 2363). The cost is R70 per hour.

Paarl Paarl Vintners (☎ 021-872 3841) can provide information on other wineries in the area.

KWV (☎ *021-807 3007,* W *www.kwv.co.za, Kohler St)* **Map 6, #18** Tastings (R10) & sales 9am-4pm Mon-Sat. KWV is no longer the all-controlling body it used to be, but it remains one of the best known of the country's wineries and its products are mostly sold overseas. Some KWV port and sherry is available within South Africa, and the fortified wines, in particular, are among the world's best. The firm's impressive offices **(Map 6, #19)** are at La Concorde on Paarl's Main St, but the cellar tours are at the complex near the railway line. It's well worth taking the tour (available in English, German and French as well as Afrikaans) if only to see the enormous Cathedral Cellar built in 1930. Call ahead for times of cellar tours, which cost R20.

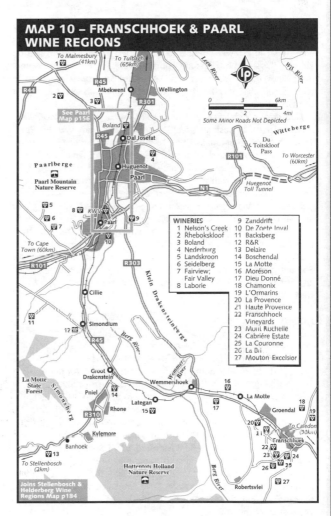

MAP 10 – FRANSCHHOEK & PAARL WINE REGIONS

WINERIES

1. Nelson's Creek
2. Rhebokskloof
3. Boland
4. Nederburg
5. Landskroon
6. Seidelberg
7. Fairview; Fair Valley
8. Laborie
9. Zanddrift
10. De Zoete Inval
11. Backsberg
12. R&R
13. Delaire
14. Boschendal
15. La Motte
16. Moréson
17. Dieu Donné
18. Chamonix
19. L'Ormarins
20. La Provence
21. Haute Provence
22. Franschhoek Vineyards
23. Mont Rochelle
24. Cabriére Estate
25. La Couronne
26. La Bri
27. Mouton Excelsior

Laborie (☎ 021-807 3390, 🖥 www.kwv-international.com, *Taillefert St*) **Map 10, #8** Tastings (R7) & sales 9am-5pm daily Oct-Apr, 9am-5pm Mon-Sat May-Sept. Singles/doubles B&B R250/500. KWV's attractive showcase vineyard is just off Main Rd. Both the restaurant (☎ 807 3095) and the new guesthouse (☎ 807 3271) in old Cape Dutch buildings are excellent value considering their quality. Picnic baskets are available for a bargain R60 for two and there's a 3.5km hiking trail through the vineyards. The restaurant is open daily for lunch and from Tuesday to Saturday for dinner; mains cost R35 to R50.

Fairview (☎ 021-863 2450, ⓔ fairback@iafrica.com) **Map 10, #7**
Tastings (R10) & sales 8.30am-5pm Mon-Fri, 8.30am-1pm Sat. Peacocks
and a goat in a tower (apparently goats love to climb) greet you on
arrival at this small and deservedly popular winery. The tastings are great
value since they cover more than 20 wines *and* the wide range of
cheeses from sheep's, goats' and cows' milk. Fairview is 5km south-west
of Paarl off the R101.

Landskroon Estate (☎ 021-863 1039, ⓦ www.landskroonwines
.com) **Map 10, #5** Tastings (free) & sales 8.30am-5pm Mon-Fri, 9am-
1pm Sat. Nine generations of the De Villiers family have been perfect-
ing their wine-making skills on this pleasant estate, which has a nice
terrace overlooking the vines. There are some good cheeses for sale;
they go very nicely with the celebrated cabernet sauvignons and port.
The estate is 6km south-west of Paarl off the R101.

Nederburg Wines (☎ 021-862 3104, ⓦ www.nederburg.co.za) **Map
10, #4** Tastings (free) & sales 8.30am-5pm Mon-Fri, 9am-1pm Sat.
This is a big but professional and welcoming operation. The vast range
of wines is among the most widely available across the country. The
picnic lunches (December to March only) are very popular and go for
R55 per person. Cellar tours are available in English, German, French
and Spanish for R12.50. Bookings are essential for picnics and tours.
Nederburg Wines is 7km east of Paarl off the N1.

Robertson
The Robertson area is worth a visit for its 27 wineries, its
scenery and the general absence of tourist coaches. Staying the night
in the peaceful village of McGregor is a good way to end a day's tasting.

Robertson Winery (☎ 023-626 3059, ⓦ www.robertsonwine.co.za)
Tastings (free) & sales 8am-5pm Mon-Thurs, 8am-4.30pm Fri, 9am-
1pm Sat. This cellar is the region's oldest (but occupies a boring
modern building), and has a small museum attached. The sauvignon
blanc, Wide River cabernet sauvignon reserve and semisweet wines are
the ones to go for. Look for the entrance on Voortrekker St.

Graham Beck (☎ 023-626 1214, ⓦ www.grahambeckwines.co.za)
Tastings (free) & sales 9am-5pm Mon-Fri, 10am-3pm Sat. This winery,
based in a striking orange aircraft hangar–like building, comes as a
breath of fresh air after all those Cape Dutch estates, as do its emi-
nently drinkable products. Its fizzers give French champagnes a run for
their money and the muscat is heaven in a glass. It's located towards
Worcester off the R60.

De Wetshof Estate (☎ 023-615 1853, ⓦ www.dewetshof.co.za)
Tastings (free) & sales 8.30am-4.30pm Mon-Fri, 9.30am-12.30pm Sat.
This estate produces some of the best chardonnay in the country, as
well as an award-winning botrytis dessert wine.

Language

South Africa's official languages were once English and Afrikaans but nine others have been added: Ndebele, North Sotho, South Sotho, Swati, Tsonga, Tswana, Venda, Xhosa and Zulu.

Forms, brochures and timetables are usually bilingual (English and Afrikaans) but road signs alternate. Most Afrikaans speakers also speak good English, but this is not always the case in small rural towns and among older people. However, it's not uncommon for blacks in cities to speak at least six languages – whites can usually speak two.

In the Cape Town area only three languages are prominent: Afrikaans (spoken by many whites and coloureds), English (spoken by nearly everyone) and Xhosa (spoken mainly by blacks).

Afrikaans

Although Afrikaans is closely associated with Afrikaners, it is also the first language of many coloureds. Ironically, it was probably first used as a common language by the polyglot coloured community of the Cape, and passed back to whites by nannies and servants. Some 5½ million people speak the language, roughly half of whom are Afrikaner and half coloured.

Afrikaans developed from the High Dutch of the 17th century. It has abandoned the complicated grammar and incorporated vocabulary from French, English, indigenous African languages and even Asian languages (as a result of the influence of East Asian slaves). It's inventive, powerful and expressive, but it was not recognised as one of the country's official languages until 1925; before then it was officially a dialect of Dutch.

Words are generally pronounced as they are spelt, with the characteristic guttural emphasis and rolled 'r' of the Germanic languages.

Pronunciation

The following pronunciation guide is not exhaustive, but it includes the more difficult of the sounds that differ from English.

a	as the 'u' in 'pup'
e	as in 'hen'
i	as the 'e' in 'angel'
o	as the 'o' in 'fort', or as the 'oy' in 'boy'
u	as the 'e' in 'angel' but with lips pouted
r	a rolled 'rr' sound
aai	as the 'y' in 'why'
ae	as 'ah'
ee	as in 'deer'
ei	as the 'ay' in 'play'
oe	as the 'oo' in 'loot'
oë	as the 'oe' in 'doer'
ooi	as the 'oi' in 'oil', preceded by 'w'
oei	as the 'ooey' in 'phooey', preceded by 'w'
tj	as the 'ch' in 'chunk'

Greetings & Civilities

Hello.	*Hallo.*
Good morning.	*Goeiemôre.*
Good afternoon.	*Goeiemiddag.*
Good evening.	*Goeienaand.*
Good night.	*Goeienag.*
Please.	*Asseblief.*
Thank you.	*Dankie.*
Thank you very much.	*Baie dankie.*
How are you?	*Hoe gaan dit?*
Good thank you.	*Goed dankie.*
Pardon.	*Ekskuus.*

Basics

Yes.	*Ja.*
No.	*Nee.*
Isn't that so?	*Né?*
What?	*Wat?*
How?	*Hoe?*
How many/much?	*Hoeveel?*
Where?	*Waar?*
When?	*Wanneer?*

today	*vandag*
tomorrow	*môre*
yesterday	*gister*
soon	*nou-nou*
emergency	*nood*

Small Talk

Do you speak English?	*Praat u Engels?*
Do you speak Afrikaans?	*Praat u Afrikaans?*
I only understand a little Afrikaans.	*Ek verstaan net 'n bietjie Afrikaans.*
Where do you live?	*Waar woon u?*
What is your occupation?	*Wat is jou beroep?*
Where are you from?	*Waarvandaan kom u?*
from ...	*van ...*
overseas	*oorsee*
son	*seun*
daughter	*dogter*
wife	*vrou*
husband	*eggenoot*
mother	*ma*
father	*pa*
sister	*suster*
brother	*broer*
uncle	*oom*
aunt	*tante*
nice/good/pleasant	*lekker*
bad	*sleg*
cheap	*goedkoop*
expensive	*duur*
party	*jol*

Getting Around

travel	*reis*
departure	*vertrek*
arrival	*aankoms*
to	*na*
from	*van*
ticket	*kaartjie*
single	*enkel*
return	*retoer*

Around Town

art gallery	*kunsgalery*
at the corner	*op die hoek*
avenue	*laan*
building	*gebou*
butcher	*slaghuis*
church	*kerk*
city centre	*middestad*
city	*stad*
inquiries	*navrae*
exit	*uitgang*
information	*inligting*
left	*links*
office	*kantoor*
pharmacy/chemist	*apteek*
right	*regs*
road	*pad*
room	*kamer*
shop	*winkel*
shop selling alcohol	*drankwinkel*
station	*stasie*
street	*straat*
tourist bureau	*toeristeburo*
town	*dorp*
traffic light	*verkeerslig*

In the Country

bay	*baai*
beach	*strand*
caravan park	*woonwapark*
field/plain	*veld*
game reserve	*wildtuin*
hiking trail	*wandelpad*
little hill, usually flat-topped	*kopje/koppie*
main road	*hoofweg*
marsh	*vlei*
mountain	*berg*
point	*punt*
river	*rivier*
road	*pad*
shanty town	*blikkiesdorp*
utility/pick-up	*bakkie*

Food & Drink

bar	*kroeg*
barbecue	*braai/braaivleis*
beer	*bier*
bread	*brood*
cheese	*kaas*
cup of coffee	*koppie koffie*
fish	*vis*
fried meatball	*frikkadel*
fruit preserve	*konfyt*
fruit	*vrugte*

glass of milk	glas melk
griddle cakes	rooster koek
hotel bar	kroeg
meat	vleis
kebabs, usually marinated	sosatie
picnic	padkos
a herbal tea, reputedly therapeutic	rooibos
small doughnuts served with honey	koeksesters
twice-cooked biscuit	rusk
vegetables	groente
wine	wyn

Time & Days

am	vm
pm	nm
daily	daagliks
public holiday	openbare vakansiedag
Monday	Maandag (Ma)
Tuesday	Dinsdag (Di)
Wednesday	Woensdag (Wo)
Thursday	Donderdag (Do)
Friday	Vrydag (Vr)
Saturday	Saterdag (Sa)
Sunday	Sondag (So)

Numbers

1	een
2	twee
3	drie
4	vier
5	vyf
6	ses
7	sewe
8	agt
9	nege
10	tien
11	elf
12	twaalf
13	dertien
14	veertien
15	vyftien
16	sestien
17	sewentien
18	agtien
19	negentien
20	twintig
21	een en twintig
30	dertig
40	veertig
50	vyftig
60	sestig
70	sewentig
80	tagtig
90	negentig
100	honderd
1000	duisend

South African English

English has undergone some changes during its time in South Africa. Quite a few words have changed meaning, new words have been appropriated, and thanks to the influence of Afrikaans, a distinctive accent has developed. British rather than US practice is followed in grammar and spelling. In some cases British words are preferred to their US equivalents (eg, 'lift' not 'elevator', 'petrol' not 'gas'). In African English, repetition for emphasis is common: Something that burns you is 'hot hot'; fields after the rains are 'green green'; a crowded minibus with no more room is 'full full' and so on.

Glossary

Bokke
   affectionate name for the South African national rugby team, the Springboks
bottle store
   shop selling alcohol
buppie
   black yuppie
comma
   used instead of the decimal point, eg, 10,5 ('ten comma five')
cool drink
   canned soft drink
eh
   pronounced to rhyme with 'hay', an all-purpose ending to sentences, even very short ones such as 'Thanks, eh'.
farm stall
   small roadside shop or shelter that sells farm produce

Howzit?
all-purpose greeting

Izzit?
rhetorical question that most closely translates as 'Really?' It could mean 'Is it?', 'Is that so?', 'Did you?', 'Are you?', 'Is he?', 'Are they?', 'Is she?', 'Are we?', 'Amazing!' etc.

just now
indeterminate future, but reasonably imminent (see 'now' and 'now-now')

now
soon; eg, 'I'll serve you now' means in a little while. 'Just now' means 'I understand that you're impatient, and I'll be with you soon', or 'When I can get around to it'.

now-now
immediately

plus-minus
approximately; eg, 'How far is Dagsdorp?' 'Plus-minus 60km.'

robot
traffic light

russian
large red sausage, fried but often served cold

Shame!
What a pity!

sif
horrible

sis
ugh

slots
poker machines

Sorry!
often used to express sympathy for someone having a minor mishap. Also used to get attention, as in 'Excuse me'.

spook and diesel
rum and Coke

supper
main evening meal

tickie box
public phone on private premises

vienna
smaller version of the russian sausage

Where do you stay?
'Where do you live?' not 'Which hotel are you staying at?'

yah well no fine
yes-no-maybe-perhaps

you must
Sometimes it sounds as though everyone's ordering you around: 'You must sit over there'; 'You must order from the waiter'. But they aren't. 'Must' is a fairly neutral word in South Africa, and doesn't have the 'bossy' connotations that it does in other English-speaking countries. Think of 'You must …' as a less polite version of 'Please …'.

Xhosa

Xhosa is the language of the Xhosa people. It's the dominant indigenous language in Eastern Cape province, and is also spoken by many blacks in the Cape Town area.

It's worth noting that *bawo* is a term of respect used when addressing an older man.

Good morning.	*Molo.*
Good night.	*Rhonani.*
Do you speak English?	*Uyakwazi ukuthetha isiNgesi?*
Are you well?	*Uphilile namhlanje?*
Yes, I am well.	*Ewe, ndiphilile.*
Where do you come from?	*Uvela phi na?*
I come from ...	*Ndivela e ...*
When do we arrive?	*Siya kufika nini na?*
The road is good.	*Indlela ilungile.*
The road is bad.	*Indlela imbi.*
I am lost.	*Ndilahlekile.*
Is this the road to ...?	*Yindlela eya ...?*
Would you show me the way to ...?	*Ungandibonisa indlela eya ...?*
Is it possible to cross the river?	*Ungaweleka umlambo?*
How much is it?	*Yimalini?*

day	*usuku*
week	*iveki*
month (moon)	*inyanga*
north	*umntla*
south	*umzantsi*
east	*empumalanga*
west	*entshonalanga*

Glossary

ANC – African National Congress

apartheid – literally 'the state of being apart'; the old South African political system in which people were segregated according to race

AWB – Afrikaner Weerstandsbeweging (Afrikaner Resistance Movement), an extremist right-wing group of Afrikaners; it seems to be fading from the scene

Bergie – homeless person

biltong – dried meat made from virtually anything

bobotie – a traditional Malay dish; delicate curried mince with a topping of savoury egg custard, usually served on turmeric-flavoured rice

boerewors – spicy sausages, often sold like hot dogs by street vendors; essential at any *braai*

braai – a barbecue featuring lots of grilled meat and beer ('and a small salad for the ladies'); a South African institution, particularly among whites

bredie – a traditional Cape Malay stew of vegetables and lamb, chicken, or fish

Broederbond – a secret society open only to Protestant Afrikaner men; highly influential under National Party rule

cafe, kaffe – in some cases, a pleasant place for a coffee; in others, a small shop selling odds and ends, plus unappetising fried food

camp site – an individual pitch on a camping ground

camping ground – an area where tents can be pitched and caravans parked

Codesa – Convention for a Democratic South Africa

coloureds – South Africans of mixed race

dinkie – the smallest size of wine bottle

dorp – a rural settlement where a road crosses a river

DP – Democratic Party

drostdy – the residence of a *landdrost*

dumpie – the smallest size of beer bottle

fynbos – the vegetation of the area around Cape Town, composed of proteas, heaths and reeds; literally 'fine bush'

hanepoot – a dessert wine made from the Mediterranean grape variety known as muscat of Alexandria

Homelands – reserves for the black peoples of South Africa, established under apartheid and reabsorbed into South Africa after 1994; also derisively called *bantustans*

IFP – Inkatha Freedom Party

jol – party (used as a verb and as a noun); also any good time: 'How was Mozambique?' 'Yah, it was a jol, man.'

kaffe – see *cafe*

karamat – the tomb of a Muslim saint

kingklip an excellent firm-fleshed fish, usually served fried

kloof ravine

kloofing – adventure activity involving climbing, jumping and swimming in kloofs

KWV – Kooperatieve Wijnbouwers Vereeniging; the cooperative formed in 1918 to control minimum prices, production areas and quota limits in the wine industry

landdrost – an official representative of the colony's governor who acted as local administrator, tax collector and magistrate

line fish – catch of the day

location – another word for *township*, usually in a rural area

malva pudding – a delicious sponge dessert; sometimes called vinegar pudding, since it's traditionally made with apricot jam and vinegar

mealie – an ear of maize

mealie meal – finely ground maize

mealie pap – mealie porridge; the staple diet of rural blacks, often served with stew

melktert – custard tart
moffie – a gay man; formerly derogatory, but now appropriated by many in the gay community
Mother City – another name for Cape Town; probably so called because it was South Africa's first colony

NNP – New National Party
nonshared taxi – a taxi available for private hire, as distinct from a *shared taxi*
NP – National Party

PAC – Pan-African Congress
Pagad – People against Gangsterism and Drugs
pap and sous – maize porridge with a sauce
poort – a mountain pass

renosterbos – literally 'rhinoceros bush'; a type of vegetation
Rikkis – tiny, open vans providing Asian-style transport in Cape Town's City Bowl and nearby areas at low prices
rondavel – a round hut with a conical roof, frequently seen in holiday resorts

SABC – South African Broadcasting Corporation
samp – crushed maize used for porridge; known in Xhosa as *umngqusho*
SANDF – South African National Defence Force
sandveld – land consisting mainly of sand dunes
shared taxi – a relatively cheap form of shared transport, usually a minibus; also known as a black taxi, a minibus taxi or a long-distance taxi
shebeen – a drinking establishment in a township; once illegal, now merely unlicensed
snoek – a firm-fleshed migratory fish that appears off the Cape in June and July, served smoked, salted or curried
sourveld – barren land; land where little will grow
Spar – a supermarket chain; becoming a generic term for any large supermarket

spruit – shallow river
stad – Afrikaans for 'city centre'; used on road signs
strand – beach
sundowner – any drink, but typically alcohol, drunk at sunset

Tavern of the Seas – Cape Town was once known this way, in the days when it had a reputation among sailors as a riotous port
Telkom – government telecommunications company
township – black residential district, usually hidden on the outskirts of an otherwise white town

ubuntu – a Xhosa and Zulu word for humanity, often used to indicate traditional hospitality, but broader than that; it has spiritual overtones that suggest the connectedness of all living things
umnqombothi – Xhosa for rough-and-ready home-brewed beer
UDF – United Democratic Front
UDM – United Democratic Movement

veld – (pronounced 'felt') open grassland; variations include lowveld, highveld, bushveld, *sandveld* and *sourveld*
venison – if you see this on a menu it's bound to be some form of antelope, usually springbok
vlei – (pronounced 'flay') any low open landscape, sometimes marshy
VOC – Vereenigde Oost-Indische Compagnie (Dutch East India Company)
Voortrekkers – the original Afrikaner settlers of the Orange Free State and Transvaal who migrated from the Cape Colony in the 1830s

waterblommetjie bredie – a traditional Cape Malay stew of mutton with faintly peppery water-hyacinth flowers and white wine
weg – literally 'way' but translated as 'street' or 'road'; eg, 'Abelweg' means 'Abel Rd'

zol – marijuana, also known as dagga

LONELY PLANET

You already know that Lonely Planet produces more than this one guidebook, but you might not be aware of the other products we have on this region. Here is a selection of titles that you may want to check out as well:

Southern Africa
ISBN 0 86442 662 3

South Africa, Lesotho & Swaziland
ISBN 1 86450 322 X

Botswana
ISBN 1 74059 041 4

Mozambique
ISBN 1 86450 108 1

Zambia
ISBN 1 74059 045 7

Namibia
ISBN 1 74059 042 2

Africa on a shoestring
ISBN 0 86442 663 1

Read This First: Africa
ISBN 1 86450 066 2

Watching Wildlife Southern Africa
ISBN 1 86450 035 2

Cape Town City Map
ISBN 1 86450 076 X

Southern Africa Road Atlas
ISBN 1 86450 101 4

Healthy Travel Africa
ISBN 1 86450 050 6

Zimbabwe
ISBN 1 74059 043 0

Malawi
ISBN 1 86450 095 6

Available wherever books are sold

Lonely Planet Guides by Region

Lonely Planet is known worldwide for publishing practical, reliable and no-nonsense travel information in our guides and on our Web site. The Lonely Planet list covers just about every accessible part of the world. Currently there are 16 series: Travel guides, Shoestring guides, Condensed guides, Phrasebooks, Read This First, Healthy Travel, Walking guides, Cycling guides, Watching Wildlife guides, Pisces Diving & Snorkeling guides, City Maps, Road Atlases, Out to Eat, World Food, Journeys travel literature and Pictorials.

AFRICA Africa on a shoestring • Botswana • Cairo • Cairo City Map • Cape Town • Cape Town City Map • East Africa • Egypt • Egyptian Arabic phrasebook • Ethiopia, Eritrea & Djibouti • Ethiopian Amharic phrasebook • The Gambia & Senegal • Healthy Travel Africa • Kenya • Malawi • Morocco • Moroccan Arabic phrasebook • Mozambique • Namibia • Read This First: Africa • South Africa, Lesotho & Swaziland • Southern Africa • Southern Africa Road Atlas • Swahili phrasebook • Tanzania, Zanzibar & Pemba • Trekking in East Africa • Tunisia • Watching Wildlife East Africa • Watching Wildlife Southern Africa • West Africa • World Food Morocco • Zambia • Zimbabwe, Botswana & Namibia
Travel Literature: Mali Blues: Traveling to an African Beat • The Rainbird: A Central African Journey • Songs to an African Sunset: A Zimbabwean Story

AUSTRALIA & THE PACIFIC Aboriginal Australia & the Torres Strait Islands •Auckland • Australia • Australian phrasebook • Australia Road Atlas • Cycling Australia • Cycling New Zealand • Fiji • Fijian phrasebook • Healthy Travel Australia, NZ & the Pacific • Islands of Australia's Great Barrier Reef • Melbourne • Melbourne City Map • Micronesia • New Caledonia • New South Wales • New Zealand • Northern Territory • Outback Australia • Out to Eat – Melbourne • Out to Eat – Sydney • Papua New Guinea • Pidgin phrasebook • Queensland • Rarotonga & the Cook Islands • Samoa • Solomon Islands • South Australia • South Pacific • South Pacific phrasebook • Sydney • Sydney City Map • Sydney Condensed • Tahiti & French Polynesia • Tasmania • Tonga • Tramping in New Zealand • Vanuatu • Victoria • Walking in Australia • Watching Wildlife Australia • Western Australia
Travel Literature: Islands in the Clouds: Travels in the Highlands of New Guinea • Kiwi Tracks: A New Zealand Journey • Sean & David's Long Drive

CENTRAL AMERICA & THE CARIBBEAN Bahamas, Turks & Caicos • Baja California • Belize, Guatemala & Yucatán • Bermuda • Central America on a shoestring • Costa Rica • Costa Rica Spanish phrasebook • Cuba • Cycling Cuba • Dominican Republic & Haiti • Eastern Caribbean • Guatemala • Havana • Healthy Travel Central & South America • Jamaica • Mexico • Mexico City • Panama • Puerto Rico • Read This First: Central & South America • Virgin Islands • World Food Caribbean • World Food Mexico • Yucatán
Travel Literature: Green Dreams: Travels in Central America

EUROPE Amsterdam • Amsterdam City Map • Amsterdam Condensed • Andalucía • Athens • Austria • Baltic States phrasebook • Barcelona • Barcelona City Map • Belgium & Luxembourg • Berlin • Berlin City Map • Britain • British phrasebook • Brussels, Bruges & Antwerp • Brussels City Map • Budapest • Budapest City Map • Canary Islands • Catalunya & the Costa Brava • Central Europe • Central Europe phrasebook • Copenhagen • Corfu & the Ionians • Corsica • Crete • Crete Condensed • Croatia • Cycling Britain • Cycling France • Cyprus • Czech & Slovak Republics • Czech phrasebook • Denmark • Dublin • Dublin City Map • Dublin Condensed • Eastern Europe • Eastern Europe phrasebook • Edinburgh • Edinburgh City Map • England • Estonia, Latvia & Lithuania • Europe on a shoestring • Europe phrasebook • Finland • Florence • Florence City Map • France • Frankfurt City Map • Frankfurt Condensed • French phrasebook • Georgia, Armenia & Azerbaijan • Germany • German phrasebook • Greece • Greek Islands • Greek phrasebook • Hungary • Iceland, Greenland & the Faroe Islands • Ireland • Italian phrasebook • Italy • Kraków • Lisbon • The Loire • London • London City Map • London Condensed • Madrid • Madrid City Map • Malta • Mediterranean Europe • Milan, Turin & Genoa • Moscow • Munich • Netherlands • Normandy • Norway • Out to Eat – London • Out to Eat – Paris • Paris • Paris City Map • Paris Condensed • Poland • Polish phrasebook • Portugal • Portuguese phrasebook • Prague • Prague City Map • Provence & the Côte d'Azur • Read This First: Europe • Rhodes & the Dodecanese • Romania & Moldova • Rome • Rome City Map • Rome Condensed • Russia, Ukraine & Belarus • Russian phrasebook • Scandinavian & Baltic Europe • Scandinavian phrasebook • Scotland • Sicily • Slovenia • South-West France • Spain • Spanish phrasebook • Stockholm • St Petersburg • St Petersburg City Map • Sweden • Switzerland • Tuscany • Ukrainian phrasebook • Venice • Vienna • Wales • Walking in Britain • Walking in France • Walking in Ireland • Walking in Italy • Walking in Scotland • Walking in Spain • Walking in Switzerland • Western Europe • World Food France • World Food Greece • World Food Ireland • World Food Italy • World Food Spain **Travel Literature:** After Yugoslavia • Love and War in the Apennines • The Olive Grove: Travels in Greece • On the Shores of the Mediterranean • Round Ireland in Low Gear • A Small Place in Italy

Lonely Planet Mail Order

Lonely Planet products are distributed worldwide. They are also available by mail order from Lonely Planet, so if you have difficulty finding a title please write to us. North and South American residents should write to 150 Linden St, Oakland, CA 94607, USA; European and African residents should write to 10a Spring Place, London NW5 3BH, UK; and residents of other countries to Locked Bag 1, Footscray, Victoria 3011, Australia.

INDIAN SUBCONTINENT & THE INDIAN OCEAN Bangladesh • Bengali phrasebook • Bhutan • Delhi • Goa • Healthy Travel Asia & India • Hindi & Urdu phrasebook • India • India & Bangladesh City Map • Indian Himalaya • Karakoram Highway • Kathmandu City Map • Kerala • Madagascar • Maldives • Mauritius, Réunion & Seychelles • Mumbai (Bombay) • Nepal • Nepali phrasebook • North India • Pakistan • Rajasthan • Read This First: Asia & India • South India • Sri Lanka • Sri Lanka phrasebook • Tibet • Tibetan phrasebook • Trekking in the Indian Himalaya • Trekking in the Karakoram & Hindukush • Trekking in the Nepal Himalaya • World Food India **Travel Literature:** The Age of Kali: Indian Travels and Encounters • Hello Goodnight: A Life of Goa • In Rajasthan • Maverick in Madagascar • A Season in Heaven: True Tales from the Road to Kathmandu • Shopping for Buddhas • A Short Walk in the Hindu Kush • Slowly Down the Ganges

MIDDLE EAST & CENTRAL ASIA Bahrain, Kuwait & Qatar • Central Asia • Central Asia phrasebook • Dubai • Farsi (Persian) phrasebook • Hebrew phrasebook • Iran • Israel & the Palestinian Territories • Istanbul • Istanbul City Map • Istanbul to Cairo • Istanbul to Kathmandu • Jerusalem • Jerusalem City Map • Jordan • Lebanon • Middle East • Oman & the United Arab Emirates • Syria • Turkey • Turkish phrasebook • World Food Turkey • Yemen **Travel Literature:** Black on Black: Iran Revisited • Breaking Ranks: Turbulent Travels in the Promised Land • The Gates of Damascus • Kingdom of the Film Stars: Journey into Jordan

NORTH AMERICA Alaska • Boston • Boston City Map • Boston Condensed • British Columbia • California & Nevada • California Condensed • Canada • Chicago • Chicago City Map • Chicago Condensed • Florida • Georgia & the Carolinas • Great Lakes • Hawaii • Hiking in Alaska • Hiking in the USA • Honolulu & Oahu City Map • Las Vegas • Los Angeles • Los Angeles City Map • Louisiana & the Deep South • Miami • Miami City Map • Montreal • New England • New Orleans • New Orleans City Map • New York City • New York City City Map • New York City Condensed • New York, New Jersey & Pennsylvania • Oahu • Out to Eat – San Francisco • Pacific Northwest • Rocky Mountains • San Diego & Tijuana • San Francisco • San Francisco City Map • Seattle • Seattle City Map • Southwest • Texas • Toronto • USA • USA phrasebook • Vancouver • Vancouver City Map • Virginia & the Capital Region • Washington, DC • Washington, DC City Map • World Food New Orleans **Travel Literature:** Caught Inside: A Surfer's Year on the California Coast • Drive Thru America

NORTH-EAST ASIA Beijing • Beijing City Map • Cantonese phrasebook • China • Hiking in Japan • Hong Kong & Macau • Hong Kong City Map • Hong Kong Condensed • Japan • Japanese phrasebook • Korea • Korean phrasebook • Kyoto • Mandarin phrasebook • Mongolia • Mongolian phrasebook • Seoul • Shanghai • South-West China • Taiwan • Tokyo • Tokyo Condensed • World Food Hong Kong • World Food Japan **Travel Literature:** In Xanadu: A Quest • Lost Japan

SOUTH AMERICA Argentina, Uruguay & Paraguay • Bolivia • Brazil • Brazilian phrasebook • Buenos Aires • Buenos Aires City Map • Chile & Easter Island • Colombia • Ecuador & the Galapagos Islands • Healthy Travel Central & South America • Latin American Spanish phrasebook • Peru • Quechua phrasebook • Read This First: Central & South America • Rio de Janeiro • Rio de Janeiro City Map • Santiago de Chile • South America on a shoestring • Trekking in the Patagonian Andes • Venezuela **Travel Literature:** Full Circle: A South American Journey

SOUTH-EAST ASIA Bali & Lombok • Bangkok • Bangkok City Map • Burmese phrasebook • Cambodia • Cycling Vietnam, Laos & Cambodia • East Timor phrasebook • Hanoi • Healthy Travel Asia & India • Hill Tribes phrasebook • Ho Chi Minh City (Saigon) • Indonesia • Indonesian phrasebook • Indonesia's Eastern Islands • Java • Lao phrasebook • Laos • Malay phrasebook • Malaysia, Singapore & Brunei • Myanmar (Burma) • Philippines • Pilipino (Tagalog) phrasebook • Read This First: Asia & India • Singapore • Singapore City Map • South-East Asia on a shoestring • South-East Asia phrasebook • Thailand • Thailand's Islands & Beaches • Thailand, Vietnam, Laos & Cambodia Road Atlas • Thai phrasebook • Vietnam • Vietnamese phrasebook • World Food Indonesia • World Food Thailand • World Food Vietnam

ALSO AVAILABLE: Antarctica • The Arctic • The Blue Man: Tales of Travel, Love and Coffee • Brief Encounters: Stories of Love, Sex & Travel • Buddhist Stupas in Asia: The Shape of Perfection • Chasing Rickshaws • The Last Grain Race • Lonely Planet … On the Edge: Adventurous Escapades from Around the World • Lonely Planet Unpacked • Lonely Planet Unpacked Again • Not the Only Planet: Science Fiction Travel Stories • Ports of Call: A Journey by Sea • Sacred India • Travel Photography: A Guide to Taking Better Pictures • Travel with Children • Tuvalu: Portrait of an Island Nation

Index

Text

Bold indicates maps.

Bold indicates maps.

Bold indicates maps.

Places to Eat

MAP 11 – CAPE TOWN & THE PENINSULA

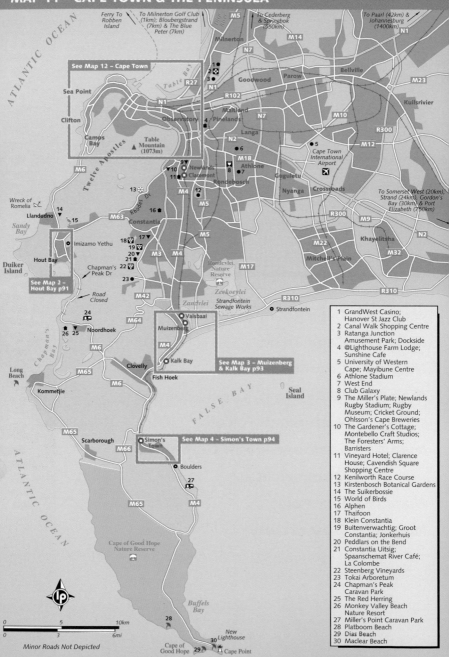

ATLANTIC OCEAN

Ferry To Robben Island

To Milnerton Golf Club (1km); Bloubergstrand (7km) & The Blue Peter (7km)

To Cederberg & Springbok (550km)

To Paarl (42km) & Johannesburg (1400km)

Milnerton

See Map 12 – Cape Town

Table Bay

Sea Point

Clifton

Camps Bay

Twelve Apostles

Table Mountain (1073m)

Wreck of Romelia

Llandudno

Sandy Bay

Hout Bay

Duiker Island

See Map 2 – Hout Bay p91

Chapman's Peak Dr

Road Closed

Imizamo Yethu

Chapman's Bay

Long Beach

Kommetjie

Scarborough

ATLANTIC OCEAN

Noordhoek

Clovelly

Fish Hoek

Simon's Town

Boulders

Cape of Good Hope Nature Reserve

Buffels Bay

Cape of Good Hope

New Lighthouse

Cape Point

Goodwood

Parow

Bellville

Kuilsrivier

Maitland

Pinelands

Langa

Observatory

Athlone

Rondebosch

Newlands

Claremont

Rhodes Dr

Constantia

Zandvlei Nature Reserve

Zeekovlei

Zandvlei

Strandfontein Sewage Works

Valsbaai

Muizenberg

See Map 3 – Muizenberg & Kalk Bay p93

Kalk Bay

FALSE BAY

Seal Island

Cape Town International Airport

Gugulethu

Nyanga

Crossroads

Khayelitsha

Mitchell's Plain

Strandfontein

To Somerset West (20km), Strand (24km), Gordon's Bay (30km) & Port Elizabeth (750km)

See Map 4 – Simon's Town p94

Minor Roads Not Depicted

0   5   10km
0   3   6mi

1 GrandWest Casino; Hanover St Jazz Club
2 Canal Walk Shopping Centre
3 Ratanga Junction Amusement Park; Dockside
4 @Lighthouse Farm Lodge; Sunshine Cafe
5 University of Western Cape; Maybuine Centre
6 Athlone Stadium
7 West End
8 Club Galaxy
9 The Miller's Plate; Newlands Rugby Stadium; Rugby Museum; Cricket Ground; Ohlsson's Cape Breweries
10 The Gardener's Cottage; Montebello Craft Studios; The Foresters' Arms; Barristers
11 Vineyard Hotel; Clarence House; Cavendish Square Shopping Centre
12 Kenilworth Race Course
13 Kirstenbosch Botanical Gardens
14 The Suikerbossie
15 World of Birds
16 Alphen
17 Thaifoon
18 Klein Constantia
19 Buitenverwachting; Groot Constantia; Jonkershuis
20 Peddlars on the Bend
21 Constantia Uitsig; Spaanschemat River Café; La Colombe
22 Steenberg Vineyards
23 Tokai Arboretum
24 Chapman's Peak Caravan Park
25 The Red Herring
26 Monkey Valley Beach Nature Resort
27 Miller's Point Caravan Park
28 Platboom Beach
29 Dias Beach
30 Maclear Beach

Oceans of desire: The Cape Peninsula is an ideal destination for beach-lovers. From the Cape of Good Hope Nature Reserve, jutting into the Atlantic Ocean, to the beach chalets of Muizenberg, there are ample places to lay your towel.

MAP 12 – CAPE TOWN

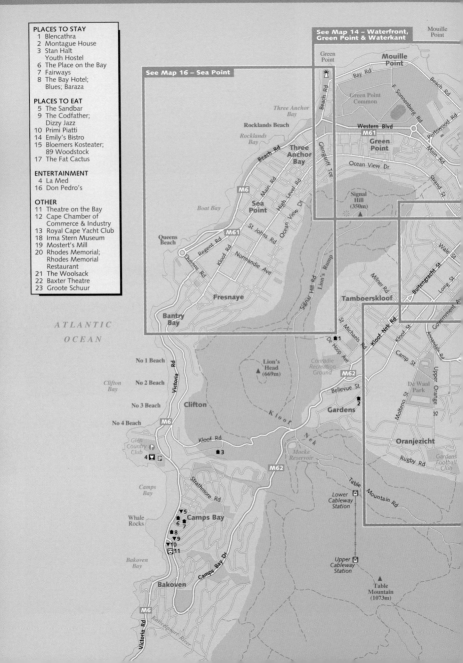

PLACES TO STAY
1 Blencathra
2 Montague House
3 Stan Halt
   Youth Hostel
6 The Place on the Bay
7 Fairways
8 The Bay Hotel;
   Blues; Baraza

PLACES TO EAT
5 The Sandbar
9 The Codfather;
   Dizzy Jazz
10 Primi Piatti
14 Emily's Bistro
15 Bloemers Kosteater;
   89 Woodstock
17 The Fat Cactus

ENTERTAINMENT
4 La Med
16 Don Pedro's

OTHER
11 Theatre on the Bay
12 Cape Chamber of
   Commerce & Industry
13 Royal Cape Yacht Club
18 Irma Stern Museum
19 Mostert's Mill
20 Rhodes Memorial;
   Rhodes Memorial
   Restaurant
21 The Woolsack
22 Baxter Theatre
23 Groote Schuur

See Map 14 – Waterfront,
Green Point & Waterkant

Mouille
Point

See Map 16 – Sea Point

ATLANTIC

OCEAN

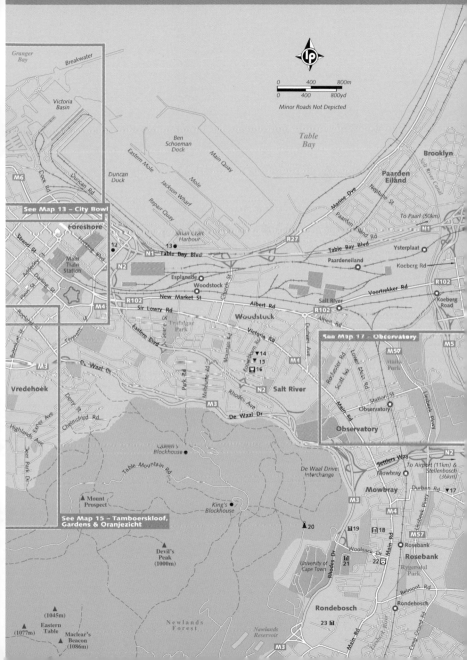

Granger
Bay

Breakwater

Victoria
Basin

Ben
Schoeman
Dock

Main Quay

Table
Bay

Brooklyn

Eastern Mole

Mole

Paarden
Eiland

Marine Dve

Neptune St

To Paarl (50km)

Jackson Wharf

Duncan Duck

Duncan Rd

Dock Rd

M6

Repair Quay

Paarden Eiland Rd

N1

Foreshore

Strand St

Shian Craft
Harbour

12

13

N1 Table Bay Blvd

R27

Table Bay Blvd

Ysterplaat

Main Table
Station

Buitengracht St

Adderley St

Darling St

Plein St

M4

N2

Esplanade

Woodstock

New Market St

Sir Lowry Rd

Church St

Albert Rd

Paardeneiland

Koeberg Rd

R102

Voortrekker Rd

R102

Salt River

R102

Koeberg
Road

Terrace St

Eastern Blvd

Trafalgar
Park

Woodstock

Albert Rd

See Map 17 – Observatory

M57

M5

De Waal Dr

Searle St

Victoria Rd

14

13

16

Duncan Ave

M1

Roodebloem Rd

Lower Dean Rd

Scott Rd

Station St

Altona
Park

Vredehoek

De Waal Dr

Park Rd

Mountain Rd

Melbourne Rd

Rhodes Ave

N2

Salt River

Main Rd

Observatory

Liesbeek Pkwy

Observatory

Devey St

Chelmsford Rd

Esher Ave

Highlands Ave

Deer Park Dr

M3

De Waal Dr

M3

Queen's
Blockhouse

Table Mountain Rd

See Map 15 – Tamboerskloof,
Gardens & Oranjezicht

De Waal Drive
Interchange

Settlers Way

N2

To Airport (11km) &
Stellenbosch
(36km)

Mowbray

Durban Rd

17

King's
Blockhouse

20

Mowbray

M3

M4

M57

Devil's
Peak
(1000m)

Rhodes Dr

Woolsack Dr

19

18

Rosebank

22

Rosebank

University of
Cape Town

21

Rygersdal
Park

Mount
Prospect

(1045m)

Eastern
Table

Maclear's
Beacon
(1086m)

(1077m)

Newlands
Forest

Newlands
Reservoir

Rondebosch

23

Rondebosch

Belmont Rd

Main Rd

Camp Ground Rd

Liesbeek River

M3

Eastern Blvd

0   400   800m
0   400   800yd

Minor Roads Not Depicted

See Map 13 – City Bowl

MAP 13 – CITY BOWL

Joins Map 14 – Waterfront, Green Point & Waterkant

Noon Gun

Viewpoint

0   100   200m
0   100   200yd

August St

Longmarket St

Schotsche Kloof

Church St

Yusuf Dve

Strand St

Waterkant St

Riebeeck St

Castle St

Hout St

Bo-Kaap

Wale St

Buitengracht St

Van Riebeeck Square

Heritage Square

Shortmarket St

Longmarket St

Bree St

Greenmarket Square

Church St

Berg St

Wale St

Bureau St

Loop St

Pepper St

Leeuwen St

Bloem St

Buitengracht St

New Church St

Olifant St

Buitensingle St

M62

Hout St

Bryant St

Jordan St

Service St

Hout St

Whitford St

Carisbrook Rd

New Church St

Chiappini St

Jarvis St

Dorp St

Company's Gardens

Keerom St

Queen Victoria St

Government Ave

Parliament St

Grey's Pass

Museum St

Buitenkant St

Rose St

Berg St

Bree St

Schotsche Kloof

Military Rd

Voetboog Rd

Pentz Rd

Upper Bloem St

Upper Pepper St

Upper Leeuwen St

Delville Wood Memorial

South African Museum & Planetarium

South African National Gallery

Orange St

Roeland St

Bouquet St

St John's St

Beckham St

Park St

Joins Map 15 – Tamboerskloof, Gardens & Oranjezicht

Joins Map 14 – Waterfront, Green Point & Waterkant

N2

N2

Table Bay Blvd

Koen Steytler Ave

Roggebaai Square

Pier Place

Salazar Square

Hans Strijdom Ave

Bree St

Prestwich St

Thibault Square

Tulbagh Square

102

101

99

100

111

Loop St

Lower Burg St

St George's Mall

106

Heerengracht

104

105

103

Merriman Square

110

Finish Walking Tour (see p108)

107

D F Malan St

108

Jan Smuts St

Martin Hammerschlag Wy

Hertzog Blvd

109

112

113

114

115

116

Barrack St

Hout St

121

117

118

120

119

Prince St

Trafalgar Square

123

122

124

Strand St

126

125

Oswald Pirow St

Grand Parade

133

132

131

129

Castle St

Start Walking Tour (see p105)

128

127

Church Square

130

Spin St

Mostert St

134

135

Corporation St

Parade St

Buitenkant St

Longmarket St

Darling St

P

136

Barrack St

Albertus St

Plein St

Castle of Good Hope

141

R102

M4

Sir Lowry Rd

137

138

139

Commercial St

Aberdeen St

140

Canterbury St

Primrose St

Citadel St

Wale St

Hanover St

Keerengracht St

Tennant St

Stone St

Muir St

M60

M59

Joins Map 15 – Tamboerskloof, Gardens & Oranjezicht

Zonnebloem

MAP 13 – CITY BOWL

PLACES TO STAY

13 Cape Heritage Hotel
21 Metropole Hotel
27 Days Inn; The Famous Butchers Grill
41 Tudor Hotel
68 Travellers Inn
71 Overseas Visitors' Club
72 St Paul's B&B Guest House
76 The Backpack; Africa Travel Centre
77 Zebra Crossing
86 Long St Backpackers
108 Hotel Formule 1
116 Cape Sun Hotel
127 Train Lodge
135 The Townhouse
136 Parliament Hotel

PLACES TO EAT

2 Marco's African Place
10 Savoy Cabbage
14 ...and Lemon
15 Africa Café
16 Biesmiellah
34 Cycles; Holiday Inn
36 Primi Piatti
37 Le Petit Paris
42 Mesopotamia
43 Cafe Mozart
45 Bukhara
47 Off Moroka Cafe Africaine
51 Shambala
55 Five Flies
57 Sooz Baguette Bar
61 Mr Pickwick's
62 Mama Africa
66 Mexican Kitchen
69 Diablo Bar Tapas; Jo'burg
70 Lola's
73 Priscilla's
74 Gorgeous
83 Long St Cafe
84 Kennedy's
92 Gardens Restaurant
128 De Waterblommetjie
140 D6 Snack Bar

ENTERTAINMENT

11 Gignet Theatre Café
12 Pa Na Na Souk Bar
23 The Fez
25 The Jet Lounge; The Baseline
29 Coffee Lounge
33 The Purple Turtle
39 The Square All Bar None
53 Long Beach
54 169 on Long
60 Rhythm Divine
64 The Lounge
91 Rhodes House
107 Artscape

MUSEUMS

7 Gold of Africa Museum
17 Bo-Kaap Museum
20 South African Missionary Meeting House Museum
40 Michaelis Collection; Old Town House; Ivy Garden Restaurant
49 Cultural History Museum; Slave Lodge
112 Koopmans de Wet House
139 District Six Museum

CONSULATES

5 Netherlands
22 Mozambique
38 Canada
81 Germany
89 Ireland
102 Australia
105 Japan
106 USA
111 Botswana; UK

OTHER

1 Tana Baru Cemetery
3 Avis Car Rental
4 Budget Car Rental
6 Lutheran Church
8 Imperial Car Rental
9 Harley-Davidson Cape Town
18 Atlas Trading Company
19 St Stephen's Church
24 Shap's Cameraland
26 City Park Hospital
28 Auwal Mosque
30 Camera Repair Centre
31 The African Music Store
32 Pan African Market; Pan African Kitchen
35 Sturk's Tobacconists
44 Metropolitan Gallery
46 African Image
48 Groote Kerk
50 St George's Cathedral
52 Noor el Hamedia Mosque
56 Palm Tree Mosque
58 Prolab
59 Alliance Française
63 African Buzz
65 Nomad Adventure Centre; Extreme Sports Shack
67 The Junk Shop
75 Afrogem
78 Le Cap Motorcycle Hire
79 Downhill Adventures
80 Long St Baths
82 Morris's
85 Adventure Village
87 The Bead Shop
88 Clarke's
90 Centre for the Book
93 Cecil John Rhodes Statue
94 Tuynhuis
95 National Library of South Africa
96 Houses of Parliament
97 Entrance to Houses of Parliament
98 Government Printers
99 STA Travel
100 Southern Life Centre
101 American Express
103 British Airways Travel Clinic
104 Jan & Maria Van Riebeeck Statues
109 Civic Centre
110 Bus Terminus & Booking Offices for Translux, Greyhound & Intercape Mainliner
113 Cape Town Tourism; Montebello Craft Studios
114 Surf Centre
115 Ulrich Naumann's
117 Woolworths
118 Taxi Rank
119 Golden Acre Centre
120 Flower Market
121 Rennies Travel
122 First National Bank
123 Stuttaford's Town Square
124 Standard Bank
125 Main Post Office
126 Golden Acre Terminal
129 Bus Information Kiosk
130 Old Town Hall
131 Lite Kem Pharmacy
132 Wellington Fruit Growers
133 Mutual Building
134 Cape Union Mart
137 Department of Home Affairs
138 Police Station
141 Good Hope Centre

In Cape Town, the good times will find you. Film makers, buskers, marketeers and musicians make for a lively cultural scene and a fun, relaxed atmosphere, especially in summer.

MAP 14 – WATERFRONT, GREEN POINT & WATERKANT

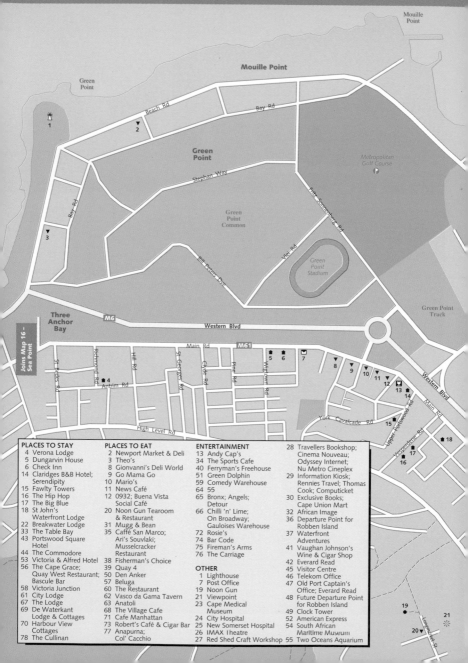

PLACES TO STAY
4 Verona Lodge
5 Dungarvin House
6 Check Inn
14 Claridges B&B Hotel;
   Serendipity
15 Fawlty Towers
16 The Hip Hop
17 The Big Blue
18 St John's
   Waterfront Lodge
22 Breakwater Lodge
33 The Table Bay
43 Portswood Square
   Hotel
44 The Commodore
53 Victoria & Alfred Hotel
56 The Cape Grace;
   Quay West Restaurant;
   Bascule Bar
58 Victoria Junction
61 City Lodge
67 The Lodge
69 De Waterkant
   Lodge & Cottages
70 Harbour View
   Cottages
78 The Cullinan

PLACES TO EAT
2 Newport Market & Deli
3 Theo's
8 Gionvanni's Deli World
9 Go Mama Go
10 Mario's
11 News Café
12 0932; Buena Vista
   Social Café
20 Noon Gun Tearoom
   & Restaurant
31 Mugg & Bean
35 Caffé San Marco;
   Ari's Souvlaki;
   Musselcracker
   Restaurant
38 Fisherman's Choice
39 Quay 4
50 Den Anker
57 Beluga
60 The Restaurant
62 Vasco da Gama Tavern
63 Anatoli
68 The Village Cafe
71 Cafe Manhattan
73 Robert's Café & Cigar Bar
77 Anapurna;
   Col' Cacchio

ENTERTAINMENT
13 Andy Cap's
34 The Sports Cafe
40 Ferryman's Freehouse
51 Green Dolphin
59 Comedy Warehouse
64 55
65 Bronx; Angels;
   Detour
66 Chilli 'n' Lime;
   On Broadway;
   Gauloises Warehouse
72 Rosie's
74 Bar Code
75 Fireman's Arms
76 The Carriage

OTHER
1 Lighthouse
7 Post Office
19 Noon Gun
21 Viewpoint
23 Cape Medical
   Museum
24 City Hospital
25 New Somerset Hospital
26 IMAX Theatre
27 Red Shed Craft Workshop

28 Travellers Bookshop;
   Cinema Nouveau;
   Odyssey Internet;
   Nu Metro Cineplex
29 Information Kiosk;
   Rennies Travel; Thomas
   Cook; Computicket
30 Exclusive Books;
   Cape Union Mart
32 African Image
36 Departure Point for
   Robben Island
37 Waterfront
   Adventures
41 Vaughan Johnson's
   Wine & Cigar Shop
42 Everard Read
45 Visitor Centre
46 Telekom Office
47 Old Port Captain's
   Office; Everard Read
48 Future Departure Point
   for Robben Island
49 Clock Tower
52 American Express
54 South African
   Maritime Museum
55 Two Oceans Aquarium

Joins Map 16 – Sea Point

MAP 15 – TAMBOERSKLOOF, GARDENS & ORANJEZICHT

Joins Map 13 –
City Bowl

Tamboerskloof

Gardens

Zonnebloem

Reservoir

De Waal Park

Molteno Reservoir

Oranjezicht

Dunkley Square

Vredehoek

School

School

School

Gardens Football Club

PLACES TO STAY
1 Underberg Guesthouse
2 Parker Cottage
3 Table Mountain Lodge
4 Leeuwenvoet House
6 Cape Mews Cottages
13 Ashanti Lodge
15 Mount Nelson Hotel
19 The Fritz Hotel
28 Cape Gardens Lodge
42 iKhaya Guest Lodge
44 Conifer Lodge
45 Gardens Centre Holiday Flats; Gardens Centre; Cape Union Mart; Flight Centre; Computicket
46 Oak Lodge

47 Cloudbreak
49 Belmont House
50 Villa Belmonte
51 Amsterdam Guest House
52 Ambleside Guesthouse

PLACES TO EAT
5 The Happy Wok
7 Melissa's; Peasants
8 Cafe Dharma
12 Cafe Paradiso
14 Nelson's Eye
18 Ocean Basket
20 Naked on Kloof
21 Cafe Bardeli
23 Rozenhof
43 Maria's

ENTERTAINMENT
9 Cafe Camissa; Fields Health Store
11 Cool Runnings
17 Labia Cinema
22 Dros
25 Little Theatre
34 The Perseverance Tavern
35 The Shed; Blue Lizard Internet Café; The Jam
37 Drum Cafe
38 Stag's Head Hotel

OTHER
10 Hotchi-Witchi
16 Bertram House
24 Spar Supermarket

26 Italian Consulate
27 French Consulate
29 Delville Wood Memorial
30 South African Museum & Planetarium
31 British Council
32 Wayne Motors
33 Rust-en-Vreugd
36 Western Cape Archives
39 South African National Gallery
40 South African Jewish Museum; Old Synagogue; Cape Town Holocaust Centre; Great Synagogue; Café Riteve
41 Mountain Club of South Africa
48 Clementina Ceramics & Fine Art

0   150   300m
0   150   300yd

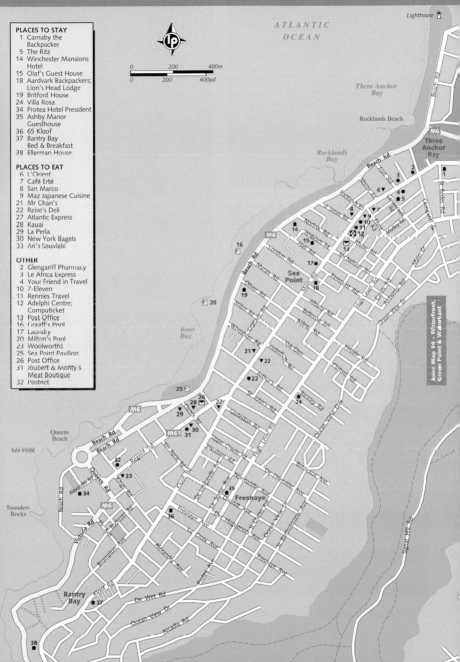

ATLANTIC
OCEAN

Lighthouse

Three Anchor
Bay

Rocklands Beach

Three
Anchor
Bay

Rocklands
Bay

Beach Rd

Sea
Point

Kloof
Bay

Queens
Beach

Sea Point

Saunders
Rocks

Fresnaye

Bantry
Bay

BETHUNE CARMICHAEL

RICHARD I'ANSON

SIMON RICHMOND

RICHARD I'ANSON

Some artefacts make overt political statements, while others are more decorative. In the art of the townships, the medium – discarded soft-drink cans, food tins or wire – is the message. Buying souvenirs directly from the people who make them is a good way to support local industries.

1 The Curve Bar at the Bijoux	7 Independent Armchair Theatre	12 Valkenberg Hospital
2 River Club	8 Pancho's Mexican Kitchen; Obz Café; A Fu Chinese	13 A Touch of Madness
3 The Lodge	9 Café Whatever	14 Café Ganesh; Green Mamba Cafe
4 Green Elephant	10 Rolling Stones	15 Senhôra Sardine
5 Cool Runnings	11 Diva	16 The Wholefood Store
6 Mnandi Textiles & Design		17 Groote Schuur Hospital; Transplant Museum

By the end of your time in Cape Town, you'll have no superlatives left to describe the city's setting.

SIMON RICHMOND

MAP LEGEND

CITY ROUTES

Fwy .... Freeway	------ Unsealed Road
Hwy .... Primary Road	--→-- One-way Street
Rd ...... Secondary Road	Pedestrian Street
St .... Street	Stepped Street
La .... Lane	→≡ ≡ ≡ Tunnel
On/Off Ramp	Footbridge

HYDROGRAPHY

River; Creek
Canal
Lake
Dry Lake; Salt Lake
Spring; Rapids
Waterfalls

TRANSPORT ROUTES

Train
Cable Car/Chairlift
Ferry
Walking Trail
Walking Tour
Path
Pier or Jetty

REGIONAL ROUTES

Tollway, Freeway
Primary Road
Secondary Road
Minor Road

AREA FEATURES

Building	Beach
Park, Gardens	Cemetery
Market	Campus
Sports Ground	Plaza

BOUNDARIES

International
Provincial
Fortified Wall

POPULATION SYMBOLS

✪ **CAPITAL** .... National Capital	● **CITY** .... City	● Village ....Village
◉ **CAPITAL** .... Provincial Capital	○ **Town** ....Town	.... Urban Area

MAP SYMBOLS

■ .... Place to Stay	▼ .... Place to Eat	● .... Point of Interest

✈ ...... Airfield; Airport	⚲ .... Golf Course	🏛 .... Museum	⊠ ..... Shopping Centre
⊖ .... Bank	⊕ .... Hospital	🐦 ...... Nature Reserve	🏠 .... Stately Home
🐦 .... Bird Sanctuary	🖥 .... Internet Cafe	Ⓟ .... Parking	🏊 .... Swimming Pool
🚌 .... Bus Stop/Terminal	⚓ .... Lighthouse	⊙ .... Petrol Station	🚕 .... Taxi Rank
🚐 .... Caravan Park	☼ .... Lookout	⊕ ...... Police Station	☎ .... Telephone
✚ .... Church	▲ .... Monument	✉ .... Post Office	🎭 .... Theatre
🎦 .... Cinema	☪ .... Mosque	Ⓟ .... Pub or Bar	ℹ ... Tourist Information
🏛 . Embassy/Consulate	▲ .... Mountain	⚓ .... Shipwreck	🍷 .... Winery

Note: not all symbols displayed above appear in this book

LONELY PLANET OFFICES

Australia
Locked Bag 1, Footscray, Victoria 3011
☎ 03 8379 8000 fax 03 8379 8111
email: talk2us@lonelyplanet.com.au

USA
150 Linden St, Oakland, CA 94607
☎ 510 893 8555 TOLL FREE: 800 275 5555
fax 510 893 8572
email: info@lonelyplanet.com

UK
10a Spring Place, London NW5 3BH
☎ 020 7428 4800 fax 020 7428 4828
email: go@lonelyplanet.co.uk

France
1 rue du Dahomey, 75011 Paris
☎ 01 55 25 33 00 fax 01 55 25 33 01
email: bip@lonelyplanet.fr
www.lonelyplanet.fr

World Wide Web: www.lonelyplanet.com *or* AOL keyword: lp
Lonely Planet Images: lpi@lonelyplanet.com.au